Finally Organized, Finally Free
For the Home

FINALLY
ORGANIZED
FINALLY
Free

FOR THE HOME

MARIA GRACIA

Published by **BlueMoon Publishing.**

This publication is designed to provide accurate and authoritative information in regard to the subject matter covered. It is sold with the understanding that the publisher and the copyright owner are not engaged in rendering legal, accounting or other professional service. If legal advice or other expert assistance is required, the services of a competent professional person who specializes in that particular field should be sought.

While due care has been exercised in the compilation of this guide, we are not responsible for errors or omissions. This reference is intended to assist in providing information to the public, and the information is delivered as accurately as possible.

Senior Executive Editor: Joseph Gracia, Laura Sherman

Index: WordCo Indexing Services

Cover Design: Cathi Stevenson of Book Cover Express

Please direct any comments, questions or suggestions regarding this book to:

BlueMoon Publishing
611 Arlington Way
Watertown WI 53094
USA

Library of Congress Cataloging-in-Publication Data

Gracia, Maria
    Finally Organized, Finally Free for the Home/by Maria Gracia
    ISBN # 0-9779777-1-4 $34.95

    Library of Congress Control Number 2006902367

    Includes Index.

    Reference: Home Organization, Goals, Self-Help, Family Resources,
    Time Management, Planning, Achievement.

ISBN # 0-9779777-1-4

First Edition 2006.

Printed in the United States of America.

Dedication

This book is dedicated to my daughter, Amanda Grace.

You make each day of my life such a delight.

You are beautiful, sweet, bright, curious and silly

just to name a few of your most lovable traits.

You're every mother's dream and I love you dearly.

Acknowledgements

Thanks to all of you from the bottom of my heart
for all your positive influence and support.

My husband, Joe

My husband's sons, Chad, Scott and Jason

My father-in-law, Bill

Table of Contents

Chapter 1

Introduction

"I've got to get organized!"

When did you last utter these words? Was it when you realized that the raging, paper beast had taken complete control over your dining room table?

Maybe it was when you were late for your son's soccer game . . . yet again.

Perhaps it was when you looked at all the clutter on your kitchen counter, computer center, home office desk, bedroom nightstand and everyplace else. You may have even contemplated tossing everything out the window!

Was it when you desperately searched for those missing concert tickets?

It could have been when you missed that important appointment or when that deadline crept up on you.

Maybe it was when you had to go grocery shopping at night with hungry, whining kids because you couldn't get to it earlier in the day.

Perhaps it was when you realized that you have enough tasks on your To Do list to last you for the next ten years and you've given up on ever catching up with it all.

Or even worse, it may have happened when you found out you had no time left for yourself, your family, your friends, that much needed vacation and basically everything in life that you love to do.

You're not alone. Those words have been expressed over and over again by thousands of people all over the world.

Disorganization can actually trap you into living a life filled with stress, frustration and chaos. It can rob you of the precious time you should be spending enjoying your life.

By overcoming disorganization, you can be set free to live the kind of life you've always dreamed of.

Teeny-Tiny tips equal big changes!

For some reason, so many people equate being organized with achieving an enormous and impossible feat. Something only lucky people are capable of having.

If this is your thinking, then let me ease your mind.

Being organized does not require you to perform time-consuming, complicated systems.

It is not rocket science.

It is not something that's going to take you years of soul searching to start.

And it's not something that only lucky people are capable of having.

Just a few small organizing tips—a few little, teeny-tiny tips, applied with a positive attitude, can help you be more organized today, than you were yesterday.

As you are able to apply tiny organizing tips to your life and those teeny tips become habits that you do each day, you will be more and more organized.

Your goal should never be to get totally organized.

That is a difficult, overwhelming, frightening, major, impossible goal and something I would never recommend you try to take on.

There is no one who is always totally organized.

Even professional organizers are occasionally late for appointments or sometimes have messy desks.

Your goal should be to apply small organizing tips today that will make your life just a little more organized tomorrow. Small, teeny-tiny tips can help make big changes in your life.

And you'll get all the teeny-tiny tips you need and more, as you read *Finally Organized, Finally Free for the Home*.

Venturing outside your comfort zone

We live a life of choices. If you had a choice between comfort and risk, which would you take? Most people would choose comfort. Comfort is the familiar and the well-known. Your comfort zone is your personal area of thoughts and actions within which you feel comfortable and safe.

Anything you haven't thought or done—something new—lies outside the parameters of your comfort zone. When you think about these things, you may feel uncomfortable. After feeling uncomfortable, you may sometimes get discouraged and tend to give up before ever starting something new.

Of course, to accomplish something new like getting organized, you're required to venture outside of your comfort zone.

You can get organized. But you have to believe it and you have to step outside your comfort zone to get started.

Start off on the right foot.

Right now, I'm going to ask you to determine exactly what it is you're trying to accomplish by reading this book.

The more specific you are in your description, the easier it will be for you to succeed in achieving your objectives.

For example, stating, "I'd like to eliminate clutter," is too broad.

It would be better to say, "I'd like to remove every piece of paper from my kitchen counter or I would like to weed out my clothes closet by 50%."

Or how about, "I'd like to be able to accomplish a minimum of four tasks on my To Do List each day, without having to work late to complete them."

You get the point.

Take a moment right now to think about and write down your personal objectives.

My objectives are:

1. _____

_____

_____

_____

_____

2. _____

_____

_____

_____

_____

3. _____

_____

_____

4. _____

_____

_____

_____

_____

5. _____

_____

_____

_____

_____

The next critical step is to set a practical deadline to accomplish each of these objectives. So, go back to each one and assign a specific date that you wish to meet each of them. Writing "as soon as possible" is too broad. It must be a calendar date such as September 26 or July 7.

Setting objectives and deadlines gives you something to shoot for. If you don't meet your goals by your deadlines, that doesn't mean that you have failed. It just means you have to re-adjust your deadlines and go for it once again, until you've achieved your objectives.

You'll benefit from my organizing experience

What qualifies me to help you get organized? To start, I worked for ten years with Dun and Bradstreet's Nielsen Media Research in New York City as an organizing and management specialist. Throughout my tenure, I managed the data analysis department, worked with hundreds of television stations and advertising agencies and developed effective, productive systems for my clients and staff.

In 1996, I moved to Wisconsin and founded Get Organized Now! My husband and I both run our business at home, while raising our daughter Amanda. Our home is very organized. Everything has a home. We can welcome unexpected guests without having to pick things up before we answer the doorbell.

I have literally helped thousands of individuals and businesses get organized since then, so what I teach is "real life organizing." In fact, my Get Organized Now! Web site is visited by over a million people each year and my Get Organized Now! Newsletter has been read by hundreds of thousands of people.

Just to name a few, I have appeared at, written for or have been interviewed by hundreds of international, national and local media and organizations such as:

Fox 6 News WITI-TV Milwaukee

World Talk Radio

KNEV Radio: The New Mix 95.5 Morning Show

11 Alive News WXIA-TV Atlanta

Fox 6 News WOWT-TV: Discover Omaha

WJR Radio 760 AM: The Internet Advisor

FM 89.3 KPCC Nat'l Public Radio, Talk of the City

WQIK-FM 99.1 Radio, Jacksonville, FL, Morning Show

WKZK Radio, Augusta, Marilyn Joyce Motivational Talk Show

Woman's Day Magazine

Country Living Magazine

Parenting Magazine

First for Women Magazine

Woman's World

Kitchen and Bath Ideas Magazine

Milwaukee Business Journal

Barnes and Noble, Milwaukee, WI

Staples Office Supplies Stores Business Expert

Delta Connections Magazine

Lifestyles Magazine of Orlando

Venice Gulf Coast Living

The News-Sun and The Evening Star

Access Magazine

I don't just teach these organizing techniques. I use them myself. I guarantee you that they all work beautifully!

What you won't find in this book

There are volumes of organizing books on the market. Believe me, bookstore and library shelves are full of them.

But this book is unique.

You won't find a whole lot of philosophy, theories, difficult-to-understand concepts or fluff. You won't have to read dozens of pages before you get to the meat. You won't have to read the entire book to begin to get organized. The second you hit Chapter One, you'll find tips and ideas you can apply— immediately!

How to use this book

Finally Organized, Finally Free for the Home is categorized into individual topics applicable to most people. There are tips, ideas and real life question/answer sessions within each to help you save time. Some can help you save a few minutes while others can help you save a few hours. Nevertheless, they are all designed to help you get better organized.

Choose a few tips and ideas at a time. Don't try to implement dozens at once. Realize that effective organization is an ongoing process. Once you begin to execute one of these ideas, continue to practice it over and over again. Soon enough, each tip or idea that you institute will become a habit.

By the way, only after you do something repetitively—a total of 21 consecutive times—does it become a habit and part of your everyday routine.

Each idea, tip, technique and system you use will bring you another step closer to achieving organizational success. Just as you learned everything else in life—one step at a time—so too will you be able to say that you're Finally Organized, Finally Free.

This is not something to be achieved in a day. Getting organized requires knowledge, implementation, practice and motivation just as it does to effectively ride a bike, play golf or cook a meal. However, taking it one step at a time, while maintaining an "I can do it" attitude, will get you there before you know it.

You can do it. I wish you the greatest success in getting organized, so that you can be Finally Organized, Finally Free!

Chapter 2

Getting Started

- **I wish I was as organized as . . .** Do you envy a friend or relative who appears to be the most organized person you know? Do you wonder how this person always seems to have a clean house, never misses appointments, completes dozens of activities and never seems to break a sweat? Do you sometimes wish you could be as organized as this person?

  If you compare yourself to someone else, you may be setting yourself up for failure. Sometimes when people compare themselves to other people, they tend to see the best in others, while seeing the very worst in themselves. These negative feelings don't help people with the motivation they need to get organized.

- **Don't compare.** You can certainly use a very organized person as a role model or as someone you could learn from. When you're trying to gauge how productive or clutter-free you are, stop comparing yourself to someone else. There's no way that your lifestyle and circumstances are exactly the same as another individual.

  Instead, set up a few reasonable goals—like uncluttering a drawer, doing three items on your To Do list or reading a chapter of that report for work. Write those goals down, along with deadlines for each, and schedule time to work on them.

  As you meet your goals, compare what you've written with what you've actually done. This gives you an excellent visual that shows how much you've done or how much effort you've dedicated to getting organized. Who knows? At the end of the week or month, you may even surprise yourself with the amount of things you've accomplished.

- **Start somewhere.** So many people say, "I have so much to organize. I don't know where to start." That's when paper begins to accumulate into piles and closets begin to burst. The fact is that it doesn't matter where you start, as long as you start somewhere. Just by getting started, you've already won half the battle.

- **What's bothering you the most?** This is usually the best place to begin. If you hate that pile of papers on your dining room table, start there. If you're getting stressed because you can't fit another item on the kitchen counter, then you've found the perfect starting point.

- **Where do you spend most of your time?** This is another good place to begin. If you spend the majority of time in your kitchen and the kitchen is the most cluttered room in your home, than organizing this room will be most satisfying to you later.

- **Make an appointment.** Block out a specific time to begin working on your goal. Keep that appointment just as you would with a doctor or a dentist. Writing it in your calendar helps ensure you don't have a conflict in your schedule.

- **Being committed means doing.** It's not good enough to "say" you're committed to organizing. The only way to prove you're committed is to physically start organizing.

- **Commit to 15 minutes.** You might not have hours to get organized, but you certainly have 15 minutes. So, instead of worrying about finding hours to work on your goal, set aside 15 minutes each day—or 15 minutes each week if it's not a pressing issue.

- **Small chunks.** Rather than thinking about the huge project ahead, break that project up into bite-sized manageable tasks. For instance, if you want to organize the boxes in your attic, you might consider going through one box per day until all boxes have been organized.

- **Rome wasn't built in a day.** Be realistic about your organizing goals and deadlines. While it's generally not possible to organize a clothes closet in five minutes, it is possible to weed out a sock drawer in that amount of time.

- **Find a cheering section.** While trying to get something organized, you may need someone to cheer you on. Ask a spouse, one of your kids, a friend or a neighbor to a) see to it that you start and b) see to it that you're continuing to work on your goal until completion. Don't choose a wishy-washy person to do this. Choose someone ruthless—someone who won't give up cheering you on until you're done.

- **Get comfortable.** If your goal is to do physical organizing, like organizing your basement, wear comfortable clothing that you're not afraid to get dirty so you can really dig in and get going.

  On the other hand, if your goal is to organize your calendar, you can wear anything you want. For many people, if they dress professionally when working on an office-type project they tend to be more productive and take the job more seriously.

- **Be awake.** You're not going to get very far if you didn't get a good night's rest the night before. The day prior to your organizing starting point, be sure to get at least eight solid sleep hours.

Organizing Clinic

Question

How can I use index cards to organize my life?

Brian Iversen
Weymouth, MA

Answer

Dear Brian,

Although there are unlimited possibilities, here are five quick ideas you can apply immediately:

- **Goal setting.** Perhaps you've always wanted to learn a new language or plant a garden. Goal setting will help you get there. Grab some index cards. Write a specific goal on each. Arrange the cards so that the goals you most want to achieve are on top. Write deadlines on each card, break each goal down into mini-goals and schedule time to achieve each of them. When you've reached those goals, make index cards for any new ones, re-shuffle and start again.

- **Cleaning.** Instead of cleaning your home all at once, clean a little bit each day. Get some index cards and write a cleaning task on each. For example: Card 1: Clean the Bathroom, Card 2: Wash Clothes, etc. Place all of your cards in a box and draw one each day. That's your cleaning task for the day. Be sure to include some FREE DAY cards in your box. If you draw one of them, you don't have to do any cleaning for the day. Hooray! Be sure to keep the cards that were already drawn in a holding box, until all the cards you inserted have been drawn. Then, start over again. This system works great for kids' chores too!

- **Organizing a letter or report.** Have to write a formal letter? Organize your thoughts on index cards. Write one thought, idea or suggestion per index card. Then, arrange them sequentially and write your letter based on them.

- **Planning an event.** Get some index cards and write an event topic on each card. For example, let's say you were planning a party. You might have one index card for each category. Example: Card 1: Invitations, Card 2: Food, Card 3: Music. Jot down steps to be done on each topic card. If you're planning a party that other people are helping to organize, perhaps you can give a card to each person. Each person's responsibilities are on their own individual card.

- **Recalling excerpts in a book.** When reading a book, keep an index card tucked into the front cover. When you want to save something for future reference, jot down the page number and either T for top of page, M for middle of page or B for bottom of page. Also jot down a short two to three word description to jog your memory. Tuck the card back in your book. Later on, just use your index card and you won't have to flip through the entire book to find exactly what you're looking for. P.S. You can even use the index card as a bookmark.

- **Make it pleasant.** If you're organizing in a dark, dank room, it's not going to be fun or enticing to start. Make the room you're working in as pleasant as possible. Open a window to let in some fresh air. Pull up the shades and let in some light. Put on your favorite tunes. Invite someone over to keep you company while you organize—or better yet, get them to help.

- **No excuses.** Excuses are the death of getting anything done. "I can't organize today because I have to walk the dog." "I can't organize because I have to entertain my kids." "I can't organize because I have to meet a friend for lunch." You are in control of whether you organize or not. It's your choice. There are very few valid excuses.

- **Read something enticing.** Keep a file folder filled with motivational quotes, articles and cartoons. Read some of the contents in this folder ten minutes prior to starting any organizing project to help boost your energy.

- **Go somewhere.** If you're working on organizing your planner, a book you're writing, your laptop files or anything portable, work on it in a local park, your backyard or anyplace else you find peaceful and soothing.

- **Read all about it.** Think of your goal and write a headline such as "Jane organizes her bedroom closet and finally gets to work on time" or "Jeff organizes his car and finally takes that long overdue family road trip." Post your headline and read it every day. Then start making that headline a reality.

- **Bribe yourself.** Make something you love to do, dependant on the completion of today's task. If you promise yourself that you will not watch your favorite television program tonight unless you work for 15 minutes on organizing your paper piles, you're sure to get that small task finished. No cheating allowed.

- **Tell everyone you know.** When you plan to organize something, tell everyone you know about your plans. You may actually feel guilty or embarrassed if you don't start.

- **Set goals.** Make a list of all the things you want to organize. It doesn't have to be in any particular order. When you're done, choose one item on it. That is your major goal. Now, take that major goal and break it down into smaller pieces. Those will be your mini goals. One by one, work on your mini-goals until each is completed. Once the final mini goal is completed, you will have accomplished your major goal. Here's an example:

  ❖ Major Goal: Organize the bathroom.

    ➢ Mini Goal 1: Organize the medicine cabinet.

    ➢ Mini Goal 2: Organize the cabinet under the sink.

- ➤ <u>Mini</u> Goal 3: Weed out the magazine holder.

- ➤ <u>Mini</u> Goal 4: Set up separate toiletry storage areas for each member of the family.

- **Establish deadlines.** "I'll get to it, when I have time," never works. You're not going to have time, unless you schedule time. You should set a specific deadline for each of your mini-goals. Here's an example:

  - ❖ Deadline for mini goal 1: March 04

  - ❖ Deadline for mini goal 2: March 11

  - ❖ Deadline for mini goal 3: March 18

  - ❖ Deadline for mini goal 4: March 25

- **Designate rewards.** In order to really get motivated, designate a reward for each mini-goal achieved by your specified deadline. It has to be something really enticing, that you will only give yourself when you reach your goal.

  Your final mini-goal—the one that allows you to fully complete your major goal—should be the reward that most entices you. Here's an example:

  - ❖ Reward for mini goal 1: Take a 15-minute nap in the backyard hammock.

  - ❖ Reward for mini goal 2: Designate tomorrow as a "Chore Free" Day.

  - ❖ Reward for mini goal 3: Listen to your favorite CD—all the way through.

  - ❖ Reward for mini goal 4: Take yourself out for a nice lunch.

- **Make them visible.** Post your goals, deadlines and pending rewards in a prominent place, where you're sure to see them every day. The kitchen refrigerator, the bathroom mirror or a home office bulletin board are all good choices.

- **Challenge yourself with a timer.** Does it take you forever to complete your cleaning and chores? Use a timer and you can finish everything more quickly. For instance, if it usually takes you 20 minutes to dust, set a timer for 15 minutes and race against the clock to get your dusting done before the alarm sounds. It may sound silly, but it actually works—especially if you have a bit of a competitive nature in you.

- **Pop in a CD.** An alternative to using a timer is to pop in a favorite CD and organize until the music stops. Once the last song is over, it's quitting time.

- **Visualize the end result.** Close your eyes and envision yourself sitting in your uncluttered kitchen. There are no loose papers in sight and you're sipping a cup of rich coffee. Imagine your friend walking in and actually telling you she's jealous that your home looks so organized and beautiful.

- **Yes, it will require you to change a bit.** If you always do everything the same way, you'll always get the same results. For instance, always toss papers on the kitchen table and the kitchen table will always be cluttered. To get organized, you're required to do things a bit differently. Just because it's different, however, doesn't mean it's more difficult. In fact, the systems required to get and maintain organization are actually easy and pay off big in the long run.

- **Believe in yourself.** It has happened so many times. Someone tells me he just can't get organized. He's not disciplined enough. She's too deeply buried in paper. He's not a very focused person. She is being pulled in too many directions. I can't. I can't. I can't.

  And that person is right. There's no way a person will ever get organized with an "I can't" attitude.

  If you tell yourself you can't learn another language, you won't learn another language. Tell yourself you can't play golf, you'll never play golf. Say "I can't get organized" and you won't get organized. Now, this is not saying that anyone in the world can do anything he or she wants to do. Not everyone could be an opera singer. Not everyone could be an Olympic gold medal winner.

  But, how will you know that you can't do something you truly want to do, if you don't give yourself a fighting chance? It's inevitable— saying, "I can't" practically guarantees you won't. Now that you know why saying "I can't," eliminates any chance of success, there's a very simple way of achieving more of what you set out to do.

  All you have to do is drop the letter T from "I can't" and suddenly you'll begin to see that everything changes. Tell yourself "I can learn another language." You'll get a few language books and you'll begin learning a whole new vocabulary. Tell yourself "I can play golf." You'll get on the green with a golf instructor who can give you the instruction you need and you'll begin playing golf. Tell yourself "I can get organized," and you'll begin applying some simple organizing concepts to pretty much guarantee you will get organized.

  You need to give yourself a fighting chance and that fighting chance begins in your own mind. The bottom line is, you have to believe in yourself and see yourself succeeding, before you ever will.

- **Pick a tip.** Want to really see how easy it is to start getting organized? Just turn to any page in this book, pick a tip and apply that one teeny tiny tip today. Once you do that, you're well on your way to becoming *Finally Organized, Finally Free*.

Chapter 3

Finding the Energy

- **Take a deep breath.** Getting overwhelmed just looking at the clutter is one of the greatest excuses not to start. Take a deep breath and focus on one small area. Once that area is done, there will be plenty of time for the rest.

- **Early bird or night owl?** There's no doubt about it. Organizing your home or office does take some energy. That's why knowing your peak energy level is so important. If you're an early bird and your energy level is very high in the morning, that's the best time for you to start. If you have more energy at night organize during that time instead.

- **Know your limits.** Some people are at their best when they work in long, marathon sessions. Others can only work for fifteen minutes at a time. Determine your limits and set your organizing schedule within that timeframe.

- **Eat healthy.** Not eating nutritious meals regularly contributes to feeling sluggish and disoriented. Most people need three nutritious meals per day. Stay away from foods that can make you sleepy such as white flour and sugar.

- **Never skip breakfast.** You've heard it before. Breakfast is the most important meal of the day. But be sure to eat something healthy. Trade in your bagels for a vegetable omelet or bowl of oatmeal with fresh fruit.

- **Catch some winks.** Eight hours of sleep, no more and no less, is just about right for most people. If you get less or more, you could end up feeling very overtired.

- **Breathe.** When you feel like you're getting tired and out of breath, it's time to breathe. Inhale some fresh air and let it out. Do this several times until you feel your energy lifting.

- **Stay hydrated.** If you get dehydrated, you're going to feel exhausted. Drink water throughout the day—at least a four-ounce glass every hour. Ditch the soda and other sugary beverages when you're trying to get something done.

- **Take a power nap.** If you feel yourself getting tired in the middle of an activity, stop and take a ten-minute nap. This may be all you need to reenergize. Be sure to set your alarm clock so you don't fall asleep for hours.

- **Pleasant aromas.** Smelling something delightful can send your energy levels soaring to new heights. Try a scented candle, lavender oil or pleasant room spray.

Organizing Clinic

Question

In the old days when the kids were younger, I was pretty organized. Then about ten years ago I was diagnosed with MS. Over the past few years, all of my organizing abilities have gone downhill. The papers, school notes and hockey schedules pile up and end up overflowing in the basket. I am unable to write or walk unaided so I do use the computer a lot, but it's just not the same as jotting something down in an organizer. Bedrooms are another story altogether, as is organizing my cupboards.

I was fortunate this past summer to have my best friend from Massachusetts come and help me out, but it's all building up again. Any suggestions?

Vickie Jillson
Corunna, Ontario, Canada

Answer

Dear Vickie,

Since you were pretty organized ten years ago, I'm assuming you know how to be organized. However, now with your illness, your energy level has plummeted. Here are some ideas that may help you get back on track.

- **Make a Tickler File.** You'll find step-by-step instructions in this book. It doesn't take much energy to make or use and it's easy for the kids to use too. If you don't have the dexterity right now to label the files, ask a friend or one of your kids to help. This will help get your active papers under control.

- **The kids can help.** I'm assuming since your children are old enough to play hockey, then they are old enough to help you keep your home organized. Come up with a chore chart on your computer and get the entire family to chip in.

- **Give yourself a daily project.** Since you don't have that much energy, give yourself a 15-minute organizing project to work on each day. This will ensure you're getting things done each day without exhausting yourself. When you're done, celebrate your accomplishments.

- **Get some assistance.** Is it within your budget to have your home professionally organized? There are plenty of great people out there who can help you organize your cupboards, bedrooms, files, and so on. Some will even come back each week to help you maintain control. If it's way out of your budget, speak to your local church or community center. They're certain to have some willing volunteers to give you a hand.

- **Get your blood flowing.** Start off your day with ten minutes of physical activity, such as riding your bike, jogging or doing some stretches. Then, get to your organizing project. Getting your body moving may give you all the energy you need to get started.

- **Keep a journal.** Are you tired on some days and energetic on others? If so, keep a daily journal indicating your energy level on a scale of 1 to 5, what you ate, what type of exercise you did, how much you slept and if there were any things that stressed you out that day. Evaluate your log within two weeks to determine if you see a pattern that may be causing those low energy days.

- **Get a check up.** Sometimes low energy has to do with a health issue. Get an annual physical each year to rule out or correct any health issues.

- **No more butts.** Smokers typically have lower energy than non-smokers. Try your best to kick the habit.

- **Don't sit all day.** If you sit most of the day, such as a job that requires you to sit at your computer, it's vital for you to get up and get moving regularly. Stand up and stretch. Walk down the hall. Go outside and take a deep breath of fresh air. If you're home most of the day, don't spend more than an hour on the sofa watching TV.

- **Music marathon.** Listening to cheery, upbeat music when you're organizing can really get you moving and keep you alert. Don't play it so loud so that it's a distraction. Keep it at an enjoyable background level.

- **Work with an energetic person.** Get one of the most energetic family members in your house to help out. His or her energy may rub off on you. If you can't find such a person in your house, find an energetic relative, neighbor, friend, student or professional organizer.

- **Meditate.** Need to regroup your thoughts? Any form of meditation can help you take a vacation from daily stressors.

- **Reduce activities.** You may be running around too much. I knew a woman once who was in the PTA, a bowling league, the church choir, a Bible study class, an aerobics group, the quilting club and the town board. To top it off, she was the mother of five young children. That's enough to make anyone fatigued. Choose the activities you enjoy the most and do those only.

  The same goes for your kids if you're constantly driving them from one activity to the next. It can be healthy and enjoyable to spend some quiet time together as a family at home, rather than moving from one outside activity to the next.

- **Plan some fun.** If your day is packed with all work activities and no play activities, no wonder you're feeling tired! Sandwich fun activities in between chores, projects and errands.

Organizing Clinic

Question

I can rarely finish a project the day I start it, due to chronic fatigue and lack of time. I don't have a room where I can leave things out. My family moves my half-organized piles making my problem worse than before. I can't go on this way. Help!

Marie Krasch
Whittier, CA

Answer

Dear Marie,

Here are a few ideas that can help you get things done with a lot less frustration.

- **Lower your expectations.** Most projects don't have to be completed in one day. When you have a project to do, break it down into smaller parts over the course of several days. This is less overwhelming and ensures an entire day isn't spent on just one project. Work for 15 to 20 minutes at a time. Before you know it, your project will be done.

- **Re-think your work area.** If your family keeps moving your unfinished projects, it's probably because they're being temporarily stored in a main living area. They are probably in the way of your family's day-to-day activities. Since you don't have an extra room, designate an out-of-the-way corner or nook or an extra portable table for your unfinished projects. If it's not in your family's way, it should not have to be moved.

- **Assess your other systems.** Everyone gets the same exact 24 hours each day. The truly organized people are those who constantly evaluate their systems to be sure they're making the most of those 24 hours. If there is a severe lack of time in your day to complete your tasks and projects, then some of your other systems need to be worked on. Over the next two weeks, fill out a daily time log, keeping track of what you're doing and how long it's taking. At the end of the two-week period, you'll immediately see what items are soaking up your schedule and you'll be able to work on streamlining or eliminating those things. Once you eliminate those things that are wasting time, you'll have more free time available to work on other projects.

- **Handle right away.** Right now, it sounds like you have piles of paper you're trying to organize. If you handle your paper on a daily basis, tossing what you don't need and filing what you do need, it won't have a chance to get out of hand in the future. In other words, if the project didn't get out-of-hand in the first place, you wouldn't have this paper pile project. Remember, if you take care of things right away, they'll only take a few seconds to handle, while when you let things go, they often turn into big, time-consuming projects.

- **Conserve energy.** If you know you only have so much energy in a given day, divide that time evenly between a project that you must do even though you're not too happy about it and a project you would prefer to do.

- **Watch where you're putting your energy.** If much of your day's energy is going to tasks that are not very important, it's a good idea to reassess. Give most of your energy to the tasks that are important.

- **Avoid work stress.** A stressful job during the day can leave you feeling tired and annoyed at night. Determine what's causing stress at your job and try to eliminate that stress. Talk to your boss or the head of the Human Resources department for assistance. If you really can't take the stress, make a goal to find a more enjoyable, less stressful, job.

- **Hang out with positive people.** Spending time with negative people can be exhausting, especially when the negativity is not due to an illness. Find some very positive friends and relatives and stick with them.

- **Avoid same old, same old.** Try to do at least one new thing each day. This will keep your mind sharp and will make your day more interesting.

- **Avoid colds.** Having a cold or the flu can be particularly draining. Take all necessary measures to avoid getting sick. Get a flu shot. Wash your hands often. Don't touch your hands to your eyes, nose or mouth, especially after activities such as riding the subway, shaking someone's hand or holding onto a railing at a mall.

- **Go outside.** Just a little bit of sunlight or fresh air can bring refreshing energy. Open your shades and your windows. Go outside at least once or twice each day. Don't use rain as an excuse. Bring an umbrella. Even if it's just for five minutes at a time, it is sure to do you good.

- **Be happy.** Read fun and motivating books. Sing happy songs. Watch funny movies. Listen to inspirational audio programs. Enjoy the clouds, the sun, the blue sky, flowers, the beach and snow. Talk with a favorite friend, relative or associate often. Make time for your hobbies. Set goals. Basically, do whatever it takes to have a cheerful, enjoyable day and the energy will naturally follow.

- **Take a cool shower.** If you're having a slow and sluggish day, jump in the shower for ten minutes—no matter what time of the day it is. Be sure the water is on the cooler side and you're sure to wake up and feel more energy. If you'd prefer not to get your hair wet, just wear a shower cap.

- **Declare a high-energy day.** Just by telling yourself over and over that today is going to be a high-energy day, you can set the stage.

Chapter 4

Busting Clutter

- **What is clutter?** Webster's Dictionary defines clutter as "an untidy mess; a state of disorder; things left around untidily." I'd like to add a bit to that description. It's also clutter if . . .

  - ❖ It is damaged and you have no aspirations to repair it.

  - ❖ Using it is more bother than it's worth.

  - ❖ You never use it.

  - ❖ You don't like it.

  - ❖ It is obsolete.

  - ❖ You've outgrown it physically.

  - ❖ You've outgrown it mentally.

  - ❖ It is uncomfortable physically.

  - ❖ It is uncomfortable mentally.

  - ❖ It is too fragile or dainty to enjoy.

  - ❖ It is too good to use.

  - ❖ It is the wrong size.

  - ❖ It is the wrong color.

  - ❖ It is the wrong style.

  - ❖ It is not flattering.

  - ❖ It has no useful purpose.

  - ❖ You wouldn't notice if it was missing.

- **Damaged with no aspirations to repair it.** If you don't plan on repairing something that's broken, either give it to someone else to repair or get rid of it. It's just taking up space you could be using for something else.

- **It's more bother than it's worth.** If you have something you never use because it's such a bother to use it, it's not worth your space, your time or your energy. Buy a more efficient item if necessary and get rid of the item that's causing you so much trouble.

- **You never use it.** A friend of mine once had very long hair and used to keep a huge bag of curlers when she wanted a wavy style. Now her hair is very short and I recently noticed she still had her bag of curlers.

  When I asked her why she was keeping them, she said that maybe someday she would grow her hair out again. But I reminded her that her hair has been short for almost five years already. At that point, she was convinced to part with her bag of curlers and she hasn't missed them since.

- **Decide that you've had enough.** Once you've made the decision that you've really had it up to your eyeballs with clutter, you've taken the most important step to getting rid of it.

Great idea!

When going through your sentimental items and trying to thin out collections, rather than hanging on to each and every item, take pictures of many of the items and keep them in an album. This way you still have the memories, but not all the clutter.

Kristy Tidrick
Stone Creek, OH

- **Make distinctions.** If you don't use it or you don't love it, it's clutter. Make two piles: a) I use it/I love it and b) I don't use it/I don't care about it.

- **Get it out of your sight.** For ten minutes each day, choose a room. Pick up two items and declare one a "keeper" and the second "clutter." Get the clutter item out of your sight. Either put it into a Donation or Rummage Sale box if it's good enough to be used by someone else or put it in your trash container. Out of sight—out of mind.

- **Delete, delete and delete.** Just like physical clutter, virtual clutter is taking up valuable space on your computer. Again, decide whether or not it's clutter and use your delete key steadfastly. Generally jokes and other email forwards can be deleted once you've read them or even before you've read them if you're not interested. Another example would be computer files on your hard drive and disks that you no longer use.

- **You don't like it.** Please don't keep something that you don't like. It may be causing you stress every time you look at it. If it doesn't have any sentimental value to you it should be fairly easy to part with. If it was expensive, sell it or give it away to someone.

Organizing Clinic

Question

My husband insists everything be left in plain sight, so he can find stuff easier. I mean everything. His drawers are empty while the top of the dresser is piled high. It's the same with our kitchen table with mail. I'm ashamed to have company. Help!

Lou Ann
NB

Answer

Dear Lou Ann,

Your husband will more likely follow organizing systems that suit his personality style.

- **Use open cubes.** Open storage cubes are wonderful for people who have "out and about" tendencies. Everything can be stored in the open, while still having a neat and organized appearance.

- **See it through.** There are tons of storage containers on the market that allow you to see what's inside without opening them up. These are perfect storage solutions for the "out and about" type of person, because even though everything is inside, it gives the illusion that everything is out in the open.

- **Make a mail station.** To prevent mail from getting tossed on the table, as soon as it's carried inside it should be brought to the mail station. The mail station should have a basket or tray for each family member's mail. Whoever brings the mail in, has the job of sorting it into the proper person's basket. This will ensure that everyone gets his or her mail, nothing gets lost, and your husband will still have his mail out in the open.

- **Designate homes.** Very often, people leave things out in the open because they don't have permanent homes assigned. Be sure your husband has enough permanent drawers and closet space to put his things so he always knows where they are. Then, be sure that specific drawers are designated for similar items. For instance, my husband has a drawer for his underwear, another for his socks and another for his pajamas. Everything has its own home. There's no way he'll have any trouble finding his socks if they're stored in his sock drawer.

- **Have a heart-to-heart.** If you haven't done so already, try sitting down with your husband in a calm and loving manner and having a heart-to-heart conversation. Tell him it's embarrassing for you to have company over when papers are left out on the table. Maybe he's not even aware there is a problem. Maybe you might even offer to help him come up with organizing solutions that will make both of you satisfied. Marriage is a two-way street and both people have to compromise to make systems work.

- **It is obsolete.** Barring antiques if you're an antique collector, if you have something you never use because it's so old, such as a record player, an old Polaroid or a clunker of a computer, think "out with the old, in with the new."

Great idea!

I keep several boxes in the house, most under my bed, labeled "bookstore," "library," "charity," "school," "church," and "friends." When I decide I don't need something anymore, such as a clothing item, I put it into the appropriate box, such as the one for "charity." Books go first to the used-book store and whatever the store doesn't take is donated to the school or library. If one box gets full, I start another. For those charities that do pickups I hold the boxes until each quarterly pick-up date. I drop off the other boxes when they get full. By having a specific place to put things, I know where they are and can pass them on more easily while ridding the house of clutter and simplifying recycling.

Marianne Rankin
University Park, MD

- **You've outgrown it physically.** If you can no longer use your old exercise equipment, clothing, shoes or anything else you've physically outgrown, get rid of it. You're beyond that stage in your life and ready for the next new exciting stage.

- **You've outgrown it mentally.** Stuffed animals, a hobby you were once interested in but have become bored with, a fetish you've once had with mittens or anything else you're no longer interested in will probably make someone else still in that mode very happy. Give someone else a chance to grow out of these things and get them out of your home.

- **It's uncomfortable physically and mentally.** If something you have is making your back, shoulders, feet, brain or any other body part stressed or painful, it's not the type of item you want laying around.

- **It's too fragile and dainty to enjoy or it's too good to use.** If this is the case, why even have it? I use my dainty crystal drinking glasses frequently. I wear my fragile and dainty pearl ring all the time. If something happens to these items, will I be sad? Yes, probably. But I'd be even sadder if they just sat in a drawer or cabinet forever.

Organizing Clinic

Question

My question is guilt I have regarding giving or throwing things away. Either the items are not in good enough condition to give away or bad for the environment to throw away. For example, a lot of times I don't feel I should give an item to Goodwill because it's not perfect, like a backpack purse with one strap torn, but it's not bad enough to throw away.

Another real problem is used computer parts. Most are obsolete by the time I'm ready to throw them out and it's bad for the environment to just put them in the trash. So now they're cluttering up my garage. Any ideas? Thanks!

Ronnie Levine
Long Beach, California

Answer

Dear Ronnie,

Don't you also feel guilty for taking up unnecessary space in your home? Don't you also feel guilty that you're allowing your guilt to prevent you from getting organized? First, let's talk about those things you feel are not quite good enough to donate. Instead of using your time to fret about it, channel that energy into actually repairing those items. The backpack purse can be sewn up and be almost as good as new.

Goodwill will generally take things that are in fairly good condition. Even if you're not handy with something like sewing or repairing, someone who shops at donation shops may be very good at this. In general, items that are donated to these donation services are in decent shape—not perfect shape. As long as they're clean and repairable, they will usually be accepted.

In addition, did you realize that much of what many thrift shops receive is sold as scrap for rags and recycling? These items are sold in bulk. Of course, if items are way out of the range of being repaired, such as those that are badly damaged or tattered and the thrift shop refuses those items, tossing them away will free up your space for nicer, more useable items.

As for the old computer parts, if they're truly of no use and are outdated, you should really get rid of them. First, try to find a computer parts recycling center in your area. Look in the phone book. If no computer parts recycling center is available and if you can't find someone else to take them, such as a computer repair shop or a person who enjoys tinkering with old equipment, contact your city's sanitation department and ask them the best way to dispose of these parts.

The sooner you stop feeling guilty about getting rid of things you never use, the sooner you'll be able to free your own environment and your mind.

- **It's the wrong size, color or style. It's not flattering.** Get rid of it. You should feel good about your possessions. Enough said.

- **It has no useful purpose.** By all means, if you have no idea why you're even keeping something, don't keep it a minute longer.

- **Don't be wasteful.** Remember, when you keep something that no longer serves a purpose or has outlived its value or usefulness, you're wasting space, time, money and energy.

- **Display your treasures.** For items you're truly sentimental about, use them and enjoy them. Don't keep them boxed up in a closet.

- **You wouldn't notice if it was missing.** If you're not sure whether you'd miss it or not, put it in a "Holding Box" with the other items you're unsure of. Seal this box and put it in an out-of-the way place, like a high closet shelf or in the attic. Go to your calendar and put the words "Holding Box" on a date that's six months ahead of today.

  When you finally see the words "Holding Box" on your calendar, whatever you still have not retrieved from that box goes to charity or the garbage collector. Obviously, you didn't miss it.

- **Don't Encourage More Clutter.** So many people have clutter because they wait to put things away or they delay tossing something out they no longer need. Things are put in a temporary place "just for now" and those temporary storage areas often become problem clutter spots.

  For instance, if there's already one sheet of paper left out on your desk will it really make a big difference if there are two sheets left out or three or four? Actually, it will make a huge difference because before you know it, you'll have an enormous stack of paper on your desk.

  What about if you toss a jacket over the back of the sofa? It's only one jacket, right? Well, what if your spouse walks in and tosses his or her jacket right next to yours? After all, you've just expressed that it's okay to do so by tossing your jacket over the sofa. Then, your kids come home from school and toss their jackets over the sofa, because they figure if the system is good enough for mom and dad, then it's good enough for them too. It won't take long for your home to be a mess.

  Have you ever heard of the broken window theory? If there's an old, abandoned factory in a town and it has one broken window that's left broken, before long there will be two broken windows, three broken windows, four, five—until the building is full of broken windows and the neighborhood begins to deteriorate.

It's just the way it goes. If nobody cares enough to fix the first broken window, others will be compelled to break more windows because there is no order or enforcement of rules in this town. The broken window theory can be applied to most areas of your life. If you let the small stuff go, the small stuff will soon turn into big stuff.

So, the next time you consider tossing the mail on the coffee table instead of going through it right now or letting the laundry pile up all week rather than doing a load a day, think about the broken window theory. Most clutter can be avoided by taking a moment to put things away now or by immediately getting rid of things you no longer need.

- **Take a photo.** Do you have something you don't like, but are keeping because you received it from someone special? Maybe a large number of your possessions meet similar criteria. If you're not using and/or enjoying these items, they're just taking up space. Take photos of each sentimental item, save the photos in a scrapbook and toss the item itself. Better yet, take digital photos and keep them on a CD. Keep the memory, rather than allowing the physical item to waste space.

- **Make a video.** Invite close family members and friends over. Go through old memorabilia—furniture, jewelry, whatever—and talk about why those items are special to you. Include everyone in the conversation. Tape the entire event. The memorabilia and the memories will be on tape and you'll be able to get rid of the actual objects since they'll be recorded.

- **Make a donation box.** Get a large cardboard box and label it "Donation Box." Under the title, write, "These are the things I don't use, but someone else could be using right now." Every time you find something in your home you no longer use and that you don't have deep sentimental attachment to, put it in the Donation Box. Bring the box to your favorite charity or Goodwill once each month. You'll feel great knowing you've helped someone less fortunate than yourself. Plus, your home will have less clutter and be more organized.

- **Get tax relief.** You may be able to deduct donations from your taxes. Keep an envelope including all donation information inside. On the receipt you get from the charity, list the name of the item you donated and the approximate value.

- **Donation drop-offs.** There is an unlimited array of choices available to donate clothing, books, furniture, toys, appliances, sporting equipment and more. To give you an idea, you can donate to Goodwill, churches, domestic violence shelters, thrift stores, hospitals, orphanages, theaters, second hand bookstores, prisons, senior citizen centers and schools.

Organizing Clinic

Question

I am 72 years old and have many items given to me by close family and friends. My children complain about the clutter. They're right. Also many items belonged to my mother. I am sentimental. What can I do to unclutter this mess? Thank you.

Catherine L. McCormick
Philadelphia, PA

Answer

Dear Catherine,

There's certainly nothing wrong with being sentimental or keeping things you truly treasure. What you've collected over the years represents the love and good memories between you, your mom, your family and your friends. First, it's important to realize that you're not going to lose the memories because you no longer have the physical symbols of those memories. What you feel for your family and friends is in your heart. What I've done with some people I've assisted over the years is to tell them to take photos of possessions that they want to remember, but to get rid of the possessions themselves. Of course, if they're in good condition, donate them. Photos take up little space and keep the memories alive.

Another possibility is to pass on some of these treasures to people in your family. For instance, if your mom gave you a set of pots and pans, maybe one of your children would like them. Ask first, of course. Just knowing that the treasured items are still in the family—but not necessarily in your home—may bring you some comfort. For those items that are incredibly important to you—you have to be discerning here—appropriate storage is a must. If you have a large home, you can always display some of it and store the rest. Every so often, put some items away and take others out of storage. In doing so, everything is not on display at one time.

If you're short on space, consider putting up some shelving. Line the shelves with pretty baskets and hat boxes. Store some of your treasures that way. Definitely only keep the most sentimental stuff though. Your mother may have given you lots of things, but everything can't have the same sentimental value. If she gave you a pearl ring, a teapot, a coffee table and a set of china, perhaps keeping one of those things would satisfy your sentimental side. Be careful about keeping everything, otherwise your home could easily be taken over and get totally out of control.

- **Lighten your load and reduce stress.** One word: simplify. If you have lots of clutter, there's no doubt you're feeling lots of stress. A cluttered, chaotic environment breeds stress and frustration. If you don't love it and/or you don't use it, it's clutter. Get rid of your clutter and lighten your load. As you do, you'll be reducing stress and feeling a sense of calm.

- **Organize to make money.** You can actually make money from your useable clutter. Consider running a classified ad, selling on E-bay or another Internet auction site, holding a rummage sale or working with a consignment shop.

  You're probably familiar with most of these methods. Consignment shops are generally the least used because people aren't aware of how they work. In general, the consignment shop accepts your donations and attempts to sell them for you. If they do, they will give you a percentage of the selling price. If they don't, they may give the item(s) back to you or better yet, some donate the unsold items to a charity for you. If they donate to a charity, of course, you won't make any money, but at least the item won't end up back in your home just to gather dust again.

- **Use a Rotation Box.** You may have beautiful things you really do enjoy, but you may not have the space to display all of them. Display just a few at a time and place the rest in a "Rotation Box" stored in the basement, attic or a closet. When the season or your mood changes, just put away some of the items currently on display and access your Rotation Box for the items in storage you now wish to display. You'll get to enjoy all of your items throughout the year.

- **Give them to someone who could use them.** If it disturbs you to dump things, even if you're never going to use them again, consider passing them on to someone else. Ask friends, family or associates if they would like them. If not, donate them. Your local Salvation Army will probably accept your donation if the items are in fairly good condition.

- **Avoid the Halfway House Syndrome.** That's when you put something someplace temporarily until you decide what you're going to do with it. These temporary areas most often turn into permanent areas—better known as clutter spots. Force yourself to make a firm decision whether to toss or keep something. If you decide to keep it, use it. If not, get rid of it today.

- **Keep or Toss Test.** The next time you're contemplating whether or not you should keep or toss, use these questions to help you decide:

  ❖ Have I used this item in the past year?

  ❖ Is it serving a specific purpose?

  ❖ Do I still like it?

  ❖ Is there a legal reason for keeping it?

  ❖ Do I have a place to store it where I will find it again?

- **The one-minute decision.** When having difficulty deciding whether to keep or toss something, set a timer for exactly one minute. When the timer sounds, force yourself to make the decision and be done with it. You won't spend all day contemplating.

- **Synchronize with trash day.** Make it a point to organize for one hour each day before trash day. Whatever junk you gather can immediately be tossed in the trash, ready for the garbage collector the next morning.

- **Live out of the box.** When you're trying to get your home organized, discarding or donating your clutter is an extremely important action that you most likely have to take. One of the easiest ways to begin getting organized is to lighten your load. However, getting rid of things is often terribly difficult for people—not physically, but emotionally. It's one of the greatest struggles for the millions of people who wish they were more organized.

    The "Live Out of the Box" Method can help. If an item is constantly in your sight, your emotions may interfere with your uncluttering process. You may think, "Well, maybe I should hang onto it as I may need it someday." Whereas, if it was buried somewhere out of sight, you'd most likely never think of it again.

    Get yourself a few very large boxes, choose the one room that currently bothers you the most and pack everything up—except for bills that have to be paid and very meaningful heirlooms or decorative items—just as you would if you were moving. Once you're done, everything should be completely packed up and in boxes. Put today's date on those boxes.

    For the next three months, live out of the box. When you need or want something, pilfer it from the box and use it. Items you use receive "OK to Keep" status. In other words, you can then put those items back in their appropriate closet, cabinet, drawer, countertop or shelf.

    After the three months have gone by, whatever still remains in that box is donated, sold or dumped. After all, if you haven't needed it or thought about it in three months, what are the chances you'll ever think about it or need it again?

    Yes, it will be a bit of a pain to live out of boxes—for that one room—but keep in mind that the things you really want and need in that room will be out of the box and in their appropriate homes within a few days. Many of our Get Organized Now! Discussion Forum members have used this technique with excellent results and swear by it.

Great idea!

My kitchen has a small amount of cupboard and drawer space. Recently, I began to remove items that I don't use often or don't use at all, such as mismatched drinking glasses, excess mixing spoons and other utensils and plastic storage containers. I am not sure whether I want to get rid of these items altogether, so I boxed them up and put them in an out-of-the-way spot.

Now, it is easier to find the items that I do use often and unloading the dishwasher is faster because I don't need to shuffle around various types of drinking glasses in order to have room for everything.

In a few months, I will go through the boxed items and it will be easier to decide which items to donate to charity. I will ask myself if I even remembered that I owned X, Y, or Z and if I do need one again someday, how difficult and expensive will it be to acquire another one?

There will always be the chance that sometime in the future, I might need something that I had given away. However, I would rather spend a few dollars on a new mixing spoon than hold on to anything and everything because "I might need it someday."

Kari Yearous
Winona, MN

- **Get help.** Invite a friend over to help you dejunk or hire a professional organizer. Sometimes the help of another person, especially one that will encourage you to be ruthless, may be all the motivation and support you need.

- **15 minutes each day.** Clutter has a tendency to grow and get out of hand. Spend fifteen minutes each day clearing off tabletops, desks and other surfaces. You won't give clutter a chance to set in.

- **Another's clutter is not your responsibility.** If it's not your clutter, give it to whomever it belongs to so he or she can decide whether to keep or toss it. This applies to your married daughter's old school report cards, your friend's stuff that she left at your home from the last rummage sale you had together, your college-aged son's artwork from kindergarten and so on.

- **Stop buying physical stuff.** You may like to shop and perhaps you're fortunate enough to have the money to do so frequently. But just because you like to shop, doesn't mean you have to buy "physical" things. Next time you get the urge, buy yourself something that doesn't clutter, such as a vacation, theatre tickets, a restaurant gift certificate, a massage or an educational class.

- **Give it a home.** Have a place for everything and keep everything in its place. Things that don't have homes are homeless. Designate a specific home for every item you have so you know exactly where to put it when you're done with it. Never leave an item stranded. When you're done with it, put it back in its home immediately.

- **Five minutes to save hours.** Is your problem paper clutter? If so, schedule a minimum of five minutes per evening to file the important stuff in your filing cabinet and to toss the unimportant papers out a little at a time.

Great idea!

I keep a large plastic bag on the closet doorknob in my bedroom. Anything I want to give away to the Salvation Army, I immediately put into this bag. When the bag is full, my husband drops it off.

Rochelle Bharath
Hollywood, FL

- **Don't expect miracles.** If you have a lot of clutter, chances are it has been building for months or even years. Since it took that clutter so long to get there, chances are you won't be able to get rid of it in a day. But if you just focus on getting rid of just a little bit each day, you'll soon begin to make a dent and eventually it will be gone.

- **Clutter—it's not only physical.** Besides physical clutter, there is also paper clutter, virtual clutter and mental clutter—all of which we'll discuss in the chapters ahead. All clutter, no matter what form it takes, wastes time, energy and money while it increases chaos, stress and frustration. Clearing the clutter paves the way for a simpler, happier, more fulfilling life.

- **Rent a dumpster.** If you have an enormous amount of clutter that includes large items such as furniture and appliances, rent a dumpster and get rid of it once and for all.

- **Don't be held hostage.** Beware of being held hostage by your possessions. When your stuff begins taking over your life and you're spending all your time climbing over things, looking for missing items and fretting over where you'll put your next "treasure," you are wasting precious time that you can never buy back.

- **It's time to let go.** When you hold on to something physically, you tend to become even more attached to it. When getting rid of clutter, have a friend or relative hold the object while you decide whether to keep it or get rid of it. Hint: Choose a friend who will sway you towards getting rid of it.

- **Heed these words of wisdom.** In the words of Henry David Thoreau, "Simplify. Simplify." The less you have, the less opportunity to generate clutter.

- **Schedule a monthly unclutter assignment.** Each month, have something scheduled to unclutter. For instance, designate January your "Kitchen Weed Out Month." Designate February as your "Home Office Weed Out Month." Schedule March as your "Basement Weed Out Month." You get the idea. Each month, concentrate on one room or one area and weed it out. Clutter will never have a chance to build up!

- **Tackle Your Clutter.** Look around your home or office and find one of your clutter trouble spots. Is it your desk? Your clothes closet? Your filing cabinet? Your dining room table? Once you find it, this clutter spot is the opposing team, just like in a football game.

You versus the Desk.

Or

You versus the Table.

Your game will be comprised of four distinct quarters of 15 minutes each.

1st Quarter: Set your timer for 15 minutes. During this time, come up with your game plan. Gather all of your supplies—trash bags, recycle container, dust rags and anything else you need. Set your voicemail up to retrieve incoming calls. Tell your family you cannot be interrupted as you're preparing for the big game. Put some energetic music on. Preparation is a major key that should never be skipped. When the timer buzzes, start the 2nd Quarter.

2nd Quarter: Set your timer for 15 minutes. During this time, begin tackling your clutter. Pick each item up, one by one and put it into one of three piles:

A. Keep

B. Donate/Sell

C. Toss

Your goal is to have each of the three piles pretty evenly distributed by the time you're finished. Work quickly and make a firm decision on everything you touch. When the timer goes off, stop. Do a few stretches and move on to the 3rd Quarter.

3rd Quarter: Set your timer for 15 minutes. Take everything in Pile B and put it in a box right by your front door. On your next trip out later today, put the box in the car and drive over to your local Goodwill or church to donate it. If your chosen organization will pick these items up from you, make a call now to arrange a pick-up time.

Take everything in Pile C and put it in your trash receptacle or recycle container, so it's ready for the garbage or recyclable collectors. Do this until the timer sounds.

4th Quarter: Set your timer for 15 minutes. Take everything in your A pile and find an appropriate home for those items. If the timer sounds before you're done, work for 15 minutes overtime.

By the time you're done, you will have conquered your opponent. Now spend some time celebrating your winning touchdown victory!

- **One in and one out.** Before buying anything new, try to get rid of something first. For example, before buying a new sweater, get rid of an old sweater. Before buying a new CD, get rid of one you never listen to.

- **Prevent clutter.** One of the best ways to prevent clutter is to stop it before it starts. Here are three simple questions to ask yourself:

  - ❖ **Am I going to use it?** Many a clutter pile originally started from an impulse buy. Perhaps you were enticed by an infomercial on TV for a handy-dandy pancake flipper. Perhaps you bought a new dress adorned with glitter and lace because it looked so pretty on the store mannequin. Before you buy something, always ask yourself a) if you're going to use it and b) if you're going to use it often enough to be worth the space it's going to take up in your home.

    The pancake flipper would probably be worth it if you use it once a week or once every two weeks. If you're only going to use it once every few months, it's probably not worth the extra money or the extra space it's going to take up in your kitchen cabinets. The same goes for the glittery, lacy dress. Unless you spend a lot of time at dressy parties and events, opt instead for something you'll make more use of. Otherwise, it's just going to be taking up space in your clothes closet.

    In addition, if you have well meaning friends or relatives who are constantly trying to pass things on to you that they no longer need and that you don't need either, learn to politely say "Thanks, but no thanks."

  - ❖ **Am I going to use it now or in the near future?** Of course, if you have a lawn, you spend a lot of time mowing. If you need a new lawn mower and you see a mower on sale in the winter—you might want to take advantage of purchasing that item while it's on sale.

    However, beware of buying things with the reasoning, "I'm not sure when I'll use it, but I'll use it someday." My friend, who never bakes, was planning to buy a springform pan because I had one. Her reasoning was that if she had a springform pan in her possession, it might entice her to bake someday.

I told her that before she goes out and buys one, I would loan her mine for a week. She could leave it on her countertop and see if the inspiration hit her. Needless to say, she returned the pan within a week and told me that she hadn't had the inspiration yet, so she would borrow it from me when she was ready to bake—that was three years ago.

In other words, she saved money by not buying that pan. It would have been gathering dust for years.

❖ **Where is it going to go?** On my last trip to Pier One—a wonderful store for purchasing decorative items for the home—I came across a candleholder that I really liked. But before making the purchase, I immediately asked myself, "Where is it going to go?" After some thought, I determined it would look great in my home office on my bookshelf on the 2nd shelf from the top.

I also came across a neat looking basket that I was considering buying along with the candleholder. But when I asked myself, "Where is it going to go?" I could not come up with an area off the top of my head. In the end, I bought the candleholder, but did not buy the basket.

Make sure you have a clearly defined home for the item you're considering getting. Otherwise, it's bound to be brought home, put someplace temporarily and eventually end up in a pile of other purchases that were not well thought out.

Chapter 5
Quick Storage Guidelines

- **Where should it go?** Aside from "how do I get rid of my clutter," the second most popular question I'm regularly asked is, "how do I determine where to put something, so that I could find it quickly later."

  Rather than making a quick and rash decision about where something should be stored, always try to remember to give this important decision some planned thought. This handy guide will help ensure your things are categorized and easy to find when you need them.

  ❖ **Daily Storage Areas:** These areas are meant for items you use at least once a day (hairbrush, blow dryer, toothpaste, keys, razor, slippers). Store these items within arms reach of the place you use them.

  ❖ **Weekly/Monthly Storage Areas:** These areas are meant for items you use on a weekly or monthly basis (nail polish, biking gear, bowling bag, shoe polish). These items should be stored in easily accessible areas, which may take a minute or two to retrieve. You know—those areas that you have to bend or stretch a bit to get to.

  ❖ **6 Month/Annual Storage Areas:** These areas are meant for items you use infrequently, such as every six months or annually (holiday lights, fine china, out-of-season clothing, tax returns). Store these items in clear, labeled, out-of-the-way containers.

- **Opened or closed?** Some people like open storage units, so they can see each item without opening a door. Others like closed cabinets. Either way is fine, as long as it's a system you like to use. My preference is closed storage units as I feel they give the room a more uniform, organized, neat look.

  For instance, in my home office I have a large computer armoire with doors that close. My home office also doubles as a guest room. When we have guests, I close the doors of my armoire and everything is hidden out of sight. My guests just pull out the sofa bed and are in a nice, cozy bedroom.

- **Categorize items into similar groups.** Keep toys and games in one area, books and magazines in another, writing supplies in another and so on. Don't mix different categories in one place.

- **Containerize and basket-ize.** Use organizing containers and baskets to keep everything together, organized and easily accessible. I like the clear plastic containers since you can see the contents in the container at a glance. I also like containers and baskets with lids so you can stack them if necessary.

- **Don't mindlessly put it anywhere.** When deciding where to store an item, don't just mindlessly look for an empty space on any shelf. Put a little more thought into it. Ask yourself where the item is generally used and store it somewhere in that vicinity. Ask yourself how often the item is used. If you use it all the time, you won't want to put it on a high shelf.

- **Store sets in one place.** This includes items such as pants that go with coordinating shirts and coffee mugs that go with matching dishes.

- **Make seasonal storage.** Stow sleds, ice skates and ski gear during the summer months. Stash kites, bikes and swimming apparatus in the winter.

- **Keep small items organized.** Ice cube trays, muffin tins and compartmentalized appetizer trays also double as drawer organizers for earrings, buttons, pocket change and other small trinkets.

Several small plastic containers with covers can fit in one large plastic container with a cover to keep contents together but organized.

Great idea!

I keep things where they will be used most often, such as clothes freshener spray in the bathroom, laundry detergent in the laundry room and linens in the bedroom closet—rather than storing in random areas around my house. I also keep scissors, pens, pencils and pads in each room so I am not running around looking for some when needed.

Susan Beatty
Menasha, WI

- **Identify.** Always label containers, baskets and cabinets so you know where to retrieve something from when you need it and where to put it back when you're done with it.

- **Don't forget about wall space.** Look around and you're sure to find quite a bit of empty wall space. There are many uses for this newfound space. Pots and pans can be taken out of cabinets and hung on walls. Tools can be placed on pegboards. Shelves can be installed for picture frames and knickknacks. Many stores now carry corner shelves that can be installed in a snap.

- **Same old product, new uses.** Think of new uses for items you find in your house. Use straw baskets to organize medications or bath soaps. Cloth make-up bags are perfect for holding hair accessories. A child's pencil case is great for holding spare keys.

Organizing Clinic

Question

I live in a house that has almost no closets. I have no idea why this is the case, but it is. I've lived here for 27 years and only just noticed that this is why the broom is always out and the bucket is always stashed in a bedroom. I simply have no place to put things.

Sharon Hanna, Writer and Urban Agriculturist

Answer

Dear Sharon,

Unfortunately, lots of homes built more than 25 years ago are short on storage space. But there are some things you can do to increase the space you do have. Here are a few ideas:

- **Make good use of the space you do have.** Increase the space in the closets. Install an extra rod so you can hang more. Use hangers with multiple tiers for skirts and pants. Hang an organizer over the closet door for accessories. Use a shoe rack to stack your shoes. Hang a few hooks for purses, hats and scarves. Hang a shelf or two for sweaters.

- **Get rid of the clutter.** It's important for you to make good decisions about what you should keep and what you should get rid of, especially since you have no storage space. Get rid of anything you don't use and/or like and save that space for the things you do use and like.

- **Buy an armoire or two.** For extra clothing storage space, consider armoires. These can be a bit costly, but they're nice furniture additions that have a good deal of function.

- **Get a hanging rack.** A less expensive alternative to an armoire would be to get a clothes rack. You could then put a decorative screen in front of the rack to hide the clothes.

- **Pick up some hanging organizers.** Get yourself some organizers that hold brooms, mops and other items you could hang. I have one in the laundry room closet that has space to hang five things. I have a mop, broom, dustpan and feather duster on mine and these are all consolidated in a pretty small space. If you can't fit them in a closet, find an inconspicuous wall somewhere, like behind a door.

- **Hide it.** Find some large Rubbermaid containers to store some stuff in. You could always cover the containers with pretty quilts that match your decor. Nobody will know what you have hidden underneath.

- **Use your wall space.** So many people forget they have wall space. Hang shelves in each room and you could store tons of stuff. You might even consider hanging a few cabinets with doors. For instance, this would give you extra space for towels—maybe right in the bathroom.

- **Don't hide small items.** Never put a larger item over a smaller item. For example, don't put the newspaper over the keys. This simple tip could save you hours.

- **Remember Fred Flintstone.** If you remember the old Fred Flintstone cartoons, you'll recall that every time Fred opened his closet, his bowling ball would drop on his head. Ouch!

Of course, Fred recovered very quickly from this injury. You might not. So be very careful about placing heavy items on top of high shelves. In fact, don't do it. Store heavy items on the bottom to prevent any accidents.

Great idea!

I hang clear shoe organizers on the insides of doors such as in my utility room, playroom and closets. In the pockets, I put anything that used to go into junk drawers such as elastics, pins, paperclips, tape, hats, gloves, mittens, scarves, lotion, mosquito spray and sun hats.

Karen Buelow
Germantown, TN

- **Divide that drawer.** Drawer organizers with individual compartments—the type that expand to fit any drawer—give you that extra needed storage space.

- **Invest in a storage trunk.** A storage trunk can be wonderful for storing bed sheets, blankets, quilts and more. It's a functional and decorative addition to your furniture. Plus, a trunk is often versatile and timeless enough to be passed on from generation to generation—for many years worth of organization.

- **Create visual storage with a bookcase.** A bookcase is not only for storing books. It's also wonderful visual storage space. Line the shelves with baskets, compartmentalized plastic trays, plastic containers and see-through jars. Then, fill these "organizers" with your stuff, keeping similar items together.

This solution is perfect for storing office supplies, kid's toys and games, craft items, baby supplies, tools and more. Everything will be contained in one place and be perfectly visible the second you need something.

- **Insufficient or ineffective?** Do you have insufficient storage space or ineffective storage space? There's a big difference. Insufficient storage space means you don't have enough space for your things. Ineffective space means you have enough space for your things, but you're not making the best use of that space.

Most closets and cabinets have the volume to hold twice as much as they are usually constructed for. Also, you probably have quite a few nooks and crannies for storage that you haven't even thought of.

Of course, it's important to make sure you don't have things you don't like or are outdated, but it is also important to have effective storage space for the things you do like and enjoy.

Great idea!

I save the large shoeboxes for organizing. I decorate them with stickers for kid's rooms, the comics from Sunday's paper or leftover wrapping paper. I store photographs, greeting cards, sunglasses, CDs, gravy mixes, food packages, makeup, and other small items and decorate the box to match the items. They are then labeled and stored in the closet, basement, garage and laundry room. You'd be surprised how inventive you can become with how to decorate them and what to store in them.

Janice Hunt
Midvale, UT

- **Diagnose first, remedy second.** Don't go out and buy yourself a ton of organizing baskets and containers before you determine exactly what you need to buy. The final decision will depend on several criteria such as what you're trying to store, how big it is, how heavy it is, if it needs an airtight seal and more.

- **Do a little shopping.** There are several Web sites that specialize in containers, baskets, shelves, cubes, storage systems and other organizing products that allow you to store your things in an organized manner—a few of which you'll find right on the www.getorganizednow.com Web site. But be sure you need that item before you buy it.

- **A basket won't get you organized.** Just like a great golf club doesn't guarantee a great golfer, a wonderful basket won't ensure you will be organized. The only thing that will ensure this is your attitude, your organizing knowledge and skill. It's up to you; not the baskets or containers.

- **Make visible storage with glass jars.** Many grocery items, like pickles, mayonnaise and olives are sold in glass jars. Rather than getting rid of the jars, clean them out and remove the labels. Label remover, such as Goo Gone, will help you get them off quickly. These jars make perfect visible storage. Fill them with anything like dried pasta, beans, cereal, buttons, safety pins and thread, paperclips, elastic bands and binder clips.

- **Label ease.** Consider purchasing a label maker to identify the contents in boxes, on shelves, and in other storage areas. These are especially helpful if you're not too thrilled with your handwriting and/or you want everything to look uniform. We've been happy with the Brother Labeling Systems, but there are quite a few makes and models to choose from if you do an Internet search.

- **Out of this world.** Use space bags to store bulky items, such as jackets, quilts and comforters for the season. You put the items in the bag and suck out all the air with a vacuum. You won't believe how much space this method saves.

- **Do the switch.** If you have lots of decorative display items such as toys and hobby materials, you may really like to use the Rotation Box system. Rather than always having everything out at once, you can display some of these things prominently, and store the rest away.

When the season or your mood changes, you simply rotate the items on display back into storage, and bring the items that have been in storage back out. This system allows you to keep all of the things you like, while preventing a cluttered look.

- **Think outside.** If you've used all possible storage space and you discover your home is truly too small for the things you plan to keep, you have a few options.

  ❖ The first option is to live in a cluttered, cramped space.

  ❖ The second option is to get rid of as much as possible.

  ❖ The third option is to move.

  ❖ The final option is to use an outside storage facility, either a paid facility or the basement or attic of someone you know that wouldn't mind storing some things for you until you get a bigger place.

Great idea!

As I reorganize and get rid of the clutter in my house, I tend to forget where I've now stored items I moved. I have a basket where I put notes such as, "Napkins in top cupboard," "Storage shed keys on blue key ring in kitchen basket," "Christmas sweaters in red/green box in shed," and "Extra seasonings in back cupboard." I will sometimes put a sticky note in the original spot for a while until I get used to the new arrangement.

Rita Carmody
Sturgeon Bay, WI

Chapter 6

Establishing Routines and Systems

- **Same day.** Set up routines for each day of your life and you'll always know exactly what you should be doing that day. For instance, you might do all your dusting on Mondays, all your vacuuming on Tuesdays and all your mopping on Wednesdays.

- **Same time.** If you regularly do the same things each day at the same time, those routines will help you get things done. You won't have to spend time thinking what you're going to be doing each day. You can just do it.

- **Same place.** Consistently perform tasks in a consistent designated area each time. For instance, if you always pay the bills in the home office, you'll never have to search all over your home for the bill paying supplies.

- **Same week, month or year.** Whenever you have recurring tasks, schedule them so they're done each week on the same day, each month on the same day of the month or each year on the same day of the year. Getting into this habit acts as a reminder and gives you a definite deadline.

> ### Great idea!
>
> Keep everything in its selected place. After you're finished using something, put it away immediately to avoid clutter.
>
> Barbara Knecht
> Florida, NY

- **Do It Daily.** While organizing and cleaning on a daily basis may sound daunting, it only truly requires about 20 minutes of your time each day. When the last person gets out of the shower, spray down the walls with some shower cleaner. Quickly disinfect the toilet bowl each night. Turn the dishwasher on. Toss a load of clothes in the washing machine. Dust a few pieces of furniture. Vacuum a room. File a few sheets of paper.

You get the picture. Each of the items mentioned above just takes a few minutes—some even take a few seconds. Twenty minutes per day comes out to just over two hours per week. This is a very reasonable amount of organizing and cleaning time for the average household.

However, leave cleaning tasks for a week or two and very often the situation will get out of control. The tub will need to be scrubbed. The laundry will be piled to the ceiling. Your To Be Filed pile will be overflowing. Let it go too long and deep cleaning and heavy organizing time is required. This is much more time-consuming than organizing and cleaning a little bit each day. Whereas you would have spent just two hours in a week, now you'll find you have to spend an entire Saturday deep-cleaning and catching up. Two hours versus seven or eight hours? That's a no-brainer.

Great idea!

I have a couple of daily rituals that help keep me organized. First of all, I use the "Today" section of my daily organizer diligently. I write in everything from the day's appointments, class assignments or tests that my children will need my assistance on. At the end of the day I can see what I have accomplished and I add the tasks that were not completed to the next day's list.

This also helps me not to procrastinate. I will most likely fulfill a task if it has been on my list for a couple of days, even if it's something I dread doing.

Secondly, I set time aside each day to go through the mail and the papers that the kids bring home from school. Important papers are filed and junk is thrown out. This keeps it from piling up and overwhelming me at the end of the week.

Kathy Harshman
Clearwater, FL

- **It sounds so boring.** Doing things so consistently may seem boring to you. You may say, "I'd rather be spontaneous." Well, if you go through each day spontaneously and you're able to get everything done with plenty of time left over and with no stress, then I would say that system works for you and you could just ignore this tip. However, if you having trouble getting things done, know that consistency always pays off in the end.

- **Write it down.** Get into the habit of writing things down. When you make an appointment, write it in your planner immediately. When you have to remember things at the grocery store, write a list first. When you're on the phone with your doctor getting instructions for your child's fever, take notes in a notepad. If you write it down, you won't forget.

- **Put it back.** Whenever you pick up anything, the second you're finished using it, return it to its home. This is a vital principle in getting and staying organized.

- **Make checklists.** Checklists are essential tools for helping you to remember. Make checklists for things you need to get done, gifts you need to buy and people you'd like to call. Write a contents checklist for the diaper bag, gym bag, library return bag and beach bag and store that checklist right in the bag.

Organizing Clinic

Question

I would love to have a system, but I never seem to follow through on putting everything in its place. I don't seem to have enough places to put all my things. I lose bills, credit cards and other important information and waste tons of time looking through my piles. I know the mantras: File it, don't pile it and only handle it once. But how do I get started and follow through?

Linda K from Pennsylvania

Answer

Dear Linda,

Thanks for your question. Follow-through is one of the most important aspects of most things in life. If you declare you're going to do something and then you don't follow through, it's obvious whatever you wanted to do is not going to get accomplished.

Let's say you tell a child that she is not allowed to go out to play until she finishes her five chores. Then the child goes outside to play after finishing only two of those five chores. If you don't follow through by telling the child to come back in to do her chores, you'll most definitely have the same exact problem with her tomorrow, the next day and the day after that.

The same thing happens when it comes to getting organized. If you say you're going to get organized and then you allow yourself to do something else, you'll most definitely have the same problem tomorrow, the next day and the day after that. You get the picture. Start holding yourself accountable and you'll get the results you want. Here are four tips you can start using right now.

- **Lighten your load.** To give yourself more space, it's imperative to lighten your load. Be sure the only things you have in your home are those things you use and/or love. The rest should be sold, given to a charity organization or dumped. It's rare that people don't have enough space for the things they make use of. More often, it's that people have too many things they never use and don't even like, surrounding them.

- **Give 'em homes.** Whether it's your bills, your credit cards, your papers or your socks, everything you own should have a home—a place where each item is always stored when you're not using it, until you decide you no longer want it. For instance, your bills should immediately be placed in a bill paying system, the papers you need to keep should be in a filing system and your socks should be in a sock drawer in your bedroom.

- **Check your priorities.** I know you said that you would love to have a system and to follow through. But your actions are not supporting that. If you truly want to do something, chances are you'll do it. Perhaps you love to watch TV. If this is so, you probably follow through on watching TV. If you won the lottery, would you follow through on cashing the check? Most people would in a heartbeat. So, if you really want to follow through on your organizing systems, you will. You have to make it a priority in your mind and then prove that it's a priority. Just saying it's a priority is not enough. You have to do it.

- **Know what you're following through on.** You have to give yourself very specific goals each day so you know exactly what you should be following through on. In your case, I would say to start with the following three items:

  ➤ Gather a minimum of five things you don't use and/or love per day. Donate or dump those things immediately.

  ➤ Each day, give five homeless things you are keeping, an appropriate home where that item is always returned when you're done using it, until you no longer want it.

  ➤ Do not put anything down on a table. Do not add it to a pile. Do not toss it on a chair—even temporarily. When you're done using something, immediately return it to its home. If this is truly your priority, then make the decision in your mind to follow through.

- **Make yourself accountable.** Sometimes, we all need a little boost to stay motivated. Ask a spouse, a close friend and the members of the Get Organized Now! Discussion Forum to help you stay on track. Post a message on the forum saying you're having trouble following through with filing on a daily basis for example and then report to them every single day and let them know whether or not you followed through each day. When people are cheered on by others who care, that may be reason enough to continue.

- **Night and day.** Go to bed at the same time every night and wake up at the same time every morning whenever possible. Your body will get into a rhythm and you'll always know what times of the day are your most energetic.

- **15 minutes each night.** Establish a consistent 15-minute tidy session each night. Involve your whole family. No one is allowed to watch TV, read, play video games, take a bath or go to bed until all stray items are picked up and returned to their homes.

- **Shake things up a bit.** Even if you have routines, that doesn't mean you can never be spontaneous. I like to actually plan free time in my day to do spontaneous activities. In other words, the time is consistent, but what I do with that time may differ from day to day.

- **Get into the habit.** Ever begin doing something that you do for a few days and then stop doing it? For example, let's say you promised yourself that you were going to file papers immediately before they got out of hand, but then something else came up and the next thing you knew, you had another pile of papers that needed to be filed.

Or perhaps, on January 1 you made a vow to yourself to exercise for 20 minutes every day. You exercised for a few days. But then, by January 5, you gave up.

This happens to everyone on one occasion or another, but you really can start getting things done! Next time you really want to do something and you want to actually start and continue doing it, realize that doing it for one, two or even three days in a row is usually not enough.

Studies show it takes at least 21 days to form a habit. This means that you have to do something at least 21 times before it begins to become part of your everyday routine. So . . .

❖ **Decide exactly what you want to do.** Write it down and post it where you can see it every day, like your bathroom mirror. Be as specific as possible.

❖ **Schedule time to do what you want to do.** Again, it takes 21 days to form a habit, so schedule at least 21 days on your calendar and don't let anything get in the way of your schedule. If you miss one of your scheduled days, it's best to start over and schedule another 21 days. You must be consistent and dedicated.

❖ **Once you reach your 21 days, congratulations!** Don't stop now though, schedule another 21 days and then another and so on, until you do what you want to do, without even thinking about it . . . like brushing your teeth.

• **Failing to Plan? Then You're Planning to Fail.** I often hear, "What's the sense of planning? For all the time I spend planning something, I could already have it done." On the contrary, things rarely work out when you don't plan. Planning is nothing more than thinking before acting. If you fail to plan, in essence, you're planning to fail. Here are five examples:

❖ Gina, Mike and their two children woke up bright and early to enjoy their first day at Disney World. When they arrived at the theme park, Mike wanted to plan where they would have dinner that evening so that they could make dinner reservations. He knew they'd be tired and longing for a nice, hot meal. Gina, on the other hand, didn't think it was necessary to make plans for dinner that early in the day. She felt it would be more fun to wait until later, so it would be a more spontaneous decision.

Later that evening, when the kids began to whine about how hungry they were, Gina and Mike discovered that all the reservations in all the available nearby restaurants were completely booked up. For over two hours, they went from restaurant to restaurant trying to get seated, unsuccessfully.

Gina and Mike began to argue, the kids were irritated and everyone was hungry. In short, this could have been easily avoided if Gina had agreed with Mike to take a mere five minutes of planning time to make dinner reservations when they were available—five minutes to plan versus two hours of wasted time, plus aggravation.

❖ On Friday night, Ellen and Jane planned to meet each other the next day to catch a Saturday matinee. They both had some errands to run beforehand on Saturday morning, but agreed to meet at 12:45 for a 1:00 movie. On Friday night, Ellen wrote up a list of the errands she had to run: drycleaner, post office and library to return some books. She determined that would take her about 45 minutes, which she padded a bit just in case there was a line at the post office or a little bit of traffic.

She knew she had to meet Jane at 1:00, so she decided to wake up at 10:00 in the morning, get showered, dressed, in the car to run her errands by 11:30, get her errands done by 12:15 and then have another 15 to 30 minutes to relax before meeting Jane for the matinee. She arrived at the movie theatre at 12:45—right on time.

On the other hand, Jane stayed up late on Friday night to watch some television and woke up at 11:00 on Saturday morning. She rushed around doing her errands haphazardly on Saturday morning, forgetting to bring back the videos that were due and arrived at the movie theatre to meet Jane at 1:10—twenty-five minutes late for meeting Ellen and ten minutes after the movie had started.

Obviously, Ellen was peeved with Jane. Because of Jane's failure to plan, they both missed the beginning of the movie and had difficulty following what was going on because the first movie scene was critical to the plot.

All of this could have been avoided if Jane had just taken ten minutes on Friday night to plan a little.

❖ James and Jack both attended the same high school and had to take a Literature test in the morning. James scheduled two hours the night before to review his study material. The next day he easily aced the test ending up with an A grade.

Jack decided to go out with his friends the night before and reviewed his Literature material a half hour before test time. He struggled through the test and ended up with a C grade.

The next day, they both found out that anyone who scored less than a B on the Literature test, had to stay after school for further instruction. Jack wasn't happy, but this could have been easily avoided if he had just done some planning.

❖ Alexandra didn't have a specific date for filing her paperwork—she did it when she was in the mood. But one day her boss asked her to find an important contract in the filing cabinet for a client she had on the phone. Immediately, Alexandra felt queasy. She knew it was in the big pile of papers she hadn't filed for three weeks.

She frantically began going through her To File pile. After 20 minutes, her boss asked her what the hold up was. Alexandra had to admit she was having a bit of difficulty finding the contract in her large pile of papers.

Her boss was furious. It took Alexandra over 45 minutes to find the paper, but even though she did, her boss told her if she couldn't get her act together within a few days, her job would be on the line.

If Alexandra had planned to file for ten minutes at the end of each day, she would never have been in this predicament.

❖ Each night before she left work, Tina regularly wrote up a To Do list for the next day. She always planned to get at least four items done or a few more if she had some time left over at the end of the day. By doing so, Tina ended work each day feeling refreshed and satisfied by quitting time. She always felt her days were productive and she rarely worked late.

Gary never wrote up a To Do list. He never really knew what was coming up next. He'd just work on his tasks randomly, feeling overwhelmed and unfulfilled at the end of the day. He figured he didn't have the time to plan. He had too much work. He'd end the day feeling exhausted, although he had few, if any, projects completed. So, he regularly worked late into the evening, trying to get more done.

Tina and Gary had exactly the same amount of work. But by planning, Tina made her job a whole lot easier. Take a few minutes to think before you act. Plan your tasks, your weekly meals, your routes, your schedule and so on. A little bit of planning can go a long way. You'll waste less time and enjoy more productive, stress-free days.

• **Do a little bit now or do a lot more later.** It only takes a few minutes each day to do many things like wiping off the kitchen countertop, washing the dishes in the sink, going through the daily mail or weeding out your email inbox. But procrastinate on any of these things for more than a few days and you now have a bunch of major projects on your hands. If it can be done in a few minutes, do it now. It will save you tons of time later.

- **The truth about lists.** Lists can be very powerful tools when you understand their importance. Here are five list reminders:

  ❖ **It's not just about making lists.** Jill diligently makes lists each and every day, from her things to do, to movies she'd like to rent, to creative ideas that pop into her head. One would think that Jill is incredibly organized and gets tons of stuff completed.

  In truth, it's just the opposite. Jill writes everything down, but never refers to her lists. She finds enjoyment in making the lists and feels more organized to have these lists in her possession. She appears organized to outsiders, but in essence is getting very little, if anything, done.

  Lists can be very powerful tools, but only if you refer to them daily and apply what you've written on them. It's good to make lists, but for them to be worth anything, you have to actually DO the things on your list.

  ❖ **Let your lists remember for you.** Jack felt that it was unnecessary for him to write things down, like errands he had to run or special dates he wished to remember. He even worked as a waiter at a local pancake house and would never write the customer's order on his pad. He prided himself on being able to remember things without the need to write them down.

  One day, while in the pancake house, I watched and listened as Jack took down an order—in his head, not on paper. In taking the order this way, he forgot two things: a) one of his customers wanted lemon for her tea, but he accidentally brought her cream and b) another customer did not want mayonnaise on her sandwich and the sandwich arrived with gobs of it.

  He thought he could remember everything, but obviously he could not. His customers were not impressed by his memory and his boss wasn't either. In fact, the boss said she would have been more impressed if everything was written down and delivered as expected.

  The bottom line is, no matter how good one's memory is, it's never a good idea to rely solely on memory. The average person has tons of things to remember in a given day and things will be forgotten. If you write things down there's no need to remember and errors will be reduced dramatically.

  ❖ **Making a list doesn't take more time.** It saves time. Margaret says that by the time she writes things down, she could have them done. She randomly does things throughout her day.

  Yesterday, she woke up and saw a pile of laundry. She started the laundry. Then, she remembered she had to pick up cat food. She got in the car and took a ride over to the pet food store. When she arrived home, the mail arrived so she decided to begin going through the mail.

Her phone rang while she was doing so, so she put the mail down. She picked up the phone and it was her daughter asking her to pick her up from school at 3:00 that day. When she got off the phone, she decided to do a little bit of dusting—and then she remembered she had to stop at the dry cleaner.

And this is exactly how her day continued on—not following any kind of list and just randomly doing tasks here and there.

In doing so and not writing anything down, she totally forgot to pick up her daughter at 3:00. Her daughter called her at 3:15 and asked what the problem was and Margaret had to dash out to get her.

At the end of the day, the clothes were still in the washing machine because she had never gone back to put them in the dryer. Her mail was still sitting on the coffee table—half opened. Her dusting was only half done. Plus, she never remembered to get the clothes at the dry cleaner.

It never saves time to try to keep everything in your head and to approach your day in a random manner. Writing things down allows you to see the big picture and to approach your day in a systemized manner that ends with you accomplishing many things and feeling productive. Taking just a few minutes to write things down, can save you hours.

❖ **It doesn't take the fun out of it.** Cathy is afraid if she writes out a To Do list, the spontaneity will be taken out of her day. She sees herself as a creative person and thinks the act of writing things down is restrictive.

At the same time, Cathy is unhappy with her many unfinished projects and her lack of free time.

On the other hand, Barb writes everything down and believes she'll have more time for spontaneity by doing so. She's right.

Making To Do lists doesn't mean you can't be flexible. Even though I make To Do lists, I have often decided to be spontaneous and take the afternoon off to enjoy a book outside or to take my daughter out to play at the park.

A To Do list is a guide that allows you to systematically get things done, but it's not set in stone and it's not restrictive. In fact, I see the list as a tool to free my mind. I don't have to remember what to do. It's on my list. And if I decide to take the afternoon off, my list will remind me to get back to my projects tomorrow.

❖ **Have many lists, but not in many places.** Marlene has a list for everything—To Do, groceries, movies to see, books to read, places to visit, ideas to remember, gifts to buy, Web sites to check out, people to call, letters to write—the list of her lists goes on and on. The problem is not that Marlene has so many lists. In fact, it's great to have the things you want to remember written down. Marlene's problem is that her lists are written on sticky notes, notebooks, scraps of paper tossed in drawers, torn envelopes attached to her fridge and random papers scattered on her home office desk and kitchen table. In other words, she has lists, but she can never find them.

Your lists won't do you any good if you don't know where they are. Keep your lists in a binder—such as the *Get Organized Now! Easy Organizer*—or in a filing system. They should all be in one place and easily accessible when you need them.

- **5 Little Sayings to Help You Get Organized.** "Spring Ahead. Fall Back." That little saying always helps us remember whether we should set the clock ahead or back one hour. Similar little sayings are also great for helping you to get and stay organized. Here are just a few:

  - ❖ **A home for everything and everything in its home.** Every item you have, no matter what it is, should have a designated home. For instance, the home for your magazines might be your magazine holder, which is located on your bookshelf. Or your home for your extra file folders and labels might be the top shelf of your office supplies cabinet. If an item doesn't have a specific home, it's considered to be "homeless." Something that is homeless tends to get lost. Designate a specific home for all of your stuff.

  - ❖ **Don't put it down. Put it away.** When you remove something from its home, the best thing to do when you're done using it, is to put it away. Yes, sometimes it seems easier to just place it on the kitchen table until later or to put it on your desk until tomorrow. Unfortunately, this often results in many items being out of place, which can leave your home or office in disarray. Never mind the fact that it presents a bad example for other family members or staff members. Don't give clutter a chance to form. Put it away now. You'll find it when you need it and your environment will remain clutter-free.

  - ❖ **File, don't pile.** It is very easy to get overwhelmed with paper. Our paper volume increases on a daily basis. Between lists, mail, bills, school papers, documentation, warranties, and more, it's often seen as a pain to take the time to handle those papers immediately. However, if those papers begin to transform themselves into piles—and they usually do—it's going to be even more of a pain to get them under control. Piles tend to get taller and taller, until even the idea of dismantling them seems colossal. Not filing results in lots of piles and even more stress. If you don't need a piece of paper, get rid of it immediately. Either recycle it or give it to the appropriate party. If you do need a piece of paper, file it right now. Don't put it down, even for a minute. Put it in your filing cabinet, your Tickler file or your bill paying system. If you take the time to file it now, it won't stand a chance of growing into a huge pile.

❖ **Quality over quantity.** Clutter and chaos go hand in hand. The more things you have, the easier it is for clutter to form and grow. Always remember to place your emphasis on quality over quantity. In other words, it's not important to have a lot of things, many of which you never use. It's more beneficial to have fewer things, all of which you use and/or enjoy. Simplify your life and you will get and stay organized.

❖ **Find everything you need when you need it. Get everything done when it's due.** Many people think that getting organized is about being neat and tidy. On the contrary, a person who is not very neat or tidy can be very organized. Being organized actually entails "finding everything you need when you need it and getting everything done when it's due." If you can master these two things, you are well on your way to being organized.

• **Don't cut the ends off the ham, without asking why.** You may have specific systems for getting things done, but can you get those things done faster? Easier? Is there a less expensive way to handle it? Always keep an open mind—and open ears—for improving what you're doing. Beware of getting stuck in a day in and day out routine, just because that's the way you've always done it. This is an old fable I heard a long time ago that continues to have enormous impact on the things I do today.

Once upon a time, a child stood and watched her mother prepare the annual holiday ham. The mother carefully cut each end off the ham before placing it in the pan. The child asked, "Mother, why do you always cut the ends off the ham?" The mother replied, "Well, that's the way my mother always did it." So, the child called her grandmother and asked, "Grandma, why do you always cut the ends off the ham?" The grandmother replied, "because that's the way my mother always did it." Finally, the child called her great-grandmother and asked, "Great-Grandma, why did you always cut the ends off the ham?" The great-grandmother thought for a moment and replied, "Because the ham is way too big to fit in my baking pan!!"

So, what's the point of this little story? Many people perform many tasks in their day. There's a very good chance, though, that they've never asked themselves why they're performing those tasks. Or if they're really necessary. Or if there may be a way to perform them better or in less time. Continuously reevaluate your time and how you're using it, and chances are, you'll be sure to find areas that could be streamlined or eliminated.

Chapter 7

Cleaning and Tidying

- **Don't do it all yourself.** Assign specific cleaning tasks to each family member. If you like, you can even rotate the responsibilities so everyone has a turn at each task.

- **Keep a box nearby.** As you're cleaning, try to find at least three things you never use or that you don't like. Put these items in a box and donate the contents to charity once each month.

- **Put it near the step.** Don't make several trips up and down the stairs. When you have an item that has to go upstairs, leave it in a basket near the step. When you have to go upstairs later, grab your basket and bring everything up in one trip.

Great idea!

Before I even start cooking dinner, I will fill the sink with clean soapy water and while I am cooking, I will clean the used pots and pans and utensils while the food is cooking on the stove. This is better than waiting until after dinner when more dishes are piled on.

Christopher Kelly
Bowling Green, KY

- **Stop running back and forth.** Use a caddy with a handle to carry around your cleansers, furniture polish and cleaning rags so you don't have to keep returning to your cleaning storage area.

- **I love music.** Play upbeat music while you clean and organize. It will make you feel energetic and it's amazing how much faster the job can get done with an upbeat tune. Try "Flight of the Bumblebee" if you're feeling real ambitious.

- **Don't buy them all.** There are hundreds of cleaning products. However, there's no reason to waste your time, money and energy buying and using a million different ones to clean your home. Minimize. Buy one all-purpose cleaner for most of your cleaning needs.

- **Don't dump one at a time.** If you have a number of small wastepaper baskets around your home, don't empty each one outside individually. Carry a large, plastic garbage bag to each wastepaper basket, starting from the furthest one and working your way through the house. Then dump the large bag into your trash can once.

- **Do the basket toss.** Put one basket at the top and one at the bottom of your staircase. While you're upstairs, any stray items that need to go downstairs can be tossed in the basket on the floor you're on. While you're downstairs, toss any items that need to go upstairs into that basket. Carry the basket up or down later on instead of running up and down the stairs all day long.

- **Have someone else do it.** If you can afford it, it is well worth the money to hire a housekeeper on a regular basis. In my area, you can get an excellent cleaning company to come in for around $50 to $65 per session. The good ones dust from floor to ceiling, vacuum, scrub the floors and deodorize and clean the bathrooms. Another alternative is to do a light cleaning each week yourself, but hire a cleaning team once or twice a year to clean your house from top to bottom.

Great idea!

As soon as I empty the dishwasher, I immediately refill the soap dispenser with either the new dishwasher tabs or dishwasher powder detergent. Then whoever loads or unloads the dishwasher will know that if the soap dispenser is still closed, the dishes are still dirty. Since we started this system, there have been no more errors in putting away dirty dishes. Plus, the dishwasher is always ready for the next wash!

Dee Engel
Anoka, MN

- **Divide and separate.** Immediately separate your recyclable items—paper, plastic and cans—from your regular garbage by having separate, colored and labeled recycle containers. If the containers are different colors, they'll be easily identifiable to all family members. If this isn't possible, at minimum, label each of your recycling containers with large, bold lettering.

Tape your town's recycling instructions to the appropriate container, in case something is in question. For instance, in our town, we only must recycle glass jars that have a 1 or a 2 in the little triangle on the bottom of the jar. We also have other similar rules, so we always keep our town requirements taped to our recycling containers.

- **Clean clockwise.** Don't randomly clean a room. Move in a clockwise pattern so nothing is missed and so you don't have to backtrack.

- **Slip and slide.** Buy pots and pans with Teflon coating. It will save you quite a bit of clean-up time. However, never put Teflon coated cookware in the dishwasher. They will get ruined.

- **Off with your shoes.** Have your family members and visitors take their shoes off as soon as they walk into the house. You won't have to clean the rug as often. My mother used to have people do this and it really drove me nuts each time—that is, until I had a house of my own. Now, I wouldn't dream of letting anyone walk on my clean rugs with their shoes on. Why bring the dirt, pebbles, rainwater and other elements into your home?

- **Add a doormat in and out.** If you don't want to ask people to remove their shoes, reduce dirt and pebbles from spreading throughout your home by putting a doormat at each door. People can then wipe their feet before entering. By doing this, you won't have to vacuum as often.

- **Can it.** Keep some empty trash liners at the bottom of each garbage can or container. When you throw away the garbage, you'll have a new one immediately without having to make an extra trip to get one.

- **A cycle a day keeps the dirty dishes away.** Don't leave dirty dishes in the dishwasher overnight. Run the dishwasher cycle in the evening while watching television or tidying up so that everything is clean and ready to use in the morning.

- **Roll it off.** Keep a "Pet Hair Pick-up Roller" handy if you have a cat or dog. These sticky rollers can be rolled over the surface of your furniture, drapery and clothing to quickly remove hair and lint.

Great idea!

With a family of four we always have a large amount of trash. I have made two changes in the way I handle it so we are not taking it out everyday. First I purchased a large stainless steel can—like one you would use in a garage or warehouse— and painted it off-white. For added beauty I stenciled it with my kitchen colors. Now I have a much larger can that uses 30-33 gallon liners/bags. Secondly, I keep the container of liners/bags in the bottom of the trashcan so when we take out the full one the next one is there and waiting.

Joann Maddox
Scott Depot, WV

- **Tired of scrubbing the shower?** Clean your shower really well one time. Then, after the last person takes a shower each day, spray a little bit of shower spray on the tile walls and glass door. No scrubbing required. If you find that you get a bit of build-up later, such as hard-water stains, then spray some cleaner like Kaboom or CLR on it once each week, leave it on for 10-15 minutes and then wipe off. By the way, if you're waiting for ten minutes for the solution to set, do something else productive in the meantime.

  Speaking of hard water stains, my husband and I saved a ton of cleaning time by getting a water softener installed. If you have hard water in your area, this is definitely something to be considered.

- **No overflows allowed.** Empty your garbage cans and recyclable containers as soon as they start getting full, otherwise you're going to spend time picking up the overflow of trash. Yuck!

Great idea!

Instead of using those new and expensive disposable dusting mitts, find a pair or two of cheap, white cotton socks—preferably at a yard sale or second hand clothing store. Spray them with your favorite furniture polish and dust away. Then just throw them in the laundry.

Judy Spencer
Chino Valley, AZ

- **The outside must be cleaned too.** Don't forget about the outside of your home. Put outdoor cleaning tasks such as window washing and sweeping the walkway on your cleaning schedule so you remember to keep it up.

- **Use an extension cord.** If you don't have a central vacuuming system, get yourself a long extension cord. When you're ready to vacuum, rather than finding a new outlet every twenty feet, plug the extension cord into a central outlet and vacuum the entire first or second floor without stopping.

> ### Great idea!
>
> My favorite organizing tip is to clean one room (or one section if it is a big job) at a time. That way if I get tired, bored or otherwise interrupted, I still get satisfaction from a job completed even if the rest of the house is not done yet. I also work from the top down. For instance, I start dusting above the door jam and on top of cupboards before I do the floor since some of the dust will fall down.
>
> There is one addition to this tip and that is that sometimes there isn't enough time to finish even one room completely. In that case, I set a timer and do 10 minutes at top speed. It's amazing just how much I can get done in such a short span of time.
>
> Anne Shaw
> Emu Plains, New South Wales, Australia

- **Change your vacuum bag every two months.** By keeping it clean, you'll maximize your vacuum's power. Plus, you'll ensure you're getting the most suction.

- **Make a cleaning schedule.** Cleaning done on a well-organized schedule, systematically, will get the job done quickly and keep your place looking great. Plus, it will help prolong the life of your possessions.

- **Squeegee those windows clean.** Forget using newspaper or paper towels to get your windows clean. Newspaper may leave traces of cleaning solution on the window. Plus if the newspaper gets wet, it may transfer the ink back to your window. Paper towels leave lint and also leave a static charge that re-attracts dust.

  Instead, use a squeegee with a good window cleaning solution. You can get a squeegee at just about any housewares or hardware store. Get one that has a scrubbie on one side and the flat rubber squeegee on the other side. Your windows will stay cleaner longer, you'll finish the job faster and you'll have a wonderfully clear view.

Of course, you can always pay a window washer if you have tons of windows, no time and your budget isn't too tight.

- **Take care of those spots.** The second you spill something, even a drip from a spoon, immediately wipe it off. Don't wait for it to set and get hardened.

- **Get rid of sticky residue.** Rather than scrubbing sticky residue for hours, use a product such as Goo Gone to remove sticky stuff like shopping labels and gum.

- **Top down.** Always clean from the top of the room and work your way down to the bottom of the room. Any dust will fall down. Also, always dust before you vacuum.

- **Dust less.** Keep refrigerator tops, wall shelves and other surfaces dust free without having to dust, by topping each with an inexpensive piece of fabric, cut to cover the area. Every month, just pop the fabric into the washing machine. Then, put it back. One reader even suggested using a few sheets of papers towels on refrigerator tops that can simply be discarded later.

- **Stash it nearby.** Stash a small spray bottle of window cleaner and a roll of paper towels anywhere you have a mirror or a stainless steel surface. Anytime you see a smudge or fingerprint, wipe it off. Select-a-size paper towels that allow you to tear off just a portion of a sheet are wonderful for this purpose.

- **Do it in the buff.** Clean your shower—naked! You can scrub vigorously without worrying about getting wet. Afterwards, you can take a shower. Wipe the shower walls and floor when you're done with a dry towel.

- **Microwave magic.** Dampen a dishtowel and place it in the microwave on high for 30 seconds. The steam will loosen any crust or stains. When the 30 seconds are up, just wipe it clean with the damp dishtowel.

- **Put a lid on it.** When you're cooking, always put lids on pots and pans or use a splatter screen. The less food that splashes outside of your cookware, the less you'll have to clean.

- **Cover things you're microwaving.** Never put food into the microwave without covering it, either with a paper towel, a coffee filter or some wax paper. Foods tend to "explode" in the microwave. If you cover it, you won't have debris all over the inside.

- **Stop walking back and forth.** After dinner, empty all uneaten scraps into one dish and empty that one dish into the garbage or garbage disposal. Stack the remaining empty dishes, put the silverware on the top dish and walk to the sink once.

- **Make a task basket.** Take ten index cards and cut each into four pieces. You should end up with a total of 40 pieces. Also, keep one envelope on hand. On each piece, write one task that you can do in five minutes or less. Some examples might be: Organize a Drawer, Wash a Window, Wipe off a Countertop, Sort Mail or Weed out a File Folder.

  Take all of these pieces and put them in a basket or a paper bag. Tape the envelope on the outside of the basket or bag. Each day, shake your basket or bag to mix the chores up well. Pull out two of these pieces and do the tasks listed on them.

  When you're done with the tasks, put those pieces in the envelope.

  Keep repeating this system until all of the pieces are in the envelope. Then, dump the envelope back into the basket or bag and start over again. In just 20 days, you will have completed 40 tasks!

- **Congratulate yourself.** Consider each cleaning task you do a great accomplishment. Reward yourself for doing them. It will motivate you to help keep everything tidy and organized.

- **Sample cleaning approach #1.** Either clean all at once, or in short intervals throughout the day. It doesn't matter, as long as it gets done. You will have to customize according to the rooms in your home.
  - ❖ Monday ------------ Vacuum all rooms
  - ❖ Tuesday ------------ Dust all rooms
  - ❖ Wednesday -------- Sweep/Mop any floors
  - ❖ Thursday ----------- Clean bathroom toilet, sink, bathtub, etc.
  - ❖ Friday -------------- Wipe down countertops, monitors, etc.
  - ❖ Saturday/Sunday-- Free Day or random cleaning job

- **Sample cleaning approach #2.** Either clean all at once, or in short intervals throughout the day. It doesn't matter, as long as it gets done. You will have to customize according to the rooms in your home.
  - ❖ Monday ---------- Dust/Vacuum Master Bedroom
  - ❖ Tuesday ---------- Dust/Vacuum Living Room/Dining Room
  - ❖ Wednesday ------ Dust/Vacuum Home Office
  - ❖ Thursday --------- Dust/Vacuum Kids Bedrooms
  - ❖ Friday ------------ Dust/Clean/Mop Kitchen
  - ❖ Saturday --------- Dust/Clean/Mop Bathrooms and Laundry Room
  - ❖ Sunday ----------- Free Day or random room cleaning job

- **Sample cleaning approach #3.** If you really want to just clean once each week, and get it done, that's fine too. Set up a marathon session and do everything on one day. Get your family to help if possible, because this could end up being quite exhausting if you take on your entire home in one day all by yourself.

Chapter 8

Kitchen and Pantry

- **Use hanging baskets.** Hanging wire baskets hold fruit, vegetables, utensils and more. Plus they utilize vertical space effectively.

Organizing Clinic

Question

I can't seem to find a good place for my pots and pans. Right now they are stored in the microwave stand. What is the best way to keep them organized and accessible?

Sarah Schlicht
Cottage Grove, MN

Answer

Dear Sarah,

Since different systems work better for different people, the "best" system is the one that works well for you.

- **Decrease supply.** If you have more pots and pans than you need, donate some to a charity organization. Put those over-sized pots and pans that you don't use too frequently in high cabinets. Here are some ideas for frequently used pots and pans:

- **Hook them.** Hang cup hooks on your walls and hang pans from the hooks. This saves on cabinet space and keeps pans easily accessible.

- **Rack them.** Find a decorative, wrought iron, hanging rack at a local home center. Suspend the rack on the ceiling. It will keep your pans handy and will look professional.

- **Add horizontal dividers.** Make or purchase horizontal dividers. These are perfect for separating pot and pan lids and keeping them organized. A really frugal idea is to put a plastic dish rack in a cabinet and store your lids in it.

- **Put them in drawers or cabinets.** Why not store those pots and pans in the microwave stand? It's a handy storage area. The trick is to only store your most-used pots and pans there and try not to nest if possible.

- **Increase cabinet shelf space.** If you're storing pots in a tall cabinet, chances are they're all nested. This means, you have to take all of your pots out if you need to get to just one. Instead, get yourself some double, wire racks for cabinets. You'll be able to put a few pots or pans on each shelf of the rack without nesting.

- **Add some space.** Stacking racks work wonders in the kitchen to expand your available storage space. Buy a few so that you can stack cans, dishes, lids, wraps and bowls inside or outside your cabinets.

- **Get a few uses out of them.** When buying tools, buy those that give you multiple functions. For instance, my blender doubles as a food processor just by changing one small attachment.

- **Find hidden space.** If possible and if your budget allows, steal some space from an adjacent stairwell and recess your refrigerator into the wall.

- **Stop reaching inside.** In your under-the-counter cabinets, install pullout shelves for maximum organization and accessibility. These work really well in pantries too.

Great idea!

I store all the sink stuff like sponges, brushes and steel wool in a decorative planter that matches the style and decor of the kitchen. That way, everything is always accessible, but yet hidden from view.

Isabelle Remy
Dorval, Quebec, Canada

- **Make use of available space.** Use stackable shelves or helper shelves inside cupboards at varying heights, especially if you have a lot of empty air space. Often cabinets can be so tall that you never use the space on top.

- **Cut kitchen clutter.** While browsing through a kitchen catalog recently, it occurred to me that the number of appliances and gadgets that you can purchase for your kitchen is infinite.

There were deep fryers, power juicers, meatballers, fat mops, popsicle cake pans, tortilla bakers, corn bread skillets, pancake warmers, bacon presses, ice cream makers, corn steamers, grating mills, fruit socks, egg slicers, fruit ripeners, fruit wedgers, salad blasters, bean slicers, shish kabob baskets, bread buddies and thousands of other kitchen-type things.

Yikes! It's no wonder that so many kitchens are bursting at the seams with stuff.

Want to increase the space in your kitchen? A sure-fire way is to get rid of the gadgets and appliances you never use.

Many of these types of kitchen paraphernalia are purchased on impulse. You see the item on a store shelf or in a catalog and you think that it might be very helpful. Then, you get home, use it for a few days and soon the novelty of it all wears off. The item then, by and large, gets a permanent home on your countertop or in a cabinet, where it gathers dust bunnies for the next 22 years!

❖ **Give them the heave-ho.** I know. I know. You paid good money for that butter warmer and deviled egg tray. However, if you never use them, they're just taking up valuable real estate. Give them to a local charity. Perhaps someone else would love them more.

❖ **Give it a second thought.** If you make bread all the time, you may want to buy a bread maker and you may even actually use it. But the next time you see a gadget or appliance that you feel might be cool or nifty, ask yourself how often you're going to use it and be honest with yourself. Chances are, you're not going to eat heart-shaped waffles more than once a year. If you do, then that heart-shaped waffle maker may be just what you're looking for. If not, save your money and keep your available kitchen space free for something you're going to use all the time.

- **Look up.** Get your pots and pans out of the cabinet and hang them on an overhead rack, along a range hood or over an island. You can also purchase wall grids for this same purpose.

- **Don't forget wall space.** Fit unused wall space with wire organizers, pegboards, dish racks or shallow open shelving. Use open areas above your cabinets for both storage and display.

- **Keep it consistent.** Try to choose matching appliances whenever possible. One color scheme always looks more organized. In my kitchen, most of my appliances are black or stainless steel. This color scheme matches my refrigerator, microwave and oven.

- **Don't hoard twist ties.** Is there a surplus of twist ties scattered among your drawers? Keep a maximum of five and throw the rest away. Don't worry. When you buy new garbage bags, you'll get new twist ties in the box.

- **Corral utensils.** Ever get frustrated searching for wooden spoons, spatulas and whisks when you're trying to make dinner? Corral your utensils and store them in attractive containers on the counter where you regularly use them. A pitcher is great for holding tall spoons, an old teapot can hold metal utensils and a bowl can hold brushes. Batch similar utensils together.

- **No more dirty dishes.** There is no reason to ever have a sink full of dirty dishes. If you hand wash, the second you are done with your meal, wash and dry the dishes right away. It will only take about five minutes. Don't leave them in the sink for later, otherwise stuck-on food will increase wash time, plus it's a magnet for bacteria.

If you use a dishwasher, load the dishwasher after each meal. When all the meals are done for the day, put the soap in the dishwasher and run it. You'll never have a sink full of dirty dishes again.

Great idea!

As I load the dishwasher, I sort the silverware into the compartmentalized basket. My basket has six slots. I use two for spoons, two for forks and two for knives. It really seems to speed up the emptying process and once you start doing it, it's an easy habit to keep up!

Becky Merker
Buford, GA

- **Rack them.** The wall space behind most kitchen countertops is often neglected. But when used wisely, you could use the wall to increase your kitchen storage space. For instance, if you install a rack or wall grid there, you could hang your cooking utensils, just like many professional chefs do.

  Another idea is to install a few hooks and hang your frying pans and lids. Why take up all of your cabinet space to store these items, when you could leave these items within quick reach whenever you need them?

  Do you have enough space to put in a wall shelf or a corner shelf? If so, you might find some new space to store potted spices, small appliances or cookbooks. With a little bit of thought and creativity, you can find space you never knew you had!

- **Don't go overboard.** If you have an immediate use for an empty jar or container, by all means use it. However, discard all those other jars and containers not serving any purpose and taking up valuable space.

- **Use roll-down can racks.** These hold canned vegetables, pet foods, soda and other items in cans. When you remove a can, another rolls down. Some hold over 60 cans at once!

- **Spice-up your life.** Keep spices and herbs in clear, labeled bottles. If the spices are stored top view, put the labels on top. If they're stored side view, put the labels on the side. Store on a spice rack on the countertop or in an organizer that fits into a cabinet drawer. Alphabetize so they're easy to find.

- **Use a separate area for storage.** Store any foods bought in advance in a different storage area than the products you've already opened. Otherwise, you'll end up with three opened mustard jars or two half-used bottles of ketchup.

- **Do not eat.** Make a bunch of "Do Not Eat!" labels—preferably on your computer. Stick a label on prepared foods you're saving for special guests or for your holiday dinner to ensure family members know they shouldn't be snacking on them.

- **Keep the next one ready.** Store paper grocery bags that you use for garbage, right behind your garbage container. By the way, you don't need a million of them. Five to ten should be plenty. You'll be picking up more on your next trip to the grocery store, so there's no need for a surplus. If you use plastic trash bags in your garbage container, store extra ones in the bottom.

- **Keep rotating.** For food in your refrigerator and freezer, rotate oldest to the front and newest to the back. The groceries you bought a while back will get used up first. Use clear, plastic, airtight containers which are wonderful for keeping food fresh and for giving you the opportunity to see everything in your pantry and kitchen cabinets at a glance. Use them for cereal, pasta, beans, cookies, breadsticks, rice and more.

Bonus: No more having to shake those cardboard cereal and pasta boxes to determine how much is left. Just look at the see-through containers and the answer will be perfectly clear, literally.

Great idea!

To make it easier to clean the microwave following an explosion, put two cups of water and one teaspoon of vanilla extract in a bowl. Microwave on HIGH for about three to five minutes and wipe clean. It smells great and the oils in the extract make cleanup a breeze.

Connie Likens
Wentzville, MO

- **Decorate with food.** Clear canisters can store dry foods, such as pasta and dried beans. Plus, they are decorative enough to store out in the open on a shelf or countertop.

- **Use trays.** Don't just toss your silverware in the drawer. Use silverware trays with compartments to store forks, spoons, butter knives and other everyday utensils. The smaller compartments are perfect for items like baby utensils and corncob holders.

- **Use a Rolling Kitchen Island.** These offer extra storage space, plus increase your food preparation space dramatically.

- **Corral small food packages.** Keep a small wood or plastic box in one of your kitchen cabinets to store small food packets, like gravy mix, soup mix, flavored rice, taco seasoning, packets of oatmeal or dry marinades. If all these small items are always contained in this one place, they'll never work themselves to the backs of your cabinets and will be there for you when you want them.

- **Clear the deck.** Your kitchen countertop should be clean and clear. This will help keep everything sanitary and give you plenty of room for slicing, dicing and other meal preparations. Limit the items on your countertop to a few everyday appliances—microwave, toaster, coffee pot—and a container of cooking utensils.

- **Make everything identifiable.** Label everything that goes into your freezer with a name and a date, otherwise six months from now you may be wondering what the heck is in that mysterious package. You might even be scared to open it! You can now buy freezer bags with a handy strip to write on directly that won't rub off.

- **Red or white?** Wine racks display your wine bottles attractively and organize them in one place. They also keep the cork moist so that when you open the wine bottle, the cork is less likely to crumble inside.

- **Keep frequently used stuff nearby.** Keep your everyday dishes, utensils and cooking apparatus in a convenient, easy to reach area. Other items that are only used occasionally can be placed in higher, out-of-the-way cupboards.

- **Wrap it up.** Don't just keep your food wrap boxes in your cabinet in a big, disorganized pile. Install plastic wrap organizers. These can be hung discreetly inside a cabinet door.

- **Designate a jewelry holding system.** Leave a small jewelry box or soap dish—far enough away from any drains—in the kitchen. When you need to wash dishes or prepare food, you can place your rings, watches or bracelets into this box until you're done.

- **To bulk or not to bulk – that is the question.** For non-perishable items that you use very often, it may save you both time and money to buy in bulk. But this only works if you have extra storage space. If you don't have the extra space, it's better to buy, as you need.

- **Keep small stuff organized.** Organize small kitchen items, like cookie cutters and fancy toothpicks, into their own plastic, Ziplock bags. This will help keep everything sanitary and together for easy retrieval.

- **Pardon me.** Fancy china and glassware used only three or four times a year can be stored in a place other than where the everyday dinnerware is stored. This will give you more space for your everyday dishes and glasses.

- **Store it where you use it.** Store objects near the areas where they will be most used. Cooking utensils can be kept near the stove. Spices are usually convenient near your preparation area. Food processor blades are appropriately stored near the food processor.

- **Vary the heights.** Two-tiered racks or step-storage keep spices, small cans and jars at varying heights for selection at a glance.

- **Separate your kitchen into imaginary quadrants:**
  - ❖ Area 1: Cooking
  - ❖ Area 2: Preparing (chopping, slicing, dicing, coring)
  - ❖ Area 3: Holding (keeping food warm, cooling, rising)
  - ❖ Area 4: Cleaning

- **Don't store bills with bananas and barley.** If you pay your bills in the kitchen, keep your bill paying supplies in a closed, portable container. This will help keep everything together, plus it can be stored out of the way when not in use.

- **Get under-counter dispensers.** With under-counter dispensers you can dispense items such as plates, napkins, cups and coffee filters and eliminate cabinet and countertop clutter.

- **Get lazy.** Two-tiered Lazy Susans are perfect for storing canned goods, spices, extracts, dressings and condiments. Just spin this organizer until you find what you're looking for.

- **Use the back door.** Install an adjustable door rack on the back of a pantry door to store everything from soup cans to cereal out of the way, but still have them handy.

- **Take inventory.** Gather all old tattered dishcloths and potholders and trash them. New ones don't cost much, but make a big difference, especially if you display these prominently.

- **Store that sponge.** Pretty ceramic napkin holders are wonderful for storing kitchen sponges. The air can get to them and keep them dry when not in use. By the way, you can sanitize sponges by putting them in the dishwasher when you're ready to run a cycle.

- **Rosemary and thyme.** If you enjoy fresh herbs, keep potted ones on your kitchen windowsill. They'll get all the sun they need, they won't take up space on your countertop, and they'll be easily accessible when you're cooking.

- **Seal them.** Use airtight canisters to store flour, rice and pasta. This is very important as these items may contain or may attract, bugs. Use the clear containers so you can see when you're running low on any of these items.

- **It's hip to be square.** Square containers take up less space than round containers in the cabinets and fridge. So, next time you go to that Tupperware party, think square.

- **Shove them in.** If you're like me, you use plastic grocery bags for trash. But how to store all of them? Easy! Stuff them into an empty tissue box or empty trash bag box and pull each one out one at a time as needed. It's a much neater looking alternative than to have a closet filled with plastic bags strewn about.

- **Use a bookcase.** A bookcase placed in the kitchen provides excellent storage for everyday mugs, canned foods or cookbooks.

- **Create order under your sink.** Affix a plastic basket on the inside of cabinet doors for soap, brushes and sponges. Place a bucket or crate inside the cabinet for cleaning products and dishwashing detergent to keep everything in one place. A sliding basket on tracks or a container can nicely hold aluminum foil, wax paper and plastic wrap. There are organizers that go around the plumbing so you're not wasting good storage space.

- **Put the tab in when you empty.** As soon as you empty out the dishwasher, put the new soap tab or soap powder in the compartment immediately. As long as the compartment is closed, everyone will know that any dishes inside are dirty.

- **Put away the cookie jar.** If your countertop is being overtaken with cookie jars and ceramic canisters, trade those in for airtight plastic containers. The containers can be stored safely inside your cabinets or on shelves and your countertops will be free for meal preparation.

- **Purge plastic containers.** If you hoard margarine containers, empty baby food jars and Cool Whip containers and your cabinets are overflowing with them, get rid of all but three or four. Use these only when you're giving some food to a guest to take home with them.

- **Turn it upside down.** When storing stemware in your cabinets, store every other glass upside down. In other words, store right side up, then upside down, then right side up, then upside down. Stemware takes up a lot less space when stored like this.

- **Attach jars.** Attach the lids of glass jars to the underside of cabinets with small screws. Store dry items in the jars like popcorn kernels, beans, nuts and pasta. Screw the jar onto the stationery lid when not in use.

- **Mount them.** When buying small appliances like can openers and coffeemakers, buy those that mount under cabinets. These space savers keep your kitchen counter clutter free.

- **File them.** Use metal file folder racks in your cabinets to hold cookie sheets, cutting boards and trays.

Great idea!

Firmly mount a long, narrow piece of wood to the kitchen wall and screw in teacup hooks. Then, instead of pots and pans taking up space and toppling in your cabinet, you can hang them on the hooks. You could also screw these hooks under a shelf or cabinet.

Erma Fogarty
Champaign, IL

- **Line your shelves.** To prevent jars and bottles from making rings in your clean cabinets, line some of your shelves with a sheet of aluminum foil that can easily be replaced when necessary. An alternative is to make use of those old plastic tops that come with your coffee cans. Place bottles or jars that tend to drip on them.

- **Keep your pantry stocked.** You had tons of things to do today and now you're exhausted, but you still have to make dinner and your pantry is bare. Sound like a familiar story?

  In the future, always keep your pantry stocked with basics, such as tomato sauce, pasta, tuna, beans, canned veggies and rice. This will greatly reduce those last-minute treks to the store.

- **Stow it away.** Almost every kitchen has appliances, oversized servers and pots that are seldom used. Obviously, items that are never used should be donated, sold or tossed. However, some of these items may be important to you at certain times of the year, so getting rid of them may not be your best option.

  In fact, you may really want to keep these items, but they're taking up valuable space on the kitchen counter or in your kitchen cabinets. Maybe you have several large cookie sheets, but you only use them during the holiday season. Or you only use the bread machine when Aunt Sally visits once or twice a year and you use it religiously during those visits.

A good solution for this dilemma is to stow these rarely used items in a closet or in the basement and just pull them out when you need them. There's no sense in keeping these in the kitchen all year if you only use them once in awhile. When you do need them, you can pull them out of storage.

By the way, so you remember where you're storing everything, it's a good idea to keep a list of these rarely used items and their storage locations, taped on the inside of one of your kitchen cabinets. This idea can easily be applied to the other rooms in your home as well as your office.

- **Use helper shelves in the pantry.** Helper shelves allow you to store pantry items on two levels instead of one, thus easily doubling your pantry space. No installation is required here and they generally come in various widths and heights to fit your needs. These are just wire shelves that fit right on top of your pantry shelves. You can store some pantry items on the lower level, and more pantry items on the upper level.

- **Group like-foods together.** When organizing your pantry, try to store similar items together, like all cake and brownie boxes in one area, all canned vegetables in another area, and all pasta ingredients in another area.

- **Labels facing front.** Don't just toss things into your pantry and cupboards any old way. Boxes should be lined up like books, so you can read what's in the box by looking at the "spine." The labels on cans, jars and bottles should be facing front so you can easily scan an area and find what you're looking for in seconds.

- **Adjust as needed.** You should be able to stack a can or two on top of each other on each shelf of your pantry. If you can't, consider adjusting the shelves.

- **Keep track.** Whenever anyone in my family takes the last can of tuna or the last box of cake mix out of the pantry, they are responsible for putting that item on our shopping list. If you do this, you'll never run out of something unexpectedly.

- **Use plastic over-the-door shoe bags.** These are perfect for storing small packets, spices, seasonings, and more.

- **Hang the TV.** Some people like to have a small television set in the kitchen to watch while cooking. If this is you, consider mounting your television to the well with a television mount. You won't be taking up valuable counter space and you'll be able to enjoy your favorite programming. This works really well if you enjoy cooking, now that cable television provides so many cooking and food-related shows.

Chapter 9

Refrigerator and Freezer

- **Keep the surface clutter free.** Don't overload your refrigerator doors with coupons, sticky notes, kid's artwork, business cards and magnets. If too much is attached to your fridge, you won't be able to find anything.

  Remove all loose papers. Toss out anything that is outdated. Put coupons into a coupon organizer. Recipes you're going to prepare should be placed in a recipe file. Place other papers into a Tickler File or a filing cabinet.

- **Be conscience of quantity.** So many people buy way more than can be eaten before foods expire, therefore a huge amount of refrigerator space is being taken up by foods that end up in the trashcan. This is a waste of space and a waste of money. Just buy enough perishables for five to seven days or freeze any perishables that can be frozen and defrost them when you're ready for them.

Great idea!

I have a good tip on how to keep your freezer organized. We have a side-by-side refrigerator and freezer. On the top shelf I have all the white meat including chicken and pork. On the second shelf, I store the red meat. On the third shelf is all the frozen leftovers. The veggies are found on the bottom shelf.

I then make up a list and have it taped on the outside of the freezer. When I buy something new I put a slash on the list. After we have eaten it, I mark another slash \ so that then it's an X. Then I know that the meat has been eaten and I can put it on my grocery list.

This helps to know what is in the freezer and ensures that things don't get pushed to the back never to be seen again.

Jeannie Koenig
Fairview Park, OH

- **Put shelves in the fridge.** Just as you can add space to your cabinets with wire racks and Lazy Susan's, you can also add these items to your refrigerator shelves to add space and keep food organized.

Great idea!

I've never had much luck labeling plastic containers and bags that go in the freezer because the ink smudges or I can't get a label to stick. Now I keep a running list on the door of the fridge. I just list what's in the freezer and which container it's in, e.g. "Italian stew, square blue Rubbermaid", or "2# ground beef, freezer bag", and then the date. When I'm planning meals for the week, I don't have to dig through the freezer to find out what's in there and I don't lose track of anything only to find it hopelessly freezer-burned months in the future. It's all listed in chronological order.

Susan Gibson
Greenfield, WI

- **Wipe spills.** As soon as there's a spill, wipe it immediately. This may sound obvious, but I've known people who let a spill go for days or even months! An old, hardened, crusty spill is a bear to remove, but a new spill can usually be taken care of in seconds.

- **Don't over pack it.** Don't overload your refrigerator. Air needs to circulate to keep your food fresh and cold. Keeping enough space around each food item will make it easier to find what you're looking for. Likewise, leftovers to be eaten within a few days will not be overlooked.

- **Don't keep inedible food.** Inspect both your fridge and your freezer once each week. Toss any expired food or food you bought on impulse months ago but never plan to eat.

- **Keep the top free.** Don't store anything on top of the refrigerator unless it is in an organizing container or basket. Loose items on top are liable to fall behind the fridge—not to be seen again for years.

Great idea!

My wife and I were cleaning our refrigerator and came up with the idea of putting small bottles, like Tabasco, Worcestershire and cocktail sauce in little containers, rather than storing them loose. Doing so keeps them from falling through the rails on the door of the refrigerator. It works great and there are no stains on the refrigerator door.

Chuck Tyrrell
Philadelphia, PA

- **Watch those heights.** Store larger items towards the back and smaller items towards the front. The smaller items won't get hidden behind the larger ones.

- **Toss.** Immediately toss out any food that is spoiled, has an expired date, is unidentifiable or that nobody in your family is ever going to want again. The same goes for the freezer. Note: It's best to do this on garbage day so that the food doesn't linger in your garbage pail and stink up your kitchen.

- **Clean.** Moving your items from one shelf to the next, empty off each shelf one at a time and wipe clean. Scrape off any leftover bits of food and wipe up any spills. Do the same for the interior refrigerator door and drawers.

- **Categorize.** Designate shelves for different categories. For instance, milk, juice and soda bottles on the top shelf. Place foods ready to eat (leftovers or foods that need no cooking) on the second shelf. Place unprepared foods that need to be cooked on the third shelf. Put soda cans and heavy items on the bottom shelf. Store veggies and fruits in the produce drawer and condiments on the interior door.

- **Eggs off the door.** Never store eggs on the door of your refrigerator. Even though most appliance manufacturers provide door storage for eggs, the eggs will go bad a lot quicker when stored in this manner. This happens because the door is constantly opened, closed and exposed to air. Always keep your eggs in their original carton on an upper shelf.

- **Update emergency numbers.** A helpful tool to have on the fridge is a list of emergency numbers, such as police, fire department and neighbors. Hopefully, they'll never be needed, but if they are, these vital numbers will be at your fingertips.

- **Move shelves.** If your refrigerator allows you to adjust the heights of each shelf—most do—then definitely move those shelves around to accommodate your groceries better. By moving my top shelf down a notch, I was able to fit lots of very tall containers and bottles.

- **Cut fruit and veggies.** As soon as you get back from the supermarket, cut up those fruits and veggies. Store them in Ziplock bags or plastic containers. When you're ready to use them, they'll be available instantly. This also helps to promote good eating habits. It's easier to eat more fruit and veggies, if they're ready for eating.

- **Use labels.** If you put leftovers in opaque plastic containers or bowls covered with foil, you won't be able to see what's inside without opening them. End this problem by labeling things. Keep a sheet of white, removable self-adhesive labels nearby along with a black marker so you and your family can identify food items.

Organizing Clinic

Question

How can I organize a chest-type freezer? Everything falls to the bottom. I cannot find anything.

Denis McGuire,
Milwaukee WI

Answer

Dear Denis,

Here are a few suggestions to help you organize your chest-type freezer.

- **Empty and identify.** Completely empty out your freezer and identify anything not clearly recognizable by writing directly on the package or by attaching a label. Write down the contents of the package and the date it was put in the freezer.

- **Raise it up.** If you have a very large freezer and don't normally fill it to capacity, put some sturdy plastic crates on the bottom and lay the food items on top of these crates. The food will be easier for you to reach.

- **Order more baskets.** Many chest-type freezers come with plastic baskets that fit in the top of the freezer and slide from left to right. If you can fit two of these in your freezer, find your freezer manual and order another basket. When you need to get to items underneath, both baskets can be temporarily removed. The smaller items can be stored in these baskets and the large items can be kept below.

- **Get some buckets or rectangular baskets with handles.** While buckets or rectangular baskets may take up some additional space, it will be easier for you to separate food items by category in each of them. Plus, when you need to retrieve something, you can just reach for the bucket handle and pull those items up.

- **Consolidate similar items.** Keep all meats in one area, all prepared casseroles in another, all frozen veggies in another and so forth. The entire freezer won't have to be emptied out every time you're trying to find something.

- **Map it.** Make yourself a quick map, identifying the main areas of your freezer (bottom left, bottom right, red bucket, top sliding basket) and what food items are in those areas. Keep this list updated and you'll always know what's inside. Tape your list to the top of your freezer or the inside of the lid and you'll always know where it is.

Organizing Clinic

Question

My refrigerator is always a mess. I take everything out and clean it, but even when I first put things back in, I still can't seem to find things. I need some hints to keep my refrigerator organized.

Carol Roberts
Austin, TX

Answer

Dear Carol,

Here are a few hints that could help you get your refrigerator chaos under control:

- **Don't overload.** One of the worst things you could do is overload your refrigerator. If you're like most people, you probably shop once every week. Just buy enough to last you that week, plus a few days. The food in the fridge is seen more easily, is eaten and doesn't go bad before you're able to make (or find) it.

- **Give each category a home.** Don't just toss things in the refrigerator randomly. Each item should have a home. For instance, all beverages on the top shelf, all unprepared food on the second shelf, all leftovers on the next shelf, all veggies in the veggie drawer and all condiments on the door. You get the picture. When an item is removed, take care to put it back in the same exact place when you're done with it.

- **Use a Lazy Susan.** Put a Lazy Susan in your fridge and spin when you need something. Food items on the Lazy Susan won't find their way to the back of the fridge.

- **Make a meal plan.** Before shopping, make a meal plan so you know exactly what to buy and nothing more. Attach the meal plan to your fridge and follow it day by day, so each food item you purchased is used accordingly.

- **Use see-through containers.** Always put leftovers or any loose food in see-through containers. You'll be able to see the food on your fridge shelves at a glance.

- **Keep it fresh.** Keep your fridge smelling fresh by always storing a box of baking soda inside. Open it or buy the kind that has a fridge vent. Change the box in January, April, July and October.

- **Clean before you go shopping**. Always weed out and clean out your refrigerator the day before you go grocery shopping. This is the day it tends to be most empty, thus making it quick and easy to clean.

- **Photo display.** Refrigerators are often used for photo display. If this is the case in your home, get yourself a few acrylic, magnetic picture frames to display your shots. This will keep the photos clean, neat and will prevent curling and tears.

- **What's on top?** Don't use the top of your refrigerator as a catchall for junk you don't know where to store. However, it is OK to store a few daily-use flat trays or flat baskets up there. If you don't use the trays or baskets every single day, but use them often enough to keep, be sure you put them in a plastic bag first so they don't gather dust.

<table>
<tr><td>

Great idea!

Use plastic baskets to group food you tend to pull out together. For instance, my husband I have a basket with margarine, cream cheese and jam for our morning English muffins. You always know where the items are and whether you are out of anything.

Nan Hawthorne
Bothell, WA

</td></tr>
</table>

- **Keep a list.** Keep a shopping list right on the fridge. You can use the magnetic type or hang your own one-sheet grocery shopping form such as the one in the *Get Organized Now! Easy Organizer*. Be sure a pen is hanging there too. The rule is, when someone uses up the last bit of mustard, ice cream or anything else, they have to be sure that item is written on the shopping list.

- **Use up your leftovers.** If you have more than a day or two's worth of leftovers, don't cook. Use up those leftovers so they don't build up.

- **Defrost it.** If your freezer isn't a self-defrosting model, be sure to defrost it as soon as the frost is one-quarter inch thick. Otherwise, it's going to be very difficult, time-consuming and messy to defrost.

- **What is it?** Before freezing meats, casseroles, and other freezable items, label the container or freezer bag with the contents, the day it was packaged and the date it expires. It's also a good idea to keep a log of what's in the freezer, so those food items are not forgotten about.

- **Oldest to the front.** Organize your freezer with oldest foods towards the front and the newest foods toward the back. The oldest food items will get used up first.

- **Categorize.** Just like it's important to organize the fridge, it's also important to organize the freezer. If you have a side-by-side model, you're really in luck. Frozen meats, chicken and fish on one shelf. Frozen veggies and fruits on another. Frozen breakfasts and desserts on another. You get the picture. If you don't have shelves, create your own with wire racks to make the best use of your space.

- **Ice anyone?** If you don't have an icemaker on your refrigerator and you're making ice in ice cube trays, be sure you have a small ice bin. Make a batch of ice and pour it into the bin. Then, immediately start making the next batch of ice. You'll always have ice on hand if you use this system.

Great idea!

To keep things sorted and tidy in my freezer I have labeled grocery bags for beef mince, chicken mince, chicken breasts and lamb chops. Because we often buy meat in bulk, this makes it so easy when I need to get meat out. I just pull out the bag of, say, beef mince, which is already packed in two and four-serving sizes, to select what I need. It also saves labeling each individual one.

Debbi Ezzy
Sheffield, Tasmania, Australia

- **Frosty the snowman.** Food items kept in the freezer will lose their quality after a prolonged period of time. Toss out anything in your freezer that has a thick layer of frost on it or that cannot be identified.

- **Don't shop until it's empty.** I usually hold off on my food shopping until I only have one or two meals left in the fridge and freezer. By using this system, nothing goes to waste because everything is used up. Plus, it's easier to clean out the fridge and organize food items back into it when you don't have to remove or move things around.

- **Put kid friendly items within reach.** If you want your kids to snack healthy, but don't want them tapping you on the shoulder every time they want a snack, designate one area of the fridge for kid's snacks. Be sure the shelf is easily within their reach. Pack Ziplock bags with veggies, fruits, nuts, trail mix and cheese. When your kids want a snack, they'll know where to go.

- **Three jars of mustard and they're all open!** Definitely purchase mustard, mayonnaise, ketchup and other food items that need refrigeration after opening when you see you're running low, but don't put them in the fridge until the old one is finished.

Chapter 10

Dining Room

- **Only appropriate things.** The only things that should be in your dining room are things you dine with or things you enjoy looking at as you dine. Everything else should be removed.

- **Designate homes.** Designate specific areas in your china cabinet and/or buffet for each dining room item. Put glasses in one area, dishes in another, silverware in another and linens in another.

- **Decorate with platters.** Rather than storing large, decorative serving platters in your hutch or cupboard, why not hang them on the wall? They'll be easily accessible when you need them, they won't be taking up valuable cabinet space and you'll be able to enjoy them every day—rather than only on special occasions.

- **Wrap them up.** If you choose not to decorate with platters, keep them in storage wrapped in plastic wrap or in plastic bags. You'll keep them dust free and you won't have to spend precious time before the holidays washing them.

- **Inspect tablecloths and napkins.** Go through your dining room buffet or hutch drawers and inspect special-occasional tablecloths and napkins. Toss any that are ratty, old and faded. Donate the ones you don't care for if they're in good condition. Someone else may enjoy them.

   Spot-check those you do like for stains. Wash or have them professionally dry cleaned if necessary. Put all sets together in clear, plastic bags. When you need them for the next occasion, just grab the entire bag and set the table.

- **Keep the holidays in a separate area.** If you have holiday or special occasion tablecloths, cloth napkins, napkin rings or centerpieces, either store these together in one area of your china cabinet or even in a plastic container in the linen closet. Since you don't use these everyday, it's all right if they're not stored in the dining room if you're cramped for space.

- **Store the matching items.** Store matching tablecloths, linens, napkin rings, and other sets in a plastic bag—one matching set per bag. When you want to use a set, everything will be together. No more rummaging through your china cabinet for missing parts of a set.

- **Polish and use.** Are you saving silver flatware for that special occasion that never seems to come? If so, why not polish it and use it once each week. It may add some charm to your regular family dinners. When not in use, store your silver flatware in a tarnish-resistant cloth.

- **The china cabinet alternative.** Glass-front china cabinets can offer beautiful storage space for displaying your favorite china, but they can get dusty and it does have to be cleaned every so often—at least four times each year. Also, not everyone is in the market for beautiful china.

  Usually, a china cabinet is made up of the glass storage space on the top and a separate closed buffet section on the bottom.

  When purchasing furniture for our home, my husband and I decided to only buy the closed buffet and forego the glass storage space. Instead, we hung a beautiful piece of artwork above the buffet section.

  Since we're not in the market for delicate china that we would never use, we use the inside of the closed buffet for storing dinnerware, table linens, dining candles and so on. We have a beautiful picture to look at when having dinner in the dining room. Plus, there's no enclosed glass storage area to keep clean.

- **Reconsider the chandelier.** Chandeliers can be beautiful, but if yours is causing you more time and trouble to clean than it's worth, reconsider it. There are beautiful, but simple, light fixtures on the market that can be cleaned in a pinch.

- **Install a dimmer switch.** Create some mood in the formal dining room by installing a dimmer switch. While you're at it, replace cold bulbs with warm, cozy, inviting bulbs.

- **Check flower arrangements.** If you have any silk or dried flower arrangements in the dining room, be sure they're still in good condition. If not, toss them.

- **Add a leaf.** Many dining room tables come with a leaf to extend the table, but where to store it? My parents used to keep theirs wrapped in an old sheet and then stored on the top shelf of their coat closet. We keep ours under our bed. Always store table leaves flat or they may warp.

- **Keep it set.** If you always keep the dining room table set with a pretty tablecloth, dishes, glasses and silverware, you'll be less likely to toss papers and other things on it.

- **Have candles on hand.** If you use candlelight on your dining room table from time to time, be sure you have a box of candles on hand. Store them in the dining room in a cabinet if possible and they'll always be there when you need them.

  If you never dine by candlelight, why not try doing so once in awhile? It really helps the mood, whether you're dining with a spouse, friends, your kids or even by yourself.

- **Tell them where to sit.** When holding a dinner party, always put place cards on your dining room table so everyone knows where they should sit. Sometimes it's fun to have husbands and wives sit next to each other. Other times it's interesting to have spouses sit across from each other. Sometimes it's best to seat children in between their parents. No matter what, your guests will be seated where you want them seated.

- **Use slipcovers.** Want to quickly change the look of your dining room chairs? Slipcovers can hide torn fabric or change the entire look of your room to suit your mood or the season.

- **Chardonnay anyone?** Keep a wine rack in your dining room to hold all of those wonderful bottles of wine you're saving for that special occasion. Next time you have guests, open a bottle and enjoy.

- **Choose centerpieces with care.** If you plan to leave your centerpieces on the table when guests are dining, be sure they're not blocking anyone's view of another person at the table and that they do not become an obstacle when people are trying to access food on the table.

  In our home, we have a very large floral centerpiece. We always remove it when we have guests and replace it with candles. Please note we never use the tall candles on our dining room table because they're easily knocked over. We prefer using tea lights or small candles in jars—unscented. The scented ones will compete with the wonderful food aromas.

- **Is it OK for me to bring a guest?** If you have extra space in the dining room, keep additional seating along one of the walls or in the corners. It will be easy and more elegant for you to set another place at the table in a jiffy without having to drag in a folding chair.

- **Think unconventional.** One of my neighbors keeps a bedroom dresser in her dining room. It's the perfect match for her furniture and it offers excellent storage space for her table linens, special occasion platters, candles and other items she regularly uses in the dining room.

  Another woman I know has a small refrigerator in her dining room. She keeps beverages in there so she doesn't have to trek into her kitchen every time someone gets thirsty.

  Yet another person I know uses his dining room as a hobby room. When he has guests over on rare occasions, they eat in his kitchen. He figures he doesn't have guests over often enough to use that valuable space as a dining room.

Chapter 11

Living Room and Family Room

- **Use the rule of three.** Never keep more than three items on your coffee table or it will become a clutter table. Try nothing more than a magazine, a remote control and a coffee table book.

Organizing Clinic

Question

My living room looks like a video store. There are yards and yards of nice bright kids' videos that I just don't want to look at all the time anymore. Yes, there are great behind-the-door video units available, but they only fit videos that come in cardboard sleeves. Disney packages theirs in big plastic boxes. Any ideas?

Anna Preziosi
Ramsey NJ

Answer

Here are a few possible ideas for you, so that you live happily ever after.

- **Closed audio/video unit.** In our home, we have a wooden storage unit for our videos, DVDs and CDs. It was purchased at Suncoast Video. The unit's shelves were the right height for each of the media, including our Disney videos. And the nice thing is, the doors actually close when you're not using the unit. While at the store, we also noticed they carried units with adjustable shelves, so you could easily adjust the heights for Disney-type videos.

- **Bookshelf.** Rather than using a video unit, you might also consider a bookshelf. Usually the shelves on a bookshelf are plenty tall to fit Disney videos. You can even use bookends to hold the videos up. While bookshelves generally do not have doors, the videos can be nicely organized and off your floor. Another idea is to purchase attractive baskets from a store such as Pottery Barn. Put those on the bookshelves and then put the videos in the baskets organized alphabetically. That will keep the bookshelf looking less cluttered.

- **Shelving.** Hang shelves in the kids' rooms to store their videos. So what if the TV is in the other room? Only one video can be watched at a time, so it shouldn't be that much of a hassle to store the videos elsewhere. Your living room will be much more peaceful and inviting.

- **Consider tossing the Disney Covers.** Only the Disney covers are larger than other video covers. Jewel cases for video tapes can be purchased fairly inexpensively. They will be easier to store because they will be the same size as the rest of your videos.

- **Put up a decorative screen.** Decorative screens can hide tapes beautifully and discreetly.

- **Replace end tables.** End tables are clutter magnets and take up space. You'll probably agree that it's easy to just walk by and place something on top of them. Replace end tables with floor lamps and overhead lighting or include nice floral arrangements on the end tables so there's no room left for clutter.

- **Empty out those magazine racks.** A few current magazines are great for reading enjoyment. Anything more is just clutter.

Great idea!

I moved all my music into extra wide 1", 3-ring binders that have 12 pages that hold eight CDs each. I put all the jewel case liner pages (for reference) into one shoebox in storage. Now instead of bulky multiple racks, I have a shelf holding only two thin binders that aren't even full yet.

Rayna Thompson
Romeo, MI

- **Keep the floor clear.** There should never be anything on the floor of the family room, except for the furniture of course. Toys should be in a toy chest or on a shelf. Books go on the bookshelf. CDs belong in a CD Holder. Jackets and coats belong in the closet. Hats belong on the hat rack.

- **Give a home to your remote.** Always have a specific place for the remote control and it won't get lost. Get compartmentalized pockets you can buy that hang over the arm of a sofa or armchair. They have sections to hold the remote control and the TV Guide. What a handy idea! Or, stick a strip of Velcro both on the remote and on the side of your television and stick the Velcro strips together when not in use.

Great idea!

If you have a lot of music, take one afternoon to put your CDs or tapes in alphabetical order by artist. It makes finding the one you want a snap!

Sherri Gillmer
Durham, NC

- **Hang ten.** Hang up framed pictures to free up space. There will be less to move when you're cleaning up and they'll always be on display for your enjoyment.

- **Know when to fold 'em.** Use the type of game tables that fold-up when not in use. The same goes for snack tables.

- **Keep them contained.** It's perfectly fine to keep your sewing supplies or hobby materials in the family room. That is, as long as they're in an organizing container and not spread out all over the place.

- **Donate outdated electronics.** Donate any outdated electronics to a charity. For instance, you may use your digital camera instead of your old 35-millimeter camera, or you may use your CD player instead of your old turntable.

- **Add a basket.** In my house, we have large wicker baskets in the living room. They have covers so they always look neat. Inside, we store several board games and toys. When we have company, there's always something for both kids and adults to enjoy.

- **Add a bookcase.** If you store books in your living room or family room, a bookcase is a must. Books should be organized alphabetically by genre. Donate books you no longer want to a favorite charity, library or half-price bookstore.

- **Prevent bookshelf dust.** Store books on bookshelves so that all the book spines are flush with the edge of the shelf and each other. This will prevent dust on the shelf edge.

- **Warm and inviting.** If you have a fireplace, be sure the mantel is free of clutter. This is a wonderful area to display some of your treasures. Also, keep fireplace tools clean and ready to use. Firewood should be stored in a box or firewood holder. Be sure to schedule flue and chimney inspection and cleaning often.

- **Flip them.** Keep sofa cushions fresh and dust-free by vacuuming them and flipping them over on the first of each month. Keep in mind that cloth sofas do attract lots of dust and need to be vacuumed. In my house, we have a leather sofa. It was definitely more expensive, but it can be quickly wiped down instead of vacuumed.

- **Vacuum those shades.** Lampshades can be cleaned easily by using a vacuum cleaner and the brush attachment.

- **Rate your knickknacks.** If what you have is not worthy of being displayed in a prominent area, it's probably not worth keeping at all.

Organizing Clinic

Question

My husband requests that I videotape programs for him. He then asks for them months later and I cannot find them. I need an organized system. Please help.

Margaret Cherry
Long Beach, CA

Answer

Dear Margaret,

Here's a very simple system you can use to help you stay organized and to ensure your hubby doesn't miss those programs:

- **Designate one place.** Be sure that you have only one place for videos you tape for your husband, such as a special box or container. When you're looking for something, you'll immediately know where it's stored. As soon as you're done taping a program, take it out of the VCR, label the tape and put it in this container.

- **Keep labeling supplies in one place.** Keep an inventory of videotape labels and a marker in that box or container. If the labels and marker are right there, you'll be more likely to mark it right away, versus having to search all over your home for these items.

- **Consider your personality.** Some people are very frugal and are able to keep lots of taped programs on one tape and actually find those programs later. Others prefer to purchase shorter videotapes and just keep one or two programs on each. You'll have to determine which system works better for you. It may be less expensive for you to put all the programs on one tape, but if you're spending too much time fast-forwarding and rewinding through each tape to find the program you're looking for, well . . . time is money.

- **Set a maximum.** Hopefully, your husband watches these taped programs fairly soon after you tape them, so he doesn't end up with a large build-up of tapes. Set a maximum of unwatched programs, such as 10 or 15. In other words, when there are 10 or 15 programs still waiting to be watched in that box, don't tape any more until he has watched those.

- **Recycle.** Make it your hubby's responsibility to affix a blank label on a videotape when he no longer wants to keep the programs on a particular tape. You'll know you can tape over whatever is currently recorded.

- **Comfortable and cozy.** If you curl up on the sofa or in front of the fireplace, you may want to have a big basket in this room to store blankets. When you're chilly, just grab one and snuggle up in it.

- **What lurks in the shadows?** Shadow boxes are perfect for displaying collections. Hang the boxes on the walls and you'll never have to pick up each collectible and dust around it again.

- **Old news.** If you get a daily paper, you should not be storing more than two in your newspaper rack. Anything older is old news. Weekly magazines should be tossed within two weeks, monthly magazines within two months.

- **Buy folding chairs.** Rather than cluttering up a room with lots of extra chairs that you only use for company, get a set of folding chairs that can be stored in an attic or closet. Only take them out when you need them.

- **On the floor.** Table lamps are pretty, but tend to take up a lot of space and generally require an end table. Whenever you're looking to save some space but need good lighting, floor lamps serve this purpose well.

- **Consider an armoire.** Armoires can house your television, cable box, VCR, DVD and music systems in one neat area. Plus, they usually offer extra storage space for DVDs and tapes. When not in use, just close the doors.

Great idea!

Each night before I go to bed, I make a 5-10 minute sweep of my living room. I return remotes to their caddy. I straighten any throws or afghans that I may have used. Shoes are put in the closet and magazines or mail is put in the appropriate station. Any videos/DVDs are put in their cases and put away. This works great as a "before bed" ritual because in the morning when you enter the room, it will be in order.

Cathy Robinson
Baltimore, MD

- **Get snack tables.** You're bound to want snacks from time to time while you and your family are enjoying your family room. Snack tables give you a surface to put drinks, chips and desserts. Folding snack tables are nice since they can be folded up and stored when not in use. Many snack table sets come with their own holders. The holder can be stored in a corner of the room and each table can be removed as needed. Another option is nesting tables that allow two or three tables to be stored in the space needed for just one.

- **Find furniture with storage capacity.** A hope chest, trunk with a flat top or a coffee table with storage inside all serve two purposes. You can use the inside for blankets, toys, craft projects and more and you can use the top as a work surface or a table to hold beverages.

- **Use your family room as a home theater.** Projection TVs are pretty popular these days. You can get the feel of being at the movie theater, while enjoying the comforts of home. Projection TVs take up very little space, as they are generally attached to a ceiling or wall and project the image onto a screen or blank wall. If your family enjoys movies and you'd like to save some space in your family room, this may be the perfect solution for you.

- **Wish you had a family room?** If you live in a home that doesn't have a family room, why not consider converting your attic or part of your basement for this very purpose? If you're very handy, you may consider doing this yourself. Or get a quote from a local contractor.

- **Add visual space.** One great way to make a small room look much larger is to paint the walls in a light color. If the room is perceived as small mentally, you're going to feel claustrophobic.

Great idea!

To keep our living room clutter-free at all times, I bought a $7 medium size wicker container that matches our living room. Now when we see something that doesn't belong, it gets put in the container. No more clutter and each person has to retrieve his own stuff at the end of the day.

Pamela Fleming
Sacramento, CA

- **Add shelves.** Shelves are perfect for the family room, as they can store games, toys, books, magazines, craft materials and more.

- **Fasten on some bars.** Fasten some pretty towel bars, like the ones you use in your bathroom to hold bath towels, onto the walls of your family room. These are perfect for holding quilts and blankets. Your family will appreciate having these cozy comforts on hand when watching TV on a cold night.

- **Unify furniture.** If you have mismatched sofas and chairs in the living or family rooms, have those chairs reupholstered to match. If this isn't in your budget, give those rooms a more unified look with slipcovers.

- **Corral pet toys.** Create a home for pet toys, such as an open basket. Each night, ask someone to gather all the pet toys and bring them to their appropriate home. You may even be able to train your furry friend how to do this.

- **Choose the right fabrics.** When shopping for furniture for your living room and family room, choose fabrics that don't show dirt and that clean up easily if something is spilled on them.

- **Treasure chest.** Rather than using a coffee table, get a storage chest instead. It serves two functions. First, it gives you plenty of extra storage space for things like quilts, games and knitting items. Second, it gives you a surface to put down a drink or some table books.

- **Add reading lamps.** If you read a lot in the living room and/or family room, reading lamps are great additions. Overhead lighting can be very harsh sometimes, especially when you're trying to get into a cozy mood. Reading lamps provide the perfect light for cuddling up with a good book.

- **Greeting card display.** Whenever we get greeting cards from friends and family members, we always display them on our fireplace mantel. We are sure to leave the space empty and clutter-free for this very purpose.

- **Electricity in the floor.** In our home, our sofa and love seat are not positioned against a wall. We had an electrical outlet positioned on the floor underneath the sofa. We run our end table lamp wire under the sofa to generate power. This is an excellent solution to ensure that nobody trips over a wire and that we don't have an unsightly wire stretched across the room to a wall outlet.

- **How do I do this?** Keep TV/VCR/DVD manuals underneath the TV, VCR or DVD player. Whenever you have a question about how something works, you'll always be able to quickly locate the instructions.

- **Make a transformation.** If you don't have a guest room, but would like to have occasional guests, get yourself a sofa bed, rather than a typical sofa. When needed, it's a bed. When not needed, it's a sofa. No extra space needed!

- **Use your living room.** Believe it or not, I once knew a person who had a beautiful living room, but the only day she ever used it was on Christmas. All the furniture was covered in plastic. What a waste of space the rest of the year.

I did manage to convince this woman to use her living room daily and to remove those uncomfortable plastic covers. She said she never really thought of using it, but now it's her favorite retreat area in her home.

Chapter 12

Master Bedroom

- **One third.** On average, one third of your life is spent in the bedroom. Keep that percentage in mind and you may get even more motivated to have your bedroom clutter-free and organized.

- **Make your bed.** Make your bed right after you get up in the morning. It only takes a minute and it will look inviting when it's time to go to sleep again that night. Plus, it gives your bedroom a fresh organized appearance. If your spouse gets up after you, he or she should be in charge of this task.

> ### Great idea!
>
> When it's too warm for winter blankets on the bed, store the blankets unfolded between the mattress and box springs. It saves storage space, each person's blankets are in their own room and they're easily located when it gets cold again.
>
> Cheryl Cavender
> Peculiar, MO

- **Keep mates together.** Keep matching bed linens together and store them in an area near the beds in a bedroom drawer, chest or linen closet. Store linen sets right in the matching pillowcase.

- **What's under your bed?** Use under-the-bed storage organizers to store blankets and out-of-season sweaters. Or purchase a bed with built-in drawers. However, don't, under any circumstances, store junk under your bed.

- **Keep reading material under control.** The only reading material on your bedroom nightstand should be the book or magazine you're reading right now. Store all other reading material in a bookcase or rack.

- **Clear the nightstand and dresser surfaces.** If the surfaces in your bedroom are loaded with paper and other paraphernalia, clear them off. Surfaces should be clear and chaos-free to ensure a restful night's sleep.

- **Be prepared for blackouts.** Keep a flashlight in your bedside table drawer. In case of a blackout, you won't stub a toe trying to find a flashlight. Keep extra batteries for the flashlight in the drawer too.

- **Add a skirt.** If you are using the space beneath your bed for storage, cover that storage space with a pretty bed skirt. Nobody will ever know you're storing stuff under there.

Great idea!

I found that making my bed was one job that did not get done. I now make my bed right after I get up and finish dressing. Since, I'm usually the last one up, I don't have to wait for someone else to get out of bed first. The only time this doesn't work is when I have to go somewhere and have to be up before my husband, but then he makes it when he gets up.

Our bedroom is located right off the living room, so if I had surprise visitors before, I had to shut the bedroom door prior to answering the door. Now I don't have to worry about that. It also looks so nice when I do go into the bedroom later on.

Karen McNeff
Palmer, NE

- **Manage your music.** If you keep CDs in the bedroom, be sure to store them in a CD holder, right near your CD player. Another alternative is putting them on your nightstand in between bookends. Keep them organized alphabetically by genre, so you can find what you're looking for quickly.

- **Use a trunk.** Invest in a storage trunk for your comforters, blankets and linens. They look beautiful in the bedroom and offer tons of storage space.

- **Put the TV inside.** If you have a TV in the bedroom, store it inside an armoire. Be sure to buy an armoire with sufficient storage space for videos and DVDs so they're not left out in the open. Of course, if you don't watch TV in the bedroom, don't leave a TV in there. It takes up too much space you could be using for something else.

- **Add a chair or bench.** Add a chair, bench or ottoman in your bedroom so it's easier to put on socks or nylons. This is especially helpful when the bed is already made up and you don't want to wrinkle it. It's also helpful when your spouse is in bed, and you don't want to wake him or her.

- **Add a bookcase or bookshelf.** Don't store books in piles on the floor or on a dresser top. Instead, get yourself a small bookcase or attach some bookshelves to the walls. You'll have your own private library in the bedroom.

- **Put the right things in your nightstand.** Empty the inside of your nightstand of anything you never use. Then, store bedroom items in it such as tissues, a sleep mask, the bedroom TV remote control and your reading glasses.

- **Keep the mirror smudge free.** If you have a mirror in the bedroom, keep it smudge free. Keep a pack of glass cleaner wipes in the bedroom and clean it anytime you see smudges or fingerprints.

- **Hatbox idea.** If you don't have much storage space, you might consider getting some pretty hatboxes. You can leave these out in the open—stacked—and store all sorts of things inside.

Great idea!

The most efficient way of storing surplus duvets and pillows is to keep them in one of those plastic bags that allow you to vacuum out the air and thereby allows you to reduce their bulk by about half. As the seasons change, you can swap over your winter duvet for your summer one and you don't have to find so much space for storage.

Morag Egan
Bath, Somerset, England

- **On a roll.** Don't have enough space in your bedroom closet? Get yourself a rolling clothing rack. To discreetly hide the rack, use a decorative folding screen.

- **Speaking of folding screens.** Folding screens are wonderful for the bedroom. You can get dressed behind one. You can quickly hide a messy area behind one or they can add interest to a very plain room.

- **Get a coat rack.** Coat racks are not only for the foyer. They're also great in the bedroom. Find your outfit the night before and hang it on the coat rack and it will be ready for you in the morning.

- **Hats off to you.** If you wear hats, buy a hat rack and display your hats on it, rather than storing them in the closet. They won't get crushed on a rack.

- **Empty that hamper.** Honestly, I don't really like having a hamper in the bedroom. I just don't like the idea of dirty clothes being in my bedroom. My family puts clothes that need to be laundered in the hamper in the laundry room. However, if you insist on a hamper in the bedroom, commit to wash the clothes in it every few days.

- **Turn the mattress.** It is recommended that you turn your mattress every six months. Switch the part your head sleeps on to the part your feet sleep on and vice versa.

- **Repair shop.** Don't toss clothes that need mending on the floor or over a chair. Designate a basket for this purpose.

- **Ironing station.** At the same time, don't toss clothes that need ironing on the floor or over a chair. A basket is good for this purpose too. Another alternative is to hang up the clothes in one area of your bedroom closet until you're ready to iron them. No sense in getting them more wrinkled than they already are.

- **Sew perfect idea.** Keep two threaded needles—one with white thread, one with black—in a pincushion in your dresser drawer. When a button or hem comes loose, you'll be able to fix it quickly. No need to have to thread a needle on a hectic morning.

- **Dress up tables.** If you have a table or two in your bedroom that do not have drawers, store things under the table in baskets or plastic containers. Then, skirt those tables with pretty tablecloths, a quilt or fabrics. No one will know what lies underneath.

- **Make your desk homey.** Many people keep a writing desk in their bedrooms. They use this desk to pay bills, sign greeting cards, and do other writing tasks. If you do, just be sure that you don't accumulate mail, bills, paper, catalogs and magazines on top of it. By the end of the day, the desk should be completely clear of all clutter.

Great idea!

I put a clean, extra queen-sized contour sheet and top flat sheet under my sheet/mattress pad, at the end of the bed and clean, folded, pillowcases inside of each pillowcase for the next time the bedclothes need to be changed.

Jackie McKee
Ashtabula, OH

- **Check the lighting and sound level.** Don't use bright white lights in the bedroom. Soft lights add to the atmosphere and make the bedroom more cozy and comforting. If you find it difficult to sleep at night due to outside noise, get a sound machine. It may be easier for you to listen to a falling waterfall, rain or even white noise.

- **Keep perfumes and colognes in a tray.** A silver tray on your dresser nicely holds your favorite fragrances. When you have to clean, you don't have to remove each fragrance one by one. You remove the entire tray and when you're done dusting, the entire tray is returned.

- **Beat those sheets.** There is rarely any reason to keep more than two or three sets of sheets for any one bed in your home. If you have more than three sets for one bed, donate the rest to charity. Avoid buying sheets that can only be used once or twice a year, like holiday-specific sheets.

- **Bed head.** If you're in the market for new bedroom furniture, consider a headboard style that has space for storage. One of our neighbors has a beautiful headboard that holds books, the TV remote, an alarm clock and reading glasses among other items.

- **Store them in a sham.** If you've been storing bulky quilts and blankets in your closets, they're probably taking up lots of valuable space. Instead, pick up a few pillow shams that match your decor. Store your out-of-season blankets and quilts right in the shams. Then, arrange the shams, which now look exactly like pillows on the beds. The display is attractive, but better yet, it's a wonderful space saver!

Chapter 13

Clothes Closet and Dresser Drawers

- **Empty it out.** In order to really reorganize your bedroom closet, the best thing to do is empty it out completely. Then, carefully make a decision whether to keep or dump each item. If you haven't worn it in a year, chances are good that you'll never wear it again. Get rid of it. Dump it or donate it.

Weed Out Your Clothes Closet

How do you decide what to keep and what to part with? Here is a simple guide:

It's too big or too small. Get it out of your closet and donate it so that someone who does fit into it can wear it. Even if you're trying to lose a few pounds, it's not worth keeping it. Live in the now. Once you reach your goal, reward yourself by shopping for new outfits to fit your new figure.

You don't like it. This is a no-brainer. Get rid of it today.

It's stained. If you really like the garment, but can't wear it because it's stained, spend some time this week getting that stain washed out. If you can't get the stain out, bring the garment to your local dry cleaner. If they can't get the stain out, and there's no other way for you to hide the stain, such as a patch or accessory, then bite the bullet and part with this piece of clothing.

It's ripped or torn. Repair it yourself, have someone else repair it or get rid of it.

It's a wear-once outfit. If you have a wedding dress, prom dress, tuxedo or other wear-once dress in your closet, you have an emotional decision to make. If you can't bear to part with these items because they bring back happy memories, then you may have to just keep them. However, if you have photographs of yourself in the wear-once outfit and that's good enough for you, consider parting with it so that someone else can make his or her own good memories in that outfit. On the other hand, if they bring back bad memories, by all means get rid of them. Bring them to a consignment shop, sell them at your next garage sale or donate them.

It's a special occasion outfit. If you have an outfit that you'll only wear if you plan to attend a special occasion, like a wedding or baptism, keep it. But only if a) you love it, b) it fits, c) it's in good condition. If you never or rarely attend a special occasion, why not set a special date with your spouse or a friend and go out on your own special occasion dinner?

It may come back in fashion. This is a bad reason to keep an outfit. It could take years before clothes come back in fashion (if they ever do). What if there's a theme party someday? You can likely recreate the look by visiting a few local thrift shops.

You don't have anything to match it. Perhaps you have a shirt that you love, but can't seem to find pants to match it, or vice versa. Make it a point to go shopping this weekend in search of that perfect match. Remember, neutral colors such as black, brown, beige and gray go well with most other colors. You might even want to bring the piece you have to the store with you and have a sales clerk help you find a good match. Try the mall, so you can get assistance from several different stores before you make your choice. You'll be thrilled that you can finally wear that shirt that's been sitting in your closet!

You never wear it simply because you have too much. If your closet is packed with clothes and you have outfits you never wear simply because of the high volume, you may want to consider putting some of those clothes into storage so that your closet doesn't feel so stuffed and cramped. One thing you definitely should not do is go clothes shopping. Don't add anything else.

- **Add a light.** It's easy for closets that are dark to get cluttered. Add a light so you can see what you're doing.

- **Customize it.** If your budget allows, consider a custom closet organization system to keep your clothing, shoes, handbags, ties, scarves and briefcases stored in a neat and organized fashion. These systems are a bit tricky, so unless you've done it before, have it installed by a professional. You'll save yourself a headache.

- **Twice as nice.** Plan to clean out and organize your closets twice a year—once in the spring, once in the fall.

Great idea!

Every time I buy new clothing, I take the exact number or more of my old, worn out items and get rid of them. This saves on the clothing clutter a bit. For instance, if I bring home six new pairs of socks, I go through my socks and take out at least six old pairs. If I bring home three new shirts, out go three old, worn out or wrong sized shirts.

Jennifer Callahan
Navarre, FL

- **Be consistent.** Consistency is imperative to good organization. How you organize your closet depends on your particular preference. Here are a few different closet organizing methods:

  - ❖ **By type of clothing:** You can store all of your jeans in one section, all of your blazers in another, all of your skirts in another, and all of your shoes in another. Try to keep all white skirts together, all blue shirts together, and so on for a more uniform look. The same goes for length. In other words, don't put a mini skirt in between two long skirts, otherwise it may not be easily visible.

  - ❖ **By outfit:** Sometimes people choose to only wear one particular skirt with one particular shirt, or one particular pair of pants with one particular blazer. If this is you, you may want to hang all clothing (and accessories) that go with a particular outfit together.

  - ❖ **By occasion:** Keep all casual clothing together, all business clothing together and all special occasion clothing together. Then, within those groups, you can organize by type of clothing, color and/or by outfit.

Great idea!

My 9-year old son pretty much wears only white athletic socks, unlike my 6-year old daughter whose every pair is unique. To minimize the number of unmatched socks he has, I buy only one brand and style of socks for him. This way, I can match any sock with a mate.

When one sock wears out, I hang onto the mate until another sock gets worn out or goes missing and I have a pair again. When the total number of socks gets low, I restock with the same brand and style again.

Lynne Assa
Danville, CA

- **Hanger art.** Buy space-saver hangers that hold five to six skirts vertically. They take up less room and keep your skirts in one area.

- **Put shoes on racks.** Get shoe racks for family members to keep in their closet. Count the shoes first, leaving room for some additional pairs. Then, measure the available space—width and height.

  There are many shoe rack designs to choose from. I went for a pretty, stackable wood design. The shoes lay flat on it, so they're not constantly sliding off as they would with the typical slanted shoe rack versions.

  I am not a proponent of the vinyl shoe bags that hang on closet doors for shoe storage. They're not the best for hygiene since they accumulate dirt and don't allow shoes to breathe. They can also be clumsy.

- **Do the seasonal switch.** If you have limited closet space, you may want to consider separating your clothing by season. You can always store the out-of-season clothing in snap-shut plastic boxes. Label the boxes with the person's name and season. Then, when the new season arrives, take a few hours to make the switch.

- **One way.** Hang all articles of clothing facing in the same direction for a nice, uniform look. The same goes for hangers.

- **Keep hangers with hangers.** When you take a hanging item out of your closet, don't leave the hanger in the original spot. When clothes are moved back and forth, it is then difficult to see the hanger. Place the empty hangers on one side of the closet or in a basket on the floor to keep them visible.

- **Have extra, but don't go overboard.** Keep a maximum of ten extra hangers in the closet. You don't need a surplus of 87!

- **Up, up and away.** There should never be clothes on the closet floor. Hang them up, put them on a shelf or fold and put them in your dresser.

Great idea!

I sometimes have had trouble getting rid of an article of clothing even if I find I'm not wearing it. I started writing the month and year when I bought the garment on the label with a laundry marker. I can then check the date later on and see how long I've really had the garment.

It makes it easier to get rid of it when you see you've had it a long time and aren't using it. No longer do I say, "maybe I'll wear it one of these days," when I've had it a few years and havn't worn it in all that time.

Sallie Brodie
Webberville, MI

- **Quality counts.** Using thin, wire hangers is not a good way to keep a closet organized. These hangers tend to twist, bend, tangle and stick up in the air. Give them to your local dry cleaner to recycle. Select plastic or quality wood hangers for your shirts and blazers. Quality metal clip hangers for your skirts and pants are recommended.

Great idea!

For years, I have kept a paper bag in my clothes closet and in the kitchen/den area. I use it to place items I'm no longer using, reading or wanting to wear.

Using a grocery bag with handles or one of the mid-size department store shopping bags with handles, I can conveniently drop items inside. This has helped me recycle more easily on an almost daily basis.

When the bag is full, I pick it up, place it in the car and take it to a women's shelter or a donation station, like Goodwill or The Salvation Army, and begin a new bag.

Ruth Campbell
Santa Cruz, CA

- **Let them breathe.** When you get home from the dry cleaners, immediately take the twist tie off the batch of clothing and remove the plastic covering, unless you're not planning to wear a particular outfit for the next 6 months.

  Replace wire hangers with sturdy, plastic ones immediately —your dry cleaner may even take the hangers back from you if you offer. Take the time to organize your clothes immediately or you're bound to get frustrated during the morning rush when you're looking for something to wear.

- **One is the loneliest number.** Who says you can have only one clothing rod? Install two or three at varying heights to utilize all your hanging storage space. Be sure, however, that your clothes are not overlapping or hanging too low. For instance, you wouldn't want to hang pants on a top rod if they're covering your shirts on the lower rod. You also don't want clothing dragging on the floor. Hanging shirts on a top rod and skirts on a lower rod usually works beautifully.

- **Closet or drawer?** There's no absolute rule, but I usually store items like pants, jeans, shirts, blouses, dresses, suits and jackets in the closet. In my dresser drawers, I usually store things like underwear, pajamas, T-shirts, sweaters and swimwear.

- **Savvy sweater storage.** Store sweaters in see-through under-the-bed storage containers during the warmer season.

- **Sort and divide.** Drawer dividers in bedroom dressers keep socks, underwear and lingerie neat and easy to find quickly. Rotate newest washed items to the back and pull previously washed items forward.

Great idea!

I tend to wear my shirts twice before I designate them as being "laundry." To keep track of the shirts I have worn once, I hang them back up but I turn the hanger around so that it's on the back of the bar instead of the front. That way I know which shirts I should wear and those I've worn before.

Stephanie Ens
Winnipeg, Manitoba, Canada

- **Save space with specialty hangers.** Collapsible, multi-tiered hangers are the latest rage, and they're wonderful for saving space since they allow you to hang multiple items at once.

- **Ready for the cleaners.** Hang a laundry bag on a hook inside the closet for clothes that need to go to the dry cleaners. When it's full, you can just grab it and take it to be cleaned.

- **Sock it to them.** If you don't have a legitimate use for those odd socks you're keeping in your bedroom dresser—you know, the ones that are missing their mates—get rid of them or use them as dust rags.

- **Add drawers to your closet.** Sometimes you can easily slip a chest of drawers or a bedroom dresser that's taking up too much bedroom space, right into your clothes closet. This is an especially nice clothing storage solution if you have a piece that doesn't match well with your other bedroom furniture.

- **Less is more.** If your clothes closet looks like an earthquake recently hit, limit the number of pants, skirts, shirts, shorts and jackets that you have at any given time. Eliminate something before buying something new. Quality is important; quantity isn't.

- **Plan first, shop second.** Plan ahead and determine what you need before you go shopping. For instance, if you have a pair of gray, woolen pants but no shirt to match, indicate this on your shopping list.

- **Schedule a monthly "Clothes Toss" date.** Invite family members that have overloaded, cluttered closets and dresser drawers. Everyone should bring at least one item of clothing they hate, will no longer be wearing, that no longer fits or is worn out. The clothing then gets bagged up and taken to the nearest charity. You can switch homes every month. It's a good way to see each other and get rid of extra clutter at the same time.

Great idea!

When trying to sort out clothes that I no longer wear, I empty my closet and drawers into our guest room closet. Then as I get dressed each day, I go into the guest room to find something to wear. At the end of the season, any clothes still in the guest room I know have not been worn, so I can box them up for Goodwill or a garage sale. I do this every couple of years to keep my closets and drawers organized.

Jolene Aylor
Mt. Pleasant, MI

- **Use a mesh laundry bag**. Toss dirty stockings and delicates in a zippered mesh laundry bag. When there are enough items inside, you can just toss the entire bag in the wash on the delicate cycle.

- **Sort your hand me-downs.** If you have several children, you may save the oldest child's clothing for a younger child and the younger child's clothing for the next youngest child. Get large plastic containers and label them with sizes. Keep these bins in your closet and add any clothing in good condition that no longer fit your older children. Before you go clothes shopping again, check the appropriate containers first. Once your youngest child no longer fits into any of the stored clothes, any clothes still in good condition will be ready for your favorite charity. Clothes in less than good condition can be tossed.

Great idea!

I have a way that I decide/determine which clothes in the closet to discard or give away. Every once in a while, or at the beginning of a season, I turn all the hangers with clothes on them backwards on the rod. When replacing them after washing or wearing, I put them on the proper way. After a few months or the end of the season, I can easily see which clothes I haven't worn. These are the ones I get rid of.

Terese Wells
Prince Frederick, MD

- **At the dry cleaner.** Many dry cleaners will clean and store bulky coats, furs and other winter clothing for a minimal charge. Some even do it for free. You may be able to free up lots of storage space, so be sure to check.

- **Store upright.** Tall winter boots can look messy if they keep flopping over. Keep them upright by stuffing them with old rolled-up magazines secured with elastic bands.

- **Freeze frame.** If you store your shoes in the original shoeboxes they came in, take a photograph of the shoes and tape the photo to the front of the shoebox. You'll be able to identify the contents without opening the box. This is especially helpful if you have tons of shoes.

- **Add canvas shelves.** There are canvas shelves available that you hang on your clothing rod. They basically look like cubbies and are perfect for storing clothing items that would be damaged if hung, such as sweaters.

Great idea!

I store my "off-season" clothing in large plastic totes. This year, instead of getting all sweaters, sweatshirts and other winter items out, I pulled clothes from the tote bags as I needed them. Some needed to be pulled the night before for ironing.

I've found that since I'm only pulling things out as I need/want them, I'm not wearing most of the winter clothes I've been hanging onto. Now that winter is about over, I've got all my "recyclable" clothes ready to go to a garage sale or Goodwill and I'm only keeping the stuff that I truly like and wear. I'm planning to do the same with my summer clothes in just a few months.

Sue McDaniel
Eldon, IA

- **Dirty work clothes.** If you have clothes you keep for painting, gardening, working on the car or other "dirty work," consider getting rid of all but one or two outfits. You most likely don't need more than that.

Great idea!

I dread going through clothes that I may no longer need. To help me not dread it so much when it is time to sort through clothes, I tell myself I only have to try on five articles of clothing before going to bed each night. I have labeled sacks that I put clothing into (give away, garage sale, to be repaired.)

This is not so overwhelming and discouraging for me as going through all the clothes in one day and trying to make a decision. Sooner than I would expect, my clothes are sorted through and I have a good feeling to go with my clean closet.

Janet Broyles
Edmond, OK

- **Don't toss them on a chair.** For anything you wear a few times before tossing in the wash, such as pajamas, don't toss them over the back of a chair or on the floor. Instead, hang a hook on the back of your bedroom closet door, hang them in your closet in a section designated for this purpose or put them on a coat rack in your bedroom and wear them the very next day.

Chapter 14

Kids Bedrooms and Kids Bedroom Closets

- **There's a monster in my closet.** And the monster's name is Clutter! Remember, most bedroom closet tips for adults are the same for the kids so definitely refer to the Master Bedroom section in this book. Below, I've provided some ideas in addition that work especially well for kids' rooms and kids' closets.

Great idea!

With two small children, they can grow out of their clothes faster than we would like or afford for that matter. Each time I do laundry, I keep an eye out for those items that are starting to fit snug. We keep a trash bag in the linen closet with all of these clothes and once the bag is full we bring it to the donation center or local homeless shelter. This ensures that all donations are clean as well as organized.

Bonnie Jordan
Boston, MA

- **Corral baseball caps.** Hang a baseball cap rack on the back of your child's bedroom door to keep all caps neat and organized. Ensure it's at a reachable level for a child's height. Show her how to hang the caps on it properly. If your child is a true hat fan, decorate one of her bedroom walls with caps. Just hang decorative hooks and store the hats out in the open.

- **Store shoes.** Give your child a shoe rack to keep his shoes organized, easily accessible and in one place. Show your child how to organize shoes, keeping all pairs together—not one shoe under the bed and the other in the kitchen.

- **Gather stuffed animals, toys and games.** Put up shelves in children's rooms. This is usually a better solution for toy storage versus containers, because the toys won't get crushed and will be easily obtainable. If you want your kids to be able to get toys themselves, be sure the shelf is not too high. However, if you prefer to get the toys for your kids, put the shelf up higher.

- **Use a hammock.** String a hammock up in your child's bedroom to store stuffed animals. You'll never have to remove them from the bed again.

- **Fling the fluff.** Decorator bed pillows in a child's bedroom may look nice, but are they worth the time it takes to pull them off at night and put them back on in the morning, every morning, every single day of your life? Consider simplifying by taking the pillows off.

- **Think vertical.** If you have more than one child, invest in loft beds. You can then fit a dresser, desk or other necessary piece of furniture in the space a second bed would be taking up.

- **Manage paper.** Create a filing system for your child, for papers such as artwork, rock star photos, blank paper and notes from family and friends. Use a portable filing container that is capable of holding hanging files and that can be transported to someplace else if necessary.

Portable filing containers with handles are nice, since they can be transported to different homes or vacation spots. Some of these containers have snap-shut compartments for pens, pencils, clips and more.

Organizing Clinic

Question

Young reader's books come in all shapes and sizes. Some are extra large and some are very small. Some have wheels and some have objects attached to them to be used with the books. Storing them in an average bookcase is impossible. Do you have any suggestions?

Theresa Swift
Windsor, CA

Answer

Dear Theresa,

Line up some baskets on your bookcase shelves. Then, put the books and any attachments inside the baskets. This should help to hold everything and keep the readers looking neat and attractive at the same time. If there are lots of little attachments, put the entire reader along with the attachments in a large, see-through plastic bag. Then, put the bag with its contents in your baskets. If you'd prefer not to take up space in your family bookcase, you might consider adding some shelving in your kids' rooms for this purpose. Then, just line the shelves with nice baskets and fill them with the books.

Another alternative is to use stackable cubbies, rather than baskets. My local library uses eight stackable cubbies for their kids' books section and they work beautifully for this purpose.

- **Put the monkey on their shoulders.** Declare each son or daughter in charge of his or her own room, bed, closets and drawers. Sound scary? It won't be if you also declare (and follow through on) consequences for any room that is

109

not cleaned up by bedtime, like no TV tomorrow until it's done. While some kids may need some initial instruction, most kids over the age of four should be able to keep their room in decent order.

- **Teach responsibility.** Teach your children to clean and organize their rooms as soon as they're old enough to do so. If you do everything for them, you're truly doing them a disservice. Devise a simple daily checklist for maintenance. Older kids' checklists can be in words, younger kids checklists can be in pictures.

- **Imaginary line.** If you have two children sharing the same room, divide the room in half with an imaginary line. Describe this imaginary line to each child. Assign each one the responsibility of keeping her side clean and organized.

- **Closet sharing.** If two of your children share one clothes closet, be sure to divide it evenly down the middle. Perhaps paint or mark the clothes rod where the dividing line is. Also, each child should get different colored hangers.

- **Dresser sharing.** If two of your children share one dresser, be sure to designate drawers for each child—preferably the same number of drawers if possible—so that each child has sufficient room for his or her clothes.

- **Bring shelves down.** Want your kids to put their toys away? Make it easy for them. Hang shelves in their rooms at eye level for easy retrieval and storage. If your kids can't reach the shelves, they're not going to be able to clean up.

- **Want to play a game?** Store loose game pieces in empty margarine containers or any other small plastic container with a lid.

- **Fix those boxes.** Board game boxes that are falling apart should have no place in your home. Repair the boxes with tape or use other boxes that are in better condition.

- **Hang shoe bags.** Vinyl shoe bags are excellent storage containers for small toys, such as Matchbox cars, Barbie clothes and more. Hang one on each child's bedroom door.

- **Store by season, gender and size.** When you are ready to store children's clothing for the season or for hand-me-downs, label the box with the season, gender and size. For instance, "Spring/Summer, Female, 0-6 Months" or "Fall/Winter, Male, 3 Years."

- **Seven-Day Organizer.** You can buy canvas, hanging organizing bags that have seven cubes labeled Monday, Tuesday, Wednesday, and so on for each day of the week. Each child chooses an outfit for each day of the week, including underwear, and stores it in one of these cubes. No more thinking of what to wear on busy weekday mornings.

- **Rotate toys.** If your kids have an abundant amount of toys cluttering up their rooms, store most in the basement or attic and just a few in the bedroom. Every month, swap some of those in the room for some of those in storage. This is an excellent way to keep the clutter at bay, plus it helps hold kids' interests a bit longer if they haven't seen that toy in awhile.

Organizing Clinic

Question

How do I organize my kids' rooms? There are Barbies and their accessories, 18 inch dolls and their accessories, horses and their accessories, other numerous dolls and their numerous accessories, beads, various other crafts, little toys, collections, photos, books, jewelry and desk supplies. The list goes on and on, but the floor and closet space doesn't!

Jenny Argue
Geneva, IL

Answer

Dear Jenny,

Here are just three small hints to help you get started:

- **Shelving.** Add some simple shelves to your walls. Then, put some decorative, functional, wicker baskets on top to keep toys organized. So many times, wall space is forgotten. Shelving adds tons of space you never knew you had.

- **Shoe organizers.** Get yourself a few plastic shoe organizers, specifically the ones that hang over the door. Hang one over the bedroom entry door (facing the child's room) and another in the child's closet. These are handy for storing items like Barbie clothing, jewelry and desk supplies.

- **Storage containers.** Large plastic storage containers with covers, with smaller plastic storage containers with covers stored inside, make great storage bins for beads and other crafts. You can leave these out in the open if you don't have closet space. If you like, you can even cover them with a pretty throw when not in use.

- **Let them decide.** Every time you see your child's room getting a bit overloaded with clutter, have him decide on at least one item to give to charity. This teaches compassion, while keeping kids rooms clutter free.

- **Stow a bed.** Stow a hideaway bed under your child's bed for sleepovers. Their guests will be comfortable and no extra space is required.

- **Bunk beds.** Bunk beds don't take up any more side-by-side space than regular beds. They're perfect if you have more than one child or if you have a visiting child fairly often.

- **Stack them.** Colorful stacking bins are wonderful organizers for a child's bedroom. Each bin can hold a different category of toys. For instance, one bin can be for Barbie dolls, another for rubber stamps and another for books.

- **Get an activity desk.** Rather than your child coloring on his bed or drawing while lying on the floor, why not invest in a child's activity desk? He or she will have plenty of area to write, color, draw or craft on top and ample storage space in drawers underneath.

- **Stack those cubes.** Stacking cubes are also wonderful storage tools for kids' bedrooms. You can buy the open type, the type that have doors, or you can buy both and mix and match. You can leave them out in the open or store them in your child's bedroom closet. You can buy as many or as few as you need. They're very versatile and can house toys, music, crafts and more.

- **Hang a corkboard.** Hang a corkboard in your child's bedroom so she can display her prized artwork, a report she got an "A" on or her favorite photographs.

- **Use an umbrella stand.** If your child has toy golf clubs, baseball bats or other tall items, give him an umbrella stand to store these items together in one corner of the room.

- **Line dressers with baskets.** Line dressers with baskets to hold kid nail polish, kid jewelry, kid cars and other small items. The baskets will keep everything organized and give the room an uncluttered look.

- **Add a computer center.** If your child has a computer in his room, a computer center is a good piece of furniture to have. Buy the type that gives him room for his computer tower, printer and other equipment so everything fits inside.

- **Divide the room.** If you have two kids who want privacy, but you don't have two kids' bedrooms, consider dividing the one room into two. You can use beads, door curtains, string lights, ready-made paneled room dividers or two-sided bookcases. Another option is to put canopies over each child's bed.

- **Create zones.** If your child's bedroom is also a playroom, create a few zones. Zone A would be for sleeping and dressing, Zone B for playing and artwork and Zone C for reading and homework. The room will be defined which will help you better decide where to put things.

- **I'm puzzled.** If your kids enjoy putting puzzles together, forget about using the kitchen table. Instead, get them a roll out puzzle mat. The unfinished puzzle can be rolled up when not in use.

- **New use for something old.** Once you're not using the changing table for your child anymore, convert that furniture into shelving for toys or books.

- **Go to the back door.** Hang a clear vinyl shoe organizer on the back of your child's bedroom entry door. Use each pocket to store toys, hair accessories or art supplies.

- **Lower the rod.** Lower the clothes rod in your child's closet so she can easily reach it. This is especially good when you're teaching her how to choose clothes and dress herself. You can move it up later as your child grows.

Great idea!

Place a plastic bin in the bottom of your child's closet. As you notice your child is wearing something that no longer fits or needs mending, use a laundry marker and place a mark on the tag of the garment while your child is wearing it. D is for donate and M for mend. While folding the cloths after laundering them, place all the M's in one pile and set them aside for a mending moment. After the mending is done place a slash through the M. While putting away laundry, take the D's to your child's room and place them in the bin. When the bin is full, drop it at Goodwill. This works for adults too!

Bonnie Jordan
Boston, MA

- **Corral comic books and kid magazines.** Use magazine boxes from an office supply store to help organize your kids' comic books and magazines. You can also make a magazine holder from an empty cereal box.

- **Use photos.** When you organize toys into plastic bins with lids, take a photo of the toys inside and tape that photo onto the outside of the box, like a photo of Barbie for all Barbie-related items. Your child will be able to find toys easily and will know where the toy goes when not in use.

- **Make a stand.** Trade in kids' nightstands for storage chests instead. The storage area in chests is much larger.

- **Shake it up.** Install decorative shaker pegs on bedroom walls to hold hats, jackets or outfits for the week.

- **The paper caper.** This is a great time to begin teaching your kids the importance of paper management. If your child is in school, he or she is old enough to having a filing cabinet to store papers such as those related to school, artwork or greeting cards.

Chapter 15

The Nursery

- **Sketch it out.** Measure your future baby's room and sketch the room out on grid paper labeled with the measurements. If you use grid paper, you'll have a guide for dimensions of the room and your furniture. Make copies of your initial sketch.

  Then, use those copies to sketch out a number of possible decorating scenarios in order to help you make smart decorating decisions.

  You can even make cut outs to scale, representing your furniture, and lay out possible arrangement scenarios on your grid.

- **Spend some time in the room.** As you're planning, spend some time in your future baby's room jotting down your observations during different times of the day and year.

  For instance, determine where the sun is shining brightest during sunrise and sunset. If your baby's crib is in direct view of the sunrise, for example, he or she might wake up earlier than you would like.

  Pay particular attention to window drafts and air conditioner vents, which you would not want near the baby.

  Know this room well before you begin to prepare it for your baby.

- **Buy furniture that does double duty.** There are many cribs on the market that easily convert into different sized beds as your child grows up. Our daughter started with a crib that converts into a toddler bed and later converts into a full-size adult bed.

  There are chests of drawers that have built-in changing tables. We never had a changing table for our baby. We had a dresser with a hutch. The changing table was built right in and was easily converted to a shelf for books, stuffed animals and games. Look for these multi-functional baby items that save space and money.

- **Less is more.** The less decorative knickknacks and stuffed animals you use in your baby's room, the less cluttered and chaotic it will look. Plus, you'll have a lot less to keep clean.

  Remember, you're going to be spending enough of time taking care of your new baby. Don't give yourself additional cleaning tasks you don't need.

Great idea!

When my daughter was born, we had a changing table for her. When she outgrew it, sentimental as I am, I didn't want to get rid of it.

Now we use it in the garage where our washer and dryer are. I have put six laundry baskets on it, two on each level. I labeled each basket in black ink for sorting whites, reds, darks, towels, sheets and hand washing. Everyone can easily and quickly sort their own laundry when they bring their laundry basket to the garage.

It works great and speeds up the laundry process because the sorting is already done.

It also helps when you are teaching your children to do laundry so they don't mix a red shirt with the whites!

Carolyn Lane
Eureka, CA

- **Keep essentials nearby.** Keep diapers, wipes, baby powder, diaper rash cream, a thermometer, hand sanitizer, a few extra outfits and anything else you need to change your baby, right near the changing table.

- **Get a diaper holder.** You're going to need to store lots of diapers. Consider a diaper bag that hangs over the railing of the crib. We had one in our house that fit 58 diapers. Don't laugh. That size bag only lasted about a week!

- **At least two sets.** Always have at least two sets of sheets, two waterproof mattress pads and two changing table covers. When your baby's diaper leaks in the middle of the night, you'll be prepared with fresh linens.

- **Buy disposable changing pads.** We always kept a disposable changing pad cover right over our baby's regular changing pad cover. When the disposable changing pad cover got dirty, we just tossed it. No more washing the cloth changing pad cover each day.

- **A few toys at a time.** There's little reason to go out and buy your new baby hundreds of new toys. Believe me, most would rather play with your keys or a box than with any of the best toys on the market. Besides, you'll probably get toys as gifts. When my baby was born, we didn't have to buy one toy. Our family, friends and neighbors gave us enough to last us more than a year.

- **Organize by size.** When family, friends and neighbors find out you're having a baby, chances are you'll start to receive clothing for the little one.

Designate two drawers for 0-3 month outfits, another drawer for 3-6 month outfits and another outfit for 6+ month outfits. As your baby grows out of one size, you'll know exactly what drawer to look in to find the next size up.

Great idea!

When I tried to get rid of some of my child's extra baby clothes, I first went to the consignment shops. They were just so picky. Everything seemed to be either too faded, out of style or stained.

So I just took the clothes, shoes and blankets to the local crisis pregnancy center. They are so desperate for baby and maternity clothes. The girls who use the services usually have little money and sometimes nowhere to turn for basic baby supplies. They appreciated all of my extras, no matter how out of style they were. Plus I got the good feeling you get when you know you've helped someone out in need.

Angie Baker
Dayton, OH

- **Already outgrown.** If you plan to have more children in the future, take all clothing your baby has outgrown and organize it into plastic containers. Label the containers by size. When your next baby arrives, you'll be all set.

  If you don't plan to have more kids, use the same idea but give the containers to relatives or friends or sell those already categorized items at your next rummage sale.

- **Organize the dresser.** Dedicate specific drawers for specific items in your baby's dresser. For instance, in my baby's dresser, we stored bibs, hats and socks in the top drawer, casual clothes in the 2nd drawer, dressier clothes in the 3rd drawer and blankets and sheets in the bottom drawer.

- **Tiny socks.** Baby socks are tiny and tend to get lost very easily. Fold pairs together and organize them into the dresser in shallow baskets or containers.

- **Shoe fettish.** Don't buy more than one or two pairs of baby shoes for your baby. Babies don't need to be in shoes until they're walking. Keep a pair or two for visiting Grandma or for some other special occasion.

- **Where's my stuffed animal?** Before our baby was born, I kid you not, we had over 22 stuffed animal gifts waiting for her. I bought some very decorative baskets and stored several in each basket. Each basket was stored on the floor or on a shelf in the corners of the nursery. They looked really cute and were contained.

- **Those wipe containers.** Baby wipe containers are excellent storage containers. You can use them in various areas of your home to store makeup, feminine products, first aid, hair accessories, small toys and so much more. Label the outside and use these whenever you need storage containers.

- **Keep the future in mind.** While you may want to go all out and decorate your future baby's room with child-like wallpaper and cute accessories, keep in mind that in just a few years, your child may be complaining that the scheme is too babyish.

   Then, you'll be faced with the prospect of having to decorate this room again very soon into your child's life. It's easier to keep the wall treatments and furniture very basic, so it can span many years of your child's life. On the other hand, you can easily change comforters, rugs and decorative accessories.

- **Keep a diaper bag in the closet.** Always keep a diaper bag that is already prepared in your baby's closet. When you have to go out, you'll be able to grab the bag, add some food or formula and get going.

- **Read between the lines.** Add a few shelves to your child's room and add decorative book ends or get a few storage cubes. You will have the perfect space to store all of your baby's books. These both serve the purpose well, since baby books come in all shapes and sizes and sometimes don't fit well into a typical bookcase.

- **Light the night.** Have a nightlight in your baby's room. When you answer her cries at night, you can just light the nightlight instead of illuminating the entire room. Doing so prevents your baby from thinking it's already daytime and helps to ensure she can fall back asleep.

- **Start a memory box.** Can you imagine how thrilled your child will be when she is an adult and you still have some of the things from when she was a baby? Now, I'm not suggesting that you keep everything—only the really special things.

   In my daughter Amanda's memory box, I have the band the doctor used to take her blood pressure at the hospital, the outfit I took her home in, her first "Welcome to the World" card from mom and dad, the one toy she really took to and a few other special items.

   This box is stored on a high shelf in her closet and I add to it from time to time as Amanda grows up . It's organized and it ensures these special items don't get lost or tossed in a junk drawer.

Chapter 16

Home Office

- **A place to do your work.** Whether it's a full-size office or a work surface, such as a table or a desk, you need a place to do your "work." I don't necessarily mean work, such as a home-based business, but any type of paper work you do in your home.

  If you're looking for tips on setting up an actual office where you will conduct business, or you work in an office outside your home, definitely pick up a copy of my book *Finally Organized, Finally Free for the Office.*

  This section, however, is going to pertain mostly to your "home" work. This means the area you use to pay bills, sign permission slips, read mail, write correspondence and file important paperwork.

- **Designate an office space.** If you have lots of rooms in your house, dedicating one of your rooms for your home work would be a great thing to do. Not everyone has that luxury though. So, your next best bet is to designate one consistent area where you handle such tasks.

  My parents have a desk and filing cabinet in their bedroom. All their home work is done there.

  A friend of mine uses a lap desk in her living room for this purpose. Her filing cabinet is in the living room. When it's not in use, it's covered with a pretty quilt. Nobody knows it's under there.

  A neighbor of mine uses her kitchen table as her work surface and keeps a portable file box for her home filing in one of the kitchen cabinets.

  An associate of mine does his homework in one of his closets. He pulled the door off his closet, found a desk that fit nicely in an inset and he goes to work at least once a week.

  Yet, another person, attached a large work surface to her kitchen wall with hinges. When she needs to use it, she flips it down. When she's not using it, she flips it up. No extra permanent space needed!

  Find an area of your home for your home work. Put all supplies you need to do your work somewhere in that room, whether in a permanent cabinet or in a portable box and do your work in that room consistently.

- **Buy an attractive filing cabinet.** Buy a filing cabinet that fits into your décor. You might want to invest in a nice wood cabinet that looks more like furniture than like commercial office equipment. You can also cover a filing cabinet with a pretty quilt when you're done using it for the day.

Organizing Clinic

Question

Even though my whole house is a mess, I realize important documents from all family members (me, a son and a daughter) have to be organized first. For example, health and car insurances and appliance guarantees are not in any sort of order. Any suggestions?

Virginia Gordillo
Guatemala

Answer

Dear Virginia,

Important documents need to be organized into file folders and then stored in the filing cabinet.

You need main categories such as Insurance, Warranties, Bank Statements, Medical Records and so on. These categories should each have a hanging file folder. Within the main categories are sub-categories. For instance, within your Insurance hanging file folder, you might store regular manila file folders for auto insurance, health insurance and home insurance.

A pre-made filing system can help you set up your home or office filing system in no time at all—without having to think of a single file category. The work is already done for you.

You also mentioned that your house is a mess. While you're working on getting your filing system together, I recommend you spend at least 15 minutes each day getting your home under control. Chances are, some important documents are hidden among the household clutter.

You would be amazed at what just 15 minutes of focused time each day could do to keep your filing system and your home in top-notch condition.

- **Every home needs a filing cabinet.** Whether you are a large family of eight or a small family of one or two, you need a filing cabinet in your home to store your home papers. Shoeboxes won't do. Drawers stuffed with papers won't do.

Go to an office supply store and get yourself a two or four-drawer filing cabinet. Be sure it's a good, full-suspension one so the drawers don't fall forward from the weight of the file folders when pulled out.

I can't tell you how many homes I've seen with file cabinets that just have the folders tossed inside the drawer. The file folders get ruined this way, they slide to the bottom of the drawer and it's almost impossible to finger through your files when you're looking for something. The bottom line is to be sure there's a mechanism included for "hanging" file folders.

If there's absolutely no way you want a filing cabinet, then at minimum, get yourself a few portable file boxes. These hold hanging file folders, have a lid that closes up on top and a handle that allows you to carry the box from one room to the next.

Organizing Clinic

Question

I have read and attempted to work with several systems to organize my genealogy research. I use the computer for many records, but I need a system that provides quick access to originals, like wills, birth certificates and death certificates. Also I need a system that gives me easy and uncluttered hard copy records in order to take family files to reunions and on research trips.

Mary Sanders
Gainesville, GA

Answer

Dear Mary,

Get yourself a portable file box with a lid and handle made for hanging file folders. Also pick up four hanging binders, index dividers and acid-free sheet protectors.

Label each binder with major categories such as, Paternal Grandfather's Family, Paternal Grandmother's Family, Maternal Grandfather's Family, Maternal Grandmother's Family, etc.

Within each of these binders, include a set of index dividers to separate each family member's records. Label each index divider with a family member's name. Insert several sheet protectors in between each of the index dividers. Finally, insert your documents into the sheet protectors.

Now you can easily organize and find information for each family member and you can carry your records with you wherever you please.

- **Double purposes.** Some home offices serve dual purposes. My home office is also a guest room. When I have guests staying in the guest room, I'm able to "close shop" by closing the doors of my computer armoire.

  The sofa I use for business reading pulls out to a queen size bed. All the furniture is wooden to convey a very homey feel. I have pretty pictures on the walls, an attractive hurricane lamp and books that are both business-related and non-business related on my bookshelf.

  When I'm not working, it's hard to tell that my office is a home office. It truly looks like and is a cozy retreat for guests.

  Bonnie, a colleague of mine, has a home office that shares space with her personal computer, sewing machine, craft items and the bed her granddaughter sleeps in when she stays over, but she is sure to keep each area separated—one corner for each separate purpose.

Great idea!

My husband and I find that we're constantly confusing our cell-phone charger cords and other similar adapters and small electrical cords. I decided to assign these small detachable cords a home in a single drawer in the kitchen. To help identify them, I put each in a Ziploc-type bag, and use a permanent marker to label each one. It also saves the frustration of trying to untangle a snarl of cords at the last minute.

Joy Conradt
Eugene, OR

- **Use a folding screen.** Folding screens are especially handy if you work in a home office. Put one up and you'll be able to easily disguise a work area or convert one work area into two. A friend of mine has a home office set-up in her family room. Each evening, she closes shop by hiding her desk behind a decorative screen.

- **Home office supplies.** Most home offices should be stocked with the following office supplies:

  ❖ Pens, pencils and hi-lighters

  ❖ A calculator

  ❖ Your checkbook

- ❖ Postage stamps

- ❖ Envelopes

- ❖ Home address labels

- ❖ Writing paper

- ❖ Correction fluid

- ❖ Scotch tape

- ❖ A stapler

- ❖ Paper clips

- ❖ A calendar or planner

- ❖ Sticky notes

- ❖ A notepad or notebook

- ❖ Generic greeting cards for Thank You, Birthday, Anniversary, Get Well, Sympathy and so on

Great idea!

I have a very large desk with a hutch and, in these quarters, had no extra room to create an "office." The desk takes up one-fourth of my living room, so I have maximized every bit of room on the desk for storage. My favorite idea is a raised shelf with a drawer and CD slots underneath that is very handy. My printer sits on top of the shelf leaving about 18-20 inches of "dead space" above the printer.

I took two small cup hooks and screwed them into the underside of the top of the hutch. I have a wooden basket with leather loop handles and I hung those handles on the cup hooks. Now, this basket hangs suspended about 4 inches below the top of the hutch and about 4 inches above the printer. No dead space and a great spot to store everything from paperclips to headphones.

Julianne Kelly
Fort Riley, KS

- **Think comfort.** Be sure the lighting in your office area is bright enough so you're not straining your eyes. You may need a few lights depending on what you're using your office for. A bright white light is great for detail-work, such as when you're paying bills, while a warmer yellow light may be better for creating a relaxing mood when you're reading.

  You will also need a good, comfortable chair. If there will be several members of your family using the work area, get a chair that allows for height adjustment. It should be a nice, sturdy, office-type chair—one that swivels if you're going to be moving around a lot.

- **Nifty holder.** Put all outgoing mail in a napkin holder. Each day, grab all your outgoing mail and mail it at once.

- **Clear work surface-clear mind.** If your work surface looks like a tornado just whipped through it, how will you be able to concentrate on the project at hand? Do you really want to pay your bills, write a letter, work on a craft or check your kid's homework among piles of scattered files, papers, mail and magazines?

A messy, disorganized work area results in scattered thoughts and stress. A cluttered desk can easily lead to unfortunate circumstances such as lost paperwork, missed appointments, late payments on your bills and missing phone numbers. It's nearly impossible to think straight when you're working in such a chaotic situation.

The only paper on the desk or table you're working on, should be the task or project you're doing right now. File everything else away or at the very least, temporarily move it to another area. Once your work surface is completely clear, you'll then be ready to work in a stress-free, productive manner.

Great idea!

I have some very nice place mats that only get used for special occasions, but I like to look at them and was wondering where in the house I could put them so I could enjoy seeing them.

I uncluttered a rectangular space in the middle of my desk and put one of my favorite place mats there. My goal this past week was to keep everything off the place mat. So far, so good. My goal next week will be to increase the empty perimeter around it and to keep increasing it until the desk is permanently clutter-free.

The pretty placemat is not only a permanent reminder, but a bit of a reward since I like its color and design so much.

Nancy Coker
Altadena, CA

- **Your computer.** If you have a computer in a computer center, then you probably have a separate work surface for writing. If your computer is sitting right on your work surface however, you may want to consider some space saving ideas to free up that work surface area a bit.

For instance, your computer tower can go on the floor under or beside your desk. You can install a shelf for your printer, scanner and/or fax machine. You can buy a flat-screen monitor—they take up less than 1/3 of the space a regular monitor does! You can put your monitor on a monitor riser. Risers leave space under the monitor.

There are lots of possibilities. Visit your local office supply store and ask the salesperson for space saving ideas.

Great idea!

Having tried many systems, I recently hit on an idea that seems to work fairly well for me. I have a small contracting company, so I have to keep up with jobs to do as a company, as well as things I have to do directly. My goal was to find a system that was easy to update and didn't take up my whole desk.

I started with a stenographer's notebook, which is lined and has a center vertical line down the middle. I then divide this by priority from top to bottom. The left side is company projects. The right side contains jobs I must finish, like quotes. My priorities are:

Top-Things that need to be done immediately

2nd Group- Things that are started or need to be started, but are waiting on something or someone.

3rd Group- Things that need to be done in the near future, but haven't been started yet.

4th Group- Things that need to be done sometime in the future, but as yet have no start time or schedule.

I divide my groups by drawing lines on each page (this takes a little time, but not too much). I start at the bottom and make a line four lines up, the next group has five lines, and the last line is seven lines up from there. This leaves the largest grouping at the top. These could be different for different companies, depending on the situation.

The biggest perceived drawback to this system is probably the biggest plus in my mind. Every day the jobs will have to be re-listed, but this forces me to evaluate the jobs as I go through them. I cross off the jobs that are done, re-evaluate the priority of every job, and I am ready with a fresh perspective every day. I also cross off every job as I transfer it, to make sure that I do not miss anything during the transfer of information.

J T Lewis
Company: RJ Lewis
Guilford, IN
www.rjlewis.net/sys-tmpl/door

Chapter 17

Bathrooms

- **Inspect your medicine cabinet.** Toss old makeup, perfumes, toiletries and prescriptions. Dump anything with an expired date, cosmetics over a year old and anything else you no longer use. Don't store medications in the bathroom. The heat and steam could ruin them.

- **Stop rings.** When storing shaving cream, store the cans upside down on their plastic caps. This will prevent rust rings, thus saving you cleaning time.

- **Increase space.** Short on cabinet space? For that extra needed storage, install shelves on the bathroom walls.

- **There's space behind your bathroom door.** If your home has tiny closets or you're looking for a little extra storage space, install towel bars on the back of your bathroom door. They can hold items you would normally keep in a closet such as extra towels or pants. Each bar can hold two or three pairs. You might even skip the bar idea and hang a few hooks—perfect for hanging your bathrobe or outfits for the next few days.

  Another bonus is that you'll have less ironing to do. Every time you take a shower, the steam will help reduce wrinkles on any of the clothing hanging on the bars or hooks.

- **Hold those brushes.** Always keep toothbrushes in toothbrush holders. Each family member should have a different colored toothbrush for quick and easy identification.

- **Use a shower caddy.** Rather than having soaps, shampoos and other items scattered about, get a shower caddy. Stock it with the items you use each day. Caddies offer convenient access to anything that your family uses in the shower.

Great idea!

I always dedicate rainy days to cleaning out my bathroom and vanity drawers. The rule with my toiletries is if I have had it for more than one year, it is time to throw it away. That way, I am always using all of the toiletries I own and there is no buildup in my vanity drawers.

Lauren Hobstetter
Palo Alto, CA

- **Use fruit baskets.** Hanging wire fruit baskets, usually used in the kitchen, double as bathroom holders for curlers, combs and more.

- **It's magnetic.** A long magnet, affixed to the back of your medicine chest will hold tweezers, shavers, clippers, scissors and other metal objects neatly in place.

- **Forget soap.** Well, at least forget soap bars. They're messy and leave soap scum behind. Use liquid soap instead. They dispense soap easily and leave no messy residue. You can even buy multi-pour dispensers that can be mounted to the tile and filled with your favorite soaps, lotions and shampoos.

- **Small space doesn't mean small storage.** If your cabinets are small, use an over-the-toilet organizer, a shelf or a wicker basket to hold powders, sprays and other essentials.

- **Add a rack.** For large bathrooms, consider putting a matching coat rack inside. It's perfect for holding robes or towels.

- **Think outside the box.** A three-tiered plate rack is convenient for holding soaps, nail polish, hairbrushes, barrettes and more.

- **Give them a tote.** Assign each family member their own basket or tote bag for their bathroom personals. Hang each on a separate hook. This will eliminate confusion over what belongs to whom.

- **Hang the dryer.** If your hair dryer and curling iron have a loop, a simple nail or hook will allow you to hang it on the side of a cabinet or on the wall.

- **Give them a home.** Designate a specific home for each bathroom item. Don't clutter one area with too many things. Leave sufficient space around each item so you can find what you need in a matter of seconds.

Great idea!

A fantastic organizing tool was putting up small rounded hooks on the inside of my medicine cabinet. These are usually used for hanging coffee mugs, but could also be used on bathroom vanity doors under the sink.

I have four hooks for different types and lengths of necklaces, chains and bracelets. These are all out of sight when the doors are closed, but easily accessible when I need to decide which to use. They stay neat and I avoid getting wrinkles in my delicate chains, bracelets and necklaces.

Marta Sherwood
Gilroy, CA

- **Use a caddy.** Consider using clear organizing caddies to store similar items together. All your lotions can go in one, hair products in another and colognes in another.

- **Store the new stuff elsewhere.** Store toiletries and paper products bought in advance in a different storage area than the products you've already opened. Otherwise, you'll have three half-used hair spray cans or two slightly finished boxes of tissues.

- **Get rid of old towels.** Toss out stringy, ripped, faded, thinned-out bath towels. Forget the "what if I need extra rags" syndrome.

- **Keep rubber ducky safe.** Store bath toys in a wicker basket right near the bathtub. Toys will dry out quickly and will be easily accessible for your children. Another possibility is to put toys in a nylon mesh bag and attach the bag to a hooked suction cup. Then store the bag on your tile shower wall.

- **News flash.** Catch up on the news without wasting time. Put a radio in the bathroom—a waterproof radio if you're putting it in your shower—and listen while getting ready to start your day.

- **Keep toilet paper handy.** Hang a plastic, toilet paper rack inside your under-the-sink cabinet or on the back of the cabinet door. These organize and store three to four extra rolls of toilet paper.

- **Add some pockets.** Sew colorful cloth pockets and then attach them to the outside of a child's shower curtain. Spruce them up with some big decorative buttons. Store barrettes and ponytail holders in one pocket, a hairbrush and combs in another, and lotion in yet another. It looks really cute and is a great storage solution. Just make sure you have a sturdy shower rod and that you don't put anything extra heavy in the pockets.

Great idea!

One of the greatest organization tips for my bathroom is to use square baskets for everyday toiletries. I have my cleanser, moisturizer and cosmetics in a basket that I can pull in and out of the vanity. This is also great for my husband's shaving cream, aftershave and everything else that he uses.

After they are used, they are put away and the countertop is ready to be cleaned with a cleaning cloth that I keep under the sink. Very fast, clean and easy.

Sonia Rebollo-McCloskey
Westminster, CO

- **Bathroom reading.** Keep reading clutter off the floor by installing an acrylic magazine rack to the wall to hold magazines for the entire family.

- **Strange but true.** Family members keep forgetting to put down the toilet seat? The "Self-Closing Toilet Seat" never forgets. Its automatic closing system begins lowering the seat a few minutes after use.

Great idea!

Keep basic sewing supplies in the area where you get dressed. Whether you find a loose seam or a missing button, you can take care of it immediately. Sure beats setting it aside for an indefinite stay in a mending pile.

Julinda Adams
Loogootee, IN

- **Make "Sleepover Kits."** Create Sleepover Kits for your guest bathroom. Place extra toothbrushes, toothpaste, mouthwash, shampoo, soap, a disposable razor and other toiletries in a pretty basket. When guests visit, they will feel right at home.

- **Dispense it.** Rather than having several bottles of shampoo and shower gel in your shower, add a wall dispenser that dispenses these liquids.

- **Add bars.** Not enough bars in your bathroom for towels? Add a few and you'll help ensure the towels go back on the rod when not in use and not on the floor. While you're at it, hang a few hooks for clothing being taken off or clean clothing you plan to wear that day.

- **Ladies only.** Store feminine products neatly and discreetly by using empty diaper wipe boxes or empty cosmetic bags. Store these close to the toilet.

- **Use a ribbon.** Clip barrettes to a length of ribbon. Hang the ribbon on a hook. You'll be able to find your barrettes quickly without having to rummage through a drawer.

- **Put cleaning supplies in each bathroom.** Rather than sharing cleaning supplies between two or more bathrooms and having to carry them back and forth, give each bathroom its own cleaning supply caddy. When you're ready to clean one of the bathrooms, the supplies will be right there.

- **Add a pen and pad.** Always keep a pen and pad of paper in the bathroom. Studies have shown that the bathroom is one of the top ten areas where one may experience a creative moment. You'll be able to quickly jot down any ideas you want to remember.

- **Add a corner shelf.** Many bathrooms are short on space. At the same time, most have room for corner shelves. You can usually find these at craft shows or in home stores. They're perfect for holding cosmetics, hair accessories, shaving supplies and more.

- **Add a hook.** Add a hook to the back of your bathroom door to hold bathrobes, clothing, or an extra towel.

- **Designate a drawer.** If you have enough drawers, assign one to each of your family members. Or if you prefer, designate each drawer to be used for a bathroom category such as hair accessories or oral hygiene.

- **Towel storage ideas.** If you have enough cabinets in your bathroom, by all means store towels there rather than in a separate linen closet. If you don't have enough cabinets, hang shelves for towels. You can even put a wine rack or a basket in your bathroom to hold rolled hand towels and washcloths.

- **Group towels.** Group towels by color and size in your bathroom cabinet. For instance all bath towels on one shelf, all hand towels on another shelf and all face towels on another shelf.

- **Stack them properly.** Stack towels with the folded edge out, like they would be displayed in a store. This will keep a neat appearance and help to ensure you grab only one.

- **Skirt it.** If you have a pedestal sink and no under-sink storage, you may want to skirt your sink, using Velcro to attach the fabric. You'll have some instant storage space behind the skirt.

- **Be careful.** If you have kids, take precautions with your bathroom storage. Get a toilet latch. Even things with childproof caps should be kept out of reach. One child I know managed to get her hands on her dad's disposable razor. Thank goodness he was able to grab it before his daughter was injured.

- **I can see clearly now.** Set up a series of see-through jars on your bathroom countertop or bathroom shelf for items you need to keep sterile, such as cotton balls, cosmetic sponges and Q-tips.

- **Put it in a tub.** Get a plastic tub large enough to fit everything you use each morning, like cosmetics, shaving supplies, hair sprays and gels, and put everything inside. Store the tub in your bathroom cabinet.

When you need the tub in the morning, pull it out and use the contents. When you're done, store the entire tub back in the cabinet. If you have several family members, you may want to give each person their own tub.

Chapter 18

Basement

- **Hang tool boards with latches**. These will keep long handled tools organized. Use hooks to hang bikes and tools onto pegboards.

- **Hold tall items.** Use a tall trash can or umbrella stand for holding tall items such as fishing rods, pool cues and baseball bats.

- **Tin can alley.** Cut the top and bottoms off of tin cans and nail them to the wall with the cut ends facing up and down. Put one long handled tool in each with the handle facing down.

- **Dispose properly.** Get rid of anything in your basement that has not been used for months. Check with your local fire department to find out how to dispose of flammable items.

- **Aprons are not only for cooking.** Hang a wraparound cloth apron with pockets and you'll have an instant tool tote. Make your own or purchase an inexpensive one from a home improvement center.

- **Keep tape neat.** Vertically mount a cardboard paper towel roll on the wall or inside a cabinet door. Use it to hold large, circular rolls of tape.

- **Use a toolbox with sections**. You'll be able to divide and separate tools into their own divisions. Dividing and separating will make it easier to find a tool when you need it.

- **Hire help.** If you live alone and your basement is really going to be a bear to clean, consider hiring a high school or college student to help.

Great idea!

I always had a jumble of electrical cords to small appliances jammed in a kitchen drawer with no way to tell which one belonged to which appliance. One day the light bulb went off and I began to save the cardboard toilet tissue rolls. They were the perfect size for a folded cord. I labeled them on the outside for instant recognition. They fit nice and organized in one small drawer now. You can also cut paper towel cardboard rolls in two. They can be covered with contact paper for strength and beauty.

Charlotte Kavan
Port St. Lucie, FL

- **Keep small hardware visible.** Keep various labeled jars for nails, screws and washers. Nail or screw the cap of the jar to the underside of a board. The jars will always be in one place and you can unscrew the jar, take out what you need and replace it again on its mounted lid when you're finished getting what you need.

- **Get a free-standing "Sports Organizer Rack."** These racks keep equipment from soccer balls to baseball mitts to golf shoes ready for play. The steel racks have roomy shelves and hanging hooks to keep gear organized.

- **The dirty dozen.** Keep loose golf balls stored and organized in empty egg cartons.

- **Hold that hose.** If you keep your garden hose in the garage, don't just leave it tossed on the floor. Wrap it around a "Garden Hose Holder" that is mounted to the wall.

- **Skip cardboard. Use plastic instead.** Clear, labeled organizing containers are perfect for the basement and garage. Store car care products in one. Store paint brushes in another. You get the picture. They will keep everything free of dust and organized for easy retrieval.

- **Let there be light.** Ensure there is sufficient lighting, especially inside any closets or cabinets. Generating clutter is easy when you can't see what you're putting in or taking out.

- **Think of it as a room, not a junk area.** Don't make your basement or garage catch-all areas for things you don't even use. If you're storing something that is not useful or that you don't enjoy, get rid of it today.

- **Store them high.** Store weed killer, paint and other toxic materials on high shelves, out of the reach of young children. But make sure that they are closed tightly so they don't fall on you when you bring them down.

- **One step up.** Keep a stepstool or stepladder handy. You'll be able to easily reach items on high shelves. Be sure you store it in a place where young children cannot climb up.

- **Create a "Pick up at the Hardware Store" list.** Include items you buy at the hardware store. Make copies of this list. Hang one up in the garage or basement. Keep the rest in a file until you need a new one. As you run out of something, check off what you need and bring this list with you to the store.

- **Shelf storage.** Use utility shelves in your basement storage area to hold items ranging from paint cans and garden supplies to car care products. While open storage is very convenient, I feel that closed storage gives the basement a less cluttered look.

- **Schedule maintenance.** Every year or so, you'll have to change the filter in your furnace. Be sure this maintenance is scheduled on your calendar.

- **Finish if off.** If you're in the market for finishing off your basement, give organizing and storage some careful thought first. Think of what you'll be using your basement for.

  For instance, if you're going to be using one section for a play area, another area for a craft area, another area for a home theater area and a fourth area for storage, create separate zones for each of these purposes.

  Either build walls around these zones, add half walls or keep things related to each zone in separate sections.

  In addition, you may want to consider getting some free standing or built in cabinets, floor to ceiling with shelves, that close.

  If you plan to have a reading area in the basement, consider some built-in bookshelves, so you don't have to purchase separate units for this purpose.

- **Space under the stairs.** Don't forget the space under your staircase. This is an excellent area for storing holiday decorations, toys and more. One daddy I know built a play area for his children under the stairs. It actually resembles a little dollhouse. Very cute and functional.

- **An extra bathroom?** Some families I know have an extra bathroom in the basement and it works out beautifully for them. On the other hand, my husband and I don't want another bathroom to keep clean, so we won't be installing another bathroom in our basement. We already have two bathrooms on our main floor. You'll have to weigh the extra convenience versus the extra cleaning time.

- **Handling sentimentals.** If you haven't organized the basement in awhile, be prepared to take a trip down Memory Lane—old photographs, games that haven't been touched in years, ice skates, granny's silverware and so on. Try to put these items to one side until you've reached your organizing goal for the day. Then, reminisce with your family later on that night after dinner, rather than right now. You'll finish what you set out to accomplish

- **Use your space wisely.** Don't forget all that wall space. Hang hooks and pegboards. Add shelving. Have a big, empty closet? Put a utility shelf unit inside. Turn an old, unused bar stool upside down and put all of your tall items, such as baseball bats and curtain rods inside. Pick up some translucent, plastic Rubbermaid containers and store out-of-season clothing, holiday decorations and other things you're not using right now inside.

- **Avoid keeping widgets.** Resist the urge to save every little thing-a-ma-jig and what-cha-ma-call-it you come across. If you (and your family members) don't know what it is or what it belongs to, it should probably be trashed.

- **Don't forget winter storage.** Squirrels store goods for the winter. You might want to do the same. Basements are great for storing canned goods. If you live in a cold climate, you'll be happy it's there—especially on those icy, cold days when you'd rather stay home than venture out to a supermarket.

  Keep it all organized with can organizers which are available at most home stores. Some hold up to 50 cans that roll forward each time you remove one.

- **Store those batteries.** Don't toss batteries into a large bucket or box randomly. Instead, get a battery rack. Then organize those batteries by type: AA, AAA, C, D, and so on.

- **Don't just toss things.** Most people use their basements as storage areas. If you're storing things in the basement, don't just store anywhere. Actually categorize items into plastic boxes with lids. Put like items together. Label everything.

- **Workshop wizard.** Keep your workshop neat and organized by creating zones. For instance, you may have one zone for electrical supplies, one for plumbing supplies and another for building supplies. Use plastic containers with lids in several sizes to keep like items together.

- **Clean and paint the walls.** Painting the interior walls will make the basement easier to clean and maintain. It will also help cut down on dust and mildew.

- **Leave some room.** Clear out the space surrounding your furnace, water heater and any other major appliances. Clutter around these can be a fire hazard and a safety hazard.

- **Keep it clean.** After you give your basement an organizing overhaul, designate 15 minutes each week to tidy up. You won't ever have to waste hours cleaning it up again.

- **It's not a storage warehouse.** Stop thinking of your basement as a storage warehouse. If you have boxes upon boxes that have been stored in your basement for years, it's time to clear them out. If it helps, get rid of them without even checking to see what's inside. If you haven't had to look in them up until now, you probably never will.

- **Have it finished off.** If you have an unfinished basement, consider having it finished off. Just having some drywall that has been textured and painted, and having a fresh clean floor or carpet installed, will make the basement feel more like another part of your home. Designate just one area of it for storage and use the rest as "living space."

Chapter 19

Attic

- **You may find unconventional storage.** Attics are notorious for holding large storage pieces such as trunks, luggage, armoires—and these are perfect for storing out of season clothing, holiday decorations or dress-up clothes for the kids.

- **Use plastic storage bins.** Rather than storing in cardboard boxes, use plastic storage containers. They will keep the boxed contents preserved better.

- **Cover it up.** Some attics are large enough to store large pieces of furniture, like antiques you'd prefer not to part with. Just be sure to cover the furniture with old bed linens to protect them from dust and sunlight that may stream in.

- **Move it out.** Don't keep tons of old furniture just because someone gave it to you. If you never plan on using it again and you never plan on selling it, it's just taking up space you could be using for something else.

  Sometimes furniture can be sentimental, such as an old rocking chair that was your grandfather's favorite. But if you have tons of "sentimental" furniture using up every nook and cranny, you may consider taking photos of the furniture for your memory book and donating the furniture itself. Furniture takes up a lot of space. Photos of furniture do not.

- **Use overhead beams.** Looking for a great storage area for seasonal decorations, such as winter and spring door wreaths? Use the overhead beams in your attic. Screw hooks into the beams and hang.

- **Label all sides.** When labeling boxes, be sure to label all sides. You can see what's inside at a glance without having to unstack boxes.

- **Get rid of pests.** If you haven't used your attic in awhile, you may have some insects or pests living there. If necessary, call an exterminator so you can begin making use of that free space.

- **Make a border.** Try not to store attic contents in the middle of the attic, as it will be difficult to access what you need. Instead, store boxes around the perimeter and keep the center empty.

- **Dress up.** If you keep dress-up clothes for your kids in the attic, store them in an old trunk. It makes dress-up time more fun, plus it keeps all of those clothes contained in one area.

- **Never store edibles.** Whatever you do, never store birdseed or any other edibles in the attic unless they're canned. Otherwise, you might end up attracting mice, insects or bats.

- **Build according to the shape.** Consider adding shelving that fits the shape of your attic. You may have to customize the shelves a bit, but once done you will have tons of extra storage space.

- **Take precautions.** Don't store things in the attic like photographs, computer disks, videos or any items that may be damaged by high heat or extreme cold.

- **Assign a space.** Assign a space for each of the categories of items you're storing in your attic. Store mementos and sentimental items in one area, clothing in another and toys in another.

- **Aged to imperfection.** If you have boxes of things stuffed in the attic that you haven't looked at for years, reconsider even keeping them at all. If you haven't looked at them in all this time, they may not be worth keeping.

- **Use a cedar trunk.** If you're storing clothing in the attic, you might consider doing so in a cedar trunk. This will protect the clothing from varmints.

- **Bring the stuff downstairs.** If you want to organize the contents of your dark, cold attic, but don't want to spend all day there, grab one of your stored boxes and bring it downstairs into your kitchen or living room. Organize that box, tossing anything you no longer need. When you're done with the first one, just grab another box.

- **It's not just for storage.** Most people think of using their attic to store things. If you don't need the extra storage, consider turning your attic into a hobby room, reading room or playroom. There's no rule that says your attic has to be a storage area. It could be a peaceful, quiet retreat for you and your family members. It could even be used as an office.

- **Add some light and temperature control.** Brighten your attic by adding lamp lighting. It will be easier for you to be in the attic if it's not spooky and dark. Also, if it's always cold up there, you might consider getting it insulated. If it's always hot, consider adding a ceiling fan.

- **Before converting.** Before converting your attic into another room, be sure there's ample headroom, a stairway or a sturdy ladder leading to the room and that the floor joists are sturdy enough to support the added load.

- **Create an inventory map.** As you're organizing your attic, make an inventory map of what you're storing up there. The map should include the areas of the attic and the types of items you're storing in those areas. Keep your attic inventory map in your filing system so you can find the map and what you're looking for in the attic, at any given time.

Chapter 20

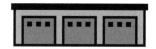

Garage

- **Make room for the car.** It's sad. My husband and I often walk around different neighborhoods and we see so many garages stuffed floor to ceiling and wall-to-wall. Sometimes, the owner's car won't even fit inside.

  If you don't have room for your car or both your cars for that matter, it's time to give your garage an overhaul.

- **Clear it out.** When you're ready to give your garage a major overhaul, the best thing to do is move as much as possible out of the garage and temporarily into the driveway. This will create plenty of room to move around and to see what you have. Plus, you'll already be starting with some empty areas to store the things you're going to keep. Move the car out into the driveway.

Great idea!

Hang each tool in your garage or basement on a pegboard. Trace around each tool with a pencil. Then, remove the tool and paint the penciled line, so that you end up with the outline of your hammer, screwdriver, saw and other tools. Now, your family members will know exactly where to return each tool.

Ed Abrigo
North Bergen, NJ

- **Keep like items together.** Put garden things in one area. Store hammers and wrenches in another area. Keep car care products in yet another area.

- **Trash containers aren't only for trash.** Clean trash containers are perfect for storing potting soil, birdseed, fertilizer and other garden materials.

- **Hang bikes.** Don't leave bicycles scattered all over the garage. Instead hang them on wall hooks or bike racks. This helps keep the garage clutter free, plus it protects bicycle tires when not in use.

- **Toss old stuff.** Get rid of old rags, buckets, tools and other items you haven't used in a year or more. Old paint cans and other toxic items usually can't be tossed in your trashcan. Call your local sanitation department for your town's hazardous waste disposal rules.

- **On the ceiling.** Mount ceiling racks for extra storage. This is a wonderful storage spot for seasonal equipment, outdoor holiday decorations and more.

- **Eek!** Do you have mice in your garage? End the problem with an exterminator or with traps before the garage problems end up in your house.

- **That's screwy.** Attach glass jar lids to the underside of a shelf in your garage. Fill each glass jar with nuts, bolts, screws, nails or other hardware. Then, screw the glass onto the attached lid. Do this with several glass jars in one convenient area.

- **Coffee cans.** Save old coffee cans and use them to store nails, screws, nuts and other small hardware. Label the cans and store them on a shelf in your garage.

- **Get a hardware storage cabinet.** If you have lots of combinations of small hardware, consider getting a hardware storage cabinet. Some have 16 small drawers; some have 64! These cabinets can be stacked, but those that can be mounted on the wall are especially nice.

- **Stack 'em.** Stacking bins are wonderful for organizing car care products, small garden tools, small power tools and more.

- **Hang a grid.** Wire grids are wonderful for keeping tons of garage items organized. They allow for multiple configurations of hooks, baskets and shelves without leaving multiple holes in the walls. The grid is the only component that mounts directly into the wall.

- **Tall and long.** Get an organizer to hold shovels, rakes, brooms and other long tools. We have one that holds 20 long handled tools. We picked it from a local hardware store. Very inexpensive, but very effective.

- **Oil them.** Speaking of tools, keep them protected from moisture and rust by rubbing them with a thick coat of olive oil each month.

- **Add a steel sports cabinet.** If your family is really into playing sports, it may be well worth it to invest in a steel sports cabinet for the garage. Most are large and provide secure storage for skis, golf bags, baseball bats and more.

- **Balls, helmets and pads . . . oh my!** Get a large netted bag and hang it from your wall or ceiling. This provides excellent storage for sports gear like balls, helmets and kneepads. Another idea is to hang a nylon hammock across one corner of your garage for this same purpose.

- **Make a garbage depot.** Designate an area of your garage for a large plastic trashcan with a lid and your recycling bins. We have a recycling bin for paper and another for cans and glass. When we walk out of our laundry room into the garage, the garbage depot is right there.

- **Finish it off.** Have an unfinished garage? It will look less cluttered and more like a room if you finish it off. Do it yourself or have it done for you if it's within your budget.

  Have your garage insulated so it's warm and toasty in the winter. Add floor to ceiling shelves or closed cabinets. Add some artwork to the walls. Think of your garage as just another room in your home, rather than a dumping ground or storage space.

  One of our neighbors has a beautiful garage. The walls are finished and painted bright white. There's not one cluttered area. Plus, there are framed posters on the walls.

- **In a bucket.** Store sponges, rags, soap and other car washing apparatus in a bucket in the garage.

- **Stop mud and snow in its tracks.** If you enter your house from the garage, add a bench right near the house entry door. Sit on it to remove muddy, wet or snow covered shoes. Put a rubber mat there too to hold that muddy footwear until you have a chance to clean them off.

- **Ladder racks.** Add racks for ladders to keep them off the floor so they won't be taking up any valuable floor space.

- **Hold that lumber.** Use PVC piping and strap to hold lumber out of the way on the ceiling of your garage. Write the dimensions of the lumber on the ends so you can easily identify the size, or designate a color for each length and color code the ends of the lumber for simple identification.

- **You've got the power.** Consider having an electrician install extra power outlets for you, especially if you're constantly looking for someplace to plug in tools you're recharging.

- **Add a window.** If you spend lots of time in your garage, you may want to consider adding a window or two so light streams in during the day. At least provide adequate lighting or skylights.

- **Mount a ceiling system.** Turn ceiling space into storage space. Stop foraging around backs of cabinets or bottoms of boxes. Mount a ceiling system on the ceiling of your garage and you'll have added an incredible amount of storage space. Ceiling systems can usually be customized for height and have strong weight capacities.

- **Add a loft.** Add a loft to store items like holiday decorations and camping equipment. Use thick boards or heavy-duty plywood across the rafters in your garage to create a separate floor and use this floor as storage space.

- **Add a worktable.** If you don't have a worktable in your garage, you might consider adding one. Before we had one, I was filling the birdfeeder and potting plants on the garage floor or in the driveway. Now, with a worktable, I can do these tasks and more without breaking my back.

- **Don't drive into the wall.** Hang a tennis ball from the ceiling so it taps your car window when you've pulled in far enough. You'll prevent bumps and scratches.

- **Paint the can.** Before storing paint, especially if you're going to be storing various colors, paint the top and side with a little bit of the paint inside. Once dry, store the can. Next time you need a little touch-up paint, you'll be able to just glance and grab the appropriate can.

- **Sandpaper storage.** Store sandpaper in a 3-ring binder organized by grits. Then, label the spine of the binder and store it on a shelf in your garage. No more searching for scraps of sandpaper when you need it.

- **Have a place for garbage.** Keep a garbage can in your garage, especially near your workbench or any area where you tend to generate lots of garbage. This way, you can toss immediately.

- **Let's twist again.** Keep a small supply of twist ties in your garage. These are perfect for keeping cords together and wrapping around power tool wires.

- **Store birdseed and pet food inside cabinets.** Never store birdseed or any pet food that is not canned out in the open in the garage. You'll just be inviting insects, mice and other rodents. If you store seed and pet food in the garage, store it in plastic containers. Then, store those plastic containers inside closed cabinets so they're extra secure.

While you're at it, Always keep a measuring cup right in the seed or dry pet food, so you can scoop out what you need without having to lift the entire bag.

Chapter 21

Laundry Center and the Laundry Mountain

- **Put them on shelves.** Get everything off the floor and hang shelves for laundry detergent, fabric softener, stain remover and other laundry necessities. Be sure the shelves are right near the washer so laundry items are easily grabbed when needed.

- **Catch the loose stuff.** Keep a box in the laundry room to collect buttons, coins, keys, and other small items. Or attach a hook magnet on the side of the dryer. Hang a pouch on the hook and use it to collect these stray items.

- **Toss the trash.** You need something for laundry trash such as lint and used dryer sheets. Either put a trash container in the laundry room or hang a plastic bag on the doorknob. Put it out for the trash collectors once each week.

Great idea!

Since we have a large closet, we keep three plastic tubs on the floor of our closet for presorting laundry. We have one for whites, one for durable colored clothes and one for delicate colored clothes. When they get full, we dump them into the washer. The wash day sorting hassle is solved! We trained our children to do this as toddlers. Now as teenagers they are experts at it.

Bruce Stahl
Overland Park, KS

- **Get a collapsible drying rack.** Wooden or plastic portable clothes dryers are wonderful for drying out clothing that can't be tumble dried, such as nylons, brassieres and so on. They fold up when not in use.

  In my home, there's actually enough space in between the washer and the dryer to store it. If you don't have this space, add a hook on the wall for yours or store it in your laundry center closet.

- **Keep a sewing kit nearby.** As you're washing, if you notice a loose button or a hem that's coming loose, grab your sewing kit and make a quick repair immediately.

- **Get a folding table.** It may be easier for you to fold, if you could fold right onto a folding table. If you can't fit a folding table, consider attaching a fold-down shelf to the wall for this purpose. Another option is folding on top of your washer and dryer or carrying the clothes to a table, a large ottoman or a bed in your home and fold there.

- **Dry clean only.** Hang a bag in your laundry room closet for dry clean only clothing. Assign a family member to take the clothes to and pick them up from the dry cleaner once each week or as needed. Some dry cleaners will even pick up and deliver.

- **Sort it out.** Get yourself a laundry sorter and keep it right in the laundry room. As each family member needs clothing laundered he or she should bring his or her clothes to the laundry room. He or she could then sort them right into the appropriate section.

This eliminates the need for you to walk around your home collecting everyone's clothing and the sorting is already done. It also eliminates the need for a laundry hamper in each room.

The laundry sorter I have has three removable canvas bags and is on wheels. It fits right in my laundry room closet. My family sorts dark colored clothing into one bag, white and light colored clothing into another bag and towels and sheets into the third bag. We also have a small mesh bag attached to the laundry sorter if anyone needs something washed that is very delicate, like hosiery.

- **Put it in the basket.** Place small laundry baskets, one for each family member, above or near the dryer. Sort clothes by family member as you pull them out of the dryer. Have each person pick up their own basket and put their own clothes away.

Great idea!

Whenever I am putting something that's going to need ironing into the laundry basket, I include a hanger. I use only the plastic variety, so there's no danger of snagging or hooking other things. I also can drop an extra hanger or several down the laundry chute when I know there are items that are waiting to be washed that will need them.

When I'm taking things out of the dryer, I can put them straight onto hangers and minimize wrinkles before I have to either a) fold them, b) rush up from the basement and hang them up with a hanger nowhere in sight because they've been left on yet another floor higher, or c) leave them crumpled letting the wrinkles set in more, making later ironing a much harder task.

Betsy Davenport, PhD, Managing Editor, ADDvance Online Magazine
Portland, OR
www.ncgiadd.org/

- **Make a list of occasionals.** Keep a list of items that only get washed occasionally over the washing machine—throw rugs, shower curtains, comforters. When you have less than a full load, just check your list and add one of these items to it. It will also help you to remember to wash those occasional items that are often forgotten.

> ### Great idea!
>
> Do you also sometimes miss a sock from a pair when you're hanging up your laundry? I put a box on top of my dryer where I store these single socks. After the laundry is dry and I end up with a single sock, I search the box for the other one. If it's not there I store this sock. Most of the time the other sock shows up a week afterwards.
>
> Trudie Tijssen
> Alkmaar, Noord Holland, Netherlands

- **Give them a home.** You should assign a specific home for each of your laundry necessities. For instance, in my laundry room, I have a shelving unit recessed into the wall. Two of the four shelves are specifically for my laundry products. On one shelf I keep my detergent and bleach on the left and my stain treaters on the right. On the other shelf, I keep my fabric softener sheets for the dryer on the left and my iron and iron's water filler on the right.

- **Learn about your washer and dryer.** Read your washer and dryer's operating instructions, even if you've had your units for years. There are often good tips included in these manuals, such as ways to save energy or eliminate stains.

- **Label them.** If you have a large family, you may want to mark clothing labels with the appropriate family members name or initials. When you're done washing and drying, you'll know instantly what belongs to whom.

- **Pre-treat quickly.** The second you spot a stain on any clothing, pre-treat it with a stain stick or some stain remover. Even if you can't get to the laundry that day, at least the stain won't set in as quickly.

- **Lay it flat.** Sometimes certain clothing will need to dry flat. Get yourself a mesh dryer rack so the clothing dries, front and back. I usually leave this rack in my bedroom near an open window or near the heating vent depending on the time of year until it dries. You may even be able to fit your dryer rack on the top of your washer and dryer, but be sure it's big enough to lay out a large sweater on top without you having to fold the arms in.

- **Keep the units clean.** The washer and dryer should be dusted and wiped regularly to keep them clean and sanitary, both inside and out.

> ### Great idea!
>
> When laundry gets me down and my kids never seem to help, I get four laundry baskets—one for each of us. As I fold the clothing, I sort the laundry into the proper basket. Once it's all done, the kids are old enough to decide if they want to live out of the basket or put it away. This is much better then folding them and placing them on their beds to put away, because my hard work seems to always end up on the floor with the dirty laundry.
>
> Lisa Pomerantz
> Danvers, MA

- **Make it pretty.** If your laundry room is not very pretty, you're going to hate doing laundry even more. Paint the room, preferably a light, fresh color such as white, light yellow or light blue. Hang a pretty picture. Be sure it's clean. Get rid of any cobwebs. The more inviting it is, the more motivation you'll have to be there to do your wash.

- **Post instructions.** So no one has an excuse for not helping out with laundry sorting, washing, drying or ironing, post a set of instructions right in the laundry room. As family members ask questions that are not posted, update and re-post your instructions.

- **Give them a bag.** Give each family member a zippered mesh bag for his or her underwear and socks. Wash those items right in the bags and then return the bags to their rightful owners.

- **Keep the laundry under control.** The best way to keep your dirty laundry under control is to wash and dry often. In my home (3 people), I wash and dry one load each day. My laundry is always caught up.

I usually start a wash first thing in the morning before breakfast. By the time I'm finished with breakfast and some morning tasks, the washer cycle is done and I toss that load in the dryer.

If you have lots of people living in your home, you may need to do two loads each day.

A friend of mine designates one day each week, Wednesdays, to doing all her laundry. She spends all day doing it, but this system works for her. She follows it religiously.

Whatever system you use, remember, the washing machine and dryer do most of the work. You just have to be around to load, unload and fold.

- **Baby oh baby.** When I first had my baby, I separated all of her clothing and washed them alone in a mild detergent. That is, until she was about three months old. At that point, I figured I'd try washing her clothes with ours.

  She had no allergic reaction to the detergent, so I decided just to wash her clothes along with ours. This worked out well for us. If you have a baby, you may want to give it a try.

- **Reduce wrinkles.** Try not to overload the dryer and be sure to get clothing out of your dryer as soon as possible once the cycle is finished. If you let the dried clothing sit in there all day, it's going to get wrinkled and you'll have to spend more time ironing. Set your dryer buzzer to sound when the cycle is over or set your watch timer to sound.

Great idea!

Every week I am left with at least five or six single socks that I can't find the matches to for the life of me. I would make sure that a pair would enter the washer together, but by the time they came out of the dryer, one was missing. I even thought that maybe they were sticking to my sheets from static cling, so I started diligently shaking out the linens to loosen their grip, but still no socks would appear. I was starting to think that there were "Sock Gremlins" that hung out in the dryer and stole them! I finally concluded that on my tight budget, I couldn't afford to lose this many socks.

I also hated the part about doing laundry where I had to sort and match a big pile of socks before I could fold them and put them away. I would procrastinate doing this chore for weeks on end. Well, I finally decided to stop worrying about the lost socks, stop putting off the sort/match job and start taking action. I knew that I would have to use my most clever mind to work on this one and this is what I came up with.

I put a small basket of large stainless steel safety pins near the hamper and one near the washer. When socks are taken off, before they are put in the laundry hamper, they are immediately joined together by a safety pin. If any slip by this process they're caught just before they go in the washer and pinned right there. Now when I take my clothes out of the dryer, the socks are together, pre-matched and ready to be folded and put away—and no lost socks, ever!

I unpin them, bundle them up and we're good to go. The next phase is to get my kids to pin their socks at the hamper by themselves.

Christy Johnson
Vista, CA

- **Fold as they come out.** Fold your clothing directly out of the dryer and put it away as soon as you're done. The typical load should take you about five to seven minutes to fold.

- **Get the kids and your spouse to help out.** It's not difficult to do the laundry and most people, including kids over eight years of age, are quite capable of doing a load of wash. Make an instruction checklist in case it needs to be referenced. If your kids are too young to do this, at least get them to load the washer, fold their clothes or sort their own laundry. The more they learn now, the better.

- **Clean out that lint.** As soon as the dryer cycle is complete, before you even unload, first clean out the lint trap. When you need to dry your next load, it will already be clean and ready to go. Whatever you do, never allow lint to build up in the dryer. Overloaded lint traps are a fire hazard.

- **Color code.** If you have more than one child, you may want to write their initials on the clothing labels. This will enable you to easily identify what belongs to whom.

- **Oh no, a tissue.** Always empty pockets before you start the wash. If you forget and discover all your laundered clothes are full of tissue lint, put everything back in the dryer along with two dryer softener sheets and air dry for 20 minutes. This should help get most of the lint off.

- **I forgot.** If clothes in the dryer already wrinkled by the time you remember them, toss in a damp towel or damp sheet and run the dryer cycle again on warm. This may help to get many of the wrinkles out.

- **Wear at least twice.** Aside from undergarments and socks, it's generally unnecessary to wash your pants, sweaters, shirts and dresses every single time you wear them. Unless you spilled something on your clothing or you were out exercising in them, you can probably get two to three wears before spending the time it takes to wash them.

- **Towels can be used a few times.** Towels used to dry yourself when you emerge from the shower are still clean. You just washed yourself. Why would the towel be dirty? Hang the towel on a towel rack, so it's dry for the next day. Then, limit your towel washing and drying to once or twice a week.

- **Save a trip to the dry cleaner.** If at all possible, purchase clothing that doesn't have to be dry-cleaned and can be tossed in the washer.

- **Use a dry cleaning kit.** Very often, you can avoid a trip to the dry cleaner and freshen up your outfits with a dry cleaning kit, available in most grocery stores. I use Dryel since it is easy to use and works beautifully.

- **Wash and iron.** After doing the wash, immediately iron everything that needs ironing. Then hang these items in your closet. You won't have to waste time each morning ironing clothes before work.

- **Forget ironing all together.** Rather than having to worry about ironing, buy machine washable clothes that don't need to be ironed.

- **Everyone's responsibility.** Enlist family members to help with the washing, drying and ironing. Try one of the following:

  ❖ Have each person do his or her own wash.

  ❖ Assign a particular person these duties.

  ❖ Rotate everyone's schedule so everyone gets a turn.

- **Don't wash half-loads.** Wait until your laundry bag, hamper or sorter is full. You'll save time, plus money on your energy bill.

- **Bedtime magic.** When you're ready to wash bed sheets, wash them, dry them and put them right back on the bed. No folding required.

- **On a roll.** If you don't have your own washing machine or dryer and use a commercial one, you're probably constantly searching for quarters. Stop at the bank once a week—or go on payday—and get at least $20 worth of quarters. Keep them in a change purse, specifically to be used for the purpose of washing and drying clothes.

- **De-dust those curtains.** To remove dust from curtains, take them down and put them in the dryer on the fluff or delicate/cool tumble setting. Toss in a fabric softener sheet and dry for 15-20 minutes. They'll come out smelling fresh and clean.

- **Laundromat smarts.** If you use a Laundromat outside of your home:

  ❖ If you're making constant trips back and forth to the Laundromat, consider purchasing your own washer and dryer. It will save you mounds of time.

  ❖ Don't carry around heavy detergent bottles. Either leave them in your car or transfer small amounts to smaller bottles so they're lighter to carry.

  ❖ Bring along a wet paper towel to wipe up soap spills, dirt and debris from the washer and dryer before you launder your clothes.

  ❖ Each week at the bank, pick up a few rolls of quarters for your laundry. Put the coins in a change pouch in the laundry hamper you use to transport clothes back and forth from the Laundromat. You won't forget to bring them.

  ❖ If your budget permits, some Laundromats offer an option of washing, drying and folding your clothes for you, to be picked up later. If you don't mind someone else doing your wash, this may be the perfect solution for you.

- **Organize during your washer/dryer cycle.** After you put your laundry in the washing machine, you'll have approximately 40 minutes of waiting time. Instead of just standing around or watching TV, do something you can get done in 40 minutes or less, such as paying your bills, preparing dinner or catching up on some reading.

  Then, toss the clothes in the dryer and you'll have another 40 minutes or so to catch up on email, make phone calls or work on a hobby. Use these two machines as timers for getting things done. It's amazing how much could be accomplished during a simple wash-dry cycle!

- **Add some amenities.** If you have the space, you may consider adding a comfortable chair and bookcase to your laundry room. While the washer and dryer are going through their cycles, you can catch up on your reading. Or, keep a television or radio in the laundry room. You can watch your favorite shows or listen to music while doing the laundry.

- **Make it bright.** If you're treating stains, you want to be sure you can see them well. Be sure you have good lighting in this room.

- **High and dry.** You can now buy drying centers which allow you to hang clothing inside (on hangers) to dry. This reduces and/or eliminates wrinkles.

- **Hang a bulletin board.** Use it as a central storage area for your laundry needs. For instance, tack up a few tiny plastic pouches for buttons, safety pins or a small sewing kit. Include a laundry checklist that you and your family can refer to. Add an area to store dry cleaning receipts.

- **Add wire shelving.** It provides an inexpensive, but very versatile holding space for folded laundry.

- **Get a laundry butler.** This is a compact 3-shelf unit that nestles between the washer and dryer. It has wheels, so it rolls around easily. Raised side rails keep all of your laundry needs—detergent, bleach, and so on—in place.

- **Install a retractable clothes line.** This is simply attached to the wall and you pull the clothesline(s) out whenever you need to drip dry clothes. Be sure to get one with a tension control knob so heavier clothes don't cause the line to droop.

- **Install wall-mounted cabinets.** Detergent and other laundry supplies will be cleverly hidden behind closed doors. Any kind of closed storage unit automatically reduces the chaotic, disorganized look.

Organizing Clinic

Question

I am always behind on laundry because I have to take it to the Laundromat. I live in an area of the country where weather frequently discourages the loading and unloading. Is there any way to make this process easier?

Sheryl
Kansas City, MO

Answer

Dear Sheryl,

Here are a few simple ideas to lighten your load:

- **Go weekly.** Don't go to the Laundromat less than once each week. If you do, it's going to pile up way too much and become difficult to handle.

- **Don't allow the weather to dictate your trips.** Choose one standard day each week to make your trip to the Laundromat, rain or shine. Get yourself a few large nylon laundry bags, some to use for dirty laundry, some to use for clean. This will protect your clothes from rain as you transport them into and out of the Laundromat.

- **Keep laundry supplies in your car.** Since you must go to the Laundromat so often, keep a plastic crate or carry-all in your car to hold all of your laundry detergent, softener, softener sheets, coins and other laundry essentials. No sense in bringing them into and out of your home each week.

- **Get double and triple duty out of them.** Limit the stacks of laundry from piling up by wearing clothing, excluding underwear, multiple times before bringing them to the Laundromat. As long as you don't stain them and you're not on your knees working in the garden, they're probably pretty clean after one or two uses and probably just need to be pressed. Bed sheets can go for two weeks instead of one and towels can be used three to five times before being washed.

- **Consider a portable washing machine and dryer.** If at all possible, consider purchasing a portable washing machine and dryer. These can come pretty compact for even small apartment spaces. You can reduce or perhaps even eliminate, your trips to the Laundromat with this option.

- **Do they have a drop off option?** Many Laundromats now offer a drop-off option for busy customers. Basically, you drop off your dirty laundry and leave. A Laundromat attendant then washes, dries and folds everything for you. You then drive back the next day or next week and pick everything up.

Chapter 22

Utility Closet

- **Things to store.** If your utility closet is big enough, it may be the perfect place to store your vacuum, your ironing board and iron—even your baby's stroller. Just be sure you can get at the things you're storing without having to move things to get at them.

- **Put them in a bucket.** If you store cleaning supplies in your utility room, store the most frequently used ones in a bucket. When you need to clean, just grab the bucket and go.

- **Get an organizer.** Hang a mop and broom organizer on the utility closet wall to keep these items off the floor and in one place.

Great idea!

I have found that the paper towel cardboard tubes make excellent storage containers for extension cords. It is such a pleasure to pull out the cord without having a major "untangle" project on my hands.

Carla Bell
Chicago, IL

- **Store an extra hamper.** When you have guests over, you can loan them the extra laundry hamper for clothing they need washed and dried.

- **Store trash bags.** Hang a hook in your utility closet and hang a tote bag on that hook. This is the perfect spot to store all of those plastic grocery bags you use for garbage.

- **Open a paper bag.** If you collect paper grocery bags for paper garbage like newspapers, open up one brown paper bag in your utility closet. Store several closed paper bags inside.

- **Make an emergency station.** The utility closet is the perfect place to keep some emergency supplies, such as a flashlight, a candle, matches, batteries and a fire extinguisher. Keep smaller supplies in a covered plastic box. Mount the fire extinguisher to the wall.

Chapter 23

Junk Drawer (We Know You Have One)

- **Get rid of that term.** The term "junk drawer" is horrible, because it invites "junk." Never designate any drawer in your home a junk drawer. Junk is something you and your family members have no use for and/or can't identify and junk should promptly be discarded. If you have a drawer that includes useful items, but the items are in a very messy state, then you need to get it organized.

- **Turn it into a help drawer.** We have a drawer in the kitchen that we use for some random items, but I would never consider it a junk drawer. Inside, we keep our phone books, our address book, a few pens, a folder with some take-out menus and some bag clips. It's never a mess. I can identify each item inside. There's no junk in there.

- **Remove everything.** Take everything out of the drawer and place it on top of your counter. If your junk drawer is removable, remove it from the track and turn it upside down onto your counter. You may want to lay a sheet of newspaper down first to help protect your countertop.

- **Sort.** Begin categorizing each widget (i.e. thumbtacks in one pile, buttons in another, toothpicks in another). By the way, when you come across a gadget that you can't identify, put it aside. Check with others in your family to determine if it a) can be identified and b) if it is truly needed. If not, toss it.

- **Categorize into compartments.** Finally, begin replacing the items you are going to keep, ensuring that each categorized item is in its own place.

- **Keep it current.** Make it a point that whenever you're on telephone hold, you're doing something productive, such as weeding out your junk drawer or organizing anything that is out of place inside.

Great idea!

Whenever I'm organizing desks and drawers (with the exception of dresser drawers), I separate everything into Ziploc baggies. For example when I was organizing my desk, I put thumbtacks in one baggie and marked "thumbtacks" with a permanent marker on the baggie. This way I can just pull out that certain bag and take it to the place I'm working.

Dara Fitzgerald
Seaford, DE

- **Typical junk drawer items.** Here are just a few items typically stored in junk drawers and some possible solutions to go with each:
  - ❖ **Office Supplies:** (Elastic bands, paper clips, thumb tacks, pens, erasers, scotch tape, etc.) These can likely be stored in your office area with the rest of your office supplies.
  - ❖ **Coupons:** Store in a coupon holder so they're not floating all over.
  - ❖ **Recipes:** Put in a recipe binder. Don't store hundreds if you rarely cook!
  - ❖ **Keys:** Determine what each key opens and label them with masking tape. Then, keep them all together in one cup or box.
  - ❖ **Take-out Menus:** Put all of them in a manila envelope, and store in a drawer or on the refrigerator side attached with a magnet.
  - ❖ **Loose change:** Add to your purse or wallet and use the next time you're at a store. If there's a huge amount, cash it in at your bank for dollars.
  - ❖ **Buttons:** Add to a container used strictly for buttons, or put these in your craft room. I can't even remember the last time I needed a button. I use them for my scrapbooking projects or I toss them if I feel I won't be able to use them in any of my layouts. If I ever need a button for a garment, I figure I'll just run over to the local craft store.
  - ❖ **Photos:** They're going to get ruined. If they're worth keeping, put them into a photo album or an acid-free photo box.
  - ❖ **Camera Film:** Put new rolls into a container with the rest of your picture taking supplies. Bring used rolls to your local photo finishing shop to be developed.
  - ❖ **Batteries:** Put all loose batteries together into a plastic box or container. Never put dead batteries in the drawer. Immediately toss them.
  - ❖ **Candy and gum:** Put them into a pretty candy dish so they can be found and eaten, before they get stale. If they're already stale, toss them.
  - ❖ **Gadgets and tools:** If you can identify them, put them into a toolbox or a box specifically designated for gadgets, like extra phone wires and pieces you need to convert toys.
- **Find dividing tools.** Find something around the house that you can slip into your drawer to keep these categorized items separated, such as an ice cube tray, drawer dividers, small boxes or three-ounce paper cups. Organize these separators into your drawer. Or, you may opt to buy a drawer organizer that includes a second lift-out tray for even more effective organizing.

Chapter 24

Coat Closet

- **Use it everyday.** Some people save their front coat closet just for guests. Unless you have lots of visitors every day, this is a waste of space. Store your everyday jackets and coats in there and keep a few extra hangers for guests.

- **Take everything out.** If you want to give your coat closet an overhaul, it's best to remove everything. Once you do this, go through your jackets, coats, scarves, umbrellas and anything else. Put everything you're keeping into one pile, everything you're dumping into another pile and everything you're donating into another pile. The keepers will be stored back inside. Dump and donate promptly.

- **Hang some hooks.** Hooks in the coat closet are perfect for holding handbags, umbrellas, backpacks and dog leashes.

Great idea!

My sister-in-law gave me this idea for clothing, but I have taken it a step further with my shoes. Lightly place a piece of tape on the clothing article or shoe in an obvious place. When you wear it, remove the tape. At the end of the season, anything that still has tape on it gets tossed out or donated to charity. This is a surefire way to see what clothes and/or shoes you no longer wear.

Adrianne Everhart
Downers Grove, IL

- **Organize by season and length.** Organize all fall and winter items to the left and all spring and summer items to the right. Keep long coats and raincoats stored towards the side of the closet, rather than in the middle. Never store a short jacket in between two long jackets. Never store more than one coat on the same hanger. Do either of these and your jacket or coat is liable to get hidden.

- **Hang in one direction.** All coats and jackets should be facing the same direction with the opening of the coats facing left and the back of the coats facing right. Face all hangers in one direction too. Consistency makes for a more organized, less-chaotic look.

- **Yes, Mommy dearest.** Wire hangers are too weak to hang most coats and jackets. Toss them or give them to your local dry cleaner for recycling. Invest in sturdy wooden or heavy-duty plastic hangers instead. Try to use the same type of hangers and color for everything.

Great idea!

For organizing hats, scarves and gloves, I got one of those over-the-door shoe organizers that has the large sideways slots and hung it over the door of our very small coat closet.

Each slot holds the matching set of each item. I tried the other type of shoe organizer that has the front slot that can hold only one shoe, but the slots ripped easily and it wasn't large enough to hold a heavy scarf. I have had my current organizer for several years and it works like a charm.

To save some money, I fill it up when the end of the season clearance sales pop up. Then we are all set for the next season. It keeps our couch nice and glove free too!

Mary Maharidge
Clinton Township, MI

- **Install a light.** If your coat closet is very dark inside even when the light is on outside the closet, consider adding a light inside. It's easier to find things when you can see what you're looking for. There are lights available that are battery operated, which means you won't even have to get an electrician.

- **Hang a mirror.** Hang a mirror on the back of your coat closet door. This is the perfect place to be sure your hat is on correctly or to touch up your lipstick.

- **Dry on a coat rack.** Avoid putting wet coats, jackets, scarves, hats, gloves and umbrellas in the coat closet. Instead, put a coat rack in your foyer, hallway, laundry room or mudroom and dry out wet outerwear there. Hang them as soon as they're dry.

- **Add a shoe rack.** If you store shoes in the coat closet, add a shoe rack with space big enough to hold all your family's shoes. Only keep daily shoes in the coat closet. Less frequently used shoes can be stored in the family member's bedroom closet. Large items like boots go in the back, smaller items in the front—so everything can be seen.

- **Get them out of your house.** If you don't have a coat closet and you're really pressed for space, ask your local dry cleaner if they store winter coats. Many do free of charge or for a minimal fee.

Great idea!

I happen to be a woman who is addicted to shoes (Imagine that?). I was finding that I was running ragged in the morning in my dark closet trying to match up which shoes to wear with what.

Being that I am an actress and work in the fashion industry, I pick up wonderfully creative ideas from the stylists who provide clothing to the talent. Recently, I was asked to come in for a fitting and lo and behold, my shoe problem had been solved.

The key is, save all of those shoeboxes that you are so eagerly ready to toss. Set each pair of shoes on a white or black tablecloth, placing one of the shoes straight at the camera and the other side ways to the camera, with the heel of the side one resting on the heel of the other.

Take digital pictures of each pair of shoes, cut each photo to fit the size of the shoebox and tape it on the end. You will never again fumble through a dark closet looking for another pair of shoes.

Carrie Zanoline
Windsor, CA

- **Weed out your wardrobe.** If you have several coats and jackets, chances are you only regularly wear one or two. Donate the ones you rarely wear. You'll be helping to keep someone else warm while giving yourself more space in your coat closet.

Great idea!

One of the greatest "overlooked" areas of space throughout all homes is that space just inside closets, pantries and the like right above the door. Seriously, open any closet in your home and look inside, above the doorway: beautiful unused space!

Install a small shelf right above the door and you have excellent extra storage. In my pantry right above the door is a shelf where I keep my paper towels and paper napkins. In a coat closet might be seasonal clothing items (i.e. gloves, hats, scarves put away in a tub or basket). In a woman's closet may be a great tuck-away for purses and clutches. Just inside a linen closet may be a great space to store extra toilet paper packages. The needs and possibilities are endless.

Harriette Jacobs
Warrenton, GA

- **Top of the closet.** In many coat closets, there's a high shelf. What do you store there? It's really up to you. My parents used to store their holiday decorations up there. A friend of mine uses it to store her donation box. Another person I know uses the area to store serving platters.

  Since it's a high shelf, you probably won't want to store things you need everyday. Otherwise, you'll probably need to drag the stepstool out every time you need something. But store something up there. Don't let this valuable space go to waste.

- **All my kittens have lost their mittens.** There are a few options to keep mittens, scarves and gloves organized:

  ❖ Give each family member a tote bag for these items and hang the tote bag on a hanger in the coat closet.

  ❖ Have each family member store one set of gloves or mittens, a hat and a scarf into the sleeve of the coat he or she wears each day. This system only works if your family members wear the same coat, gloves, scarf and hat each day.

  ❖ Put storage containers in the closet and designate one for each person. Try to get different colored ones for each family member so they're easily identifiable or at minimum, label them.

  ❖ Use a shoe organizer. Get a vinyl shoe organizer that can be hung in your coat closet on the rod. Store one outerwear item in each pouch. Since the pouches are clear, everyone should be able to find what they need instantly.

  ❖ Give each family member a basket for these items and line the baskets on a shelf in the coat closet.

- **Keep your "Donation Box" inside.** Every time you have something you want to donate to a charity, add it to the Donation Box and store the Donation Box in your coat closet. Once each month, drop off your donations.

- **Add a shoe rack.** We keep a shoe rack on the floor of our coat closet to store all of our everyday shoes. It has four shelves, one for me, one for my husband, one for my daughter and one for guests.

- **Seasons change.** If you have the extra space in your home, consider keeping only the current season's coats and jackets in your closet and the others in another storage area. Rotate as the seasons change.

- **Use garment protectors.** Store clean out-of-season clothing in cloth garment bags to keep them clean. Don't use plastic bags that do not allow clothing to breathe properly and can cause moisture to collect, later causing mold.

Organizing Clinic

Question

My husband is a cap person. He has a cap for everything. The problem is they lay all over the house wherever he takes them off. Can you tell me a way to organize them?

Amy Fielder, Olive Branch, MS

Answer

Amy,

You actually have two problems to work on. First, you need a storage solution for your husband's caps. Second, you need to get your hubby to use the storage system, rather than leaving his hats all over the place.

For now, we'll give your husband a break, since he doesn't currently have a storage system. But once you have that system in place, no more excuses for him.

- **Buy one.** Purchase an inexpensive cap storage system. There are tons of cap racks on the market that can be installed in a closet or behind a door.

- **Make one.** Make your own cap storage system. Hang some hooks along one of the walls in your home, such as the mudroom or a utility room. Store each cap on its own hook, or hang a clothesline along the wall in an extra room and clothespin each hat to the line. Either one of these systems will ensure a) it's easy to find the right cap and b) it's easy to return the cap to the system.

- **Get hubby to comply.** Get your husband to use the system. You can try just asking him to use the system. For some people, that may work out beautifully. However, if you're still running into problems, tell your hubby that every time you find a hat tossed somewhere instead of in his new cap storage system, that you're going to hide the hat for three weeks and stick to your guns. Don't give the hat(s) back until your hubby begins using the system.

Chapter 25

Garden

- **Consider the important stuff.** When planting your garden, it's important to keep certain criteria in mind, such as location, soil type, sunlight, watering needs, wind and size.

- **Plan in the winter.** Plan your garden during the winter months. Measure it and sketch it out on paper. When spring arrives, you'll be ready.

Organizing Clinic

Question

I love gardening and have the usual array of tools, mowers, trimmer, soils and amendments, mulch, stakes, hand tools, sprays fertilizers and bags of various powdery substances like green sand. Do you have any garage or garden shed organizing tips? I have to keep my things in my garage because I do not have a shed. Thanks.

Dan Green, Wallingford, CT

Answer

Dear Dan,

I challenged our Get Organized Now! Discussion Forum readers with your question and the tips they shared were excellent ones. Hope they help!

Response 1: I have my gardening things organized in the front part of our garage on an industrial shelving unit I purchased at Sam's Club. Our garage is prone to flooding, so everything gets lifted off the floor and placed in plastic buckets when possible. On the bottom shelf, I have a series of larger former kitty litter buckets, with handles. They are similar in size to a five-gallon bucket.

I keep hand tools in one plastic kitty litter bucket with handles. Next to this bucket, I keep another empty bucket and can easily grab both buckets when going to one garden area to deadhead or do some other quick garden task. I try to work 15 minutes at a time and keeping these buckets together has made it easy to grab and go, instead of spending my time hunting for things. On my way back to the garage, I dump the yard waste into the compost pile.

In the tool bucket, I also keep a can of WD-40 spray oil and a rag for quick cleaning of tools when I'm done. I keep larger hand tools such as loppers in a larger five-gallon can.

In another bucket I keep a few things I use when fertilizing. I have a coffee can I use as a scoop and other such tools for fertilizing, easy to grab and go independently of the other gardening functions.

Of course, there is a container for tapes, garden stakes, marker, a sharp utility knife and duct tape.

The shelving unit is sturdy and when I have bags of dirt, they lay nicely stacked on one of the shelves off the floor, as we are prone to flooding. I cut off the caps of a couple of liquid laundry detergent jugs and these act nicely as watering cans our kids can easily use. I keep any liquid weed killers in one red dishpan. This color alert reminds me to bring these things in the house after the gardening season and store them in our laundry room.

I purchased a small Mantis Tiller two summers ago and I keep all the tines and tools in one bucket. I keep a five-gallon bucket on the floor by the shelving unit, filled with sand and one quart of clean car oil. This is for pushing shovels and larger tools into for cleaning. A wire brush for stubborn dirt hangs nearby. Next to the sand, I have a Rubbermaid garbage can on wheels, that I keep most of our larger tools in shovels, my favorite skuffle hoe and pitchfork. They're all stored handle down.

My husband rigged a beam that we are able to hang a variety of tools from. The weed trimmer hangs nicely, as well as the Mantis Tiller.

Response 2: We bought a rack for hanging rakes, hoes, and other items along the front wall. Really handy! We used to just place those items in a large trashcan, handle-down.

Response 3: I keep my seeds, hand tools and pots in drawers and old kitchen cabinets that were installed in the garage after a kitchen remodel.

We installed a plywood counter on top for potting. I have half for my gardening activities; my husband has the other half for a workbench. My potting soil is kept in a five-gallon bucket nearby. Large bags of fertilizers are on a shelving unit, smaller boxes on a shelf unit mounted on the wall.

Since our garage is an older one, the tools are hung on the wall between the studs. The previous owners had chalked the outlines of the tools on the boards.

Response 4: I keep my gardening soil in a big metal trashcan with a lid. I keep it outside. A plastic one with wheels probably would be even better. I have a bucket with a deal that fits around it that I use for my small hand tools. It has everything I use and I can just pick it up and go.

You can get five-gallon buckets from grocery store bakeries. They always have them to get rid of and will even save them if someone has beaten you to that day's. They're a really good grade, better than you can buy yourself.

- **Research first.** Do your homework before planting. Determine what plants and flowers look best together. Find out where you can purchase your plants and seeds at the best value.

- **Set a schedule.** Schedule time each week—or more if necessary—to take care of your garden before weeds add to your work. Keep garden tools in flowerpots and wagons. Large terra cotta flower pots filled with sand are wonderful for holding small garden tools. They'll stay clean and sharp and they won't bang against each other. Plus, they look pretty stored this way. An alternative is to use children's wagons, which are easy to haul around the garden and yard.

> ### Great idea!
>
> I have found a couple of great uses for the hangers that hold five pairs of pants and have the arms that swing out. I use them to hang my garden flags. They are the perfect size and they are stored neatly and flat. They don't get ruined. I hang them in the closet that is closest to the garden flag stand.
>
> Andrea Guastadisegni
> Grayslake, IL

- **Plant fresh veggies.** If you love fresh vegetables and you love gardening, planting veggies could save you trips back and forth to the supermarket.

- **Buy perennials.** If you love flowers, but don't have time for too much gardening, buy perennials. They bloom year after year and you won't have to keep buying and planting.

- **Neat garden tool storage.** Keep your garden tools in an upright tool container with slots to keep each tool organized and handy when you need it.

- **List your garden chores.** Set up a written schedule of garden chores so you don't forget to do what you have to, when you have to.

- **Don't choose green.** When choosing garden tools and equipment, avoid buying green. Green tools blend in with the lawn and can be difficult to find if you put them down. If you already have green tools, spray paint them a bright color or wrap the handles with bright reflective tape.

- **Top tools.** Don't waste time with old, rusted, outdated tools that are hindering you from getting the job done, rather than helping you.

- **Empty spots.** When your spring bulbs start emerging, you may see bare spots. Stick a wooden stake or a Popsicle stick in the area where you wish there was a tulip or other bulb flower. Mark the wooden stick with the type of flower you want planted there. In the fall, you'll know exactly where to plant that bulb.

- **Protect your car.** If you enjoy buying plants from your local garden center, be sure you always have protective plastic, like large trash bags, in your car.

You will then be able to line the back seat or the trunk, before you put your plants inside, to prevent dirt and water stains.

- **Use Popsicle sticks.** These can help you identify various plants and vegetables in your garden easily. Just write on the Popsicle stick and stick it in the ground next to the plant.

- **Consider container gardening.** If you don't have the space to plant a garden, consider a container garden instead. You buy appropriate sized containers and grow your veggies or flowers right in the container.

- **It can water itself.** Rather than wondering how much to water and when, pick up some self-watering containers. You just fill them when the indicator shows it's running low, and your plants and flowers always get the exact amount of water they require.

- **Mulch, mulch, mulch.** Put enough mulch in your plant beds—at least a few inches. Good mulch will feed your soil, seal in moisture and reduce weeds.

- **May I have some water please?** It's much better for your lawn and plants to receive a few days of a good long watering session, than a tiny, little watering session every day. By doing this, you'll encourage deep root systems.

- **Get a hedge trimmer.** One year, I wasted almost two days cutting down spent flowers in my garden using a small pair of garden shears. The next year, my husband came home with an electric hedge trimmer. I was able to trim in one hour, rather than two days!

- **Plant bulbs.** Bulbs, like tulips, come back on their own with no additional work on your part. Plant them in the spring or fall, and enjoy their beautiful colors year after year.

- **High and dry.** Remember to store pesticides, chemicals and fertilizers in a high, dry spot in your garden shed. In doing so, they won't freeze and can't be easily accessed by wildlife, pets or inquisitive children. Lock them up whenever possible, just to be on the safe side.

- **Keep feeders full.** Determine how many days pass before the tiny creatures empty them out. Then, make a consistent schedule to be sure you fill those feeders when needed. Send yourself an automatic email reminder to fill each Tuesday, for instance. Or, fill the bird feeders every time you put out the trash.

Chapter 26

Lawn

- **Do it yourself, without working.** Rather than watering your lawn manually, invest a little bit of money in an automatic sprinkler system, or create your own using connectors and timers. Set it on automatic pilot, while you rest in your hammock sipping lemonade.

- **Get a good mower.** If your budget allows, a self-propelled gas powered mower, rather than a manual one, will help get the job done quicker and with less exhaustion.

Great idea!

When mowing the lawn, I always run into weeds here and there. Even when I do the weed and feed thing monthly, the weeds will always pop up. I used to try to find them again after I finished cutting, but would always have a hard time trying to spot them as they blend so well into the grass—especially Bermuda grass.

Now I just take the hand spray bottle with me when I'm cutting and when I see a weed, I stop right there and spray it. Then I continue cutting. I found that this cuts my time by not having to go over the whole lawn searching for the weeds again. I keep the bottle attached to my lawn mower or on my pants pocket.

Frank Galica
San Jose, CA

- **Set timers.** Set your sprinklers with automatic timers that are set to go off at the same time each day. If you have a large lawn, use several sprinklers and several timers.

- **Use soaker hoses.** Use soaker hoses around your plants and trees. Attach the soaker hose to your outside faucet (or to another regular hose if necessary), wrap the hose around your trees and plants, stake the hose down if necessary and turn the water on about a quarter of a turn. The water will slowly seep out of the soaker hose's holes and keep all of your trees and plants watered. Once the soaker hoses are in place, you can say good-bye to manual watering.

- **Don't wait too long.** In the summer and early fall, the lawn tends to grow very quickly. If you wait too long, it's going to be very difficult to cut it even with an excellent mower. Cut twice each week and leave the grass at around four inches high.

- **Rake those leaves.** While it may seem like a waste of time to rake up fall leaves, if you don't take the time to do so, the leftover leaves can smother turf and leave dead patches come spring. Then, you'll have to take the time to add new grass seed, and all the work that goes along with that. You don't have to get every last leaf off, but give the lawn a good raking when most of the leaves have fallen off the trees, or a little bit each day when autumn hits.

- **Use the pooper scooper.** If you have a dog, get yourself a long-handled pooper scooper and clean up your pooches leftovers each day.

- **Mulch grass clippings.** Do you really want to have to collect all of your grass clippings and go through the trouble of having to dispose of them? When you mulch the clippings, you're providing your lawn with valuable nutrients. If your lawn mower doesn't currently mulch, consider investing in one that does.

- **Maintain your equipment.** Clean your mower well after each use. Be sure you have enough gas. Change the oil and sparkplugs as per the recommended guidelines for your particular model.

- **Keep off the sidewalk.** If you turn your mower on the sidewalk, you're bound to end up with grass clippings all over the walk. You'll then have to power wash the sidewalk to get the grass clippings and grass stains cleaned up. Turn on the mower on the grass. The same thing goes for when you're edging. Do it so the mower shoots out the grass clippings over the lawn—not the sidewalk.

- **Keep it trimmed.** Your lawn should always be approximately 3 ½" long. Cut it when it's about 4" long so that you're only cutting off about a ½" and you don't end up with clumps of long grass clippings all over your lawn.

- **Use the tuna trick.** Strategically place 4 empty tuna cans on the east, west, north and south sides of your lawn, so that the water from your sprinklers goes inside the cans. You'll be able to see how much water your lawn is getting. Your lawn needs at least an inch each week.

- **Go west, young man.** East, north, south and diagonally too! When mowing your lawn, don't always mow in the same direction. Vary your mowing route so that your grass doesn't "lean" in one direction all the time.

- **Get someone else to tend the lawn.** According to a Gallup Survey, more than 22 million households each year hire professional landscape, lawn care and tree care services. We hire a lawn and landscape company that provides us with services to keep our lawn green and weed free, keep our plants fertilized and keep pesky insects at bay. If your budget allows, take a break and have someone else do it for you.

Chapter 27

Outside Quarters

- **Recruit family members to help.** If everyone has a particular duty they're responsible for, the job can get done quicker and everyone can reap the rewards of his or her accomplishments. Older kids can help out with mowing. Young kids can pick up their toys from the lawn.

- **Bring toys inside.** Instruct your kids to always put any toys they bring outside, back in the house. No matter how nice your neighborhood is there's always the possibility that something will be stolen. Plus, you will have to spend unnecessary time each evening gathering everything left outside.

- **No toys in the driveway rule.** Instruct your kids to never leave toys or bikes in the driveway. A serious accident could occur.

- **Barbecue anyone?** Prevent initial food build-up by using Pam cooking spray designed for the grill. Then, use oven cleaner after your barbecue to clean up the rest. Remove the grill grates and put them on old newspaper. Spray on oven cleaner and let sit for a few hours or overnight. Then wipe and hose off.

- **Should we eat outside?** Keep all the non-food things you need when you eat outside in one basket or plastic storage container. Include items like paper plates, napkins, paper cups, plastic flatware, a tablecloth, wet wipes, bug repellant, a citronella candle and a means to hold down the tablecloth so it doesn't fly away. When you want to eat outside, you'll just have to grab your storage container and walk out the door, rather than spending time gathering everything in your kitchen.

- **Get a serving tray.** It's easier to put a bunch of things on a tray when you're carrying things outside, than having to make several trips back and forth into the house to gather everything you need.

- **Keep the tools outside.** Store gas grill tools right inside the gas grill when it's not in use. When you're ready to use the grill, the tools will be ready and waiting.

- **Get a gauge.** Don't wait until you're in the middle of barbecuing a roast to discover you have no more propane in your tank. Get a propane tank gauge and get more propane when you're running low. Better yet, if you have the space, keep a spare tank on hand.

- **String up some fish netting.** This is perfect for helping you keep outdoor toys in one place. Just two heavy-duty hooks to hold everything in place and you're good to go.

- **Get a bin with a lid.** Another option for storing outdoor toys is to put them in a bin with a lid. Everything will be contained in a consistent place.

- **Put up a clothes rack.** If you have a pool, add a clothes rack to the pool area. This is the perfect tool for drying out wet towels.

- **Slip and slide.** Is the bottom of your kids' wading pool pretty slippery? Just stick on some bathtub decals for safety.

- **Fence it in.** Consider adding a fence around your pool area. It will help to keep children and animals out of the pool when it's not being supervised. Plus, it helps to provide some privacy.

- **Add some light.** Be sure the area around your pool is well lit so that nobody accidentally falls into the pool and so that you can keep an eye on the pool area easily.

- **Keep pool supplies together.** Designate an area specifically for pool supplies. If you have young children, keep the pool supplies on a high shelf out of reach, or in a locked box.

- **Fill a kid pool with balls.** If you have a hard plastic pool that you store during the non-swimming months for the kids, consider also making use of it indoors this year. Rather than filling it with water, fill it with balls—obviously balls that are large and not able to be swallowed. Your young kids will have a ball sitting in the pool playing with all the balls inside. For a small pool, you'll have to get at least 50 balls—often available on clearance at large toy stores.

- **Organize the shed.** Don't just toss things randomly in your shed. Hanging hooks, pegboards and/or shelves allow you to keep equipment off the floor. Containers help you to keep similar items together.

- **Under cover.** Consider covering your patio furniture and barbecue with covers when not in use. It will keep them cleaner and more protected from the weather.

- **Would you like to take a stroll?** Never leave the baby stroller outside where it could get damaged from the weather. We don't even like to leave ours in the garage, because sometimes crickets and other little creatures may like to take up housing in it. Your best bet is to fold it up and store it in your house. We have enough space in our utility room, but you can also use your basement or a spare room.

If you only use the stroller when you're out for the day, you may consider just storing it in the trunk of your car. Or, store your large stroller at home and store a smaller umbrella stroller in the car.

Chapter 28

Car and Other Vehicles

- **All aboard.** According to a recent study, the average American spends a minimum of 15 hours per week behind the wheel. That's probably just as much time as you spend in some of the rooms in your home. Just like clutter doesn't belong in your home, it definitely doesn't belong in your car(s).

- **Make a clean sweep.** Climb into your car and remove all clutter. Toss empty soda cans and fast food wrappers. Gather all coins strewn about. Collect magazines and newspapers. Corral the maps.

- **No food or drink.** Institute a no food and no drink rule in the car. You'll never end up with empty soda cans, cracker crumbs or sticky surfaces from candy and fruit roll-ups.

- **Use the visor.** There are some nice organizing products on the market that can be attached to your car visor, such as a visor CD holder and a visor sunglass clip. Use these to keep items right at your fingertips and ready when you need them.

Great idea!

Every year I get my car detailed. Twice I have had the intention of selling the car and upgrading, but my car comes back looking so new that I keep it for another year. It kick-starts me into maintaining it in top condition again. Then after 12 months of the kids' messes and driving along a dirt driveway, it's truly ready for a big spring clean.

There are two benefits. First I am keeping the car longer than intended, so I'm saving repayment costs. Second, because it's well maintained, my car is worth more on the resale market when I do decide to upgrade.

Kari Esplin
Eden, New South Wales, Australia

- **Back seat organizer.** Back seat organizers hang from the back of the front car seat and have pockets and mesh compartments. These are perfect for organizing and hauling things like toys, umbrellas and books.

- **Half full or half empty.** Never let your car's gas gauge fall below the quarter tank mark. The second you hit a quarter tank, fill her up.

- **The great crate.** Keep a crate in your trunk. You'll be able to place items that you don't want rolling around, like grocery store bottles or cleaning supplies.

- **Tie a ribbon.** Tie a bright colored ribbon to your car antenna. It will help make it easier to spot at the mall or even after a heavy snowfall.

- **An extra $20.** Keep an extra $20 stashed in your glove compartment for emergencies. Just remember to remove it temporarily if your car needs to be serviced so it's not stolen.

- **Make a "Car Kit."** Include items like tissues, napkins, straws, plastic utensils, non-perishable foods, a pad of paper, a pen and anything you feel you may need while you're on the road. This is especially helpful if you have children.

- **Where am I?** Always keep a local map and perhaps a state map in the side door pocket of your car. You may need it when out on the road, especially if the road you originally wanted to take is under construction.

- **Tuck the trash bags.** Tuck a box of trash bags in the back seat pocket of your car. Whenever you need a trash bag, you'll have one. Toss the trash bag regularly or immediately if you've put food items or a dirty diaper into it.

  It's also handy to have these spare bags on hand for carrying things into the house or for one of those days when your grocery bag rips.

- **At the car wash.** Either wash your car regularly yourself or bring it to the local car wash at least once every two weeks. It's as important to keep the outside looking good, as it is the inside.

  Vacuum thoroughly and clean the inside windows while you're at it.

  My husband and I leave a package of electrostatic cloths—you can even use fabric softener sheets—in one of our car compartments. Whenever we bring the car to the car wash, we grab a cloth and dust off the surfaces inside while we're waiting for the car wash to finish.

- **Store a sheet.** Always store an old bed sheet in the trunk, folded up. Whenever you need to lay something messy in the trunk, such as dirty pumpkins from the pumpkin patch or plants, just lay the sheet down and you'll keep the dirt from touching the car.

  When you get home, you can either shake the sheet out or launder it.

  Another option is to always have a few large, plastic lawn and leaf bags in the car. These can easily be torn into a sheet and placed in your trunk or the back seat for protection.

- **Clean out the glove compartment.** Your glove compartment should only contain a few necessary items, such as your car manual, sunglasses, one local map, one state map, a pen and a small pad of paper. Clean the rest of the junk out.

Organizing Clinic

Question

I am wondering how and what to keep in regards to automobile maintenance and repair. I keep the title, registration, and other important car-related papers in a safe place, but don't have a good system to record information about when tires were rotated, oil changed, motor mount replaced and other maintenance information. Any assistance would be appreciated.

Barbara Huss
Topeka, KS

Answer

Dear Barbara,

Here is a simple system that anyone with a vehicle can easily follow:

- **Know what needs to be done.** In general, you probably know you need to get regular oil changes, tire rotations, brake service, transmission service and so on. However, refer to your vehicle owner's manual for specific details on your car. If you don't have the owner's manual, ask a trusted car dealership representative or auto mechanic for a maintenance schedule.

- **Keep a log of your car maintenance.** Either make your own log or use the pre-made one you'll find in the *Get Organized Now! Easy Organizer*. You'll want to record the date, the mileage on your vehicle on the date of repair, a description of the maintenance completed, the company the car was serviced by and the cost.

- **Keep paperwork in a folder.** Keep all maintenance regarding your vehicle in a file folder. If you need to look something up, you'll be able to find it easily. Keep the file folder in your filing cabinet for safekeeping. If you have several cars, make one folder for each car. Keep a copy or printout of your car maintenance log in each car's file folder.

- **Hold your media.** Don't just toss audio cassettes and CDs in the glove compartment or on the floor. Get yourself cases to hold them instead. You don't need dozens of cassettes and CDs in your car. Just keep a few to get you through the week or your family vacation.

- **A few toys.** There's no need to store volumes of toys in the car. For our baby, we had one toy bar that she played with for months. For older kids, keep enough books and toys to fit in a small plastic lidded container and no more.

- **Photo shoot.** It's always a good idea to keep a disposable camera in the car for those unexpected times you wish to take a photo. Plus, if you get into an accident, you can take immediate documentation.

- **Extra phone books.** Rather than tossing last year's phone book, consider keeping that one in the car. When you're out and you need to call for a reservation or contact a company for directions or other information, you'll have the phone book at your fingertips.

- **Use your cruise control.** Many cars have it, but very often this feature is left unused. As long as you're awake and alert and the weather is good, set your car slightly above the speed limit and cruise. You'll ensure your speed doesn't drop down too low, which will increase trip time. Don't worry. It's generally an easy feature to use and you can always tap on the break to disengage it when necessary.

Great idea!

As a busy mother of two little girls (ages 3 and 1) trying to stay organized is something I am always trying to achieve. With numerous trips in our vehicle to places like school, shopping centers, play centers or visits to friends and family, we are frequently in the car. My girls have never been the biggest fans of their car seats even in the best of times. So I have a large clear storage bin between their seats filled with various toys and games.

When we are on longer trips there are lots of things to keep them busy if they are not interested in snoozing. This bin of toys also comes in handy when we are visiting someone who might not have age-appropriate toys for them to play with. I try to rotate the various items in this bin as I do with their other toys to keep them exciting.

Lori Tinella
Alton, Ontario, Canada

- **Cooler in the trunk.** Keep a cooler in your trunk at all times. When you go grocery shopping or you need to keep a dish-to-pass cool, the cooler will keep everything at the right temperature until you get there.

- **Clean it up.** Keep cleaning supplies in your trunk, like window cleaner and leather cleaner and paper towels. You'll have these supplies in a pinch when you need them.

- **Trash it.** Keep a trash container in your car to collect the daily garbage you accumulate. At day's end, empty it out into a large home trash container. If you don't like the idea of having a trash container in your car, keep a stash of plastic grocery store bags instead. Collect your trash in one of these, and dump the entire bag into your home trash container at the end of the day.

- **Make an "Activity Kit."** When your kids get bored, they can open up the kit and play. Include crossword puzzles, travel games and fun activity books.

- **Get a portable DVD player.** When we're out on long drives and our daughter starts to get restless, we pop in one of her favorite DVDs and she's generally quiet for the remainder of the trip. We've even brought it into restaurants, with the volume on low of course, on occasions when we know the meal is going to be drawn out.

- **On the road.** If you have a lot of waiting time, like waiting in your car to pick up your kids from school or soccer practice, you may want to invest in a mobile desk. These usually come with storage space and a writing surface. While you're waiting, you can make out some bill payments, work on your grocery list or write to a friend.

- **Map it out.** If you regularly reference maps in your car, you may want to get yourself a map case organizer. These separate maps into their own compartments, so you can keep everything accessible.

- **Keep a reference journal.** My husband and I always keep a reference journal tucked into the passenger side door pocket. It started as a blank journal, but now it's a treasure trove of restaurants we like in various towns, driving directions to favorite walking trails and parks and other notes we may want to reference when we're out for a Sunday drive or looking for someplace to eat.

 Great idea!

I keep spare, disposable cameras in a diaper bag for spontaneous shots of my children. Once, at a big church event, the historian's camera failed to work, so I had a spare to lend her.

Karen Buelow
Germantown, TN

Chapter 29

Purse and Wallet

- **Purge your purse.** Go through your purse at least once each week and purge any trash. This includes, but is not limited to, receipts you don't need, cosmetics you never use, lists that are no longer relevant, business cards you have no clue why you took in the first place, pens that don't write and advertisements that no longer interest you.

- **Don't overstuff it.** If your purse is so heavy that it's breaking your arm, it's time to lighten your load. You don't need to carry everything under the sun with you. In my purse, this is what I have at all times:

  ❖ A tube of lipstick and a mirror

  ❖ Floss

  ❖ My wallet (includes 1 credit card and 1 ATM card, my driver's license, my insurance cards, a few store discount cards I frequent at least once each week and enough money to get me through the week)

  ❖ My keys

  ❖ A small notepad

  ❖ A small calendar

  ❖ My sunglasses

  ❖ My cell phone

  ❖ Any receipts, lists or coupons I need for "that day only"

  These items don't take up a whole lot of space, which means I don't need a huge purse and it's not heavy at all.

Great idea!

Always keep a spare key in your wallet. If you accidentally lock your keys in the car or even worse, lose them, you'll have a spare on hand.

Michael Pisano
Plainsboro, NJ

- **Change colors.** Choose a wallet in a color that is different from the inside color of your purse. For instance, use a red wallet in a black purse. It will stand out and you won't have to waste time fishing around for it.

- **Bag it.** Organize your purse with zip-lock bags. Keep cosmetics in one, lists in another and store discount cards in another.

- **Get a few versatile bags.** Don't change bags every day. If you do, you're going to misplace something when you're transferring contents. Or, keep all of your purse contents in a separate cosmetics bag. When you change purses, just transfer the one cosmetics bag from one purse to another.

- **Pack your stuff consistently.** When putting things in your purse, never toss in anything randomly. Have a consistent home for your keys, your phone, your sunglasses and your other stuff so you can find what you need without having to dig.

- **Keep a medication list.** Always keep a list of medications you're taking in your wallet. In the event of an emergency, you'll have all of this information on hand. If your spouse takes medications, keep a list of his or her medications also. Be sure you have these medications clearly labeled with the person's name, medication name and the dosage being taken.

- **Hide some money.** Hide a $20 bill in your purse or wallet for emergencies—and only use it for real emergencies.

- **Keep a purse/wallet list at home.** Inventory the contents of your purse and wallet, and keep this inventory list in a safe place at home. In case you lose your purse or your wallet is stolen, you'll have a ready-reference to help you get your life back in order.

- **Weigh your options.** On some occasions, you may not need to carry a purse around. For instance, if you're a new mom, you may want to double the use of your baby's diaper bag and store your purse necessities inside. If you use a briefcase, you can store your purse contents or your wallet inside.

- **Downsize.** Purchase a very small purse. Since you won't be able to fit much inside, you'll be restricted to only carrying around your essentials.

- **Where is my purse?** Be sure your purse has a home when you're not using it. In your house, it may be on a hook or a designated shelf. In your office it may be locked in the bottom drawer of your desk.

- **Prevent theft.** In restaurants, never leave your purse slipped around your chair or on the seat next to you. Doing so makes it very easy for a purse snatcher to complete his mission. Leave it on the floor with the strap around your ankle or hold it on your lap.

  When in the grocery store, carry your purse on your shoulder. If you absolutely must put the bag in your shopping cart, wind the cart's seatbelt around your purse's handle or strap.

Chapter 30

Accessories and Jewelry

- **Tie one on.** Ties and belts stored in drawers are difficult to find and take up unnecessary space. Use tie and belt racks in your closet.

- **Hook, line and sinker.** Keep necklaces and bracelets untangled and easily accessible by hanging them on hooks inside your bedroom closet, on a peg rack or on a hanging jewelry organizer. Keep earrings together by using an earring tree or an ice cube tray in your drawer.

- **Organize accessories.** Over-the-door, clear shoe bags are wonderful for holding light items such as hosiery, socks and handkerchiefs.

- **House your jewelry.** Get a jewelry armoire or a jewelry box for all your good jewelry, rather than storing it loose in a dresser drawer. Jewelry armoires allow necklaces to hang, so you won't end up wasting time untangling them.

- **It's in the drawer.** Keep accessories in clear plastic drawers. These drawers are usually stackable, so you can stack three or four on top of each other and have the perfect divided compartments for all your accessories.

- **Corral caps.** Corral caps and put them on a cap holder. There are some holders that hold a dozen or more caps neatly and together. Alternately, you may decide to put some hooks into a wall, such as a bedroom closet wall or a mudroom wall and hang them there.

- **Eye of the needle.** To organize pierced earrings, use a square of needlepoint material. Just stick the earring post through and attach the earring back to the other side of the mesh.

Great idea!

I have a lot of necklaces, all kinds from 14K gold and sterling silver to costume pieces. I never could find the right chain I was looking for or a particular set of beads or pearls. I bought an inexpensive bulletin board and mounted it on my closet wall. I line up pushpins on the board and hang my chains and things from the tacks. Now I can easily see everything and select what I want.

You can also put the tacks anywhere you want, higher for longer pieces, lower for shorter ones—like bracelets. I love this! It has saved me a lot of hassle. Hope you enjoy it.

Lynn Cohen
Boynton Beach, Florida

Great idea!

To find buttons or beads that originally came with a particular piece of clothing when you need to make a repair, stick them on an index card with an identifier such as a photo or a handwritten description of the garment. No more guessing! Store in an index card box labeled "Buttons and Beads."

Catherine Plunkett
Memphis, TN

- **Shoo those shoes.** Avoid buying shoes in colors like bright pink or red polka dots that you can only wear with one outfit and that usually end up tossed into the back of a closet. Plain black, brown and other neutral-colored shoes go with most outfits.

- **Take a step forward.** Put your best foot forward and get all of your shoes organized. I generally don't recommend—strangely enough—the hanging plastic shoe organizers for shoes. When you remove shoes, they need to breathe. Those plastic organizers don't allow this to happen and you're just going to end up with sweaty shoes that never have a chance to air out.

  Instead, use plastic or wooden shoe organizers that sit on your floor or on a shelf. Try not to get the kind that is slanted, as shoes without heels will slide right off. The one that I have is wooden, has two flat shelves (you can add more shelves to it) and can accommodate men's, women's and children's shoes.

  Count up the shoes you're keeping and get a rack to fit that number of shoes, plus a few more just in case. Many shoe racks stack and keep shoes beautifully organized. Buy a rack for each family member if necessary.

- **Banish lost barrettes.** Attach barrettes to a length of ribbon and hang the ribbon from a hook in a cabinet or closet. Pairs of barrettes will always be together and ready for you when you want them.

- **Pocketbook parade.** No, you don't have to toss out your many pocketbooks—just the ones you never use. Organizing them on shelves or on pegs will keep them looking good and make them much easier to locate when needed.

  Dedicate a shelf (or wall) for all your bags. For your dressier bags used less frequently, store them in see-through plastic bags to eliminate dust.

Organizing Clinic

Question

My question has to deal with the storing of scarves. I have several dozen and they are presently stored in a bureau drawer, neatly folded according to color and size. As I search for one in a hurry, the rest get out of order. Therein lies the problem.

I'd like to be able to hang them individually, but there is no room left in either the closets or wardrobes. Yes, I know, I have too many clothes, but I'm quite happy with that situation.

Unfortunately, floor space is also at a premium, so a very tall, narrow, multi drawer unit may also be out of the question. I thought about stringing a clothesline with pegs from wall to wall. Looking forward to any ideas you may have to offer.

Catherine West
Fall River, Nova Scotia, Canada

Answer

Dear Catherine,

Here are three possibilities that may help:

- **Bag 'em.** Keep the scarves in your bureau, but put each one into a plastic bag. You'll be able to find what you're looking for, without each scarf unfolding as you're looking. Another possibility is to buy or make drawer dividers and store each scarf in its own compartment.

- **Use a few tie racks.** While you may be short of space in your closet, you can probably squeeze in a few tie-racks. Display each scarf just as you would a tie.

- **Hang pegs on the wall.** Use your idea of stringing a clothesline with pegs. You can also hang lots of decorative pegs and hang a scarf on each one. Now that's a different kind of wall art!

- **Use the jewelry store method.** Jewelry stores often store jewelry in little white envelopes. Each envelope is labeled with the contents and then all of them are stored in a box—usually the size of a photo storage box. You can use this same tried and true method at home.

- **It's a wrap.** If you're going to be traveling with your jewelry, consider getting a jewelry wrap that can be hanged or rolled, has many jewelry compartments and that has a special closure so you don't lose anything.

- **Go to your local hardware store.** Traditional jewelry boxes aren't always the perfect fit for your needs. But you may find exactly what you're looking for at your local hardware store. Try an inexpensive nut and bolt tray instead.

Chapter 31

Decorating, Remodeling and Repair

- **What's this?** If you purchase "Assembly Required" products, you probably have random packages of extra nuts, washers and screws that manufacturers include. If you have no idea what these items go with, dump them. And remember, next time you purchase a put it together yourself product, immediately label the little plastic bag of widgets.

- **Find tips for organizing your specific hobby.** If you own a lot of collectibles—baseball cards, figurines, spoons, dolls—use available information sources such as magazines or appropriate Web sites to get ideas on how to arrange them in an organized manner. Purchase the manufacturers suggested organizing containers to prolong the life of your collections.

- **Sketch it out.** Before rearranging or redecorating your home, plan ahead. Sketch your thoughts out on paper. Carefully measure, especially prior to buying expensive furniture.

- **Keep your ideas with you.** When we were having our home built, I came up with a handy system that really helped with decorating. My husband and I gathered samples of our wall paint colors from our paint supplier, swatches of our carpeting, samples of our countertops and flooring, and so on. We then measured areas that we were currently looking to decorate, such as the dimensions of our windows for window treatments and the size of our tables for lamps.

  I found a small plastic photo book—small enough to fit inside my purse. In each photo slot, I included a fabric swatch or a carpet remnant or a floor sample or a list of dimensions. I keep that photo book in my purse, so when we're out on the weekends searching for new things for the house, we have all of the information we need readily available.

  It's much easier to choose a shower curtain when you have the color of the walls in your hands and it's a cinch to choose a tablecloth when you are certain of your table dimensions!

- **Strike a pose.** When remodeling, take before-and-after photos. You'll be able to preserve the memory, plus you'll have proof of improvement value.

- **Virtually move it first.** Before moving around heavy furniture, just to discover you don't like the way it looks, consider first using one of the many software products available. They can help you plan your design to ensure you're going to like the way it looks, before you move the furniture.

Organizing Clinic

Question

My house is very cluttered with things accumulated over the past 11 years of marriage. I want to change the decor and I have been getting rid of some of the decor we've had in the past. That's a start. I also have paper, catalogs and magazines. I throw out those that I am done with or don't want, but the ones I want to keep have nowhere to go. I have no clue what to do with the kids' rooms, my room or any of the other rooms in the house. How can I organize all this stuff? We really have nowhere to put it. Do you have any ideas on making more space or hiding the stuff?

Melissa McNeil
Hanson, MA

Answer

Dear Melissa

The typical couple married over 11 years can definitely accumulate quite a bit. Lots of good memories, but sometimes also lots of clutter. Here are a few simple ideas:

- **Old decor.** You already started by getting rid of some of the old decor. Good for you! Oftentimes, people keep old home decorations thinking they may come back in style someday. A good rule of thumb is, if you haven't used it in the past two years, you're probably never going to use it again. Get rid of it and make room for the new.

- **Paper, catalogs and magazines.** You need a good filing system for your papers, but only keep those you truly need to. Anything outdated should be recycled. Most catalogs are available online, so there's little need to keep the paper copy more than a month. Cut articles out of your magazines and file the articles. Toss the rest of the magazine.

- **Rooms in your home.** You mentioned "all the rooms in your house." That's part of the problem. You're focusing on too much. Focus on one room at a time. Lighten your load in each room by a minimum of fifty percent. Pick up two items at a time and get rid of one of them.

- **Now you see it, now you don't.** You can make more space with shelves, closet, cabinet and drawer organizers, hooks on walls and more. You can hide your stuff with pretty tablecloths over open tables, under bed storage and furniture that doubles as storage space.

- **So sentimental.** If you're sentimental, keep your true treasures—those items you would miss desperately if something happened to them (think of what you'd take with you if you had 10 minutes to gather up your most important things and move to an island forever.) That will add some perspective to what you should keep and what you should get rid of.

- **Throw a painting party.** Enlist some friends to help you paint your house. To entice them, throw a painting party. You supply the pizza, sandwiches, soda and dessert. It will hardly feel like work!

- **Is it worth it?** Have you ever put aside items that were broken with the expectation that you'll get them fixed one day? Chances are, these items are still where you left them and they're still broken.

  When this situation occurs, determine if the item is really worth the repair or not. If it isn't, throw it away. If it is, immediately schedule a date and time on your calendar to take care of the necessary repair—and get it fixed when the date rolls around.

- **The art of hanging art.** Prior to hanging artwork, take the time to sketch out your thoughts on paper, especially if you're planning on hanging a number of items in a creative arrangement. Measure carefully before hanging. Use a level to ensure pictures are straight. Draw a pencil mark where the top of the frame will be and stand back to ensure it meets your requirements, before you start hammering.

- **Watch those wires.** Disorganized, tangled wires are not only unattractive, but are hazardous. Disconnect any wires that are not being used. Ensure that no one will trip over wires, by running them along baseboards and behind furniture.

- **Use wire covers.** Organize wires from electronics and appliances into one tube. Split-loom tubing or wire covers can be purchased in houseware, hardware or electronics stores.

- **Keep it simple.** When redecorating, keep color schemes simple and light to make space appear larger.

- **On loan.** If you loan a tool to someone, immediately set a date on your calendar when you expect it back. If it hasn't been returned to you by then, contact the borrower and ask how much longer she/he will need it. Then, write the new expecting date on your calendar again. Follow up until you receive your tool back.

  If you borrow a tool, try not to keep it over a week. If you must keep it over this amount of time, call the person and ask if it's OK.

- **Keep them straight.** If you're building something with someone who brought his/her own set of tools over, be very careful not to get those tools mixed up with yours. Code your tools with labels or a spot of florescent paint for quick identification.

- **Form and function.** When purchasing furniture, look for both form and function. For instance, consider a coffee table with a built-in cabinet for storage, a lamp with an attached magazine rack or a bench with storage space under the seat.

- **Directions first please.** When you purchase do-it-yourself furniture and appliances, don't attempt to put it together without first reading the directions. I know how intimidating and long some of those direction booklets are. However, it will be a real waste of time if you skip reading the instructions, put it together and then discover you missed a very important step.

- **Decorate with dusting in mind.** No matter how much you dust, you're bound to have to do this task again fairly soon. But you can dust so much quicker if you don't have to keep picking things up to do so. Rather than decorating with lots of little knickknacks, decorate with one large floral arrangement or one big bowl filled with fruit or potpourri. It only takes a second to pick up one thing, but it takes lots of time to pick up and return lots of little things.

- **Minimize furniture and knick-knacks.** Are you saying, "It will look so bare?" Would you say that about a sunset, the ocean or the sky? Empty space is peaceful to look at. It allows you to free your mind and release your creative juices. There's also less work, since there is less to clean, less to buy and less to break. Think about it.

- **Communication and calendars.** When you hire contractors to have a project completed, work with them to ensure a productive schedule. When we were having our basement finished off, it was our responsibility to choose cabinets, carpeting and paint and to be sure all of those items were delivered on time for installation. Good communication with your contractors is key. Always have a calendar set up for a large remodeling project, so dates, times, contractors and vendors are all listed in one place.

Chapter 32

Safe and Sound

- **Better safe than sorry.** Keep a list of emergency phone numbers near the telephone. Program a few numbers directly into speed dial if your phone has this feature. Keep this list of speed dial numbers on or near the phone.

- **Make a "First Aid Kit."** When you or a family member gets a cut or bruise, it can be upsetting. Even more upsetting can be rummaging through your bathroom cabinet searching high and low for a band-aid or ointment. Think ahead and make a first aid kit. A simple plastic container with a lid will do just fine—we use an empty baby wipe container. Include first-aid items such as band-aids, adhesive tape, gauze, scissors, hydrogen peroxide, Bactine, cotton balls and ointment.

- **Create a "Home Emergency Kit."** Store it on the main floor in your home, preferably by your entry door, or your garage entry door, but away from the reach of young children. Include candles, matches, a flashlight, batteries, first aid kit, fuses and anything else you could think of that you might need quickly in case of a power outage or other emergency.

- **Create a "Car Emergency Kit."** Store a car emergency kit in your trunk. Hopefully, you'll never need it, but it will be there if your car breaks down or an unforeseen fender bender occurs. Some possibilities include a flashlight, jumper cables, water, antifreeze, blankets and flashing lights.

- **Open and close.** Be sure on any windows you have secured with bars, that the bars have quick-release mechanisms so any family member could escape in case of an emergency, such as a fire. Also, install window guards if you have kids.

- **Make a "Home Inventory List."** Include your valuables. Write down the item name, make/model and any serial numbers. Store this list in a fireproof box. While you're at it, make a copy of your driver's license and any other documents that you may need to retrieve as proof in case of a loss. Keep your list up-to-date and you'll be totally organized when the time comes to gather any of these.

- **Make a video.** Protect yourself by using a camcorder to document valuables in your home. Keep this video in a fireproof box, along with other inventory records including lists and photos.

- **Design an "In Case of Fire Plan."** Draw up a home floor plan, clearly identifying all exits. Hold practice fire drills with your family until everyone knows the procedures in case of an emergency.

- **Pack a phone.** When used for emergencies, cell phones can be lifesavers. Consider a separate one for each family member. Ask each person to carry it when they go out. If you're on a budget, instruct them to use the cell phones strictly for emergencies.

- **Tub safety.** Never leave young children alone in the bathtub for even a few seconds. They could drown in even a tiny bit of water. Attach non-skid decals or put in a bathmat to prevent slips and falls, and never let young children stand in the bathtub. For extra support for getting in and out of the tub, attach a grab bar to the shower wall being sure to install it with studs. Keep hairdryers, curling irons and other appliances away from water to prevent shock.

- **Create a "Just in Case List."** Everyone in your family should be aware of solutions to potential problems. Have checklists for things such as turning off the water shut off valve, setting the VCR or cleaning up a spill on the carpet. Keep these checklists in a binder and be sure all family members know where the binder is stored.

- **You light up my life.** Store a flashlight in the nightstand of each family member. In case of a power outage, everyone will be armed and there will be no bumps and bruises from trying to walk in the dark.

- **Shred it.** With the abundance of identity theft these days, every home should be equipped with a paper shredder. Before tossing papers with personal information in the trash, shred them first. This includes anything with your social security number, credit card numbers, bank account numbers or any other information you would not want an identity thief to see.

- **Keep it charged.** A cell phone is of no use if it isn't charged. Charge your phone every night, or at least when the battery goes below the halfway point.

- **Have at least two sets.** Whether it's your house keys, your car keys or the keys to your storage shed, always have at least two sets. Keep one set with you and the other with a trusted relative, friend or neighbor who lives nearby. I actually have three sets of car keys. One stays with me, another with my husband and another in my wallet—just in case I accidentally lock the keys in the car.

- **Consider a home alarm.** No matter how safe you feel your neighborhood is, there's always a chance of a break in. Consider getting yourself a home alarm. We use ADT. We have motion sensors set up throughout the home that we can turn on or off depending on what room we're in. We also have alarms set up just in case someone attempts to enter through one of our doors.

- **Check batteries.** Smoke alarms are worthless if the batteries aren't working or if there aren't batteries inside. When you change the clocks in the spring and the fall, change your smoke alarm batteries at the same time.

- **Don't have a cooking accident.** Never leave pots on the stove unattended, and turn the handles of pots and pans inward so they're not accidentally knocked off the stove. Keep pot holders away from the burners.

- **Clean out the filters.** Always clean the lint out of your dryer filters. Excessive build-up has been known to start fires. Never leave the dryer running when you're not home.

- **Store a stash.** Always keep a stash of non-perishable food items in your home, such as beans, tuna, canned vegetables, peanut butter and drinking water. You'll be prepared in case you can't get to the supermarket during a storm.

- **Make a copy.** Make copies of your driver's license, insurance cards and the front and back of your credit cards. Put these copies in a locked filing cabinet. In the event of loss or theft, you'll be able to cancel your credit cards immediately and you'll have a much easier time at the Motor Vehicle office in your town.

- **Passport please.** When traveling abroad, make two copies of your passport. Keep one with you in an area separate from your actual passport and give the other to a family member at home. In case you lose your passport, it will be easier for you to identify yourself at the embassy or consulate's office.

- **Get them inspected.** Make an appointment each year to get your chimney and fireplace cleaned and inspected.

- **Keep it in your wallet.** Always write down important medical information, including medications you're on and tuck it in your wallet. In case of a health emergency, this is the first place emergency workers will look. It can save your life.

- **Have a fire extinguisher.** Every home should be equipped with a fire extinguisher to put out small fires. Hopefully, you'll never have to use it, but better to be safe than sorry. Hang it up in your utility room closet or your coat closet.

- **Review insurance regularly.** Every year, meet with your insurance agent to review your health, auto, life and home or renter's insurances. This meeting will be to ensure you have enough coverage and that you're not paying too much for the coverage you currently have.

- **Put it in the bank.** Never leave large sums of money in your home. Determine an amount that you'd like to have on hand. Anything over that amount can be deposited safely in your bank.

- **Too many cords.** Look around your home for potential fire hazards, such as bunches of power cords plugged into one set of outlets. It's not necessary to have all appliances plugged in when they're not being used.

- **Contact plan.** Do you have a plan for connecting with family members if you're separated in an amusement park or mall? What about if you can't reach a friend or relative by telephone? I regularly leave my cell phone on, even when I'm home, as a back up.

- **Label.** Are your shut-off valves for water, gas, oil and electricity clearly labeled? If not, now is a good time to take care of that task.

- **Be careful on the web.** Never give your passwords to anyone for any reason. Be particularly careful about giving out personal information. Identity theft is rampant these days. Never open email attachments from people you don't know and be wary of attachments even from people you do know. Protect your computer with virus protection and firewall software. Never allow young children to use the Internet without adult supervision.

- **Create an "In Case of Emergency" file folder.** In this colored folder, preferably red so it stands out, you should store your bank account numbers, your will, passwords, your lawyer's phone number, the key to your safety deposit box and any other important information that only you are aware of. Put it in an inconspicuous place and only tell one or two trusted people such as a spouse or close relative where this folder is. In the event of an emergency, one of these people can retrieve the folder and handle any decisions for you.

- **Baby proof.** If you have young children, you'll need to organize keeping precautions in mind. For instance, anything poisonous or sharp should be stored up high and out of baby's reach. Use outlet covers, drawer and cabinet locks and toilet locks. Get child gates so kids don't climb up or fall down stairs. Keep medications out of their reach. Also, keep child safety in mind when positioning furniture such as cribs. Place them away from the windows, away from lamps, or other areas that may pose a hazard.

- **Plan your estate.** No matter how young or old you are, you should take care in planning your estate. In case something ever happens to you, your money and possessions will be distributed as you would like them to be. Plus, your family will have peace of mind knowing everything was handled as you would have wanted it to be. Look into getting a will, a living will and possibly a trust.

- **Take the ticket.** When you drive into a parking lot and have to take a ticket to enter, use the other side of the ticket to write down what floor you parked on and what space. Take the ticket with you and use it when you return to determine exactly where you parked.

- **Buy furniture with your family in mind.** When shopping for furniture for our newly finished basement, we opted for a fabric covered ottoman, rather than a coffee table. When kids visit, we knew we wouldn't have to worry about a bumped head on the edge of a coffee table. Think of your needs before you go out and shop.

- **Check credit card statements.** Always scan through each charge on your credit card statement for suspicious charges. You don't want to be paying for something you did not buy.

- **Never give it out.** Be very wary about giving any information over the phone, especially if you did not initiate the call. For instance, if someone ever calls to say she is just calling to verify your social security number, it's more than likely a scam to steal your identity.

- **Up and down.** Light switches should be available at the top and bottom of each staircase, and all staircases should have handrails. If you put mats or rugs at the top or bottom, be sure you get the type that are heavy and non-skid.

- **Take a step.** If you live in a two-story house, have a rescue ladder than can be used as an emergency escape route.

- **Install another alarm.** That is, a carbon monoxide alarm. According to Real Simple Magazine, carbon monoxide poisoning — often caused by defective, improperly vented, or poorly maintained heating units — causes nearly 300 deaths a year in the United States. You can't see it and you can't smell it, but it can be deadly. Have your heating system checked once each year for carbon monoxide leaks.

- **Have a romantic evening.** Candles can add a romantic touch, but never leave burning candles unattended.

- **Away from the barbecue.** Designate the grill area a kid-free zone. We totally block this area off on our deck whenever we have a barbecue so kids can't get anywhere close to it.

- **Clutter is a safety hazard.** A cluttered home can be a safety hazard. Someone may trip and fall. A fire could start from piles of loose newspapers and magazines. Dust settling on items never touched could cause severe allergic reactions. Clutter is just as much a stressor as it is a safety hazard.

Chapter 33

School Days

- **Get a planner.** For students ages 14 and over, student organizers or planners are essential. They're perfect for holding and categorizing tests, homework, forms, permission slips and study materials. The good ones include calendars, schedules, To Do Lists and other planning tools.

Organizing Clinic

Question

I have two daughters, ages 15 and 17. I have kept all those special art projects, awards and birthday cards that have been accumulating throughout the years. Now I am wondering what to do with them, so that my daughters may enjoy remembering what they did without going through containers and containers.

Sandra Lankey
Baraboo, WI

Answer

Dear Sandra,

If you were just starting to collect memorabilia, I would have recommended that you only keep one or two very special items for each year of each daughter's life. In doing so, you would have only ended up with one box each for each of your daughters. This is always my recommendation for new parents as it prevents tons of boxes, but still provides children with valuable memories that represent each childhood year when they get older.

However, it sounds like you've already kept a large collection of projects, awards and birthday cards. To give each girl several containers of things to go through may prove to be overwhelming and not as fun as enjoying these memories over a period of time. Choose one consistent day each month called "Memory Day." On Memory Day, give each of your daughters one or two of the special items you've been saving.

In doing so, you will be able to spend a few minutes of quality time with each daughter, telling her what you loved about this item you kept or a special memory associated with it. In addition, your daughters can decide which of those items they wish to keep in their own memory boxes that they can take with them when they get married and/or move out.

- **Look at the month.** Rather than using Day-at-a-Glance calendars, talk to your child about using Month-at-a-Glance. They should have large enough spaces to include a number of notes. They can be used to plan and schedule time for assignments, homework, tests and other school-related activities.

- **A binder is more flexible.** Instead of a spiral notebook, three-ring binders with pocket folders are generally the better choice for students. They're more flexible for inserting and removing handouts, notes, tests and readings.

- **Limit activities.** Limit your child to a few meaningful activities. Help him to make a quick grid of the time needed for schoolwork, homework and activities. Don't forget the time it takes to get from one activity to another.

- **Schedule in study time.** As a general rule of thumb, your child needs at least two hours of study time for each hour of class time. Study time should be scheduled and written on her calendar.

- **Enhance your memory.** The better the memory, the better the grades. There are many books for enhancing ones memory. Why not read through one with your child to learn some key memory principles?

- **Get into the computer age.** Instead of handwriting drafts of book reports or other homework, have your child use the computer and a word processing program. It will help increase her productivity, while reducing her workload by 50% or more—plus it almost always looks a lot neater.

Great idea!

To keep track of all the papers for school-age children, purchase an expandable file folder labeled January through December for each child. Replace the January label with Kindergarten/1st grade, February with 2nd grade and continue until you replace December with 12th grade.

This is a great way to keep track of report cards, test scores, shots and other important information. I found it very helpful to place items for the future, such as tips for college tours, in the 12th grade file. When you are planning a graduation display or filling out health forms or college applications, all this information is very easy to locate.

Cheryl Peterson
St. Peter, MN

- **Little bits of time.** Scheduling half-hour study sessions are more effective than marathon sessions. Your child will remember more and won't get exhausted as easily.

- **Write it down.** When you learn of an upcoming test, event or anything your child must prepare for, teach him to immediately jot it in his planner. Tell him if he waits until later, there's a good chance he'll forget.

- **Meet the master.** Have your child make a Master List of everything she wants to accomplish. Then, have her transfer those items a little at a time to her daily To Do Lists. As she completes each item, have her cross it out with a hi-lighter and it will become her "accomplishment list."

- **Surf the web.** Rather than looking through countless books at the library, introduce your child to the available encyclopedias, dictionaries and other educational resources on the Internet instead. It's much quicker to have the computer look things up and the information is generally more current.

- **Keep that combo.** For students who use combination locks, it may help to jot the combination down on a small piece of paper and store it in a purse, planner or carrying case. She may think it is easy to remember something so simple, but when she's in a rush or has something else on her mind, she may not be able to recall it quickly.

- **Life in the fast lane.** Be sure your child wakes up early enough to get ready for school without rushing. If she needs 45 minutes to shower, dress and have breakfast, teach her to set her alarm clock accordingly.

- **Move the clock.** To ensure he gets up when the alarm clock goes off, put the clock on the other side of the room. When the alarm sounds, he'll have to walk all the way to the other side of the room to turn it off. The rule should be, once up, stay up.

- **Last Minute Louie.** If you're driving your son or daughter to school, don't leave at the last minute. Prepare ahead for traffic and other unforeseen circumstances that will cause a late arrival. If it generally takes you 15 minutes to get to the school, leave home at least a half hour early.

- **Prepare the wardrobe.** Before you go to bed each night, choose, iron and lay out your clothes and your child's clothes for the next day. Everyone will be set to dress and go in the morning.

- **The night before.** Is your child always scrambling to get together everything she needs for the school day each morning? Instruct her to get everything ready and set to go the evening before. Assign a specific time at night for her to do so. Have her pack her bag so she can grab and go. If necessary, make a checklist of everything she has to do the evening prior and have her check off each item as it's accomplished.

Organizing Clinic

Question

I have a very bright 8th grader, but he has a horrible time with organization. It stems, I believe, from the fact that for years in elementary school he never had to be organized or really study. He does assignments and loses them or he doesn't follow through and often hands in assignments late. His locker and backpacks are both very messy. These problems are killing his grades. Please help.

Cathy Miller
Canton, GA

Answer

Dear Cathy,

It's never too early to begin teaching good organizing techniques. If you have children younger than your eighth grader, definitely begin to help them learn how to be more organized as early as possible so that they don't experience the same problem your son is now having. Does your son use a three-ring binder or student planner? He needs a good system that holds pocket file folders for assignments to be done, completed assignments and special projects. If you assist him with getting everything into one consolidated place, this should help eliminate the problem of papers getting lost.

If he is handing in assignments late, he is starting them too late. Each night, sit down with him and go over all of his pending assignments until he can do this independently. Help him develop a system for starting each project on time. A minimum of two to three hours should be designated for completing assignments each weekday. Estimate how many weekday sessions it will take him to complete his project, depending on other assignments, school activities or difficulty of the project. Pad that time by at least a few days. Then, backtrack on the calendar to determine when that project needs to be started. As soon as the project is complete, it should immediately be placed in his planner or binder system.

Be sure he is using a backpack with compartments. Everything can be organized into its own compartment. Assist him in doing this each night until he can do it by himself. If necessary, make something he enjoys doing, contingent upon straightening out his backpack so he is encouraged to do it. For instance, there will be no TV viewing or video games until the backpack is organized. It's difficult for many students to keep an organized locker. Most have one tiny shelf on top and then a very long, vertical space without shelves that makes it very difficult to organize. Rather than this large empty space, have him measure his locker and get him some Rubbermaid containers that fit inside his locker. Be sure they're the type with covers that stack. In doing so, he will have more compartments to keep similar items together. If the containers are clear, he will be able to see the contents without even opening them. Teach him how to sort like-items like all books in one area, sporting equipment in another and clothing in another.

- **Set goals.** Help your child set realistic goals at the beginning of the school year and break those large goals into mini-goals. These goals should be written down on index cards and kept in a highly visible place where they can be seen every day.

- **Avoid clutter.** At the beginning of the school year, your child has no school clutter. Help her to avoid building clutter as the year progresses. Help her create separate folders for school announcements, tests that have been graded, papers that must be signed and so on. As papers become outdated, such as an event that has passed, they should be tossed immediately.

- **Make To Do Lists.** Help your child invest a minimum of 15 minutes per day, preparing a To Do list for tomorrow. In doing so, he will know exactly what tasks he has to accomplish the next day. This is excellent preparation for adult planning.

Great idea!

I pack my children's school lunches for the week on Sunday. I use the small snack bags and sort the foods into them (pretzels, grapes, carrots, etc.) Each morning or the night before all I have to do is grab a few bags and their lunch is ready to go. It takes about 30 minutes on Sunday afternoon to do all the packing and sorting and the kids can help too.

Katey Flores
Dallas, TX

- **Use an effective study area.** Designate a quiet, well-lit area for your child to study that is not front of the television or in an area of your home where he's bound to be distracted. Hang a "Do Not Disturb" sign on his door if other brothers and sisters make it difficult for him to focus.

- **Get comfortable.** Your child should study while sitting at a table or desk rather than in a very comfortable chair or a bed, which may cause him to feel drowsy.

- **Get beauty sleep.** Be sure your child is getting a good night's rest. This will ensure she is alert and ready to learn the following day. An 8:00PM bedtime for young children will generally ensure ample sleep time.

- **Use one calendar.** Have your child use one calendar to plan all school and personal activities, rather than two or more. Otherwise, she will run the risk of scheduling conflicts and missed appointments.

- **Color code.** Teach your child to color code similar activities on her calendar or planner. For example, all upcoming tests can be in yellow, study time in green and recreational activities in pink.

- **Break up study time.** Time management is not taught in most schools. Help your child determine how many study hours he needs. For example, if he needs six hours of time to study for a test, you may help him break that time up into six sessions of one hour each.

- **Schedule consistent study times.** Have your child set aside time every day for study and make it consistent. For example, set study time for each afternoon from 4:00PM to 6:00PM.

- **Break it up.** Break up big tasks, into smaller, bite-sized jobs. For instance, if your child has to study three chapters in her history book, instruct her to study one chapter at a time each day. If she has to work on a project, break it down into three or four stages.

- **Get the difficult stuff out of the way.** Instruct your child to do her homework for the most difficult subjects first. Then, everything else will be a breeze and therefore, more enjoyable.

- **Put together an emergency kit.** That is . . . an emergency "school supply" kit. Fill a plastic container with pencils, crayons, construction paper, pipe cleaners, glue and other items regularly needed for school. Stash it on a closet shelf and only use in case of an emergency, like when your daughter has to finish her science project and discovers she's out of glue just as the local stores are closing shop for the day.

- **It's OK to ask for help.** If your child doesn't understand a lesson, encourage him to immediately ask for help. Teach him not to let it get to the point that he's totally confused. A sibling, friend, parent or teacher can be a lifesaver.

- **Reap rewards.** Help your child designate enticing rewards for each goal set, such as an afternoon at the movies. As he achieves each goal, he should reap his rewards. This will help keep him motivated throughout the year.

- **Set up a carpool.** If several kids on the block go to the same school, set up a carpool. Each parent takes turns driving all the kids to school. It saves on gas and each parent is only responsible for driving one or two days each week.

- **Put their names on.** Kids are notorious for taking off their jackets, mittens and so on, and misplacing them. Add name labels to your kids' wardrobes to help identify. This will help make the teacher's job easier at the end of each day. If your child forgets something at school, the teacher will know it's his.

- **Schedule a homework check.** Each night after dinner, meet with your son or daughter and review his or her homework. Be sure both you and your child keep this appointment. Use this time to also sign any report cards or permission slips.

- **Tuck the lunch money.** If you need to give your child lunch money for school each day, tuck it right in his or her backpack—or whatever will definitely go to school each day—so it's not forgotten.

- **Get at least three.** If your child wears uniforms to school, your best bet is to buy at least three for the school year. If you wash often, like daily or every other day, your child will always have a clean uniform to wear while another is being laundered.

- **Give them chores.** Kids that have assigned chores at home are generally more responsible in the classroom. Give your kids at least 20 minutes worth of chores each day.

- **Check the Net.** These days, many schools and teachers provide important information for parents on the Net, via email, Web sites or blogs. Check with your child's school to determine how you can best be kept abreast of school projects, homework assignments, upcoming events and deadlines.

- **Have a family meeting.** Each night, hold a 10-minute family meeting to catch up on your kids' school day. If your kids don't offer information, you'll have to ask. If you don't ask, many students will never tell.

  Some questions might be . . . What did you do in school today? What was today's lesson in history class? What does today's homework assignment consist of? Did they mention any upcoming activities or events? Did you meet any new students? Can you tell me the most interesting thing you learned today?

- **Put the computer in the living room.** To ensure your child is doing her homework and not hanging out in Internet chat rooms or other sites you don't want him to frequent, keep the computer in your main living area so you are aware of what's going on.

- **Going on a field trip.** Always make a checklist the night before your child has to go on a school field trip. Since it's not like a normal school day, chances are your child will need things she normally would not. For instance, if the fieldtrip is in an outdoor setting, will she need sunscreen or a water bottle to keep hydrated? Also, always be sure to get your child to school early on field trip days. If she misses the bus, she misses the fun.

- **Home school.** If you home school, you'll really have to be on top of things. It basically should be run as a normal school day should be run, with designated hours for each subject and an accurate way to track what your student is learning.

Chapter 34

Work

- **Finally Organized, Finally Free—for the Office.** Below are just a few basic tips for anyone who works. If you want hundreds of tips specifically related to getting organized at the office, be sure to read our book, *Finally Organized, Finally Free for the Office* available on the www.getorganizednow.com Web site.

- **Time for work and time for play.** If you're always working late, you're probably having trouble finding time for yourself and your family. Work on streamlining your work systems until they're so organized that there's absolutely no reason to stay after-hours.

- **Cramming is crummy.** No matter what, preparation is the key. Don't wait until the very last minute to begin getting ready for an important event or project deadline. Make a list of everything you need to do and work on that list a little bit each day. This ensures that you'll do the best you possibly can when the date or deadline arrives.

- **Get your beauty sleep.** The people with the highest productivity are always those who catch their full forty winks each evening. Determine what time you have to wake up in the morning in order to arrive at work on time. Then, backtrack a minimum of seven to eight hours so you know what time you should be in bed and sleeping.

- **Planning power.** It doesn't matter if you're a student or a high-level executive in a Fortune 500 company. You must, I repeat, you must use a planner—print or electronic, whichever works best for you. When you learn of a meeting, appointment, event or any other task, immediately jot it in your planner and get it off your mind. Just remember to check your planner each and every day, so nothing is missed.

- **Goals are golden.** Set at least three goals each month and you'll have a clear, manageable path to stay on throughout your work tenure. Be sure those goals are specific and measurable. A specific and measurable work goal might be to convert five prospects to customers each month. Evaluate your results at the end of each month. Reward yourself for goals met. Don't beat yourself up for goals not met. Just commit to reaching those goals the following month.

- **Cut the clutter.** At work, you're going to get inundated with memos, invoices, customer account files, mail and so on. Keep the paper under control by 1) weeding out the old and outdated every single day and 2) keeping the papers you do need to keep in one area such as a filing cabinet or a binder with pocket folders. Be sure folders are always clearly labeled.

- **Fuel up.** So many people think they can get plenty done by skipping breakfast or lunch. But how can you work if you have low energy or a hunger headache? These important meals provide you with the energy you need so that you can produce the highest quality work. They don't have to be difficult or time consuming. Breakfast can consist of a yogurt, some fresh fruit and some cereal. Lunch can consist of tuna on 100% whole wheat bread with an apple or a chef salad.

- **Same place, same days, same times.** When scheduling, consolidate similar activities for the same place, same days and same times. If you do so, you'll always know exactly what's expected of you each day. For instance, make all of your prospect follow-up phone calls in your office with the door closed, Mondays, Wednesdays and Fridays, at 3:00PM.

- **Broccoli first, brownie second.** When eating dinner, most people eat their broccoli way before they eat their brownie. In other words, they save the best food for last, since they know it's the most luscious reward. The same goes for your work. Do the hardest, most grueling, least-loved work first. Then, do your easiest, more-likeable tasks last. Once the hard stuff is out of the way, the easier tasks and projects will be a breeze.

- **Pound perfection.** You can't dedicate 100% of your time and effort to 100% of the things in your life—you'll end up frustrated, tired and unfulfilled. Striving for perfection is an obstacle that prevents you from getting things done. It's rare that anything is going to be done perfectly. Instead, strive for excellence in everything you do. You'll end each day feeling good about yourself. Plus, you'll have more completed projects.

- **Take mass transit.** Rather than driving to work, take a bus, train or ferry. Use the riding time to read a book or to catch up on some work. It can be more relaxing than driving.

- **Chit chat is Ok, as long as it's not all day.** If you're a people person, part of the enjoyment of your work day may be when you get to chit chat with your co-workers. However, if you spend too much time chatting and too little time working, your productivity is going to suffer. Designate 10 minutes here and there for chit chat (no more than three 10-minute chit chat sessions per day).

- **All work and no play makes Jack . . . exhausted!** While you're going to be busy working on tasks and projects, being involved in activities and running back and forth to meetings, classes or events, that's no excuse for not enjoying your life. Always make the time to do the things you love to do—painting, having fun with friends, golfing, going to the movies, whatever! When you have both work (or school) and fun activities planned, you're living a balanced and full life. Isn't that what living is all about?

Chapter 35

Shopping and Errands

- **Take the squeeze out of your schedule.** If you're constantly running around from one place to the next, while hardly taking a second to breathe, your schedule most likely has too much stuff squeezed into it. Prioritize and streamline.

  If you're involved in too many activities, choose the most important ones and eliminate the rest. Spending too much time running errands? Determine if you can run these same errands every two weeks, versus weekly, or do all of your errands in one trip, rather than running an errand or two each day. The more time you save each day, the more free time you'll have on your schedule.

- **Look first.** Before you go grocery shopping, look through your fridge. Discard any stale food. Wipe shelves with a damp cloth. When you get back from shopping, the new groceries will fit right into this clean space.

- **Make a waiting bag.** No matter what, every once in awhile, you're going to find yourself waiting. You might be on telephone hold, sitting in the dentist's office waiting your turn or at the train station anticipating your train's arrival. Make that waiting time count by always carrying around a "Waiting Bag". Stock that bag with a few things you have or want to do. You may pack a book to read or your latest knitting project.

  Perhaps you might bring your cell phone to make some necessary calls, stationery to catch up on correspondence or an audio cassette player to listen to the latest book on tape. The "Waiting Bag" ensures you're always doing something productive with your time.

Great idea!

Whenever one of our children asks me to remember to bring something from home to work or from work to home, I write myself a note and staple the paper to my purse handle. This has worked for my daughter as well. She advised the children in her classroom to staple a note to their book bag or backpack handle. This way when you see the note, you are reminded there is something extra needed for the day or whenever.

Sheryl Tiedt,
Readlyn, IA

- **Go during slow times.** Try to go to the supermarket during slow periods—late at night or early in the morning—when lines are short and parking isn't a hassle. Weekdays are generally less crowded than weekends. Avoid grocery shopping the day before a holiday, especially big family holidays such as Christmas or the 4th of July.

- **Buy in bulk.** If you have lots of room for storage, consider purchasing paper items, cereals and cleaning supplies in bulk to save unnecessary trips back and forth to the store.

- **Make one trip.** Shop in a shopping center where you can consolidate many of your errands—dry cleaner, post office, ATM, grocery store—into one trip. You won't be spending hours driving around town.

- **Bag well.** If you bag your groceries at the supermarket, try to keep organization in mind. If I bag myself, I pack all the bathroom items together, all the freezer items together and so on. This makes it easier to unpack when I arrive home. If you have someone else bagging your groceries, at minimum ask the person to keep all the cold things in one bag, all fruits and vegetables in another and all items not cold in another.

Great idea!

I frequently run errands on my lunch hour or stop for takeout on my way home from the office, but would get frustrated when I'd discover that the coupons and receipts I needed were left at home or crumpled up somewhere in my wallet or purse. To solve this problem I purchased a small photo album from the dollar store. Mine has 20 pages, which is 40 sleeves. I made labels on the computer for the stores I frequently shop at and stuck them on some of the pages, plus I left some pages unlabelled.

I grouped them together logically, such as restaurants, crafts, auto, household and errands. Now, as soon as I clip something out, I file it in the album. When I drop off photos or dry cleaning, the receipt goes into its designated pocket. No more frantic searches through my wallet at pickup time.

For some of my favorite stores, I make a list on a piece of paper of the items that are on sale in the flyer and file it in one pocket, with the coupons in the opposite pocket. I also keep a list on one page of the clothing sizes of family members. This album is compact (4 1/2 inches x 6 1/2 inches) and doesn't take up much room in my handbag. It goes everywhere I go, so I am always prepared, even for a spontaneous dinner treat. Best yet, when the pages get worn or ripped (as they eventually do from constant use), I can easily replace it with another album from the dollar store. This is a very effective, low cost, low tech solution to a vexing problem!

Kathleen Wheaton
Fairport, NY

- **Create a "Master Grocery List."**

  [1] Type or write up a list of groceries that you regularly pick up at the supermarket. Do this on your computer if you own one.

  [2] Once your list is complete, print it out and make copies.

  [3] Keep one posted conveniently on the refrigerator, attached with a magnet; keep the extras in a file folder labeled "Grocery Lists" so you know where they are when you need a fresh one.

  [4] Every time you or another family member notices something running out, check it off on your list.

  [5] Bring your list to the market and cross out each item as you put it in your shopping cart.

Great idea!

You know when you go to the store and think that something will work only to get it home and find out it doesn't? We have set up a shelf in our garage to store all returns. We tape the receipt on the return and when someone is going to a store, they have to check the return slot. They can keep the money from the return to use as they like. Older kids love to take the returns back!

Syndy Daily
Raton, NM

- **Open the fridge once.** When you come home from grocery shopping, put items that need to be cooled right by the refrigerator. Then, put all these items into the refrigerator at once. This will save time and electricity.

- **Do a bit of planning first.** Plan your meals before writing up your shopping list. It will be easier for you to write up your list. In addition, you won't spend money on groceries that you don't really need this week.

- **Make and take a list.** When you run errands, don't leave the house without a list telling you where you need to go and what you have to get. Also bring a list along with items you must bring with you when you go. For instance, list clothes for the dry cleaner, bank deposit slips for the bank, car keys, checkbook for payments and any other applicable items. Take your lists into each store and check off items as you go.

- **Leave some breathing room.** When organizing your schedule, don't jam-pack it full of tasks, activities and appointments. If you do, you're going to constantly be running around like a chicken without a head and you're bound

195

to fall way behind every single day. Always leave time for things that take longer than expected to complete, special circumstances or emergencies, traffic delays, telephone hold, thinking moments or a few minutes to relax and re-energize.

- **Last one is a rotten egg.** Make it a rule. Whoever empties the peanut butter jar, uses the last bar of soap or takes the last sip of milk, is responsible for writing that item down on the shopping list.

Great idea!

With regard to shopping, we have used a layout of the grocery store to plan our shopping list. Our list is in the order of the products on the shelves. This saves time backtracking for regular items. Although the grocery store does move items occasionally, they generally stay in the same area so you will still pass these items.

Also, when at the grocery store, we put all the heavy items together and put them through first. The crushable items, like fruit, vegetables, cakes and bread, are put through last. At the car, the crushable items are placed on the back seat or floor of the car. The heavy items are put in the trunk.

Noel Lipscombe
Brisbane, Queensland, Australia

- **Don't run in circles.** Don't zig zag all over town. Start with the errand farthest from home and work your way back.

- **Call ahead when you run errands.** Before you make the trip, call the library to be sure the book you need is in or call the video store to see if the DVD you want is available. If possible, you can request that your purchase be left at the counter so you can walk in, pay and leave. A few minutes on the phone can save you an hour or more.

- **Shop in your pajamas.** Have you ever driven all the way to the store, just to find out the store is out of the size jeans you wanted? Consider shopping by catalog or on the web. This is also a great way to comparison-shop and your size will be available most of the time.

- **List mall stops.** If you're going to a mall, indicate the exact stores you'll be stopping at and why. You'll get your shopping done in a jiffy, stress-free and without spending extra dough.

Great idea!

I find that using a dry cleaner located on my route to and from work is very convenient for cleaning my husband's suits and shirts and for cleaning my own work suits and silk blouses. My husband and I have freed up spare time by not washing and ironing as much because we don't have time in our schedules. Now, my laundry load is much lighter during the week with just the kids' clothes and towels.

Lori Pastucha
Diamond Bar, CA

- **Find your car quick.** Malls are getting larger and larger. With big malls come big parking lots. With big parking lots comes the possibility that you won't be able to remember where you parked your car.

  Always note the number of your parking spot or parking area name on an index card and keep it inside your wallet, purse or shirt pocket. If the parking lot doesn't post where you are, determine where you are parked in proximity to where the mall entrance is.

  Another idea is to tie a wide, bright colored ribbon to the top of your antenna to more easily identify your car among others.

Great idea!

I have a PDA and I write my grocery list on it under the memo pad. When shopping I delete the item after putting it in my cart. If the store should be out of something it will not be deleted and the next store or next time I go to the store it will still be there and won't be forgotten.

Another thing that can be done is to put prices next to the item so I can comparison shop from one store to another. I use my PDA all the time for writing reminders for all subjects, not just groceries. It has a To Do List that is great for that.

Shirley Truitt
Harrington, DE

- **Keep library books away from your own books.** Designate a shelf or basket in your home specifically to store books borrowed from the library. Be sure your family is aware that any books borrowed from the library and any books that must be returned to the library should be stored in that one place. You'll never have to rummage through all your books to find the borrowed ones again. The same goes for videos, audio cassettes, CDs and/or DVDs borrowed from the library.

- **Take note of the entrance.** As soon as you walk in the mall, make a written note of what store you see. When you're done shopping, you can glance at your note and determine what entrance you came in. This will make it much easier to locate your automobile later.

- **Avoid rummage sales.** If you're a pack rat or a hoarder, please avoid rummage sales at all costs. You don't need to add more clutter to your environment. Go shopping in a store instead. Since you're paying for what you're buying, you may be less apt to buy useless or frivolous items.

Great idea!

I'm always in my car, so I keep all my coupons (for department stores special discount days and product coupons) in the glove compartment. This way if I happen to be in the right location, my coupons are always with me.

Anita Dobin
Super Organizing Solutions
www.organizingbysos.com/

- **Create a virtual folder.** Most stores, when you order from their Web sites, will send you an email confirmation of the order you placed. Set up an email folder specifically for Internet order confirmations when you shop. Drag and drop these email messages into the Shopping Folder so you can refer to them when necessary. Keep each confirmation until you're sure you'll be keeping the item. If you have to return something or contact the company you purchased from for any reason, you'll have the necessary "paperwork."

- **Use catalogs and the web simultaneously.** I love to receive the JC Penney catalog each season, as well as several other store catalogs. They're fun to look at while relaxing in a rocking chair or on the sofa.

As I see items I want, I just jot them down on a sheet of paper being sure to include the page number, item number, color, size and any other pertinent information.

When I'm ready to order, I just go on the store Web site and enter the item number. The item is located very quickly and I enjoy special Internet-only discounts the stores provide.

Chapter 36

Coupons

- **Cut coupons and time.** Cut coupons while you're doing something else. This allows you to get at least two things done at the same time. For instance, you can cut while you're watching TV, while you're on telephone hold or while you're waiting for an appointment.

- **See what you already have.** If you already have several coupons for a certain product, like toilet paper or room deodorizer, chances are you don't need to cut more until you use those old coupons. Check before you cut.

- **Just because.** Don't buy grocery products just because you have a coupon. You're not saving money, if you don't use the item. I generally only cut coupons for the items I will definitely use, like paper products and frozen vegetables.

- **Dump the old.** If you have a disorganized drawer full of coupons, immediately dump the entire thing in your trash container. Get rid of the old. Start from scratch.

- **That's expired.** Prior to clipping a coupon, glance at the expiration date. If you're most likely going to need that product by that expiration date, clip it and store in your coupon organizer. If not, don't waste your time clipping it.

- **Kiddie sort.** If you have a bunch of coupons and are not sure whether they're expired or not, have your kids go through them for you. This is a nice little project for young ones who are able to determine if the date has passed or not.

- **Check dates prior to shopping.** Check all of your coupons prior to your shopping trip to be sure they're not expired. Otherwise, you'll be wasting your time and your cashier's time, at the store. One person I know actually hi-lights the expiration dates so she can see them at a glance.

- **Don't cut millions.** Each week, go through your current coupon file, for duplicate product deals. Beware of clipping doubles and triples of each product, unless you know for sure that you're going to use all of them.

- **Only clip if you use them.** Clip grocery coupons only if you use them consistently on your visits to the supermarket.

- **Have your coupons when making your list.** When you're making out your grocery list, keep your coupon organizer nearby. Pull out only those coupons you need, put them in an envelope and bring the envelope to the store.

- **Use a coupon organizer.** Coupon organizers are divided by type of grocery. When you clip, simply file your coupon into the appropriate section.

Organizing Clinic

Question

I've always had problems with coupons. I realize they can save a lot of money if used wisely. However, I've never come up with a good system of storing them for easy accessibility and readability. Any ideas?

Pam Kramer
Kent, WA

Answer

Dear Pam,

Here are a few quick ideas that may help you organize a bit to make better use of your coupons.

- **Use a coupon holder.** Look around in your grocery store, dollar store or drug store chain for a grocery store coupon holder. These are generally small books with pockets for individual coupon categories. If you can't find one, get a purse-size photo album and make your own. Simply label each photo slot. Category examples are, Baking and Baked Goods, Beverages, Canned Goods, Cereal and Breakfast, Cleaning and Laundry, Condiments, Dairy, Dressings and Seasonings, Frozen Foods, Meat, Fish and Poultry, Medicines, Paper Products, Pasta, Rice and Mixes, Personal Care, Snacks and Candy and Other.

- **Use your coupons to make your list.** When you're ready to make your grocery list, be sure you look through your available coupons. Plan your list around items that are on sale. If you see an expiration date approaching on an item you use all the time, but don't need quite yet, you may want to buy it anyway and store it away if you have the space. This way, you can take advantage of the coupon savings.

- **Make a "Favorite Stores" coupon holder.** Using the method above with the purse-size photo album, make another coupon holder organized by your favorite stores. Categories might be Walgreens, Home Depot, Target, the dry cleaner and other stores you frequent. Each photo slot is labeled with the store name and whenever you go to your favorite stores, the coupon book should go with you. This idea can be used for many other types of coupon books, such as one for your favorite restaurants or another for entertainment-type coupons.

- **Bring them with you.** Of course, in order to make the best use of your coupons, you have to remember to bring them with you when you go shopping. You might choose to store your coupon book right in your purse or possibly in your car.

- **Make it consistent.** Clip your coupons on the same day at the same time each week. This will help you to establish a routine.

- **Do a monthly sort.** Label 12 plastic, see-through bags, one for each month. Sort your grocery coupons into the appropriate month and keep all the bags in a container.

- **Use a recipe box.** You can make your own coupon organizer using a recipe box or a photo box. Use the tabbed dividers to create your own categories.

- **Let's play ball.** Use a binder and baseball card organizer sheets to organize your coupons. You'll be able to easily see what you have. Be sure each page is designated for a particular category, such as baby food or cleaning products.

- **Put an envelope on the refrigerator.** Attach a #10 envelope to the refrigerator with a magnet right by your grocery list. Then, look through the Sunday paper to determine if there is a coupon for anything you need. If so, clip it and add it to your envelope.

- **Plan meals around coupons.** Plan your meals and grocery list based on the coupons you have. This will help you save money and you're sure to use up the coupons you clipped.

- **Use your store card.** Skip coupons altogether and use your store discount card instead. No need to clip. You just go shopping and then have the cashier swipe your card at the register. Any money saved is a bonus!

- **Coupons on the web.** Make a virtual email folder to collect web coupons. When you need something, first glance in your email folder to determine if you can get a discount or free shipping.

- **Sometimes it's not too late.** Some stores actually accept expired coupons. I know of a store in Wisconsin that accepts them up to six months after the expiration date. If you don't ask, you'll never know.

- **Competitor coupons.** Many stores accept coupons from their competitors, because they don't want to lose your business. For instance, my dry cleaner in town accepts coupons from any other dry cleaning company in town. Don't be afraid to ask your local retailer if they accept other company's coupons. Generally, the competitor has to be in the same genre. For instance, many hardware stores accept other hardware store coupons and some carpet cleaners accept other carpet cleaning company's coupons.

- **Give them to the military.** Military families can use expired coupons up to six months past their expiration date. So if you have extra coupons, expired or not, you may consider sending them to someone who can use them. Since addresses change so often and I don't want to give you outdated information, I can't list these military acceptance addresses. However, just do a Google search on: *expired coupons military*. You will find many addresses and instructions.

Chapter 37

Cooking and Meal Planning

- **Stack 'em.** As you're cooking, put each ingredient on a paper plate and then stack them in the order you need them. You'll save space and cleanup will be a breeze.

- **Scoop and measure.** Keep a half-cup measuring cup in both your flour and sugar canisters. You can scoop and measure at the same time.

- **Paper plate lids.** Keep a stack of inexpensive paper plates right near the microwave to use as lids when cooking in the microwave. They'll prevent splatter and cover food better than paper towels.

- **Nifty knives.** Make sure you have a good set of knives to chop and dice. Over 25% of your time could be wasted using the wrong or dull knives.

- **Don't struggle.** Get yourself a good set of tools to grate, peel, dice, core, puree—you get the point. There's no sense spending time struggling with poor equipment.

Great idea!

When I purchase meats, I put the pack in a plastic grocery bag. That way if I freeze the meat and then thaw it, there is no mess. Plus, I have a bag right there to put any fat trimmings in. If I am opening cans or cutting up veggies at the same time, I can put all that trash in the grocery bag too. When I'm finished, I just toss the bag in the trash. It makes clean up faster and easier and it also makes for a double barrier in the trashcan to guard against smell.

Diana Cotton
Lansing, MI

- **Have an occasional take-out treat.** Once or twice a month, treat your family to take-out food and use paper dishes and cups. You will get a day off from cooking and cleaning. Keep take-out menus handy in a file folder right near the telephone.

- **Wear an apron with a pocket.** It will protect your clothing and keep small items like a pen and paper pad handy.

- **Ease your workload.** There is an overwhelming selection of pre-cut, de-boned and de-shelled items in your supermarket. They may cost a little more, but if you're not on a strict budget or you're in a hurry, the time you save will be well worth it.

- **Slip and slide.** Buy Teflon pans and/or use cooking spray on your pots and pans so that foods come off quickly, without extra effort.

Organizing Clinic

Question

Help! I have been doing very well with my organizing but my problem area seems to be food. I am single, get home pretty late and don't know how to cook many things at all. I have no energy to do so even if I did! I end up going out for fast food instead and that is putting on the extra pounds.

Are there any meals I can easily and quickly cook that aren't meant to feed a family of six and that I don't have to freeze all the leftovers? I never end up eating the leftovers anyway.

Mary
Hackettstown, NJ

Answer

Mary, while it's okay to eat fast food once in awhile, it's definitely not the healthiest diet in the world. So, it is highly recommended that you learn to prepare some simple meals that take hardly any time at all. Here are four quick ideas:

- **Slow cook.** Get yourself a crockpot and search for some quick and easy crockpot recipes on the Internet. You can spend 15 minutes preparing your dinner before you leave for work in the morning and it will slow-cook all day. When you get home later on, it will be all done.

- **Make less.** Most recipes can be cut down so you only get two dinners out of them. You can also go to your bookstore and find recipes for 1-2 serving meals.

- **Store it in the fridge for Day Two.** Leftovers that are frozen are sometimes not eaten for months, either because they're forgotten about or you think it will take too much time to defrost them. However, when you cook, you can make a double-batch and put the leftovers in the refrigerator. Most foods will still taste delicious the next day (some will taste even better) and you'll never end up with a freezer full of leftovers.

- **Enjoy a salad.** Why not spend just a few moments preparing a hearty salad for dinner? Bagged lettuce, some pre-cut veggies, cooked pasta and beans will make a wonderful salad that can be prepared in less than ten minutes flat.

- **Grill it.** Get yourself an indoor electric grill. It can cook chicken, fish, beef, pork, veggies and more in a flash. Serve up the meal with some microwaved frozen veggies and a baked potato or microwaved brown rice.

- **Make a cave.** When peeling vegetables, place a plastic grocery bag on the counter so that it's open, like a cave. Peel veggies in the bag and throw the bag away.

- **Work and toss.** Keep the kitchen wastebasket right where you're preparing food so when you open a box or bag that you can toss, you will immediately do so. This will help keep the work area clean and you'll waste less time moving unnecessary items out of the way.

- **Read and assemble first.** Before making a new recipe, carefully read through the entire recipe. Assemble everything you need first, to ensure you haven't forgotten a needed item. Once you're absolutely sure you have everything necessary, have fun creating your new dish.

- **Plan your meals with the following criteria in mind**:

  ❖ Should be well balanced and nutritious.

  ❖ Should offer variety.

  ❖ Should be within your family's food budget.

  ❖ Should fit your time and energy limits.

Great idea!

I line a cookie sheet with waxed paper and spoon out cookie dough as if for baking, but place it in the freezer instead. Since I'm freezing, not baking the dough, I don't have to worry about it spreading. Therefore, the cookie dough mounds can be very close together.

When they are frozen hard, I peel them off and place them in a Tupperware container. Since the small dough mounds thaw very quickly, we can have an impromptu treat of homemade cookies quickly and easily, without the additives and preservatives of the commercial brands.

Victoria Schellhase
Gaithersburg, MD

- **Clean as you go.** Around 50% of cooking time is generally spent waiting. Use that time to wash bowls, utensils, dishes, pots and pans.

- **Make use of waiting time.** Don't wait for your meals to be done and then set the table. Set the table completely with dishes, utensils, condiments and beverages during cooking waiting times. Better yet, enlist another family member to do so.

- **Time it.** Don't be caught in the kitchen without a kitchen timer. Always set it to sound off a few minutes before the food is supposed to be done. This will avoid burning, plus give you time to make any other last minute preparations. Look for timers that sound a warning beep ten minutes prior and then five minutes prior to the time the actual alarm goes off.

- **Make it look good.** When your meals are done cooking and you're filling everyone's plate, be sure to organize the food in a complimentary, appetizing way. Put contrasting colors next to each other. Don't overfill the plates. You can always keep extras on the table in case anyone wants a second helping.

- **Cut them up.** When preparing lots of sandwiches, make them easier to designate which is which. Cut those with mustard horizontally and those with mayonnaise diagonally.

- **Double the pleasure.** When cooking a main dish for dinner, double everything so you get two dinners out of it. Refrigerate the second portion for one or two nights later.

- **Refrigerator talk.** If you or someone in your family is on a strict diet, leave a reminder right on the refrigerator door of what can or cannot be eaten. Anyone on a strict diet should keep a journal of what they've eaten so that they can adjust their diet. Likewise, they could bring this journal when they visit their doctor to help the physician help them.

- **One-pot meals.** Look for nutritious recipes that you can prepare in one pot, such as chili or stews. Cleanup will be a snap.

> ### Great idea!
>
> Making a weekly menu list helps me enormously with meal planning and grocery shopping. Each line lists the main dish and sides for a meal and reflects what I have "in stock." If necessary, I list the cookbook and the page number where the recipe instructions are located so I (or my husband) can quickly find the recipe when needed.
>
> I cross off each meal once it's prepared. Each evening, I look at the list and decide what to make for the following night's dinner. Also, if I have time, I might pull out the cookbook and do some advance prep such as defrosting meat or chopping veggies.
>
> Kim Cramer
> Apache Junction, AZ

- **Save extra trips to the supermarket.** Extend the life of food products by refrigerating them, even if they don't require it. This works great for bread, coffee, flour and dried fruits.

- **Choose your coffeemaker carefully.** If you enjoy a cup of fresh coffee in the morning, it may be well worth it for you to get a coffee maker with a time and brew mechanism. Just fill it with coffee and water, set the timer the evening before and relax with your fresh brew the next day. An alternative is to buy coffee bags. Just place one in a mug of water and microwave.

- **Organize your cookbooks.** If you love to cook, cookbooks are a godsend. Keep them ready-to-use in the kitchen on a shelf or with bookends on a countertop. However, if you never cook and have little aspiration to do so, then donate, sell or dump those old cookbooks.

- **Quick leftover tip.** Have some frozen veggies left over from last night's dinner? Place them in a plastic bag and freeze them for later use in soups or salads. Why waste money tossing them or waste time making another trip to the store?

> ## Great idea!
>
> My husband and I both have very busy and changing schedules each week. While working on our budget, we realized we overspent on lunches everyday. To minimize the costs we began making our own. On Sundays we review our schedules and each pick a few days to be in charge of lunches. We go grocery shopping to get all our necessities.
>
> We have fun surprising each other with new meals and it has become somewhat of a friendly competition. It also allows the person with the busy schedule that day to not rush. It relieves the pressure in the morning and we have even found time to have breakfast together a day or two a week.
>
> Kristen VerHaagh
> DePere, WI

- **Nuke them.** Use your microwave for cooking vegetables while you're waiting for your main dish to finish cooking.

- **Cook early, enjoy later.** Expecting company for dinner? Cook everything in the morning or the day before. When your company arrives, warm everything up. You won't be caught running late or stuck in the kitchen while everyone else is having fun.

- **Cook only once each week.** Prepare a whole week's worth of food on one day. You'll just have to heat up your pre-made meals every other day for the week. This is a great idea if you want a healthy meal, but get home too late from work to cook.

- **Size them.** Measure your baking pans. Write dimensions and capacity on the bottoms with permanent black marker. When you're ready to bake, you'll know exactly what pan to pull out.

- **No all day roasts on weeknights.** Opt for less time-consuming meals during the week, especially if you work long hours. Pasta, sautéed chicken or grilled turkey burgers, along with some microwaved veggies are nutritious meals that can be prepared and cooked in record time.

- **Ask others to start dinner.** Have family members start dinner before you get home from work. This is a time-saver, even if it's as simple as preheating the oven, preparing the salad or dicing some vegetables.

- **Be fair but firm.** You can't make everybody happy all of the time. So don't even try. If you do, you'll run yourself ragged cooking four different dinners every night. Make it a rule that everybody must eat what you're making for dinner tonight or they can whip up something themselves as a substitute. Be firm here or you'll exhaust yourself.

- **Have everyone pick a meal.** Ask each family member in your house to give you a favorite meal idea and fill that meal in on one of the days that week. This allows everyone in the house to have his or her meal choice at least once that week.

  Note: If your youngest child chooses pancakes, that's okay. Make them healthy by adding ingredients such as blueberries or fresh strawberries. Add a side of eggs and everyone should be a happy camper.

  If your teenager chooses macaroni and cheese, that's okay too. Add black beans, broccoli and ground beef for a hearty, delicious meal for everyone.

Great idea!

Although we're Indian, my husband and I love various cuisines. This led to a variety of spices, sauces, and seasonings in my kitchen cabinet, making me thoroughly confused. I could never find the required spice immediately.

Now I separate the Indian spices from the rest and place the spice bottles, sauces and marinades in alphabetical order. Even my friends who come over for parties find it very easy to use my kitchen.

Suparna Vashsiht
Houston, TX

- **Stop sifting.** When a recipe calls for sifting lots of dry ingredients, just put all those ingredients in a bowl and stir them with a whisk.

- **Save your cookbooks.** When following a recipe, cover the pages with clear plastic report covers. If you spill something on the page when cooking, you'll be able to wipe it right off. If the cookbook is small enough, you could put the entire book—opened—right into a large see-through plastic bag and read the recipe through the bag. This is a great way to keep it clean.

- **A handy holder idea.** I'm not a big fan of kitchen sponges, but my husband likes to keep the type of sponge with the scrubby backing in the kitchen to wash pots and pans. A neat idea is to store the sponge in a porcelain napkin holder. The sponge stays out of sight and air circulates around it. While we're on the subject of sponges, you can keep yours clean and fresh by putting it in the dishwasher and cleaning it with your other things every few nights.

- **Fill 'er up.** Putting the corn in one serving bowl or plate, the potatoes in another, the green beans in another and the pot roast in yet another, can add up to a lot of things to be washed after dinner. Fill each person's dinner plate directly from the pot or pan.

- **Use a slow cooker.** Assemble the ingredients the night before and put them in the crock. In the morning, put the crock in the pot and start cooking. When you're ready to eat dinner that night, it will be waiting for you.

- **20 meals.** Have a rotation of about 20 meals. Put this on paper. If you like to try new recipes, try a new one every 21st day. Determine if you'd like to replace something in your current rotation with that new recipe or put that new recipe in an "occasional recipes" file. This will take the guesswork out of meal planning and will ensure you don't get sick and tired of the same old meals. It will be three weeks before you have the same meal again.

- **Shop the fruit and vegetable aisle.** The more you stick to this aisle, the less garbage you'll accumulate. Anything that comes in a box, jar or can will really fill up your trash can and recyclable containers.

- **Shear madness.** I find that kitchen shears are a must in the kitchen. I consider them the best tool for jobs like trimming chicken fat, cutting up green beans and snipping fresh herbs. They're also handy for cutting open plastic packages.

- **Bring home the bacon.** Frying bacon makes a mess. You're bound to end up with grease splatters. Put it in the microwave instead in between paper towels and cook until done—a few minutes. You'll eliminate the mess and the paper towels will sop up much of the grease.

- **Funnel your eggs.** Need to separate an egg? Use a funnel. Just carefully crack the egg and drop it into a funnel, with a bowl under the funnel. The white will slip out into the bowl and the yolk will stay inside the funnel.

- **Line your pans.** Line your pans with non-stick aluminum foil. When you're meal is done cooking, just crumple up the foil and toss it. No more scraping and scrubbing stuck-on food.

- **No more onion odor.** When you're done chopping onions, run your hands along a stainless steel faucet or sink. Then wash them. Bye, bye stinky, onion hands. If you don't have a stainless steel sink, run your hands on a stainless steel butter knife instead.

- **Peel later.** Peel potatoes after they are cooked. When they're cool enough for you to handle, the peels will slip right off.

- **Oh, honey.** Spray a touch of non-stick cooking spray on your measuring spoon when measuring honey or molasses. It will slip right off.

Chapter 38

Recipes and Cookbooks

- **Create a "Recipe System"** Want to finally make those recipes you've always been meaning to get to? Here's a great system:

  ❖ **Make a "Temporary Recipe Binder."** Put ten 3-hole punched pocket folders into a 3-ring binder. Label each pocket folder with one of the following categories: Appetizer, Bread, Chicken, Fish, Meat, Pasta/Rice, Salad, Soup, Vegetable and Dessert

  ❖ **The rule of 10.** Whenever you come across a recipe, put it in the appropriate pocket folder. The only rule is that the maximum number of yet-to-be-attempted recipes allowed in each folder is ten. The rest must be dumped.

  ❖ **Make a "Permanent Recipe System."** Get yourself a second binder with Index Tabs. Label the tabs with the categories listed above.

  ❖ **Make "one" new recipe.** Each week, choose one new recipe from your recipe binder and make it.

  ❖ **Is it a keeper?** Once you attempt a recipe, you must decide whether or not you're ever going to make it again. If you are, it should be transferred to your "Permanent Recipe System." If you're not going to make it again, throw the recipe away.

- **Is it worth the time?** If you have aspirations of attempting a recipe, first determine if it is worth your time and effort. If not, throw it out. If you are going to attempt it, schedule a specific date to do so on your calendar.

- **What's in it?** Make a list of all ingredients you need and pick them up on your next trip to the grocery store. The longer the list of ingredients, the less of a chance you're going to actually make it. Hint: I rarely clip any recipe with more than ten ingredients!

- **Use your computer.** If you prefer to store your recipes in a computer database, just make sure the only recipes in there are your permanent recipes. Organize each recipe into computer folders, such as appetizers, beverages, and kids meals.

- **Speed it up.** The time it takes to prepare a recipe from start to finish could be drastically reduced by using the microwave whenever possible. Check your microwave oven manual for timesaving tips.

- **Hold a "New Recipe Party" at your house.** Prepare a bunch of new recipes with your friends and family. Make each person responsible for a different portion of the meal; someone handles appetizers, another person handles the main dish and so on. You can all enjoy your new treats together.

- **Use a photo album.** A neat way to keep recipes is in a 4" x 6" photo album. Since each recipe will be protected in a plastic sleeve, you won't have to worry about damaging the recipe if you accidentally splash it. You can just wipe it right off.

- **Use a cookbook holder.** These hold your recipe open and upright so you're not straining your eyes to see it while you're cooking. It helps to keep food spills and stains off your cookbooks.

Great idea!

I had several recipes from magazines, but no way to organize them. I went to the local Dollar Store and bought photo albums. I put tabs throughout the albums, subtitling them as Appetizers, Main Dishes, and so on. These have helped me get my recipes in order and I can just flip through to see what recipe I want to try next. Plus, the covered sleeves keep the recipes protected.

Trudy Clagg
Milton, WV

- **Make a meal from that cookbook? Are you kidding me?** If you have several cookbooks, chances are there are a few that you have never tried a recipe from. This may be because all the recipes in it contain food items you can't get at your grocery store or the recipes are too difficult or too fancy. Be realistic. If you have had a cookbook for a while and have never attempted even one recipe from it, it's just taking up space you could be using for something more useful. Donate it or sell it.

- **Make a "Secret Family Recipes" cookbook.** Don't take the chance of losing that luscious apple pie recipe from Grandma Millie or Uncle Jim's spicy chili specialty. Gather all the wonderful family recipes from your family members and make a Secret Family Recipes cookbook.

Type or write each recipe on a sheet of paper. Organize each recipe by category such as main dish, side dish, dessert, etc. Type or write a few words to make a cover. Gather all the pages so they resemble a book.

Have your local copy store make several copies of your book and bind each. Give these books away to anyone in your family who wants a copy. Make several editions if necessary.

These make great shower gifts or "leaving the nest" gifts for the newest independent member of the family. You can even ask aunts and other family members to add their favorite recipes with a little note (e.g. Uncle Joe's favorite or Jan loves this one.)

- **Cookbook storage.** If you enjoy cooking, you probably have several cookbooks. If you want to keep all of them in the kitchen, consider installing some shelving. If necessary, put bookends on the shelf to keep the cookbooks from toppling over.

I only keep the one or two cookbooks that I use regularly in the kitchen. I store them on my kitchen counter in between book ends. You can do the same or store yours on top of the refrigerator, if your refrigerator is not recessed into the wall and you have sufficient space on top.

I store the remainder of my cookbooks in the guest room on the bookshelf and retrieve them when I need them. Since I only use them for occasional parties and get-togethers, I don't feel they should be taking up that valuable space in my kitchen. I keep them in the guest room, because many of our houseguests enjoy flipping through them when they stay overnight.

Great idea!

To organize recipes I print off the Internet, I take 3-hole punched, clear plastic sleeves and slip the recipe inside. I place two back-to-back and store them in a binder. When I use them, if I spill something on the page, it can be easily wiped clean. This has come in very handy.

Dorie Anderson
Powell River, British Columbia, Canada

- **Tag them.** Label spiral-bound cookbooks with tags rimmed with metal. These are often found in craft stores in the scrapbooking aisle. You can easily write directly on the tag, and then attach them to each spiral binding with a ribbon. When you need a cookbook, you won't have to pull each one out to find what you're looking for.

- **Cooking on the Web.** There are volumes of recipe sites on the Web that allow you to search for recipes. Some of these will allow you to print recipes on large sheets or 3" x 5" size, save recipes you enjoy in their online database and access them with a user name or password, print out ingredient lists that correspond with particular recipes, generate nutritional information and more. If you enjoy cooking, the Web could be a wonderful tool for you.

Chapter 39

Health and Well Being

- **Skip the escalator and elevator.** Rather than taking the elevator or escalator at work or the shopping mall, take the stairs instead.

- **Go on an active date.** Rather than meeting with a friend for lunch, consider going biking, jogging or swimming together.

Organizing Clinic

Question

I have three family members who take several prescription medications that are mail ordered (90 day supply). I also have the usual over-the-counter medications on hand, such as Tylenol, ointments and cough syrups. There are 50 bottles and inhalers bouncing around a kitchen cabinet.

How do I keep track of the meds, determine when they need to be reordered and organize them in a cabinet so we can easily find all medications when we need them?

Sharon Belisle
Grove City, OH

Answer

First, get a plastic box with a cover for each family member taking prescription medication. Each person's medication should go in his own box. It's dangerous to have all medications mixed together as someone may accidentally take the wrong one. Label each person's box with his name.

In addition, get one additional plastic box for your generic medication, such as Tylenol or aspirin and label it "Generic." Place all boxes in your cabinet. Now, instead of having all of your medication tossed in a cabinet, it will all be organized and easy to find.

To keep track of each person's medication, tape a log to the inside cover of each person's box. On the log, indicate the name of the medication(s), the dosage and when it should be taken. Finally, get a small monthly calendar specifically for re-ordering medication and indicate re-order dates as needed throughout the year. At the beginning of each month, re-order anything necessary.

- **Multi-task.** Do some calisthenics or ride a stationary bike while watching your favorite television program. Do some simple stretches while you're on the telephone and you're on hold. Waiting for the washing machine or dryer to finish or for a computer file to download? Now is a great time for some sit ups or leg lifts!

Great idea!

For organizing medicine bottles, like the small ones from the pharmacy, I have a small metal "utensil" basket that is usually used for drying utensils by the sink in a dish-drying rack. It's narrow, tall and fits perfectly in my medicine cabinet. Because it's a metal basket, you can see through it to locate each of the bottles.

Heather Hull Hart, Professional Musicial
Pasco, WA
www.HeatherHull.com

- **Commit to 10 minutes .** Schedule just ten minutes of exercise per day on your calendar. By the time the month is over, you will have exercised over 300 minutes!

- **Start a walking club.** Talk to your friends and neighbors and see if you can set up a walking club. It's a great way to stay in touch and exercise at the same time. Some of my neighbors walk together on Tuesday and Thursdays nights from 7:00PM to 8:00PM. This is a great time, because most people are done eating dinner by then, and those that have younger kids will be back in an hour to tuck them in.

- **Walk to work.** Trying to fit exercise into your day? If your work is within walking distance—less than a few miles—why not walk to work? You'll have to leave a little earlier to get there, but the fresh air and the exercise will do you good.

  If you commute to work using mass transit, get off the bus or train a few stops earlier and walk the rest of the way. If you drive to work, park a few blocks away and walk the remainder.

  When I worked in New York, I walked over 20 blocks to get to work, and 20 more blocks to get back to the Port Authority at the end of my workday.

- **Schedule an annual doctor's appointment.** Please don't skip this important appointment. Your health may depend on it. It will only take an hour or two and you'll be better informed about your health and if there's anything you need to change.

- **Stop smoking.** It's a terribly unhealthy habit. Talk to your doctor about systems you can use to quit.

- **Know your numbers.** Have your blood pressure and cholesterol checked every six months or annually. If you have any sort of problem, it may be easily corrected with a change of diet, medication or exercise. If it's a serious problem, it's best to handle it as soon as possible. Once you know your numbers, you'll know what you have to do—if anything at all.

Great idea!

I have had knee surgery and cannot get down to work in lower cabinets or the bottom of closets. I bought one of the seats on wheels that they sell for gardening. Now I can work in low places. Plus, in the compartment below, I have the supplies I need for the task at hand. Sure beats the frustration of looking at a messy space or asking others to do something I would rather organize myself.

Joyce Hopper
Helotes, TX

- **Get a pedometer.** Walking is one of the easiest ways to stay fit. Get yourself a pedometer that counts your steps. Try making 10,000 steps each day your goal.

- **Keep hydrated.** Many people get so busy that by the time they get themselves a drink of water, they're already partially or fully dehydrated. Keep a water bottle filled and nearby at all times. Get into the habit of sipping throughout the day. Set a timer to go off every ten minutes to remind you until you get into the habit of drinking water without the timer.

Great idea!

My elderly mother takes many different medications. I keep a list of all her medications and dosages in our family computer. At the top of the list I put her name, address and date of birth as well as all of her ailments and the date of diagnosis or occurrence.

Whenever we have to go to the doctor's office or to the hospital, I just print a copy of the list. When the nurse asks about medications and ailments, I just hand her the list.

One time we had to call rescue to come help my mom. I had a copy of the list waiting when they got there. We did not have to waste time talking about medications or ailments since all of the info they needed, including name and date of birth, was already on the list I gave them.

Tom Polk
Jacksonville, FL

- **Organize your medications.** If you have to take medication, organize it into medication organizers. The ones that have separate compartments for each day of the week work well. Organize your pills into the compartments and you'll always know whether or not you took your medication that day.

> ### Great idea!
>
> Taking medications has loomed as a totally unpleasant task each morning as I face fourteen pills. It seemed to take forever to get them all down. Now, I take the pills into the computer room and take them whenever there is a wait for the next step in logging onto the computer. Before I know it, my pills are gone and I have used my time at the computer without any gaps in getting something accomplished. The time seems to have flown by.
>
> Beth Fleischer
> Hacienda Heights, CA

- **Cut them up.** It's not convenient to snack on healthy foods when each time you want a stalk of celery or a piece of fruit, you have to stop everything you're doing to chop, dice or wash. When you get back from grocery shopping, take an extra 10 minutes to "prepare" your veggies and fruits.

  I first wash everything. Then anything just washed drip dries in a colander. The celery gets peeled, the bell peppers get diced and the cloves of garlic get separated from the bulb. Each item is stored in either a dish or a plastic bag and placed in the fridge.

  Whenever we're looking for something healthy to snack on, it's easily available. Plus, when I want to make an omelet in the morning, the peppers, onions and mushrooms are ready and waiting.

- **Keep a diary.** Write down the foods you eat and the exercise you do. It will help you to see the big picture, so you can assess whether or not you're reaching your health goals. You'll be able to more easily see what you need to improve on.

- **Vary your activities.** To prevent boredom, try to vary your menu and your activities each day. In doing this, you'll be more excited about keeping up with your healthy living program.

- **Keep up.** Keep up with the latest health findings. What was once thought to be "good for you," may not be the best advice after all. Scientists make new discoveries every day and it's in your best interest to know all of your options.

Chapter 40

Everyday Grooming

- **Put a mirror by the door.** If you look good, you'll feel good about yourself all day. Put a mirror by your door so you can check yourself before you leave the house. This is the perfect solution for quick lipstick touchups, combing your hair or to remove that pesky piece of parsley stuck in your teeth.

> **Great idea!**
>
> Always keep an Emery board in your purse. You'll be prepared for a quick fix if you break a nail. In addition, carry clear nail polish with you when wearing panty hose. If you get a run, put some polish at the top and bottom of the run to prevent it from getting any worse.
>
> Margie Pisano
> Plainsboro, NJ

- **Towel-dry your hair first.** After you wash your hair, squeeze out the excess water and then wrap your head in an absorbent towel. Towel-drying your hair, rather than drying it when it's very wet, will reduce your hair drying time by half. Plus, you could use that towel-drying time to do other morning tasks!

- **Get a simple, natural haircut.** Rather than having to fuss with your hair each day, get a simple, natural haircut that you can just air dry or blow-dry quickly, without the need for curlers, a curling iron or brush styling.

- **Cut down cosmetics.** If you're spending tons of time putting on cosmetics each day, determine your bare minimum. Many women can get away with just a light foundation, blush, mascara and lipstick. Save the more intricate cosmetic applications for nights out on the town.

- **Do something good for yourself.** Every single day, do at least one thing to help you keep up with your grooming. For instance, on Mondays you may clip your nails, on Tuesdays you may give yourself a home facial, on Wednesdays you can get a 10-minute massage from the salon or from your better half—and so on and so forth. You're more likely to keep up with your grooming if you spread it out.

- **Get waxed.** I've given up on the tedious task of plucking my eyebrows every week. It's too time-consuming and I hate to do it. So, I just get my eyebrows waxed every 5 weeks or so, just plucking the occasional hair if absolutely necessary. There are other types of waxing available in addition if you're interested, such as upper lip waxing and leg waxing.

- **Shave in the shower.** Not sure if this will work for guys or not—you decide if you're a guy—but if you use a disposable razor, you may want to shave while you're in the shower. I shave my legs weekly right in the shower. It gets done so quickly and I don't have to use extra lotion. If you are a guy and you need a mirror to shave, there are mirrors that attach to the shower walls with suction cups.

- **Choose your shower time.** Some people prefer taking showers in the morning and others prefer to do so at night before bed. Don't feel you're locked in either way. Choose whatever works best for you and your schedule.

- **Put a radio in the bathroom.** I find that I get done a whole lot faster in the morning if I'm listening to music. I put on the pop or country station, and I'm done with showering, dressing, hair drying and other general grooming within 40 minutes or less. I also get to hear any weather, news or traffic updates that may affect my day.

- **Use those 30 seconds.** While you're swishing mouthwash in your mouth for 30 seconds, do something else in the meantime, like setting up your cosmetics on the countertop or towel drying your hair. You don't have to stand there while you're waiting for the mouthwash to do its job.

Great idea!

As someone who sleeps until the last second every morning, my morning grooming routine can be hurried resulting in toothpaste in the sink, water splashed around the vanity surface, towels not hung back up and hair care products scattered everywhere. So, I use the top drawer in the vanity and just throw all the hair care stuff into it. It literally takes ten seconds to throw the bottles, brush and hair dryer in there and the surface is then clear.

Instead of using a standard towel bar that can look messy the second someone touches a towel, I have a coat rack mounted to the wall. I hang my bath towels on there for a maybe more casual, but "no excuses not to do" look.

Lastly, I went out and bought a paper towel holder that matched the room. Now every morning after I've gotten ready, I tear off a couple paper towels, wipe down the vanity, wipe out the sink and toss the paper towel in the trash. It takes maybe 20 seconds.

The bathroom is always ready for company and it literally only takes a minute every morning.

Amanda Gardonyi
Hamilton, Ontario, Canada

- **Use a makeup remover pen.** When applying eye shadow, mascara or eyeliner, if you accidentally smudge it a bit, don't take everything off and start over again. Just use a makeup remover pen to correct the error without disturbing the rest of your makeup.

- **The cutting edge.** According to www.free-beauty-tips.com, after shaving, thoroughly clean and dry your razor blades and then completely immerse the razor head in a shallow dish filled with mineral oil. Use rubbing alcohol to wash away the oil next time you need to use the razor. By immersing the blades in oil, you stop the oxidization process that dulls their sharp edges. A daily mineral oil soak can double or even triple the life of your cartridges.

- **Cleanse at night.** Cleanse your face and neck thoroughly before you go to bed and you won't have to do this same routine in the morning. When you wake up, just splash your face with warm water for 30 seconds or so, and you'll be good to go.

- **Shampoo every other day.** Rather than washing and drying your hair every single day, wash one day and skip the next. On the second day, wear your hair up with clips if needed to make you feel fresh. If you shower every day, you can wear a shower cap every other day so your hair doesn't get wet.

- **Put your face on, on the bus.** If you commute to work, but don't do the driving, consider applying your makeup on the bus, train or ferry. As long as you're sitting down, and you have a small makeup mirror sitting on your lap, you may be able to save time by doing this morning task on the go.

- **Wear a cap.** If you are always rushing to get your kids to school in the morning, rather than trying to get your hair fixed before the school day starts, just top off with a baseball cap. You can then take care of your hair after you drop the kids off.

Great idea!

I have four needles, each threaded with a different color thread (blue, black, white and red) on hand. I keep these on the side of my calendar so I can find them quickly if a crisis arises. If I need to sew on a button or mend a hem, I can do so quickly and easily.

Betty Arnot
Glasgow, Scotland

- **Teach your kids while they're young.** Even a child as young as 15 months old can begin to learn how to brush his teeth or comb his hair. While you'll certainly have to help out, teaching them while they're little will make them more independent. By the time they're three years old, they'll be able to handle much of their morning grooming themselves—which will free up your precious morning time.

- **Put them in the line-up.** Keep your everyday cosmetics conveniently stored in one makeup bag or basket. I usually remove everything I need and line each item up on the counter in the order I use them. Directly after I apply each, that foundation, or blush or mascara gets placed back into my cosmetics bag.

- **Do it in the same order.** If you keep your morning routine fairly consistent, you'll get done a lot quicker. For instance, I always put my makeup on as soon as I'm dried from the shower, while waiting for my hair to towel dry.

Great idea!

Fishing tackle boxes are great! I frequently participate in amateur community musical theater performances, and over the years I've accumulated quite a collection of stage makeup. A fishing tackle box is perfect for storing all this stuff. The small pots of rouge, eyeliner and other cosmetics go in the compartments on the lid and the larger things go inside. Easy to grab and go on performance night.

I also use a tackle box as my toolbox. Nails and screws are sorted by size and type in the top compartments, and my other small tools are in the bottom section. I have a different brightly colored tackle box for each, so that I don't grab the wrong one and end up with wood screws when I need eyeshadow!

Kathleen Moore
Associate Editor, Rochester Healthy Living Magazine
Rochester, NY

- **Polish at night.** I never waste time polishing my nails in the morning. Instead, I polish right before my favorite television program is on in the evening. This way, the polish has time to dry and set while I watch TV.

- **Keep backups.** To prevent running out of foundation or lipstick at the last minute, I always have a second supply on hand. The second I run out of one of my cosmetics, I immediately start using the back up one, and order my next supply.

Chapter 41

Photos

- **Double the fun.** Many film processors offer double photos at no extra charge or for a nominal fee. However, only take them up on their offer if you have a need for them, such as giving extra photos to your sister in another state, otherwise you'll end up with tons of doubles taking up space.

- **Share duplicates.** Don't hold on to duplicate photos. Either share them with friends, make a scrapbook for a loved one or give them to your kids to use with stationary or craft projects.

- **Use photo boxes.** Photo albums are wonderful, but not everyone is disciplined enough to organize hundreds or thousands of photos that haven't been organized in years. Acid-free photo boxes are a quick and easy way to get those photos organized. Get a few boxes and organize by year—or decade if this is easier. Organize your photos for ten or fifteen minutes each day until they're all in boxes.

Great idea!

My sister and I scrapbook. We have begun using those accordion style file folders—the ones that are like a case with a little clasp—to keep our specialty papers sorted neatly. We labeled each file divider by colors such as blue paper in one segment and white in another. No more looking for a certain background through a 1-inch high stack of paper. We've doubled our progress in getting our photos in order since getting the scrapbooking supplies organized.

Elisabeth and Joanna Carolan
Walled Lake, MI

- **Save only the good ones.** When you get your photos back from the processor, quickly toss those that are blurry, dark or otherwise bad. Some developers even give you credit for photos you're not happy with.

- **Bring film in.** When your done taking photos, get those rolls of film to your photo developer right away and pick them up as soon as they're ready. If you already have a drawer-full of undeveloped film, make it a point to gather all of it today and bring it in.

Yes, it's going to cost you to get this backlog developed, but perhaps it will prevent you from getting this far behind in the future.

- **Put them in albums.** If you like putting photos in photo albums, once you have your photos back from the developer, get them into albums within a day or two. It's a good idea to always have albums on hand for this purpose. Put them in the album as you're watching TV or waiting for a meal to cook.

> ### Great idea!
>
> I love having photos in albums, but for many years, I've let that chore go undone because of the many other demands while working full time, having kids, and everything else. I never had the courage to face that ever-growing pile of pictures.
>
> We have recently purchased a digital camera. There will be far less pictures to place in albums. Instead I will burn CDs of all and only make a few prints of the "best." I have also decided to start placing all of those old pictures in albums, but I am starting backwards.
>
> It is a much less daunting task to go in reverse chronological order. I just file a few packs after the kids go to bed and I am already making a huge dent in that pile.
>
> Victoria Dennis
> Berwick, PA

- **Negative energy.** Some people have boxes and photo pouches of negatives that they've never used and never will. I don't have even one negative of my past photos—and I have a lot of photos—and I've never missed them. Consider tossing your negatives or only keep those of your most prized photos. If you absolutely refuse to toss negatives, store them in their own photo album or photo box in acid-free labeled, pouches.

- **Organizing boxes of photos.** If you have several boxes of photographs in no particular order, no indication of the date the photos were taken and you wish to organize them, it can be very overwhelming.

First, let go of the idea that these are ever going to be "perfectly organized." Keep a positive outlook and get started, even if for only ten minutes each night or thirty minutes each week.

Start with one box and one box only. Try first sorting by time of your life, coming up with four or so categories such as Childhood Years, Teenage Years, College Years and Married Years.

Begin sorting your photos into these four categories only. Photos that took place around the time of your childhood years goes into the Childhood pile.

Photos that took place around your married years, goes into the Married pile. This will give you a good start.

Another alternative is to sort by events, such as Vacations, Holidays and Family Shots.

Once all of your photos are sorted into groups, you can then start your next sorting process. For instance, you may begin to go through your childhood photos, getting those into categories such as Kindergarten to Third Grade, Fourth Grade to Sixth Grade and Seventh Grade to Graduation.

It doesn't have to be perfect. Just try your best.

Once they're sorted into sub-groups, just put each category into store-bought photo boxes, making sure to label the category with an index. By the time you're done, you should have pretty organized memories.

- **Get a digital camera.** When you take a photo, you can immediately view it to see whether or not you like it. If you don't, just delete it and take it over if you wish. Ever since my family got a digital camera, we have not had even one bad shot to contend with.

- **Get the photos off your camera.** If you have a digital camera, immediately get photos off your camera after each photo-taking session and download to a CD or print them out. If you wait, they're going to build up on your camera. Remember, virtual clutter can be even worse than physical clutter.

- **Get your photos on disk.** If you don't have a digital camera, when you get your 35mm photos developed, ask your developer if he can give them to you on a CD, rather than hard copy prints. Then, view the photos on your computer instead of having to store photo albums. You can always print out the one or two photos you truly love to add to your scrapbook or a wall frame.

- **Categorize your CDs.** If you store several photos on CDs, label each CD properly and add virtual folders to each so you can locate photos quickly. For example, we have a photo CD labeled Amanda's Baby Photos.

  On that CD, we have folders for Birth, One Month Old, Two Months Old, Three Months Old, etc. We have another photo CD labeled Vacations. On that CD, we have folders named after each destination we took, such as Disney-1995, Caribbean Cruise-1996, Washington DC-1997, etc.

- **Back up.** Always have backup copies of your CDs, preferably stored in a different area than your original CDs. With electronic media, there's always a chance that something will happen to the original CD. If you have a back up, you'll never have to worry that your photos will be lost forever.

Organizing Clinic

Question

We have a large number of photos that we have come into possession from my mother-in-law. They need to be organized. Some are of family long ago and are great treasures, some we have no idea who the people in them might be. How do I organize them?

Deborah Greenlee
Spruce Pine, NC

Answer

Dear Deborah,

- **Make a weekly date.** Choose a day of the week and a specific time, to work on your photo organizing project each week. I recommend an hour if possible or 30 minutes at minimum.

- **Designate where you're going to work.** If you have a hobby room or an extra room where you can spread this project out without having to pick it up, that would be great. If not, get yourself some photo boxes or envelopes. Your project can be temporarily moved out of the way until you're ready to work on it again.

- **Determine some initial categories.** Flip through some of the photos and come up with some initial categories. In your case, the categories would most likely be timeframes such as 1931-1940 and 1941-1950. It doesn't have to be perfect. Also make an "I Don't Know Who These People Are" pile. If necessary, label photo boxes or envelopes with these categories (use sticky notes to temporarily label) and form your categorized piles inside them.

- **Divide and conquer.** Pick up each photo one at a time and put it into one of the piles. If you feel you need other categories as you go through each photo, just make them up as you go. Little by little, your photos will be combined with other photos from the same time period.

- **Then organize each pile.** Once you have all of your photos in their respective categories, choose one of those categories and begin organizing the photos in that category. You might start organizing all the photos from the '40s first. Organize them by event or perhaps holidays or people. It doesn't have to be perfect. Just make sure they're in some sort of logical order.

- **Arrange photos in photo boxes or albums.** The easiest way to store your photos is in photo boxes. Just put dividers in the boxes to separate your categories. If you're feeling ambitious, you could store them in photo albums or scan them and display on your computer or the Web.

- **If you're not sure, ask.** Pass around the photos in your "I Don't Know Who These People Are" pile, at your next family gathering. Someone who attends is bound to know. You could also scan the photos, put them up on the Web and ask family members from around the world to help you figure out who these people are. This is a great way to keep in touch with family members, while organizing your photos.

Chapter 42
Hobbies and Crafts

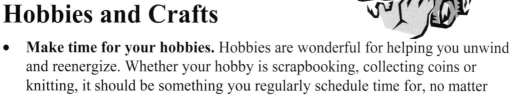

- **Make time for your hobbies.** Hobbies are wonderful for helping you unwind and reenergize. Whether your hobby is scrapbooking, collecting coins or knitting, it should be something you regularly schedule time for, no matter how busy your schedule may be.

- **Designate your hobby headquarters.** Designate a consistent, quiet space in your home to work on your hobby. By doing this, you can store all of your hobby materials in your hobby headquarters, so everything you need to use is easily accessible. Also, if you prefer to work on your hobby alone, try to make this space an area of your home where you can get some peace and quiet to work without too many interruptions.

- **Organize your stuff.** Many hobbies require lots of materials. For instance, if you scrapbook, you're probably overflowing with paper, photographs, stickers, brads, and embellishments. Scrapbooking paper can be stored in a case specifically for this purpose, organized by type of paper, color or category. Photographs can be stored in acid-free photo boxes organized by year or category, until you're ready to use them. Other supplies can be stored in clear, plastic containers, or a scrapbooking supply holder so they can be seen at a glance. The same idea holds true for any other hobby.

Great idea!

I am an avid quilter and pick up fabric odds and ends everywhere I go. The hardest thing about this is "where to store it." My grandfather often walks the junkyard and comes home with great treats. His latest find was an old baby crib. We used the two long sides and hinged them to the inside of my sewing closet door. I use the rungs as fabric hangers. Not only does it keep out the clutter, it's also a great way to recycle old furniture.

Bobbie Ann Garner
Richmond, IN

- **Put it away.** When you're done using your hobby supplies, put them back in their designated homes. Leave things strewn about and they're bound to get lost. Plus, your hobby area is going to look chaotic—which has a tendency to reduce creativity and increase stress.

- **Use an organized shopping system.** Make a list of the supplies you use when you work on your hobby. Then, make copies of this list. As you run out of a particular item, just check it off on your list. On your next trip to the supply store, bring the list with you and get everything you need. Use this system religiously and you'll always be well stocked and ready-to-go when the mood strikes.

- **Hang it up.** If you don't have a whole lot of room to organize the things you need for your hobby, use your walls. Most hardware stores have shelves you can easily attach and you may be amazed at how much extra storage space you never knew you had.

- **Store in shoe organizers.** Clear, plastic shoe organizers that hang on the backs of doors or on wall hooks, are perfect for storing several small craft items such as fabric squares or thread.

- **Think outside of the box.** Other boxes or containers you have just laying around may be the perfect storage tools for your craft or hobby items. Empty baby wipe containers are fairly large and deep and have lids. Tin containers originally meant for cookies, can double as bead holders. Large hatboxes can hold tons of yarn.

- **Go fishing.** If your hobby requires lots of small items, consider storing these things in a fishing tackle box. These are wonderful tools when you need a storage system with lots of little compartments.

- **On-the-go.** Perhaps you have a hobby that you regularly take out of your home and do on the road or at a relative's home. If so, try to get a rolling organizer that goes with your hobby. It will make it very easy for you to transport tools and materials.

- **Tote it.** A tote bag is also a nice, frugal possibility for hobbies on-the-go. Whenever you're ready to do some cross-stitching at a friend's home, just grab your tote bag and you're all set.

- **Got connections to a pizza shop?** Large, clean pizza boxes are great for storing scrapbook and other crafting papers flat, and keeping them protected from the elements.

- **Shop online.** Wasting lots of time running back and forth to the store when you need something? Tired of getting to the store just to discover what you need is out of stock? If so, save yourself a bunch of time by shopping for your hobby supplies online.

- **Get your kids involved.** Why not use your hobby as a way to get in some quality time with your kids? For instance, if your hobby is writing, perhaps your kids can be enticed to do some writing of their own and they can share what they've written with the entire family after dinner.

Organizing Clinic

Question

Since my two grown boys have moved out, I have used one of their rooms as my room. I can't seem to get the organization of the room under control. I have a large inventory of beads, scrapbook materials, pictures, craft magazines and household bills and paperwork. I just can't seem to find the best way of organizing this, utilizing the space I have and not making it look cluttered.

I have a closet with double foldout doors, a bookcase and a corner computer desk with a file cabinet in the room. But I still have to drag everything out to find one thing.

Cathy Barker
Troy, AL

Answer

Dear Cathy,

You mentioned four distinct groups: 1) beads and scrapbook materials, 2) pictures, 3) craft magazines and 4) household bills and paperwork. Here's a possible solution for each.

- **Beads and scrapbook materials.** Remove the doors from your closet and use this as your bead and scrapbook material storage area. Be sure there is enough shelving inside. If there isn't, remove what's there and install new shelving. Every foot or so, you should have a shelf and depending on the height of the closet, hopefully you can fit seven or eight shelves. Keep beads and scrapbook materials in clear glass or plastic containers on the shelves. Label each jar or container. Everything will be out in the open and at your fingertips.

- **Pictures.** I'm assuming by pictures, you mean photographs. Get yourself several acid-free photo boxes and organize photos by year, event or person into these boxes. Place the boxes on shelves or stack them on the floor. If you stack them on the floor, be sure you clearly label the front side of the box (not the top), so you can find what you're looking for without having to remove each box from the stack one by one.

- **Craft magazines.** Since you have a bookcase, this is the perfect storage area for your magazines. First, put them in cardboard or plastic magazine boxes. Then, store them in your bookcase. Organize by type of craft such as painting or woodwork, or by magazine title.

- **Household bills and paperwork.** For paperwork you're keeping, file it in the filing cabinet. For household bills, I recommend the *Get Organized Now! Easy Bill Paying System*. You can keep this system right in your bookcase and all of your pending bills and paid bills for the year, can be stored inside this wonderful little system.

Chapter 43

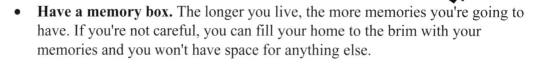

Memorabilia and Collections

- **Have a memory box.** The longer you live, the more memories you're going to have. If you're not careful, you can fill your home to the brim with your memories and you won't have space for anything else.

  Have one or two decorative boxes to store your memorabilia. It's then time to determine what you truly wish to keep and what you can do without. When these containers are full the rule is to remove and get rid of or give away, one item before you put another item inside. This will ensure only the most precious memories are stored in your Memory Box(es).

Great idea!

I use a clear glass top on my antique desk. It didn't cost much to have it cut to size, even with the notched shape of the desk.

I display stickers and souvenirs to remember. I'm a NASCAR fan and even have a bumper sticker of my favorite driver. Photos work well too. There's no clutter laying around, but the mementos are right in front of me to inspire me throughout the day. It's also a great place to put tickets so I'll remember where they are!

Cheryl Lynne Drouin
Newport News, VA

- **Make a memory quilt.** Do you have lots of clothing that reminds you of special times or special people? If so, make a quilt from scraps of each item. A quilt lets you keep the memory, without keeping the bulk.

- **Get a special case.** A friend of mine collects Precious Moments figurines and used to display them out in the open, but was always worried that something might happen to one of them. Perhaps a child visitor may knock one off the cabinet or one would fall off the shelf during a cleaning session.

  She eliminated this worry by purchasing a glass cabinet with 4 shelves. She stores her entire collection inside and no longer has to worry about any getting damaged. In addition, the entire collection is now in one place and she rarely has to clean the inside of the cabinet.

- **Keep track.** You may consider keeping a log of all your keepsakes, being sure to include the name of the item, the financial and/or historic value and whatever you know about its history. If, years from today, you pass on your collection to someone else, this information may prove to be very useful. Plus, you'll have a handy reference for yourself in the meantime.

Organizing Clinic

Question

I love to collect anything country, but I don't have any more room to put my collections that I have been keeping for all these years. I don't want to get rid of my treasures or give them away because they mean so much to me. I just want to display them somewhere in the house without having too much clutter. What should I do?

Judy Miranda
Accokeek, MD

Answer

Dear Judy,

I have the perfect solution! Just because you enjoy your collectibles, doesn't mean all of them have to be displayed every single day of the year. Choose a few treasures to display per room and store the rest in large, plastic storage boxes. Put those boxes in an out of the way area. If you need more storage space, install some additional shelving in your closets, basement or attic.

When the season or your mood changes, bring some of the stuff that's in storage out and put away some of the items you now have on display. This rotation system will keep the clutter down, but will ensure you're enjoying your collection year round.

- **Memories for generations to come.** Storage and preservation of memorabilia from the past and for the future can be held in a cedar chest. These act as "time capsules" and are generally passed from generation to generation.

  While a high quality cedar chest may be expensive, it's the perfect storage solution for treasures like your great grandmother's prized quilt, or love letters your favorite uncle wrote to his wife or old military uniforms your dad wore when he was young.

- **Consider scrapbooking.** Scrapbooking is a wonderful hobby for helping you preserve your prized photos and thoughts in a concise, organized album. Plus, you can journal your thoughts, which is very helpful in allowing you to recall what restaurant you ate in, or what city you visited, or the words your son was saying when he was two years old.

In order to keep up with my hobby, I only scrapbook my prized photos, and any other memorabilia that goes along with those photos. Since I use a digital camera, the photos I don't use are still preserved, but stored on CDs, which take up very little space.

- **Time to dress up.** Do you have lots of clothing that reminds you of special times or special people? If so, make a quilt from scraps of each item. A quilt is multi-purpose. It lets you keep the memory and it keeps you warm.

- **Use a filing system.** Some hobbies require the use of a filing system, such as genealogy research. You can keep a hanging file folder for each person or each family you're researching, along with any documents pertaining to that person, inside a portable file box. If you plan to transport your file box to the library or other research facility, be sure to get one with a lid and a handle.

Organizing Clinic

Question

My husband collects Hot Rod magazines that he can't part with. They have invaded all the drawers in our coffee table, end tables, a trunk, are stacked all over the perimeters of our bedroom floor and in boxes in the guest room. What can be done with them? He does go through them from time to time, but still won't part with the majority of them. There are year's worth and they keep coming.

Connie Burgard
Spokane, WA

Answer

Sounds like your husband really enjoys his magazines. Therefore, the last thing you want to do is ask him to get rid of them, which may cause hurt feelings. However, you can work something out with him, so that his collection isn't invading your entire home.

The best thing for you both to do is agree on a more appropriate storage system for his magazines. Office supply stores sell magazine files—which are basically holders that hold a stack of magazines. You can help your hubby organize his magazines by date into these holders and store the holders in a bookcase—or a few bookcases—specially designated for the Hot Rod magazines.

An alternative to a bookcase would be wall shelves. Your husband should like this solution as he gets to keep all his magazines, plus he will be able to find one he's looking for much quicker. As for you, yes, you'll still have to live with the magazines, but they will be contained, rather than randomly tossed about in your home.

Chapter 44

Rummage and Yard Sales

- **Not for everyone.** Rummage sales are not for everyone. They're time consuming and it's often difficult to make a significant amount of money without a significant amount of work. You're the only one who can determine if it's worthwhile to you or if your time is better spent doing something else. You can always donate instead. However, if you enjoy doing rummage sales and you become good at it, you can definitely get rid of a whole bunch of clutter and make money at the same time.

- **Check restrictions.** Some towns have restrictions on rummage sales. Check to see if your town has any regulations, such as permit requirements or sign rules.

- **Set up the night before.** Don't wait until the day of your sale to set up. If the sale is going to be in your garage, park outside and set everything up. In the morning, you'll be able to open your garage and start selling. If the sale is going to be in your driveway, at minimum, put the items in your garage so they can quickly be pulled out onto the driveway the morning of your sale.

- **It doesn't have to be all day long.** So many people think they have to forfeit the entire day when having a rummage sale. Most rummage sale buyers arrive in the morning and early afternoon hours. Try starting your sale by 7 or 8:00AM and ending it by 2:00PM.

- **Price using the color-coding system.** Rather than marking separate prices on each of your rummage sale items, use the color-coding price system. Get round, removable, multi-colored stickers. Designate a different price for each sticker—everything with a red sticker costs 50 cents, green costs one dollar, yellow costs $3 and blue costs $5.

  Place one of these round colored stickers on each of your small ticket rummage sale items. Of course, you'll have to individually price your more expensive items.

  Finally, hang a large sign that shows the colors and the prices that go with each. It will be a lot easier on you and rummage seekers will be able to see what your items cost at a glance.

- **Price each item.** An alternative to the above idea is to put an individual price on each item. Use removable labels so it's easy if you want to change a price. Plus, it will be easy for your customer to remove when she gets home later.

- **Price cheap.** If your main goal is to get rid of things and you don't have any aspirations of becoming rich that day, price your things cheap.

- **Large, multi-family sales.** If several people are involved in a rummage sale, be sure to mark each item for sale with not only the price, but also the person's initials. The person collecting the money should be keeping a log of all sales that belong to a particular individual. For instance, if there are four people selling, you'll need a legal pad with 4 columns—one for each person selling. As someone purchases the item, the appropriate amount of the sale should be noted on the log under the appropriate person's name.

- **Tell the world.** Tell everyone you know about the sale. Run an ad in your local newspaper, three days prior to your sale and the day of your sale. Put up posters and signs at nearby intersections if your town allows.

- **Rain, rain, go away.** Be prepared for rain. Either be ready to hold your sale in your garage or include rain dates in your newspaper ad.

- **Make it legible.** If you're going to bother putting up rummage sale signs, be sure they're easily read from a car passing by. This means you have to use a thick, black marker and write in big letters. Use arrows. Then, get in your car and see if you can clearly see your sign when driving past it.

- **Be specific.** Be very specific about the date and time of your sale. If you don't tell people the sale is on Saturday, June 4, from 10:00AM to 4:00PM, people may show up on your doorstep at 7:30 in the morning or 9:00 at night! You might want to indicate "No early birds" in your ad as a safeguard.

- **Involve the kids.** Let them reap some of the benefits. If their toys or clothing is being sold at the rummage sale, let them keep some or all of the profit if they help you with the sale.

- **Dress comfortably.** On the day of the sale, wear comfortable, weather-appropriate clothes and especially comfortable shoes.

- **Don't forget to eat.** Unless you're running the sale with someone else, it's going to be difficult to step inside to eat while potential customers are milling around. Eat a hearty breakfast before the sale starts. Also, make your lunch before the sale starts and put it in the fridge. When lunchtime rolls around you'll just have to run inside for a second, grab your sandwich and come outside quickly.

- **Make it inviting.** Make the atmosphere of your sale as inviting as possible. Cover tables with decorative tablecloths. Play soft music in the background. Dress nicely. Instill an air of friendliness. Have free refreshments like lemonade and cookies.

- **Sitting pretty.** Don't forget to have a chair or two outside so you can sit down and relax while potential customers are browsing. A cooler is a good idea too, so you have cold beverages for yourself on hand.

- **Categorize.** Organize items into categories such as clothing, games, dinnerware, tools, video/audio, collectibles and blankets.

- **Let's make a deal.** Make sure they're reasonable. In fact, make sure they're a bargain. Use "Buy One - Get One Free" tactics. Offer items at a volume discount.

- **Have newspaper and bags on hand.** Customers will need something to place their purchases in, so be sure to save your plastic grocery bags when you go shopping. Keep your daily newspapers for a few weeks before the sale, so you can wrap any breakable items when a customer makes a purchase.

- **Not for sale.** Try not to have items that are not for sale in the rummage sale area, but if you absolutely have to, be sure to put a "Not for Sale" sign on those items.

- **Pet patrol.** Always keep your dog in the house, behind a fence or leashed. Even if your dog is friendly, people who are afraid of dogs may be annoyed or scared if a dog is walking around.

  A friend of mine recently had a rummage sale and their dog ended up scaring the daylights out of a potential customer. The dog, although friendly, was quite large and the potential customer got so frightened that she fell over a stereo speaker. Luckily, she wasn't hurt, but she was quite embarrassed and angry—and left immediately without buying anything.

- **Do you have change?** Have plenty of change on hand—especially dollar bills, five dollar bills and quarters.

Great idea!

Keep a box in the garage or basement near the door. When you discover things that you are ready to sell to someone else at your upcoming yard sale, put those items in the box. To avoid hours of endless pricing the night before the sale, keep a pen and sticky labels right there near the box. As you put the items in the box, put the price on too.

Sharon Day
Georgia

- **Decide where the loot goes.** You will need a cash box, a fanny pack or an apron with a pocket. If you use a cash box, be very careful about letting it out of your sight. It's very easy for an unscrupulous person to pick up your cash box and leave. Fanny packs and aprons are generally safer. Rubber band $1 bills together, $5 bills together, $10 bills together and $20 bills together.

- **Accept cash only.** Cash is the easiest method for you to collect rummage sale funds. If you accept checks, also accept the fact that you may get some that bounce and you most likely will not get that money back.

- **Don't be odd.** Don't price items with odd amounts like $2.49 or $7.22. Price in numbers divisible by $0.25, such as $5.50, $11.75 or $4.00.

- **Don't store someone else's clutter.** If you hold your rummage sale with a neighbor or friend at your home, be sure that person collects anything of his that was not sold at the end of your rummage sale. Don't, under any circumstances, store his junk in your home.

Great idea!

I like to host rummage sales. To save time, I keep ready-to-use price stickers on hand. Whenever I have something that I want to put in the next sale, I think up a fair price and immediately place a price sticker on it. Then I place the items in the designated rummage sale boxes that we keep in the basement.

When I'm ready to have a rummage sale, everything is in one area and ready to be sold. I don't have to go all over the house trying to remember what I wanted to put up for sale. Since I priced everything out ahead, there's another detail I don't have to worry about.

Kathy Pankow
Hubertus, WI

- **Reduce at the end of the day.** If you don't sell it, you'll be dumping it. Towards the end of the day, drastically reduce your prices. Another alternative is giving everyone a large paper bag, and telling them they can have whatever they can fit in the bag for just $5.00.

- **Hold a pre-sale.** If you belong to a social club or your neighbors regularly shop at rummage sales, you may want to hold a pre-rummage sale the day before your actual sale, by invitation only. People tend to buy more when the sale is especially for them.

- **Make a delivery.** If you held your rummage sale specifically to get rid of your clutter, whatever is not sold at the end of your rummage sale should be loaded in your car and donated to a charitable organization. No sense bringing that clutter back into your home again.

Chapter 45

Moving

- **Use a moving checklist.** Make yourself a moving checklist outlining everything that needs to be done before and after your move.

- **Leave it behind.** Avoid moving anything you don't really need. It is expensive, time-consuming and physically unnecessary to move things you won't be using. If you don't use it now, you most likely won't use it later.

- **Get rid of clutter.** Dispose of broken tools, old toys, old clothing and other items that you no longer need, before you move. Give usable items to charity or hold a garage sale.

Great idea!

I have moved a lot over the past 10 years, and have found one practice absolutely invaluable. I make sure I take the "old" phone book with me. This has saved me lots of time, not to mention the charges for calling Information, because it never fails that there are a couple of calls I forgot to make before I left or something that I forgot to take care of. Having the phone book handy has made life so much easier.

Tricia Doane
North Conway, NH

- **Use the A-B-C system.** Everything you pack does not have to be unpacked the first day in your new home. If it contains essential items, mark it Priority A. If the contents are important, but not crucial, mark the box Priority B. If the box contains out of season items, holiday items and other things you won't need right away, mark the box Priority C. Unpack in A, B, C order.

- **Mark it.** Felt pens are ideal for marking boxes with information such as its contents, destination room, fragile or this side up.

- **Don't skimp on your moving service.** Choose an experienced moving firm with an established reputation for good service and reliability. Choosing someone that is unreliable or inexperienced will waste more time and money than you can imagine.

- **Enlist any help you can get.** You will get a lot more done, with some family members and friends helping you pack and/or unpack. If your children are old enough, they should be helping too.

- **Box it.** Get boxes in assorted sizes. Be sure they're clean, in good condition and have covers so they can be closed and sealed with tape. Start collecting them from your local merchants or purchase them from your moving company.

  Liquor boxes are excellent. They are sturdy and contain dividers making them ideal for packing drinking glasses, goblets and vases, but make sure these boxes have lids.

  By the way, an easy way to store boxes so they do not take up storage space is to open both ends and flatten them out. Cartons can be resealed with tape as you use them.

- **Wrap it.** You will need plenty of wrapping paper and heavy-duty tape. Anything wrapped in newsprint will most likely be soiled from the ink and will require cleaning after unpacking. Movers use unprinted newsprint. For items you prefer to keep clean, you can purchase this packing paper from your mover.

  Kraft paper, tissue paper and shock-resistant corrugated paper make excellent wrapping materials and may be purchased at most major department stores, craft stores or your mover. These papers also make excellent cushioning and lining material.

- **Label it.** As you're packing, place removable, colored, circle stickers on your boxes to easily distinguish kitchen items, from bedroom items from bathroom items. Use a different color for each room.

  If necessary, make a master list so you'll know what is in each box. If you can go to your new home ahead of time, you may wish to stick a corresponding colored sticker (removable stickers only please) on the door or doorframe, of the room that the box will be delivered to.

- **Lighten up.** Cartons can be handled easier if they do not exceed 50 pounds fully packed. Keep this in mind when you're packing.

- **Pack room by room.** Pack on a room-by-room basis, keeping the contents of each room in separate boxes. This will eliminate confusion and save time when you're unpacking.

- **Pack early.** Even if you only pack two boxes a day, in thirty days you will have packed sixty boxes. Start in areas where the goods are not in frequent use such as the cellar, attic and garage.

Organizing Clinic

Question

My house has been a living nightmare for years. I have too much stuff. Now, I'm moving and am paralyzed even thinking of this. How do I start getting rid of things now when it is an emergency? To make it even worse, I'm moving 1,000 miles away to Florida where there are plenty of bugs to get into junk! I have been buying Rubbermaid by the bulk, but I can't keep doing that. I don't need everything I have. One big problem is paper and craft supply items. Help!

Debbe
Washington, PA

Answer

Debbe,

Congratulations on your pending move to the Sunshine State. It's the perfect time for you to get organized. You definitely do not want to move your clutter with you. Here are a few quick ideas:

- **See the opportunity instead of the problem.** Put yourself into a different state of mind. Rather than concerning yourself about your current state of disorganization, focus on how much more organized everything is going to be in your new home. Every time a worry creeps up, chase it out of your mind with that organized visual.

- **Start tagging.** Every time you use something in your home for the next two weeks, put a sticky note on it. Anything without a sticky note at the end of the two-week period is a prime candidate to be considered for your donation box or trash bin.

- **Get someone to help.** Ask someone who is very organized—a friend, relative or professional organizer—to help you try to get rid of at least 25 percent of your stuff. As the person raises his or her eyebrows at the bread machine you never use, the dozen glasses caked with dust and the exercise machine covered with cobwebs, it will be a lot easier for you to part with.

- **Limit your paper and craft supplies to one box.** Take one of those large Rubbermaid containers you just purchased (size approximately 3' x 1' x 1') and use it to store your paper and craft supplies. Limit yourself to just this one box and donate the rest to charity.

- **Say goodbye to winter.** Except for a sweater or two and a few outerwear items that you may want to use if you travel someplace cold, give away the rest of your winter clothes. You're moving to warm weather now. You don't need them anymore. Of course, this also means other winter items like shovels, heavy blankets, comforters and so on.

- **Look at the smaller picture.** Rather than seeing this move as one huge project, look at the smaller picture instead. Tell yourself you're going to toss for 15 minutes each night, until you're done. Work in one room at a time. Within a few weeks, your load will be much lighter.

- **Order address labels.** Order address labels before you move into your new home. They will be great to have on hand when you need to indicate a change of address on anything. Leave a few behind with the people who move into your old home or apartment so they can forward anything that gets delivered to them for you. Give them a few bucks to cover any postage costs.

Organizing Clinic

Question

Currently, my husband and I are living in a very small apartment. A love seat and a recliner fit arm-to-arm and wall-to-wall across the width of the living room. We have one closet and we are not allowed to hang up shelves. Needless to say, our apartment is full of clutter and disorganization. We recently found a bigger apartment and we are preparing to move in a couple of weeks. I do not wish to continue our disorganized habits into the new apartment. How do I go about making the move an organized and a smooth process?

Jennifer Weaver
Denver, PA

Answer

Dear Jennifer,

Sometimes a move can be a blessing for getting rid of current clutter. First of all, you definitely don't want to carry your clutter from your old apartment to your new apartment.

What you need to do right now is simplify your possessions. I always recommend this rule: if you don't love it and/or you don't use it regularly, it's clutter. Go through each of your items. If it meets the clutter criteria I just described, donate or dump those items. Try to lighten your load by at least 25 percent, if not more, BEFORE you move.

I'm not sure if you will be able to hang shelves in your new apartment or not. But even if you can't use shelves, you can use portable storage systems that don't require installation, like plastic containers and cabinets. There are even plastic cabinets with drawers. These can be stored in a closet or if closet space is at a premium, even right out in the open. They're neat and can help you keep your stuff organized.

If you're planning to buy new furniture, keep both form and function in mind. You can get beautiful furniture that has lots of storage space. For instance, rather than getting a coffee table, consider an ottoman with inside storage. Instead of an open end table, think about an end table with drawers and shelves. You get the idea.

- **Make a survival kit.** Make a survival kit for your first night in your new home. This should include items that will get you through the night if it's too late to unpack or the movers didn't show up.

  Helpful items to include might be non-perishable food, a can opener, paper plates, plastic utensils, bottled water, a flashlight, a few towels, sheets, toiletries, a blanket, toilet paper, pen/paper, a few small games or magazines and a change of clothes for everyone.

> ## Great idea!
>
> We recently moved into another house. To make the move somewhat less of a chore, I color-coded the move. Each room had a color and the box that contained stuff for that room had a color chip right on the box. I also wrote on a sheet of paper the contents of each box. The head mover received a copy of my color chart and my husband and I also had copies. I also had a color board at the new house, so if there was any doubt as to where the boxes went, the movers could refer to the chart. It worked very well. The movers thought it was the best idea they had ever seen.
>
> Josephine Dutchak
> Saskatoon, Saskatchewan, Canada

- **Have someone watch the kids.** If you have children, especially young children, it might be a good idea to have someone babysit them while you are doing anything that involves your move, such as packing or unpacking. Your kids won't be interrupting your progress and you'll accomplish more.

- **Use the one room rule.** Set up one room in your new home as quickly as possible. You'll have a quiet retreat that is free of boxes. You and your family will then have a place to go when you need a break from all of the unpacking activities.

- **Make it pet safe.** If you have pets, be sure you have a plan for when the movers arrive. Perhaps keep your cats in the bathroom with the litter box and the toilet seat down or put your dogs in a fenced in yard.

  Also, take care to do what you can so your pets feel comfortable in your new home. Bring their favorite toys, give them attention and don't leave them alone for long periods of time for the first few days.

- **Make the first night special.** Make the first night in your new home as special as possible. It can be take-out Chinese food or pizza, but you may sweeten the evening with flowers, candles and music. It will really make a big difference and will help you to unwind and de-stress.

- **Devise a plan.** Before you begin unpacking randomly, sit down with your family. Discuss a plan, including where things will go and who is responsible for what. It will help things run smoothly.

- **Have a tool kit on hand.** One of the most important things to have on hand when you're setting up your new home is a basic toolbox that includes a hammer, screwdrivers, nails, hooks and other basic hardware items.

- **First things first.** It is best to first arrange your furniture and then unpack accessories and personal items.

- **Get ready for bed.** As soon as the bedroom furniture is delivered, set it up and put the sheets on the bed. You'll be grateful that everything is ready for sleeping later that night when you're really tired.

- **Let everyone know.** Inform everyone that you've moved with simple "We Have Moved" postcards or email. Include your new address, your new phone number and perhaps directions to your new place.

- **Get acquainted.** Once you arrive at your new home, schedule some "get acquainted" days on your calendar. This is a great time to figure out where the supermarket, bank, post office, and other local businesses are and will give you a chance to get familiar with your area. If there is a tourist bureau in town, stop by and see what events and opportunities your town will be offering. Your town may also have a "Welcome Wagon" program for you.

- **We're moving . . . again.** Some families move quite often. Certain jobs, such as military careers, require frequent transfers. If this sounds like your family, it's even more crucial for you to simplify your possessions. When you buy furniture, don't buy the heaviest there is. Buy multi-purpose furniture so you have less to move from place to place. Limit decorative items. Decorate with neutral colors. If you decorate like this you won't have to buy new things every time you move.

- **Kids are people too.** Moves can be difficult on children. Be sure to do what you can to make your kids feel at home in their new community. Help them get acclimated to their new surroundings. Get friendly with new neighbors, especially those you notice that have kids in the same age group as your kids. Allow them to sign up for activities they're interested in, even if it makes it a bit difficult on your schedule. Be patient with them and give them time to get used to the idea of a new home.

Chapter 46

Parties

- **Schedule in advance.** If you're holding a fairly large party, such as a bridal shower or a baby shower, schedule it at least one to two months in advance. Please be sure to verify that the guest of honor is available on that day—don't laugh. I've been to two surprise parties where the guest of honor could not be there.

- **Index cards can be a lifesaver.** Get some index cards and write an event topic on each card. For example, let's say you are planning a party. You might have one index card for each category. Example: Card 1: Invitations, Card 2: Food and Card 3: Music. Jot down steps to be done on each topic card.

  If you're planning a party that other people are helping to organize, perhaps you can give a card to each person. Each person's responsibilities are on their own individual card.

- **How many?** Don't invite more people than your home or the facility you're holding the party at will hold. Nobody likes to be stuffed into a room like a sardine. Plus, it's a safety hazard.

- **You're invited.** People should receive invitations to small events like birthday parties and picnics at least three to four weeks prior to the event—or a few months ahead for a wedding or very large event. You can now buy beautiful, blank invitations that you can run right through your computer inkjet printer, which means no need to write out every single invitation one by one. Give people at least a week or two to RSVP.

- **Use place cards.** Before guests arrive, organize where each guest will sit by putting place cards on the table. If you're going to be getting up and down to serve, make sure your chair is the one closest to the kitchen.

- **Plan meals early.** Carefully plan your party meals at least a week or more before the party. Don't forget to ask your guests about diet restrictions or make sure you have a variety of foods to choose from.

- **Make a checklist.** Don't leave all those details to memory alone. Create a "Party Checklist" and ensure everything is taken care of.

- **Gather everything before guests arrive.** Take plates, bowls, glasses, utensils and coffee cups out in advance. You'll be sure to have everything you need within arms reach, without having to fumble while your guests are waiting.

- **Use a tray.** When having a dinner party, instead of making several trips from the kitchen, use a tray. If you have lots of food to carry in and you hold parties often, consider using a rolling cart.

- **Don't under-do or over-do it.** Planning food for a crowd? To avoid wasted time and a refrigerator full of leftovers, use this guide. Just multiply the individual serving size by the number of guests—or servings—you anticipate:

  - ❖ Appetizers ....5 pieces (1/2 cup)
  - ❖ Meat/Poultry/Fish ......4 ounces
  - ❖ Side Dishes.................1/2 cup
  - ❖ Condiments ....2 teaspoons (mustard, mayo, etc.)
  - ❖ Dips............................1 tablespoon
  - ❖ Ice Cream ....1/2 cup

- **Have a rain plan.** If you're planning to have your party outside, come up with a plan in case of rain. Can it be moved inside? Perhaps you might rent a tent. Should you set a rain date?

- **Use paper.** If you're just having a casual party—such as a Super Bowl get-together or children's birthday party—consider using paper plates and cups. Clean up will be a breeze.

- **Make a record.** Keep a journal of the parties you host. This is great for future reference to avoid serving or wearing the same thing next time you entertain the same guests. Some items to include:

  - ❖ Meal/dessert you served
  - ❖ Type of party (formal, casual, theme, etc.)
  - ❖ What you/other family members wore
  - ❖ Names of your guests
  - ❖ What your guests brought
  - ❖ Special diet restrictions
  - ❖ Party favors

- **Have it catered.** If you don't have to take the time to make everything from scratch, have your meal catered. You can always add your own personal touch with dessert or party favors.

- **Prepare meals ahead of time.** If you make everything the day before, it will just have to be heated up the next day when your guests arrive. The host or hostess shouldn't have to be stuck in the kitchen, while guests are present and having fun.

- **Have a BBQ.** Instead of holding an indoor party, consider an outdoor barbecue. There's less to clean up later and less to prepare beforehand.

- **Bring a dish.** Rather than making everything yourself, ask everyone to bring a dish to pass. You'll end up with a nice variety of food. Consult with people about what they're bringing, so you don't end up with four fruit salads or all desserts and no main dishes.

- **Decorate and set the table.** The day before your party, decorate and set the table. You'll have enough to do on party day without having to worry about getting the room in order.

- **Get a babysitter.** If you're holding an adults-only party, get a babysitter to watch your children for a few hours. You won't have to tend to your guests and your kids at the same time.

- **Make an itinerary.** When holding a children's party, come up with a planned schedule of events so the kids don't get bored. Consider various games like a dancing contest, time to eat, time to open presents and story time. Make an agenda and review it with everyone at the beginning of the party. Everyone will know what to expect and look forward to.

- **Names and games.** If you have a party where the guests don't know each other, consider nametags and ice breaker games. Everyone will feel more comfortable and have a better time.

- **Get a head start.** Always start your party with an empty dishwasher and an empty trash can. This will ensure you don't end up with a sink full of dishes and an overflowing trashcan at the end of your party. If you're holding a big party, you may have to run the dishwasher cycle in the middle of the party and/or empty out the trashcan.

- **Don't cry over spilled milk.** In case something doesn't work out exactly as expected, make do. If you burned the roast, order out for pizza. If the dog ate the beautiful cake you just baked, pick up a store bought one. Bring the party inside if it rains. You get the picture. Don't get annoyed at something you can't change. Make the best of every situation.

- **Give away the food.** If you end up with tons of food after the party, and you know your family will never be able to eat all the leftovers, hand out doggie bags to your guests as they're leaving. Always keep inexpensive, disposable containers with lids on hand.

- **Get a clean-up crew.** Assign after-party clean-up duties to a group of people. Clean-up will be quicker and you won't get exhausted doing it all yourself.

Chapter 47

Cold Weather Organizing

- **Take inventory of your winter wardrobe.** This winter, plan to be prepared and look your best. Take an inventory of your winter coats, jackets, scarves, hats, boots, gloves and winter underwear. Is everything in good shape or do you need to let go of some well-worn gear for some new warm apparel? Does everything match or is your inventory made up of a red jacket, brown boots and blue gloves? Be sure you have warm, practical choices for work and cozy fashionable choices for casual winter weekends.

- **Initiate the seasonal equipment switch.** Prepare to hibernate your lawn, garden and barbecue paraphernalia for the winter. Be sure everything is hosed down and prepped for the cold months ahead so that you'll be ready for the first thaw in spring. Drain and store your hoses. Remove gasoline from mowers.

  At the same time, get your winter equipment ready. The snow blower should be ready in a pinch when the first snowflake falls. Get it serviced early if necessary. Be sure you're equipped with a shovel, salt, firewood and anything else you need.

- **Winterize the house.** Check your furnace filter and change if necessary. If it's still in good condition, temporarily remove the filter to suction off any dust with a vacuum. Cover your air conditioner to prevent drafts and to protect the unit.

  Inspect the fireplace and flue. Have them serviced. Browse around for drafty areas like doors and windows and seal them. Check the chimney to be sure it's clear. Check smoke detectors and change batteries.

- **Get the car ready for Jack Frost.** Check your vehicle's anti-freeze, hoses, snow tires and so on to be sure it's ready for Jack Frost. While you're at it, stock some winter vehicle apparatus in your trunk, such as an ice scraper, a portable shovel and emergency gear such as a warm blanket, a flashlight, motor oil, a compass, jumper cables, emergency lights and some non-perishable snacks. When you're out on the road this winter, be sure to carry along your cell phone. It can be a lifesaver!

- **Grill it. . . inside.** When it's just too chilly for your liking to grill outside, it's time to whip out your indoor electric grilling machine. Who says barbecuing is only for the warm months? Warm up your body and soul by grilling those wonderful dishes inside. Grilled chicken, ribs and burgers, along with grilled veggies make wonderful dinner choices for the frosty season.

- **Get in shape.** What are your exercising plans for the season? If you're a winter-outdoors type of person, you might opt for some winter sports, such as skiing, hockey, football or snowball fights with the kids. If you are an indoor type of person, perhaps you'd rather use the treadmill or exercise bike, go bowling or play racquetball at your local club. Use Ol' Man Winter to get in shape this year for your health and well-being. Just remember to avoid over-exertion in winter months. Your heart is already working hard in the cold to keep your body warm.

- **Stock up on food.** It's a drag to leave a toasty warm house to trek over to the supermarket in a snowstorm or blizzard. Reduce those errands and spend more time indoors by stocking up on foods for the winter. Buy and freeze meat, chicken and seafood. Hoard winter veggies and store them in your basement freezer. Get plenty of canned goods and fill up your cabinets. Don't forget about stocking up on medications too.

- **Make plans for winter outings.** Start surfing the net for some winter outing ideas to enjoy with your family and your friends. Take advantage of those off-season vacation deals. Plan to do something you haven't done in awhile that reminds you of your childhood such as sledding or ice skating. Get tickets ahead of time for those holiday events. Surprise your significant other with a weekend trip to a cozy bed and breakfast to relax and rejuvenate.

- **Light up the fire and your mind.** Think up some fun ideas to do while you're relaxing in front of the blazing fireplace. Reading, with the sound of a crackling fireplace in the background and a hot cocoa by your side can be delightful. Gather board games like Scrabble, Pictionary and Scattegories and place them all in a large covered basket. Make an appointment with your family at least one day a week to enjoy one of these games together. Cuddle up with your spouse in front of the flames, wrapped in a warm blanket and talk about your dreams and plans with each other.

- **Work on a project you've been meaning to get to.** Winter is the perfect time to begin working on that pending project. Perhaps you've been meaning to build a workstation, organize your office, straighten out the basement or start a home business. There's never a better time than the present to begin listing some goals and making a daily go of it.

- **Spring ahead, fall back.** When you adjust your clocks twice each year, check smoke and carbon monoxide detectors and weed out expired medicine. Make a list of spring and fall duties to handle when you spring ahead or fall back one hour.

Chapter 48

Spring Cleaning

- **Different task each day.** Make yourself a schedule that is comprised of one hour and one task each day. Your schedule may look something like this:

  Monday: Uncluttering
  Tuesday: Dusting
  Wednesday: Vacuuming
  Thursday: Scrubbing
  Friday: Organizing and Rearranging
  Saturday: Laundering
  Sunday: Decorating

  Then, spend one hour each day doing your assigned task for each room throughout your house. You'll be amazed at the difference you can make in your home by following this simple system.

- **Use the proper tools.** When cleaning and organizing, it's important to use tools that help you get the job done as quickly as possible. For instance, there are now dusting cloths that allow you to dust quickly and easily, without any additional sprays. Just dust and be done with it.

  Rubber gloves will help you deep clean, without drying out your hands, exposing them to harsh chemicals or burning them in hot water. Racks can hold mops, brooms and other cleaning supplies in one organized place, rather then storing them loose and having them constantly tip over. An apron with lots of pockets, can help you transport cleaning products from room to room easily, so you don't have to keep running back and forth to get what you need.

- **Donate or sell.** If you have items that you don't use, but are in good condition, they are prime candidates to sell or donate. Gather all of these items together in boxes or plastic bags. Then, decide whether you would prefer to donate them or sell them. If you choose to donate, consider giving them to your local Salvation Army or perhaps even a shelter or orphanage in town. Many of these organizations will even pick up your donations for you. If you choose to sell, you might set a date for a yard sale. You could even take some photos of these items with your digital camera and put them up for sale at an online auction Web site.

- **Make it fun.** Don't think of it as a chore. Instead, think of it as a "feel good" exercise—one that will really help you to feel good about yourself and your clean and organized environment. Play some lively, fun, upbeat music. Dance your way through your home or office with your dust rag or vacuum. Get the family involved. Give everyone a task and then do something relaxing afterwards, like watching a movie together or going to the park for a walk. Set timers and play "beat the clock." Give yourself time limits for completing small tasks and try to complete those tasks before the timer goes off. Ask a friend to help or do a swap. You clean her living room if she'll clean your kitchen.

- **Eliminate distractions.** Turn off the TV while you're cleaning and organizing and let your answering machine field your calls. If a friend stops by while you're working, simply tell him/her that you've scheduled this time for spring cleaning. He or she is free to stay, as long as you can continue working. Perhaps, you might even get some help.

  If not, tell your friend you'll stop by his or her house later on when you're done. If you have kids, give them their own jobs to do or at minimum be sure they're occupied with something else. The quickest and best jobs are accomplished when there are no distractions.

- **Make yourself a checklist.** Make a checklist of all springtime jobs that you only do once or twice a year. Perhaps you might take your large comforters to the Laundromat, take your drapes and winter coats to the dry cleaners, store your winter clothes and bring your warm-weather clothes out of hiding, or check the smoke detectors. If all of these odd jobs are on a list, you won't forget to do them. Try to do at least one or two of these odd jobs per week, throughout spring.

- **Don't forget about the insides.** While it's important to clean and organize things that are in sight all of the time, don't forget to clean and organize the areas that are out of sight. Spring is a great season to organize your closets, cabinets, drawers, bins, boxes, pantry and other inside storage areas. Give yourself that spring feeling, both inside and out.

- **Enjoy the weather while you're working.** Do some outside organizing and yard work, so you can be accomplishing something, but also enjoying the nice weather at the same time. Gather your gardening and planting supplies in one place. Replace old and broken tools. Perhaps you might even get a gardening caddie to store your good gardening tools. Clean the garage. Keep the garage door open while you're cleaning and enjoy the nice weather.

- **Open your windows.** There's nothing like taking in a breath of fresh air. As you're cleaning, open the windows. You'll be removing musty winter odors, protecting yourself from inhaling harsh cleaning product fumes and the fresh air will keep you going. While you're at it, let the sun shine in. Open curtains and drapes to give yourself plenty of light for an energy boost.

Chapter 49

Cards and Gifts

- **Once each month.** Buy cards for birthdays, anniversaries and other recurring events at the beginning of the year. Each month, on the 20th of the month, send out all greeting cards for the following month. Receiving one early is much better than receiving one late or not at all.

- **Make a birthday binder.** You'll need a two-inch, three-ring binder, 12 pocket folders and 12 index cards. Fill your binder with 12 pocket folders. Label the first pocket folder JANUARY, the second FEBRUARY and each following month accordingly through to DECEMBER.

  Tape an index card to the front of each pocket folder. On the January pocket folder's index card, write all of the January birthdays you wish to remember. Write the person's name and birthday. Do this for the remaining index cards.

  When you purchase or make your greeting cards, insert them into the proper month's folder. You can buy a whole bunch of cards at the beginning of the year if you wish or every few months, so you don't have to keep running back and forth to the store.

  Finally, choose one day each month as your Birthday Card Mailing Date and write that date on your calendar. Make the date consistent each month and send all the cards for the next month out on that date. For instance, send all your April cards out on March 26th and send all your May cards out on April 26th.

- **Kids parties.** Buy three or four videos, books or games for your children to give as birthday gifts when they are invited to parties. Wrap and stick a sticky note on each to indicate anything important, such as "Girl's Craft—Ages 7+." Store until an occasion arises to use that gift.

- **Ask the person.** When I'm not sure what to buy, I just ask the other person if there's something special they may like or perhaps ask about a subject they may be interested in such as scrapbooking, photography or history. Although some people may be really opposed to this idea because the gift is not a total surprise, it really ensures that I never waste time, money or energy buying something that is just going to be tossed in a dark closet forever.

- **Ask family or friends.** If you don't want to ask the actual recipient for his or her choice of a gift, ask their family members or friends. They may be able to give you the perfect idea.

Great idea!

To simplify gift wrapping and gift wrap storage, I only buy white ribbon and all-occasion paper that will look good with white ribbon. If there's a ribbon sale, I can stock up on white. If I pick up new gift wrap, I know I'll have ribbon at home that already matches.

Sara Heard
New York, NY

- **Please, no clutter.** Ask for gifts and give gifts that don't clutter. There are lots of great choices including dinner gift certificates, theatre tickets, music lessons or a day at the spa.

- **Get it now.** Rather than trying to find the perfect gift at the last minute, when you see something in a store that you know someone would just love, pick it up now and store it until his or her birthday or for another appropriate occasion.

- **Make a list.** Make a list of people who you always send special occasion greeting cards to. Then, buy a year's worth of cards at the same time. You will definitely save time and you may be able to save money by buying in bulk. You can even address the cards the same day if you like.

- **Buy extra cards.** Buy additional, general greeting cards for unexpected occasions—birthday, anniversary, thank you, get well, graduation—in bulk so you'll always have them on hand.

- **Keep a gift log.** Make a written log indicating people for whom you frequently purchase gifts. Include their name, clothing sizes, hobbies, favorite colors and any other information that will make it easier for you to buy a gift for that person when a special occasion rolls around.

- **Jot it down now, remember later.** When you think of a great gift idea, but you don't have time to buy it immediately, jot the idea down in your gift log. You won't forget what your idea was when you're ready to buy it.

- **Use a card notebook organizer.** Consider a greeting card organizer to organize cards for birthdays, anniversaries, holidays and other events. This looks like a notebook, except that each page has a pocket to hold cards for a specific month. There is usually space for you to pencil in events for that month. Since you can easily see what's coming up, you'll never send out a greeting card late. Plus, you can buy cards ahead of time and store them in your organizer until the date rolls around.

- **Get a greeting card box.** This is an alternative to the greeting card notebook. It's basically a box containing categorized index dividers that holds many cards for many occasions.

- **Be prepared if mailing from the store.** If you're planning to have a gift wrapped and mailed directly from the store, be sure to indicate your recipient's name and address on your gift list to give to the store clerk. You can even make out a personalized card at home and have the store clerk include it in the box before he or she wraps the gift so you don't have to spend extra time or postage mailing the card separately from the present.

Great idea!

Do you have a hard time getting that birthday card to your sister before her birthday? Write anyone's name you want to remember on a sticky note with his or her birth date. Have one sticky note per month and put that note on the coordinating month. When the first of the month rolls around you can put the sticky note in your purse as you go to the store and buy all cards for that month. Save the sticky note and put it at the end of the calendar to be placed on next year's calendar. That way you will never have to write those dates on your calendar again!

Deitra Shoemaker
Buford, GA

- **Shop on the Web.** Save time by doing your gift shopping on the Internet. Order books, candy, flowers, CD's, toys and more in minutes—without leaving the comfort of your home.

- **Department store treat.** Can't think of what to buy for that person who has everything? Don't waste time or money trying to come up with something your recipient may or may not enjoy. Just get them a gift certificate to a major department store. They'll be able to choose what they prefer.

- **Give your time.** Time is one of the greatest and most precious gifts to give. Instead of giving expensive gifts, consider visiting a friend or loved one for an hour or a weekend.

- **Hide N' Seek.** Hide gifts well so wandering eyes can't snoop, but make sure you jot down a note to yourself as a reminder of each hiding place. Keep this note in a secure place, such as a filing cabinet with a lock or a password-protected file on your computer.

- **It's a wrap.** Keep wrapping paper neat and organized by using a wrapping paper holder. An alternative is to use an umbrella stand to store each roll.

- **All wrapped up.** Don't waste time wrapping the gift yourself. Get it done in the store whenever possible, especially when it's offered free of charge.

- **Keep the 3 P's of effective gift giving in mind:**
  - ❖ Planning
  - ❖ Personalization
  - ❖ Price

- **Fun combo ideas.** Organize homemade gift baskets for family and friends. Here are some fun combinations:
  - ❖ **Italian Dinner Basket.** Bottle of red wine, box of pasta, container of Parmesan cheese, bag of mixed lettuce, bottle of Italian salad dressing, loaf of Italian bread and assorted imported candies.
  - ❖ **Take Me Away Basket.** Relaxation audiocassettes, bath salts, aromatherapy candles, lotions and assorted soaps.
  - ❖ **Children's Birthday Basket.** A few travel-sized games, a stuffed animal, some McDonald's gift certificates, a box of animal crackers, a bag of M&M's™, a book or video.
  - ❖ **Housewarming Basket.** Pretty dish towels, oven mitt, refrigerator magnets, copy of Better Homes & Gardens Magazine, potpourri and candles.
  - ❖ **Especially For Him Basket.** Shaving cream, shaving lotion, a copy of Sports Illustrated and TV Guide, microwave popcorn, a video and a new tool.
  - ❖ **Movie Buff Basket.** Microwave popcorn, cans of soda, a video or DVD, movie tickets and some favorite candies.

- **Don't go overboard.** When you receive a gift you don't like, certainly be polite and say thank you. But don't go overboard saying you just love the item. If you do, the person may give you the same thing next year.

- **Exchange them.** Don't hang onto gifts you're never going to use. Immediately exchange them for something you could use. If the original gift giver asks you later, you might say, "That outfit was nice, but didn't fit, so I exchanged it for something just as lovely" or "I really appreciate the new knitting needles you gave me, but I had a pair so similar in my collection that I decided to exchange them for this wonderful new yarn, this way your gift is used each day!"

Chapter 50

Keeping in touch

- **Start a forum.** Start an online networking forum—a.k.a. message board—to exchange ideas, tips, recipes and thoughts, rather than spending time on the telephone. Everyone can post and read messages when convenient to them. It's more cost effective and less time consuming.

- **Contact them today.** Having trouble staying in touch with your good friends? Don't let them slip away. Schedule an appointment to call, write or email them on a consistent basis. Work it out with them so that you contact them one month and they can contact you the next.

- **Use a web cam.** We live in Wisconsin and are able to call our friends in Vegas from our computer. When we're connected, we can see them and they can see us! Web cams are the future. Why limit yourself to only hearing your friends and family when you can see them too?

- **Use a reminder service.** If you have a computer, a great way to remember birthdays of friends and relatives is to use a reminder service. There are many free online services available that email you when the date arrives.

Great idea!

For those friends that live far away, I keep a stack of postcards on hand, either ones from my city, ones that I purchased when I was on a trip or ones with beautiful artwork on them. The thought of writing a letter to someone makes me put it off, so it never gets done. But it only takes two minutes to write a postcard and stay in touch. It works really well for older friends and relatives who are so pleased to get personal mail or for the young nieces and nephews in your life. "Real" mail, instead of email is something many people rarely get.

Your postcard also serves as a lovely visual reminder for the person to whom you sent it and you'd be surprised how often you will get a reply. An art postcard also works as a lovely birthday card to go with a gift when you don't have the real thing on hand.

Clara Stiles
Toronto, Ontario, Canada

- **Send an e-card.** Send an e-card and make someone feel great. There are many free e-greetings available that allow you to send your thoughts in minutes, without ever going to the store. Try www.hallmark.com

- **Combine your time.** Rather than running your errands and eating lunch alone, invite a friend or loved one to do both with you. You'll get your errands done, have a nice lunch and have your social time all at once. You might even combine your exercise time with a loved one. You can both work out together and catch up at the same time.

Great idea!

I use index cards as my address book. On each family's index card I keep last name, first names, children's names, phone numbers, birthdays and Christmas card list. If a family moves, I only have to replace their index card, not a whole address book.

Suzi Schwartzenberger
Strathmore, CA

- **Just call.** If you don't have time to write a long letter or note to a friend, a simple, ten-minute "how are you?" phone call will keep you in touch while saving time.

- **Don't have time for a long letter?** A simple "Thinking of You" card may be all it takes to show someone how much you care.

- **Make labels for people you frequently mail to.** Make a list of the people you mail to all the time, such as a parent, sibling, friend, landlord or business associate. Using Microsoft Word or whatever word processing software you have on your computer, make a full sheet of mailing labels for each of these people.

    Leave these labels in a folder marked "Mailing Labels" on your desk or wherever you frequently write. Next time you have to mail something to any of these people, just seal the envelope and stick a mailing label on the outside. It sure beats the drudgery of always writing out names and addresses.

- **Send a care package.** Send friends or family members a box full of some of their favorite things, such as your famous chocolate chip cookies, some fun photographs or a mini scrapbook you made, a quilt or special mementos.

These are perfect for family members in the military, away at camp, teaching overseas, or just to show you care.

- **In an instant.** Arrange a time when you and a good friend will be online. Then, use an instant messaging service to "talk" to each other. No long distance fees!

- **Write a blog.** A blog is basically an online journal—a diary of sorts. You can write about what's happening in your life and your interested family members or friends can access it anytime.

Great idea!

Several years ago for my new years resolution I vowed to stay in touch with family and friends through letter writing, cards and post cards. To make it easy, I printed labels for all my most common correspondents and kept the labels at work. In my day planner I kept a selection of blank cards, fancy notepaper and stamps.

Now, whenever I'm the first to arrive at a meeting, need a break from a hectic day or want to do something productive during my lunch hour, I pull out a card and start writing! I easily send out between two to five per week. It's so easy to make someone's day with just 5 minutes and a little preplanning.

Molly Gapp
Birmingham, MI

- **Phone home.** Even if you work out of state most of the week, you can stay connected with family members by giving them a quick ring on the phone. Even if it's only for a minute or two, you'll be able to make contact and stay in touch.

- **Plan a get-away.** Make it a tradition that each year you and your friends all meet for a 3-day weekend to catch up, socialize and enjoy each other.

- **Make a recording.** Get a 90 minute audio cassette and tape record yourself for approximately 10 minutes. Include things you've done this year, news, a funny story—whatever strikes your fancy. Then, pass on the audio tape to one of your friends or siblings and have him or her add to the tape. Instruct each person to keep passing the tape along so the next person can add a message. The final person should send the tape back to you.

You can then listen to everyone's message and forward the tape onto the next person, the third person and so on, so everyone has a chance to listen to all the messages. Or, you can duplicate the complete tape and send everyone his or her own copy.

- **Host a barbecue or two each year.** Invite your family and friends. You won't have to set individual dates with each person, but will still get to see everyone!

- **Make a handmade card or craft.** Sending something from the heart, made with your own hands, is a very thoughtful gesture and a wonderful way to keep in touch with your loved ones.

- **Post photos on the web.** Using your own Web site or a photo sharing Web site, post photos of your family members, vacations and more on the web. My sister lives in New Jersey and one of my aunts lives in Florida. When we take photos, we post them on the web, and just send our relatives the web address so they can view.

Chapter 51

The Paper Puzzle

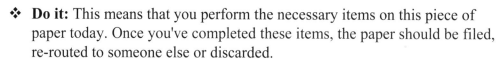

- **Start with the 4 D's of Effective Paper Management:**

  ❖ **Do it:** This means that you perform the necessary items on this piece of paper today. Once you've completed these items, the paper should be filed, re-routed to someone else or discarded.

  ❖ **Delegate it:** This means that you immediately give this paper to someone else who can perform the necessary action, whether this person is a family member, associate, friend, relative or someone you outsource to.

  ❖ **Delay it:** This means that further action needs to be taken on this paper, but not right now. File it away, so it's ready to be referenced when you need it. File it in a Tickler File if action is needed in the near future or in a filing cabinet if this paper needs to be referenced at a later date.

  ❖ **Dump it:** This is the greatest one of them all. It's probably safe to say that a huge percentage of the paper that enters your home can be immediately discarded.

Great idea!

I take the owner's manuals for CD/DVD players, TV's, Cassette players, VCR's, Audio/Video control centers, and Dish Network boxes and place them either on top or underneath the device. I also staple a copy of the receipt and any other warranty information inside the manual.

Rose Combs
San Jose, CA

- **Corral the paper clutter.** The problem often starts small. Jack brings the mail in the door and leaves it on the coffee table. Jill puts the insurance forms she has to fill out for work on the kitchen table. Jane comes home from school and drops her permission slips on the home office desk. Jeff flings his college applications on the living room coffee table. In just a few days, paper piles are forming all over the house!

Contain this problem by designating one place where all paper is handled. Have a wire basket for each family member in one room. When a paper can't be read or attended to immediately, at least it can be placed in an assigned wire basket for a day or two, where it's not going to be lost.

Organizing Clinic

Question

I'd like to find a way to organize non-essential papers that I may need as reference or like to make copies of for different groups I belong to. I can get to my important papers such as bank statements and bills in an instant, but it's the newspaper articles like job search information and resume writing that I just don't know how to get control of.

I have sticky paper with Web sites and phone numbers that I've used but not regularly, articles about restaurants, people and technology that I'm interested in and a plethora of other subjects. I need to be able to access them, but they don't merit file cabinet space. I have numerous piles of these little miscellaneous papers that I just don't know how to organize.

Fern Wolgel
Atlanta, GA

Answer

Dear Fern,

It sounds like you're keeping an awful lot of paper. You need to consolidate what you have. For Web sites, phone numbers, restaurants you wish to visit, and all of the other data in your life, all of this information could be consolidated in a three-ring binder. The *Get Organized Now! Easy Organizer* is perfect for this purpose. It's not necessary to keep full sheets, or worse, scraps of paper, for each restaurant you wish to visit or each Web site you wish to check out. One single page can list all of those restaurants you're interested in, etc. The *Easy Organizer* has an area for you to store all of your lists. It's just one binder, everything is in one place and you can find everything instantly.

Some of your articles may warrant keeping, such as an article you plan to use for an upcoming job search. However, be careful. If you can easily get this information on the Web when you need it, there's no sense in keeping tons of paper. For instance, if you need information on interviewing, you can access that information on the Web in seconds. No need to keep every article you find on interviewing, when it's so easily accessible. For articles you wish to copy for groups you belong to, keep a To Copy file folder. Each week, make the copies you need and distribute them to your group(s). Don't allow these to pile up.

You mentioned that many of your articles don't merit filing cabinet space. Actually, if the articles you're keeping are important enough to keep, these DO warrant file cabinet space. If you don't feel they're that important, you should recycle them. Articles you are saving in your filing cabinet should be in file folders labeled appropriately with headings such as Career and Gardening. Dedicate one file drawer for interesting articles. When the drawer is full, weed it out before adding anything else to it.

You might also consider scanning some articles and saving them on your computer. However, be careful about this. Wasting computer space can be even more detrimental than wasting filing space, if you hardly ever use the articles.

- **Handle paper daily.** Handle your papers within a day or two and you'll be able to keep them under control. Wait a week or more and you'll be drowning in a flood of paper. Go through your mail on a daily basis, immediately recycling anything you don't need and putting all important papers into their designated homes (e.g. pending bills in the bill paying binder or bank statements in your filing system.)

  Go through your in box once per day and empty it out each night before you leave the office. Read at least one item in your To Read file each day to keep it under control. Then, immediately file or recycle those papers. Don't let your To File papers pile up. If you have a sheet of paper to file, file it in your file cabinet right away. Don't first put it in a To File tray and then file it later after lots of papers begin to grow.

  It will only take a second to file one or two sheets of paper now, but if you allow it to grow, it's going to require quite a bit of time. That's one of the main reasons people hate to file. They allow it to pile up until it's out of control.

- **Don't print everything.** You would think because more people have computers these days that the paper clutter has been reduced. No chance of that. It has immensely multiplied. One of the reasons for an increase of paper clutter is that people are printing things that don't need to be printed.

  One person I know was complaining he didn't have enough room in his filing cabinet for his important papers. I then found out he was printing every single email he received. When I asked him why, he said that he might want to reference one of those email messages someday.

  Let's put this in perspective. He gets around 20 email messages each day, prints each of them and puts them in his filing cabinet. Twenty messages times 365 days per year equals a minimum of 7,300 sheets of paper annually. That's almost 15 reams of paper in his filing cabinet. No wonder he has no room for his important papers!

  Upon further exploration, I found out that he hasn't referenced even one of those messages in months. When I looked closer, it was over 70% jokes and funny stories that friends had sent him over the Internet. Wow. Let me assure you that 95% of the email most people read on a daily basis can be immediately responded to and deleted. The rest of it can be temporarily stored in email folders until you're ready to handle it. As a rule of thumb, don't print out your email. I print less than 1% of the email I receive.

- **Eliminate scraps of paper.** Use one binder system, such as the *Get Organized Now! Easy Organizer*, to hold all of the information you must keep on hand, such as phone numbers, birthdays, To Do lists, cleaning schedules, grocery lists and meal planning logs. This will eliminate lots of sticky notes and loose sheets of paper—which tend to get lost if they're floating around. Plus, you'll save time since you won't have to search for your important information when you need it. It will be all organized together in one place.

Great idea!

I purchased two expanding file boxes that go from A-Z to keep my paperwork at hand. One file has all of our household manuals, such as the freezer, washer/dryer, TV's and digital camera. Whenever we purchase a new appliance or electronic device, I write the date of purchase, attach the sales receipt, and file it away. When we have to do repairs, or need to know a how-to, it is easy to find. Also, we can see how "old" the item is by the date of purchase.

The second file is used for my children's electronic toys and games. Seems like everything you buy now has specific instructions that come with it. Since they are purchased mostly at Christmas, I usually file them after New Year's and trash instructions to anything that no longer works or they no longer have.

Cyndi Parsons
Athens, OH

- **Banish a paper pile.** Get yourself a box of 10" x 13" manila envelopes, a box of removable labels and a large, open paper grocery bag. Start with a paper pile, picking up the sheet on top and skimming it for content. If it's trash, immediately put it in your paper grocery bag. If you have to keep it, put it into a manila envelope, stick a blank label on the envelope and write the subject matter. If it's a recipe, write "Recipes." If it's a pending bill, write "Pending Bill." If it's a financial statement, write "Financial Statement."

Go through each paper in the pile, working from the top down, in the same manner. Of course, as you come across other pending bills, you can just insert it into the Pending Bills folder with the other pending bills you've come across. The idea is to have everything sorted when you're done. Once the pile is gone, you should have several categorized envelopes. At this point, you'll have to give the papers in those envelopes appropriate homes, like your filing cabinet or your bill paying system.

Great idea!

I love binders and find their storage potential is much greater than file folders. I keep a binder near our telephone desk with different tabs such as School Newsletters, Ballet, Piano and Summer Activities. When I get pamphlets and registration forms throughout the year for kids activities like summer camp, I put them in the pocket in the front of the binder and know that when the time comes to register the kids, everything is in one place and the completed registration forms can then be filed under the appropriate tab.

I also use this same storage system for recipes I find on the Internet and elsewhere. The binder allows me to store the recipes on a bookshelf alongside my other cookbooks.

Mavis Reynolds
Victoria, British Columbia, Canada

- **Don't be a copy cat.** These days, it's very easy to make duplicate copies of a sheet of paper. Don't be tempted to do it, unless you have an absolute need for it right now. In general, unless it's a form you use on a daily or weekly basis, you don't need two or three copies of letters, articles, comics, and so on.

Great idea!

I was always searching for the best place to store all of the small miscellaneous, yet valuable papers like gift certificates, restaurant coupons, pizza coupons, recreation passes (like free passes for ice skating, roller skating) and long distance phone cards. After trying various storage places, I finally found the answer. I purchased a decorative, inexpensive recipe card file that holds 4" x 6" cards. I used the index cards to create dividers and now I have a convenient, easy-to-access place to house those papers that used to be scattered everywhere. In addition, the first divider lists the telephone numbers of our family and neighbors as handy reference for my daughter, Lillian.

Tambra Wagner
Springfield, IL

- **I've got the measles.** To determine if you're paper shuffling—moving a sheet of paper from one place to another without ever handling the task on it—every time you pick up a paper, put a red dot on it. When a sheet of paper has more than 5 dots on it, your paper has the measles, which means you're not being productive with it.

- **Don't keep piles of scrap paper.** Lots of people who are environmentally conscious like to keep any sheet of paper they receive, figuring they could use the reverse side of the paper as scrap paper for notes and phone numbers. This only works if you're very organized. If you're not, scrap the scrap paper and keep your written information in a single notebook or binder instead.

- **Pending paper.** Do you keep paper out in the open because it's pending, such as the bid for a landscaping project that isn't yet done, or an invitation for a birthday party that's coming up? Instead of keeping tons of pending papers out in the open, use a "Pending Holding System" instead. You will need:

  o One 2 inch, 3-ring binder and a pen or marker

  o 10 pocket folders: these can be purchased at office supplies stores. They are 3-hole punched and fit into any standard 3-ring binder.

  o Removable file folder labels, approximately 1" to 2" in size

  ❖ To assemble:

  o Insert the pocket folders into your binder.

  o Put a removable file folder label on the bottom right of each folder.

  o On each label, write a category that corresponds to one of your pending projects, such as Landscaping, Upcoming Events or Basement Remodeling.

  o When you're done, place all of the papers that pertain to each of your pending categories in the properly labeled pocket folder.

  ❖ To use:

  o Now all of your pending papers are categorized, in one place, and ready to be flipped to whenever you're ready to use them.

  o Once your pending papers are no longer current (the project is done), those papers should be removed from the pocket folder and filed in your filing cabinet for future reference if necessary, discarded if you don't need to keep these papers any longer or passed on to an appropriate recipient.

  o Peel off the old category label, and stick a new one on with a new category.

Organizing Clinic

Question

I've been in the habit of filing important papers like medical papers and bank statements, but I'm beginning to run out of space because I'm not sure when to let go of these things. Is there a suggested timeframe for how long to keep these types of documents?

V. Davis, Cincinnati, OH

Answer

Since everyone's situation is different, it is recommended that you speak with your accountant about which important papers you should keep and which you should toss. However, here are a few general guidelines:

- **Tax returns and supporting documentation.** Keep for seven years. Each year, put that year's tax returns and its supporting documentation (i.e., bank statements, credit card statements that include tax-deductible purchases, loans and receipts for major purchases) in a manila envelope and store it in a box, with all previous years' tax documentation—away from your everyday filing area. The only tax-related documents in your filing cabinet should be this year's.

- **Receipts or cancelled checks.** For big purchase items, like cars, television sets or anything that has a warranty, keep the papers for as long as you have the item you purchased. Papers for items you no longer have or small ticket items like groceries or video rentals, can generally be recycled/discarded as long as you don't plan on returning the purchase.

- **Utility bills or bills for non-tax-deductible items.** Shred one year after you receive them.

- **Credit card statements.** Retain three years for those that contain no tax-related purchases.

- **ATM and other credit card receipts.** Shred and toss after the monthly statement comes.

- **Investment or property records.** Keep for six years after the sale of the investment. The monthly statements can be shredded/discarded once you receive the annual summary that reflects yearly activity.

- **Medical records.** For any serious medical problem, keep forever. For any minor medical problem discard after one year.

- **Pay check stubs.** Keep until you receive your annual W-2 statement with your gross pay for the year. Then shred and recycle the individual check stubs.

- **Bank statements.** Keep until you receive your annual statement. You can then get rid of the individual monthly statements.

- **Insurance Policies.** Keep until you can no longer legally file a claim.

Chapter 52

Mail

- **Check for your mail every day.** Even if it's raining outside and you have to walk to the end of the driveway to get your mail, grab an umbrella and make it a point to get it. The more it builds, the longer it's going to take you to go through it. Retrieve your mail every single day and give yourself every opportunity to keep it under control.

- **Stop paper in its tracks.** When you get a bill in the mail, immediately open the envelope and remove the contents. Tuck the bill in the flap of the payment envelope. Toss out everything else including all inside advertising and the outer envelope.

- **Sort it out.** Mail should be sorted each day. Junk mail should be immediately discarded. Bills belong in a bill paying system. Papers that may need to be referenced, such as insurance documents, belong in your filing system. Magazines belong in magazine racks or magazine baskets. Invitations or other events should be noted on a calendar, and then inserted temporarily into a Tickler file until the event has passed. Mail for other family members should be organized into a mail sorting system.

- **Create a Family Mail Center.** Use a Stackable File Sorter with a separate level for each person and one level for outgoing mail. Incoming mail can be easily separated and found by whomever it belongs to. Outgoing mail will be in one place and ready to be sent. Take turns delivering the mail to the post office or designate a family member to drop it off once or twice a week.

- **Use a shredder.** With the influx of identity theft these days, consider shredding any mail you no longer need that contains any personal information, such as your social security number or birth date.

Great idea!

I have a large, easily opened outdoor trash receptacle that I keep in front of my garage next to my front walk. This allows me to sort and purge mail as I walk from the street into the house. It also is great for easily disposing of trash each time I get out of the car, especially when I eat on the run. It's also handy for throwing a handful of weeds that I pull or for cleaning up after my dog each and every morning.

Nancy Werth
Plymouth, MI

- **Create a holding spot.** If it's necessary for you to visit your post office fairly often to ship out packages, have a holding spot for all mail and packages until your scheduled post office day arrives. When you're ready to go, everything will be in one place and you won't forget anything.

- **Keep mailing and shipping supplies together.** We keep all of our shipping boxes, tape, mailing labels, return address labels, packing bubbles and other related mailing supplies in one cabinet. It's a very quick and easy task when we need to prepare a package for shipping.

- **Buy stamps online.** If the only reason you visit the post office is to pick up stamps, consider buying them online instead. The post office will deliver the stamps right to your door, generally for no additional charge.

Great idea!

For years, we were disorganized about our mail. Whoever came in the door first, took charge and the mail ended up a variety of different places. I purchased a basket with a handle—Red Riding Hood-style. It has become our mail basket.

We have a mail slot in the front door, and a basket near it. Whoever comes in the door first places the mail in the basket. No more asking "where's the mail?" We always know where to find it.

Pat Griffith
Wilmette, IL

- **Open the mail with your calendar open.** When you see something in your mail pile that you may be interested in attending, such as an upcoming event or a free week at the gym, read thoroughly to determine if you need to make a reservation or pay a deposit. Take care of that task right away. Then, jot any information onto your calendar like dates, times or places. Then, insert that postcard or letter into your Tickler system if you need to refer to it when the event date rolls around.

- **Have some courier forms available.** If you ever ship packages out, you might want to keep some courier forms for companies such as Fed Ex and UPS available. It's best to have these filled out ahead of time, especially if you need to request a pick up.

- **Use return address labels.** Rather than writing out your return address on all outgoing mail, stick on a pre-addressed return label instead. I get tons of these for free in the mail from companies who request donations. But if you prefer special ones, you can always order them online from companies such as Current, Inc. By the way, always keep a few of these labels in your purse or wallet. Whenever you have to fill out a mailing list form or a contest card at a store, you can just stick a return address label on rather than filling out all of your information by hand.

- **Reduce your junk mail.** Some consumers would like to receive less advertising mail at home. The Mail Preference Service (MPS) is designed to assist those consumers in decreasing the amount of national non-profit or commercial mail they receive at home. Basically, you sign up to request that your name is removed from mailing lists. Doing so, over time, can reduce your incoming junk mail by more than 50%. For more information on the steps you need to take to reduce junk mail, please visit: www.dmaconsumers.org

- **Get off mailing lists.** If you're currently getting mail from a company that you no longer wish to receive mail from, write RTS (Return to Sender, Please remove from mailing list) on the envelope before you even open it and drop it in a mailbox so it gets returned to the company who sent it.

- **Pass it on.** Every once in awhile, you may get a piece of mail that was delivered to your address, accidentally. If you know who the mail belongs to, bring it over to that person's home as soon as possible, or call them to pick it up from you. If you don't know who the mail belongs to, put it in the mailbox so it gets forwarded to the correct person.

- **Stop the mail.** If you're going on vacation for more than a day or two, consider stopping mail delivery while you're gone. Your mailbox may not be able to hold all the mail you accumulate, and prowlers may detect that you're not home if you have lots of mail piling up in your box. You can usually then request that the post office drops all your mail at your home on the day you return from vacation, or you can pick it up at the post office yourself upon your return.

- **Tip the mail person.** Every year for the holidays, we always give our mail carrier (and some of our regular couriers) a tip or a gift certificate for delivering to us. It's just a small gesture, but often results in the mail carrier being extra nice to us—often bringing packages and mail right up to our door so we don't have to walk to the mailbox at the curb.

Chapter 53

Newspapers, Catalogs and Magazines

- **Daily dump.** If you get a daily newspaper subscription, make it a rule that at the end of the night the paper gets put into the recycle container whether you've read it or not. Since you're getting a new newspaper the next day, that day's news will be more current and you won't give newspapers a chance to build up.

  Of course, if you are constantly putting the paper in the recycle container before getting a chance to read it, cancel your daily subscription. Consider a Sunday paper only, skip the paper, get your news on the radio or access your local newspaper online.

- **Read all about it.** Set up a system to recycle your newspapers easily. Each day when we're finished reading our paper, it immediately goes into a paper grocery bag in our garage. On recycling day, we leave the filled paper bag outside for pickup. Note: Some recycling companies require you to tie your newspapers in bundles.

Great idea!

I used to have stacks and stacks of magazines sitting around. Due to the sheer number, I never got around to reading most of them. Two things have made a complete difference in my management of magazines.

1. I only order one magazine subscription a year. This forces me to choose very carefully and pick something that I know I will really use and enjoy. Plus, I inevitably get other subscriptions as birthday and Christmas gifts. At least I can limit the subscriptions I receive.

2. As soon as a magazine comes in the mail, I place it by my bed where I know I will have occasion to read a little bit at a time. Each time I pick up the magazine, I tear off each page I pass. This is great because if I get stopped in the middle, I won't have to waste time flipping back through advertisements I have already read to find my spot. Plus, if I come to something I want to save, I put the torn off page(s) in a separate pile and file (instead of trash) it.

Other great benefits of this system are that you can actually see yourself making progress as you read through the magazine and you will never again be tempted to save a magazine just because of one great article.

Lynna Sutherland
Richmond, VA

- **Cancel subscriptions.** Cancel subscriptions to magazines you're no longer reading or benefiting from. If you haven't read the last three or four issues, it's probably not worth continuing. Very often, you can actually get a refund on the issues you haven't received yet.

- **Out with the old.** When the new issue of one of your magazines arrives, it's a good idea to get rid of the last one. If you haven't yet read the last one, do so this week so you can move on to the new information that just arrived.

- **Sweep out the sweepstakes.** When you receive sweepstakes mailings, don't think that you'll increase your chances of winning if you purchase magazines from that mailing. Whether you purchase magazines or you don't, the company is required by law to include your entry.

- **Save only the articles.** When reading a magazine, tag pages you may want to reference later. As soon as you get through the magazine, tear out the pages you want to keep and discard the rest of the magazine. This will help to prevent excess magazine clutter.

Great idea!

My house was once awash in catalogs, but I've discovered a great way to contain catalog clutter. As I go through catalogs, I dog-ear the pages of interest and mark the items that interest me. Then I tear out those pages and either the order blank or the cover page with the customer number and source code on it. I staple those together and toss the rest of the catalog.

If I am not sure that I really need an item, I let what I've saved sit for a week before taking action on it. It's amazing to find that after only a week you sometimes wonder why something attracted you in the first place.

At that time I either toss the pages or order the item(s). If I order by telephone I put the order number and cost on the page. When the order comes in, if everything is satisfactory I toss the page with the information.

When ordering via the Internet, I save all email confirmations in a separate mailbox folder, deleting them only when the item has been received and no further action, such as returning or exchanging, needs to be taken on it.

Sig Stiles
Dameron, MD

- **Use magazine holders.** If you get photography or other hobby magazines, you may want to keep those magazines for reference. If so, don't store them horizontally in a huge pile. Buy magazine holders and store the magazines upright with the spine facing towards you. I keep scrapbooking and paper crafting magazines, for inspiration and ideas, stored in heavy-duty, mesh magazine holders, organized first by title and then by date.

- **Set aside reading time.** The only way to find time to enjoy your magazines is to *make* time to enjoy them. Set aside time each day to flip through them even if it's for only a few minutes at a time. Sometimes I enjoy reading my magazines in bed for a few minutes before going to sleep. A friend of mine always has her favorite magazine in her car. While she waits in her car to pick up her kids from school, she always makes use of that time by reading.

- **Cut the catalog clutter.** If you enjoy receiving catalogs, have a consistent place where you store them—preferably the area you generally flip through them most often. A basket near your reading area is a good solution. Only keep those catalogs you truly enjoy looking at. When a newer issue of a particular catalog arrives, toss the old issue.

- **Keep the details only.** Many people keep catalogs because they contain things they may want to buy for themselves or for others as gifts. When you're interested in a particular item, tear out the page that item appears on and circle the item number/description.

Finally, tear off the back page of the catalog, which is generally where the ordering information is and staple it to the item(s) you tore out. Put these in an "Items to Purchase" folder until you're ready to call in your order or place your order on the Internet.

Great idea!

When one of my magazines arrives, I go to the table of contents and see what articles are in the magazine for the month. Then I tear out the articles I want to read and discard the rest of the magazine. I carry articles with me so whenever I have a couple of minutes in line, waiting or just a little break, I can read them.

Debbie Mrazek
Plano, TX

- **Shop online.** Forego printed store catalogs and use store Web sites instead. You'll have less catalog clutter and you'll always have the latest information and prices.

- **More than one reader.** There are a few magazines that both my husband and I enjoy reading. I usually get to the magazines first and then he reads through them. We have two magazine racks. When I'm done reading a magazine, I put it in my husband's magazine rack. He can then decide whether or not he wants to read it, and when he's completely done, he can recycle that issue.

  If you have a similar situation in your house, but various family members read the magazine, you may want to work up a system to indicate who has already read a particular issue. You can have each person initial the magazine when he or she is finished with it. When everyone's initials are on it, the magazine can then be recycled.

  Or, you can mimic an office routing system. Type small slips of paper that include each family member's name. Make copies and attach one slip to each magazine. As each person is done reading it, he crosses out his name and passes the magazine to the next person on the list.

- **Don't renew every time you get a renewal.** I have a few favorite magazines and I'm constantly receiving renewal notices for them—even those that aren't set to expire for the next three years! Learn how to read your subscription label. It almost always includes the date your subscription ends right on the label in month/year format.

  If your subscription is already renewed for the next few years ahead, don't bother to renew every time you receive a renewal slip. You may not still be interested in this particular magazine five or more years from now. Wait until the magazine only has a few months left. Since magazine companies want you to re-subscribe, you'll probably get an excellent deal if you wait to renew until the subscription is near expiration.

Organizing Clinic

Question

I have tons of magazines that I'm finished reading. Do you know who would accept all these magazines as a donation? I hate to throw them away once I'm done with them because it is such a waste! This is one of my clutter issues that I hope to resolve with your help.

Christi Renger

Answer

Dear Christi,

If your community has a recycling program, the magazines you recycle will likely be used to make other paper-based products. So, if you do toss your magazines, be sure to toss them into the recycling bin so they don't go to waste and are re-used for something else. But if you'd like to donate your magazines or make better use of your subscriptions, there are several options you might consider. Just be sure to remove your subscription labels before making the donation(s).

- **Do a magazine swap.** You buy one magazine subscription and your friend buys another. Each month, swap the most current issue you've read. This allows two people to get the benefits of two magazine subscriptions, but only pay one price.

- **Give them to your library.** Call your local libraries and ask them if they would be interested in your magazine donations. If the magazines are the popular ones and they're fairly recent issues, it's possible your library will take them. Try high school and college libraries too.

- **Check with your local medical facilities.** Doctors, dentists, optometrists and other medical practitioners generally have magazines in their waiting areas. Same with local hospitals. Ask them if they would like your donations. Chances are one or more of them will gladly accept.

- **Try a teacher.** Some magazines, such as news, geographical or historical magazines, can be appropriate to use in the classroom. Art teachers may also be interested in magazines for school art projects, such as making collages. Ask teachers in local schools if they're interested.

- **Give back to your community.** Organizations in your community like shelters, nursing homes, retirement homes, soup kitchens and orphanages might be glad to have extra reading material on hand. Give them a try.

- **Bring them to work.** If you have a lunchroom or reading room at work, perhaps leave a few of them there each month. Co-workers can then enjoy magazines you've already read.

- **Give them to the local auto mechanic.** Others can read them while waiting for car repairs.

Chapter 54

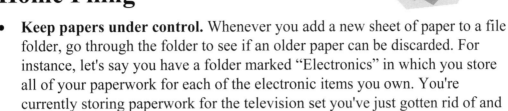

Home Filing

- **Keep papers under control.** Whenever you add a new sheet of paper to a file folder, go through the folder to see if an older paper can be discarded. For instance, let's say you have a folder marked "Electronics" in which you store all of your paperwork for each of the electronic items you own. You're currently storing paperwork for the television set you've just gotten rid of and you're ready to store paperwork for the new set you just purchased.

  A good time to discard the old paperwork that is no longer of any use to you is when you're ready to insert the new paperwork. Weeding out, each time you open a file folder, helps reduce the amount of unnecessary paperwork in your files and your life.

Great idea!

I had been trying for months to beat the paper piles. I knew about the credo "file, don't pile," but I did not know how to effectively implement it. As a result, I had stacks of papers both on my office and home office desks. I purchased an inexpensive label maker and bought a box of colored file folders at the office store. Suddenly, I had inspiration to file.

I really liked the look of the labeled and colored folders to hold my paperwork. Now, I will not lay a paper down without putting it into a pretty colored folder and labeling it neatly with my label maker. It looks sharp and I feel so organized.

I can now drop the folder into my file cabinet or stage on my desk for processing. And I can grab a folder or folders and go to a meeting looking well organized and professional. The "Pile Monster" has been clobbered!

Rebecca Mott
Chattanooga, TN

- **Banish miscellaneous.** When it comes to filing papers, the way you label your file folders will determine how quickly or if you find the papers inside those folders later on. If you write the words, Miscellaneous, Stuff, Future or any other indistinguishable term on the tab of your file folder, you'll never know what's in that folder without spending wasted time going through each sheet of paper one by one.

Take a few moments to first determine the major category. For home, it might be Financial or Family or Health. Once you know the major category, determine what an appropriate sub-category might be. For instance, in a Financial file you might have categories such as Savings Account, Mortgage and Stocks.

A rule of thumb: if the paper is important enough to file, it should be clearly categorized in your filing system.

Great idea!

I had two whole drawers in my filing cabinet related to notes and handouts I received in college. Since I went into a field directly related to my majors, I felt it would be wise to keep all of this information.

Then one day I realized that many of these papers would never be used. If I had a question about Latin verb conjugations, I would never go to a filing cabinet full of hand-written notes, even if I knew right where to find the paper. Instead, I would go to the reference book on the other side of the room, because the explanation would be far more thorough and easy to find.

I began measuring all the papers I consider saving by the same standard. "If I had a question about this, where would be the easiest place to look for information?" If the answer to that question is "in a textbook," "on the Internet," or something that is not "on this piece of paper," that particular paper immediately gets recycled.

Lynn Sutherland
Mechanicsville, VA

- **Disguise it.** A metal filing cabinet can be an indispensable tool for organizing and storing your paperwork. But its harsh, industrial look often takes away from the warmth of a room. This is especially true if you live in an apartment or a smaller home and the unit has to be stored right out in the open, in a main living area or bedroom. If you don't have a filing cabinet, consider a wood-finished one that matches your décor. Otherwise, disguise the metal cabinet you already have.

Measure your filing cabinet—length, width and depth. Then go to your local fabric store and tell the clerk you'd like to drape some fabric over the filing cabinet so it's covered when not in use. Look for some fabric that will fit in well with your decor. Another possibility is to paint the metal cabinet in a color that compliments the room. When you get home, drape the fabric over your filing cabinet and top it with a lamp, vase or other decorative item so it looks more like a table or stand than a filing cabinet.

For short metal file cabinets, you might even get yourself a round plywood top, attach it to the top of the filing cabinet and then drape the fabric over it. This will make it look even more like a table. When you need a file inside, just lift up the fabric, get what you need and then drape the fabric down over it again. Now you see it, now you don't!

Organizing Clinic

Question

A family situation occurred, which required retrieving many files. During that time many things were misplaced and later found again, but put to the side. The massive problem is trying to get all the files and many pieces of paper back into the filing cabinet. I need help! Any suggestions?

Alita McIntosh, Detroit, MI

Answer

Dear Alita,

Definitely set aside a few minutes each day to get your papers and files back under control. I recommend about 15 minutes at a time, until the job is done. Having a timer on hand will help.

It sounds like you already have file folders made up for the papers you removed from your filing system. In this case, start by putting the file folders back into your filing system—even if they don't include all of the papers that belong in them. Set the timer for fifteen minutes at the beginning of your session and work until the timer goes off. If you wish to continue, set the timer for another fifteen minutes. Do this each day, until all file folders are back in your filing system.

Once you're finished with that part of the job, your next step is to begin filing your papers into your file folders. Set your timer for 15 minutes, grab approximately 20 papers that need to be filed and begin filing them one by one into your filing system. When the first stack of 20 papers is filed away, grab another 20 and continue. Work until the timer sounds. Again, if you wish to continue for another 15 minutes, feel free to set your timer again. If not, just stop and work for another 15 minutes tomorrow, the next day and so on, until the job is completed.

I also recommend that you set a pending reward before you start each session and reward yourself at the end of each fifteen-minute session. This will keep you motivated along the way. Yes, this is probably going to take a bit of time. But each day, you'll be one step closer to completing the job. And before you know it, everything will be back in your filing cabinet.

- **Be careful about what you're filing.** Eighty percent of papers most people file are never looked at again, but most people are not satisfied with the amount of space they have in their filing cabinets.

Ally from New York filed everything from travel brochures to recipes to decorating ideas. Once those items were filed, she never referenced any of them. What did she end up with? A filing cabinet full of stuff that was just taking up space. First, before you file anything, be sure it's truly necessary to keep. In a nutshell, you only want to file papers that:

a) You need to keep for legal or financial reasons and

b) You are very likely to reference in the near future, but that you won't be able to easily access somewhere else, such as the Internet

For example, travel brochures tend to get outdated very quickly. If you're not planning on traveling somewhere within the next few months, don't get the travel brochures until the last minute. The prices and other information will be current. You could always use the Internet and skip the paper brochure completely.

Great idea!

Instead of taking up valuable space in the filing cabinet with product guides and manuals, I have purchased decorative photo boxes to store them. I am able to keep them in the kitchen and living room where most of those products are located for easy reference if I ever have a problem.

Kari McLaren
Windsor Heights, IA

- **Use folders.** One of the cardinal rules of organizing paper is to never leave it loose. Keep organized folders for each category of paper.

- **Categorize.** A filing system is only effective if you can find everything you need, when you need it—without a struggle. All good filing systems have different categories of papers.

  Your papers are either going to fall into a "main" category or a "sub" category. For example, a main category might be "Financial. Some sub-categories within Financial, may be Savings Account, Checking Account and Money Market Account.

  In your filing cabinet, your main categories should always be hanging file folders with a labeled tab. Your sub-categories should be labeled manila file folders inside the appropriate main category hanging folder.

- **Choose your system.** For the most part, people choose to use one or a combination of, these basic filing systems:

- ❖ A. Alphabetical (A, B, C, D, etc.)

- ❖ B. Numerical (1, 2, 3, 4, etc.) or

- ❖ C. Chronological (Jan, Feb, Mar, Apr, etc.)

The one you use depends on what you're using it for. For example, if you need to keep files for all of your friends, alphabetical by last name usually will work best.

For sequential projects, such as order numbers for a home business, a numerical system would probably work best.

If it is necessary for you to find things by date, then chronological may be your choice.

Some people get really creative and use a combination of these systems. For example, you may want your main categories to be chronological, but the sub-categories inside to be alphabetical.

Great idea!

In the past I've had trouble sorting through my filing cabinets deciding what's needed and what's not. I started keeping a sheet of self-adhesive stickers by the cabinets and now whenever I access a file I put a sticker on it.

After six months or so, I go through all the folders and pull out the ones without stickers. If I haven't accessed it in six months, I probably don't need it. I might put the ones I've pulled out into an archive box for another six months or a year, just to be certain I don't need it for taxes or another purpose later.

If I pull a file out of the box, I put a sticker on it and return it to the cabinet. Anything that hasn't come out of the box after that extended time is destroyed.

I'm also thinking about changing the stickers after a year, like flowers for 2004 and birds for 2005. It's turning out to be a great way to both organize and decorate my file folders!

Beth Ashton-Hilton
Congresbury, N. Somerset, England

- **Hanging tabs to the front.** When attaching tabs to hanging file folders, put the tab in the front of the folder rather than the back. You'll still be able to easily read the tab even if the folder is full.

- **New papers to the front.** When filing paper into a file folder, insert new papers into the front so the most current information is on top as soon as you open the file.

> ### Great idea!
>
> Have you ever lost the instruction booklet for that new camera, crockpot or telephone? The puzzlement and annoyance as you search frantically can be frustrating.
>
> Whenever we purchase a new item, the instruction booklet, and/or other paperwork, is immediately inserted into a "light-weight" sheet protector. These protectors are capable of holding 8-1/2" x 11" papers and are usually strong enough to withstand normal family use. The protector is then inserted into a three-ring binder that is then placed on a shelf for safekeeping. We have three binders: A-K, L-R, and S-Z. Within each binder no attempt is made to alphabetize – i.e. toaster, VCR, television.
>
> Anytime we need to refer to the instructions for a particular item, the correct binder is retrieved, opened, and thumbed through to find the correct protector. The binder is snapped open, the protector removed and carried to the working site for use. When finished, the protector is returned to the binder until needed again.
>
> J A Angus
> Lynnfield, MA

- **Label properly.** If a file isn't labeled properly, it's not going to be quick and easy to find. Write the subject on the tab of the file folder close to the top of the tab, so you can easily see it when you're looking through your files. Use a medium point, black marker to label your files. Print; don't use script. Use as few words as possible on the tab.

- **One-inch rule.** Once a file folder is one inch thick, it's time to either a) weed it out or b) start another.

- **No paperclips.** When putting papers into file folders, staple any items you wish to keep together. Don't use paper clips that tend to grab onto papers you don't wish to be together. They also tend to fall off.

- **A cabinet of their own.** School age children can benefit greatly from having their very own filing cabinet. In it, they can store school papers they wish to keep, memorabilia, artwork, articles and more. It's the perfect way to get them used to filing and keeping papers organized.

Chapter 55
Your Calendar or Planner

- **Be careful about using more than one calendar.** Use one calendar for both personal and business use. Heed the old Chinese proverb, "A man who wears two watches never knows the correct time." If you keep one calendar in your briefcase, another on your desk and another on the kitchen refrigerator, you're guaranteeing that something scheduled on one will never get written on the other, and you're bound to experience a scheduling conflict.

- **The family calendar.** One exception to the "use only one calendar rule" is when you wish to have a family calendar posted. A large write on/wipe off wall planner is usually good for this purpose. Assign each person his or her own colored marker (keep the markers in a cup right near the calendar) and make each person that is old enough responsible for filling in his or her own schedule.

  Of course, as the parent, you'll have to do two important things. First, you'll have to check the family calendar each day, especially if some of the events involve you or your spouse driving your kids to the particular event. Second, you'll have to ensure all events that involve you are transferred to your personal calendar.

- **Abbreviate and hi-light.** To save space, save time and eliminate lots of scribbling on your paper calendar, use abbreviations to help remind you of special dates or tasks. Here are my favorites, but be creative and make up some personal ones of your own:

  - PU = Pick Up (PU Dry cleaning or PU Videos)
  - VAC = Vacation (VAC Florida or VAC Retreat)
  - CL = Call (CL Jane or CL Mike)
  - BD = Birthday (BD Ellen or BD Ralph)
  - MT = Meeting (MT Ryan or MT Staff)
  - AN = Anniversary (AN Mom and Dad or AN Ed and Grace)
  - AP = Appointment (AP Doctor or AP Haircut)

  In addition, you can hi-light similar events or tasks with a fluorescent marker or with a sticker. For instance, all birthdays can be hi-lighted in pink and all appointments can be hi-lighted in yellow. Another alternative is putting a heart sticker on any anniversary dates and a candle or balloon sticker on all birthday dates.

- **Use the FILI technique.** First Item, Last Item. In other words, when you get up in the morning, the first item and the last item for that day, should be to look at your calendar.

- **Start each day with a written plan of action.** Don't just go through your day in a random manner. Write down what you need to accomplish and work on those items, checking them off one by one. If you find yourself getting sidetracked, stop what you're doing and immediately get back to your list.

- **Plans are meant to be improved.** The goal is not to create a plan and stick to it, but to create a plan and ask the question, "Is this still working?" When your answer is "no," it's time to revise the plan.

- **Purchase the right planner for your needs.** Make sure the lines are large enough for your handwriting. Ensure the pages are big enough for you to fit all your important tasks.

- **Look into the future.** Use a calendar that displays an entire week or month at a time, rather than just a day or two. You have to look into the future to be able to make time for projects, goals and enjoyment.

- **Lost and found.** The first entry in your calendar or planner should be:

  If lost, please return to:

  Name _____

  Address _____

  Phone _____

  Reward $10

  (Or whatever amount you feel you'd be willing to give in the event of loss.)

- **Once each day.** Check your daily planner every day—hence the name daily planner. If it isn't checked religiously, something will be missed or forgotten.

- **Use what you need.** There is no need to use every planning page that comes with your daily planner. Decide which pages will help you the most and pull out the ones that you'll never use.

Great idea!

Don't leave your planning until the last minute. Always write down everything you need to do tomorrow, the night before. I use my Daytimer for this purpose and it works beautifully.

Lance Flanagan,
Boulder City, NV

- **No scraps of paper.** Don't plan your projects, tasks and activities on scraps of paper, Post-it™ notes or napkins! There's a 99.9% chance that those papers will get lost.

- **One place.** When you schedule something, immediately jot it down on your calendar or in your planner. This ensures all of your information will be recorded in one easy-to-locate place.

- **Make a trade.** If you're constantly running around from appointment to appointment or if you travel frequently, consider trading in your loose address books, appointment books, To Do lists and calendars for a single planner that does it all and more.

Great idea!

There are a couple of things that I do to help keep activities and appointments organized. The first is I keep all activities and appointments on one calendar and have different colors for each person. There are seven of us and it really helps when checking the calendar at a glance. I also check my calendar every evening when I go to bed so I know ahead of time what the next day will be like.

Second, when we get an appointment card I clip it to my refrigerator with a magnetic clip. I keep all the appointments in order by date. When we finish with one we take it off the clip. It makes it easy to double-check who has the appointment and the date and time. It also helps when I need to change an appointment. The phone number is right on the card.

Kim Frisby
Spencerville, IN

- **End of year task.** Make an appointment with yourself at the end of each November to buy a calendar for the upcoming year. Transfer your recurring events from the old calendar to the new one. Mark recurring dates, such as birthdays and anniversaries, with brightly colored markers so you'll be able to see those events coming up at a glance.

- **Write it down.** Don't scramble at the last minute searching for where you put those tickets for the ball game, workshop or theater. When you mark the event on your calendar, also jot down where you put the tickets. A few days ahead of time, put the tickets in an envelope and tape them to the inside of your front door or on your light switch so you immediately see them as you're leaving.

- **Use bookmarks.** When using a calendar that you don't keep open constantly, use bookmarks on the most frequently used pages so you don' t have to flip through the book each time. Don't use a pen to hold your place. It will destroy the binding and your calendar may fall apart before the year is up.

- **In the palm of your hand.** If you're on the road often, a PDA or other digital organizer may be a good choice for you. They hold addresses, To Do Lists, calendars, virtual notepads and more. They're a bit pricey, but are perfect for keeping the frequent traveler organized.

- **Make a copy.** Instead of bringing your entire calendar on the road with you, just make a photocopy of the page—the entire week or month—and bring that copy only. You'll have less to carry. Plus, there won't be any chance of losing your calendar.

- **Days of yore.** Desk blotters were originally used to keep fountain pens from leaking on the desk. Now, they're more of a fashion statement. If you would like to use a desk blotter, by all means do so. But I would like to address the calendar/desk blotter combinations. These very large, generally month-at-a-glance, calendars act both as a blotter and a calendar in one. When you're done with the current month, you just tear away the top sheet. Two major drawbacks in my professional opinion are 1) papers often get placed on top of the calendar hiding your appointments and events and 2) it's easy to start scribbling random notes that really shouldn't be scribbled on a calendar in the first place.

- **The online calendar.** Some people have decided to get rid of their paper calendars completely, and trade them in for online calendars. Many companies who offer this service allow you to login to your account, look at your calendar in different views, enter events, receive email reminders and more. Personally, I don't want to have to go online to see my calendar. My paper calendar is simple, reliable and doesn't depend on me having an Internet connection to access it. But that's just me.

There are two things, however, that I do like about online calendars. First, a very good feature of many online calendars is the email reminder service. Just in case you forget to write something on your paper calendar or forget to look at the paper calendar, the email reminder is an excellent backup tool.

Second, two or more people (for instance, all family members in a particular household) can use one account of an online calendar, see what each person has entered, and avoid any scheduling conflicts. For example, my husband uses the free calendar offered on Yahoo. If I need to schedule an appointment that involves both of us, I login to his account, view other appointments he currently has scheduled and I am able to schedule any new appointments without there being any conflicts.

Chapter 56
Lists and Notes

- **Make lists.** A list is your own personal assistant, constantly tapping you on the shoulder, reminding you of the things you have to do or get. Leave it up to your memory alone, and something is bound to be forgotten.

- **Master lists.** A Master List is a laundry list of everything you need or want to do. It doesn't have to be in any particular order, but is a reference so you don't forget anything.

- **To Do Today lists.** You can only create your To Do Today List, once you have a Master List. Simply pull 3 to 6 tasks (3 if you're having a difficult time completing things, 6 if you have no problem completing things) from your Master List and transfer them to your To Do Today List. Don't put anything else on your To Do Today list until all items are completed.

Great idea!

I write my To Do list on my bedroom mirror using a dry-erase marker. This helps me to start planning my day while I'm getting ready in the morning. As I complete each item, I can wipe it off with a tissue. I accomplish more—and my mirror is always clean!

LaBeth Pondish
Houston, TX

- **Shopping lists.** Even if you only need one or two things at the grocery store, it is highly advised that you bring a list. It's very easy to get distracted by a new item, or a friend walking down the aisle or someone handing out samples. Without a list, you may end up driving all the way home, just to discover you never purchased the original things you set out to get.

- **Errand lists.** Whenever you have to run more than one errand, make a list of everyplace you have to go. As you complete each errand, check it off on your list.

- **Planning lists.** Whether you have to organize a project, plan a small party or plan a major event, planning lists are essential. Once you have all things-to-do listed, you can then begin categorizing and delegating.

Organizing Clinic

Question

I have a terrible time with notes that I write to myself as well as piles of papers. I write so many notes, it's ridiculous. Then, I subdivide them into too many piles. I am afraid if I throw papers and notes out, I'll lose something important. What to do?

Jane Alaimo
Freehold, NJ

Answer

I'm happy to hear you're writing your notes and not trying to keep all of your thoughts and ideas in your head. Just writing them down is the very first step toward getting them all organized. Your problem isn't the act of writing your notes. It's WHERE you're writing your notes.

Rather than jotting your thoughts on several sheets of paper, keep them consolidated in one notebook. I highly recommend you use a system such as our *Get Organized Now! Easy Organizer*. It will help you keep all of your notes, concerning a multitude of subjects, organized into appropriate categories and easy to find when you need them. When you keep your notes consolidated, you won't have to worry about sorting them into piles and you won't stand the chance of losing them.

If you don't like to carry around an organizer and a notebook when you leave your home or office, carry a tiny notepad in your purse or briefcase. You can jot down your notes when you're out. When you return to your home or office, transfer your notes into your notebook or planner system.

- **Reference lists.** There are so many reference lists that could be helpful including movies you'd like to see, books you'd like to read, gifts you may buy, places you'd like to visit, your goals and more. By writing these things down, you have a ready reference so you're less likely to forget. Plus, when things are written down, you make them more concrete, and more likely to do or see.

- **Checklists.** Checklists provide step-by-step instructions on how to do something, such as programming the VCR or using the washing machine. These essential tools help ensure that every member of any household (as long as he or she is old enough) is able to perform a task.

Tessa, a public speaker, has a binder full of checklists that her family can refer to whenever she is on the road. She has dozens of checklists including step-by-step instructions for setting the house alarm, washing a load of laundry, using the microwave, sorting the mail and changing the computer printer paper if it runs out.

- **It's not enough to have lists.** I know someone who makes so many lists, but never gets anything accomplished. Let's face it. You're not in the list making business. Therefore, it's not enough just to have lists. The most important thing about lists is that you use them to get something done.

- **List storage.** If you have many lists that you refer to often, it's important to keep them organized in one central system. This is typically a binder, but could also be a filing cabinet or file box.

  Of course, I highly recommend my *Get Organized Now! Easy Organizer* for all of your list keeping needs. It contains lists for family information, goals, to do's, projects, wishes, prayers, home maintenance, gardening, inventory, groceries, meals, budget, orders, chores, cleaning, diet, medication, people to contact, email and Web sites, travel, vacations and much more.

- **The infamous sticky note.** Someone once said to me, "Oh, you're a professional organizer. You're probably one of those people who hate to use sticky notes!" On the contrary, I use sticky notes fairly often. But, I certainly don't have sticky notes plastered all over the place.

  For instance, if I plan to visit a friend in the morning, I might leave a sticky note on my purse reminding me to return the book she loaned me. Once I do, I get rid of the sticky note.

  On occasion, I leave the house while my husband is in the shower and stick a sticky note on his computer monitor indicating that I've gone to the library, or the park or wherever. Once he reads my note, it gets discarded.

  In other words, I use sticky notes for very brief notes that are not intended to hang around for more than a day or so. The sticky notes reminds, and then gets tossed.

Great idea!

I keep all of my To Do lists on my laptop computer, using Microsoft Word. I begin each bulleted item with a few standard verbs such as "call," "mail," "buy," "email," "talk to," and "copy." Then I select the entire list and use MS Word's "Sort" feature (go under the "Table" menu and select sort) to group all the related tasks together. I can see at a glance all the calls I need to make, things I have to buy, people I need to talk to and so on, because those tasks are all grouped together. If needed, I can easily print out this sorted list and tuck the sheet of paper into my planner and manually check off each item as it's completed.

Lori Lizakowski
Crookston, MN

Chapter 57

Avoiding Morning Madness

- **Do just one more thing.** At the end of the day, ask yourself, "What task do I have to do tomorrow that will take me less than ten minutes to complete?" Then, do that one final task right now. When you wake up tomorrow, you'll already be ahead of the game!

- **Turn your breadbox into a lunch station.** Include everything you need to make lunch for your children such as sandwich bags, twist ties, bread, snacks, lunch bags and plastic utensils. You'll get your kids out the door and off to school in a jiffy.

Great idea!

We keep all or our breakfast spreads on a tray. The jam, marmalade, honey, peanut butter, Vegemite, sugar, pepper and salt all come out the morning or even the night before. This keeps them all together and saves time.

Jan Coghill
Melbourne, Australia

- **Time to get up.** Avoid a line of family members at the bathroom every morning. Stagger the time everyone gets up by 15 minutes. Rotate the schedule so the same person doesn't have to get up the earliest each day.

- **Make a timer sound.** If you're having a problem with one or more of your kids taking forever in the bathroom, set a timer to go off when his or her allotted time is over. Also, get older girls a makeup mirror for their bedroom. If she needs a few extra moments, she can put on her makeup in the bedroom rather than the bathroom.

- **What to wear?** Help your children lay out tomorrow's clothes the night before. Help them assemble their entire outfit and hang it on a hook or place it on a dressing table. This will save tons of time the next morning.

- **Give yourself a quick dress start the night before.** Each evening, lay out the clothing you plan to wear tomorrow. Iron if necessary. Assemble everything, including your accessories and then hang on a hook behind the closet door. When morning arrives, as soon as you hop out of the shower you'll be able to get dressed in seconds.

- **Prepare your breakfast table the night before.** Rather than rushing around in the morning, set the table for breakfast the night before. Include all bowls, plates, cups, napkins and non-perishable foods such as boxes of cereal or plastic-wrapped muffins. When morning arrives, just get out the refrigerated items.

- **Make breakfast the night before.** Who says you can't have a quick egg in the morning. The night before, mix together eggs (or egg substitute), shredded cheese, bell peppers, mushrooms and/or any other vegetable. Add a bit of breadcrumbs to the ingredients. Mix and divide evenly into a muffin tin using Pam cooking spray prior to prevent the eggs from sticking. Bake until done, pop out of the muffin tin, put on a plate and put the plate in the fridge. In the morning, just pop a few egg bakes into the microwave for a minute and you'll have a hearty, quick breakfast in seconds.

Great idea!

Making lunches in the morning can be stressful. I put together the week's lunches Sunday evening. This way my son can pack his own lunches, stress free!

I have a basket that I keep on a lower shelf in the fridge, that includes 5 yogurts, 5 snack bags of meat and cheese rolled up (he doesn't eat sandwiches), 5 snack bags of fresh fruit, and 5 snack bags of cut up fresh veggies. I switch up and give him different varieties in each of the categories above. Today he may want squash, tomorrow he may want broccoli. It's his choice, so he tends to eat it all up.

I also include two little disposable containers of different salad dressings for his veggies. Then I have a basket kept outside of the fridge with his choice of juices, water, snack bags of peanuts, crackers, trail mix, napkins, and spoons—the incidentals that he needs to make his lunch complete.

His confidence gets a boost and because he's making his own choices I find that he tends to eat everything and never complains about any aspect of lunch. Stress free!

Meridith Carsella
Orlando, FL

- **Make smoothies for breakfast.** Put all your fruit, yogurt, tofu, and other smoothie ingredients in the blender the night before and put the blender pitcher in the refrigerator overnight. In the morning, put the blender pitcher back on its mechanism and blend your smoothies. Sure beats having to chop up fruit during the morning rush.

- **Sandwich savvy.** Make a week's worth of sandwiches, put them in individually labeled freezer bags and freeze them. If your kids like lettuce or tomato, when you make the sandwiches also make a week's worth of sandwich topping bags and put those in the refrigerator. Each day, pop a sandwich (and a topping bag) in a brown paper lunch bag and it will be ready to eat by the time your kid's lunchtime rolls around. Note: Mayonnaise and jelly do not freeze well.

- **Don't oversleep.** If you're always oversleeping, it's time to kick the habit. Don't keep your alarm clock where you can easily reach over and turn it off. You'll probably fall asleep again. Place it at the far end of the room. You will actually have to get out of bed and walk across the room to turn it off.

- **Set the clock ahead.** One trick many people use to ensure they wake up on time is to set the bedroom clock anywhere from twenty minutes to one hour ahead.

- **Keep a clock in the bathroom.** If you're on a tight schedule, you might want to put a clock in the bathroom. This will help you keep on track.

- **Give everyone a clock.** Why should you always be the timekeeper? Give all of your kids their own alarm clock and teach them how to use it.

- **Give them fair warning.** Always give your family at least a ten-minute warning before they have to leave the house. Ring a bell ten minutes prior to the time you have to leave so everyone can finish up what they're doing and get in the car.

- **Put it in the car.** Anything (not perishables) you need to bring with you the next day can be stored in the car the night before. This will save you lots of time in the morning.

- **Turn off the tube.** If it's difficult to get your kids away from the TV in the morning, set a "No TV in the morning" rule, or a "TV goes off 10 minutes prior to departure" rule.

- **Shower the night before.** If you shower at night, you'll shave tons of time off of your morning routine.

- **Rise and shine.** If you're always rushing around in the morning, it's possible you're waking up too late. Try going to bed a half hour earlier, so you can wake up a half hour earlier.

- **Listen to the local news.** Very often, the local news can help you schedule your time better in the morning. For example, if the current weather advisory calls for snow, you may have to give yourself an extra hour to get to work. If the traffic analysis reveals there's a backup on the freeway, you may want to take the backroads instead.

Chapter 58

Getting There On Time

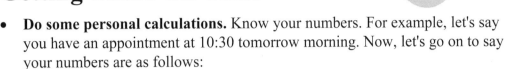

- **Do some personal calculations.** Know your numbers. For example, let's say you have an appointment at 10:30 tomorrow morning. Now, let's go on to say your numbers are as follows:

Evening

- ❖ You need 8 hours of sleep.

- ❖ It takes you 30 minutes to fall asleep.

Morning

- ❖ Always pad your time needed by a minimum of 30 minutes.

- ❖ You need 90 minutes to wake up, shower, dress, etc.

- ❖ You need 10 minutes to walk the dog.

- ❖ It's winter and you have to warm the car for 5 minutes.

- ❖ It will take you a maximum of 40 minutes to get to your appointment. Note: Always plan on the trip taking longer. With traffic, construction, etc., it usually does.

What time should you wake up? Add up your morning numbers. In this case, you'll need 175 minutes—approximately three hours, from the moment you wake up, to get there with enough time to spare and without rushing. So, if you have to be there at 10:30AM, you should wake up no later than 7:30AM and do everything you have to do without getting distracted. Use a timer to ensure you're staying on track and not taking too long doing any one activity.

Also, be sure you get enough sleep the previous night. In this case, you should go to bed no later than 11:00PM. Go to bed earlier if possible.

- **Watch out for those distractions.** Imagine this scenario. You went to bed early, woke up on time and were currently on schedule. That is—until the phone rang. Instead of allowing the answering machine to screen your call, you decided to pick up.

You soon discover it's Aunt Martha who just had to tell you about her wonderful birthday party. She just rattles on and on, until you can finally get a word in and tell her you'll have to call her after your appointment. She says, "Ok, I just have to tell you one more thing . . ."

Needless to say, you're now late. When you have to go somewhere, always have your answering machine screen your calls. Chances are, it won't be an emergency and you'll be able to return the call later, when you have more time.

- **Count on it taking longer.** There are very few things you can do that will only take five minutes or less to complete. For example, you may think it takes five minutes to check your email, but very often, it takes 15 minutes or more. Once you get into your email program, dial up, read a few letters, perhaps respond to a few and then close your program, that original five minutes often is long gone. Three words: Pad your time.

- **Sound the alarm.** Alarm clocks are not just for waking you up in the morning. If you have to leave your house or office at 3:00 in the afternoon, set the alarm to buzz at that time. You can also use a watch alarm or a computer software reminder alarm.

- **Get ready the night before.** Don't wait until the morning arrives before deciding what you're going to wear or what you have to bring. The night before, lay out your clothes, have the kids' lunches ready to go in the refrigerator, organize your materials and put them near the door and make sure you have enough gas in the car. If you do everything you need to do the night before, you'll be able to dress and go, without stress, in the morning.

- **Set the clock ahead.** Set your clock and/or watch ahead the number of minutes that you're usually late. For instance, if you're usually ten minutes late, set your watch so that it's ten minutes fast.

- **Beware the snooze button.** Most alarm clocks come equipped with a snooze button that temporarily stops the alarm and allows you to sleep for a few more minutes. Try placing your alarm clock on the other side of the room, so you actually have to get up out of bed to turn it off. Once you're up, don't go back to bed. If you must hit the snooze button once or twice, set your alarm clock earlier to make up for the extra time you need.

- **Know where you're going.** If you're traveling to an unfamiliar place, it is very important to get proper directions well ahead of time. Read through the directions beforehand and study a map if necessary. Consider making a test run a few days prior to be sure you know exactly where your destination is. If you're taking public transportation, determine the scheduled departure and arrival times, and keep accurate notes.

- **Plan an alternate route.** Your original planned route may not turn out to be the quickest route. Traffic delays happen for all sorts of reasons: construction, accidents, weather and so on. If you discover you can't take your original route, you'll have to go another way.

Know your alternate routes, before you leave your home or office. You'll be able to allow for extra time. Listen to the local traffic report on your radio while you're dressing or when you get in your car and use the best route for that day.

- **Plan to get there early.** If you have a meeting at noon, plan to get there between 11:30AM and 11:45AM at the very latest. You won't be late. Plus, if you happen to get there early, great! Now you have time to read that article you packed in your totebag last night.

- **Ask for flexibility.** If you drive your kids to school and it's interfering with you getting to work on time, perhaps you need to speak with your boss about you starting work a half hour later in the morning. Maybe you can take a half hour lunch versus an hour, or stay later in the evening, to make up for the time.

- **Make a time log.** A great way to determine exactly why you're late often is to make a two-week time log, listing every single activity you do during the day. Each time you're late for an appointment, for work, and so on, put a big L on the log. Review your activities that day to determine the cause of the lateness. Then, make a list of some possible solutions so it doesn't happen again.

- **Divide the responsibilities.** Maybe you're always running late, because you're the only person responsible for home tasks, errands and chores. Ask your spouse or kids to take on some of those responsibilities. It should be a team effort. Also, keep in mind that there may be some things you're currently doing during certain times of the day, that may be better suited for another time of day.

- **Is it worth it?** Is there something in particular you're always running late for, such as town meetings or an organization you belong to? Determine if that scheduled meeting or appointment is worth you even going to in the first place. Maybe you're going out of habit, rather than going because you really want to be there.

- **Get them there earlier.** I once knew someone who, even if you told him to arrive at 3:00PM, would not arrive until 3:30 or sometimes even 4:00. This was causing a lot of stress and frustration for the people who were waiting for him. To combat this, if we needed him to arrive at 3:00, we would tell him we needed him to arrive at 2:15. In doing this, he would generally make it by 3:00, which made everyone happy.

- **Stick to your To Do's.** Make a To Do list and follow it strictly. Don't do anything that's not on the list. It's often the extra tasks you feel you could fit in that cause late arrivals.

Chapter 59
Remembering

- **Bring questions.** When shopping for a major purchase, carry around a list of questions you need to ask. Jot down notes. It's easy to forget the details, especially when you have a variety of choices. Make a grid if you plan to do price and feature comparisons.

Did you know?

Where did the name "Tickler File" come from? Legend has it that the name "Tickler" was also the name of a long feather commonly used by farmer's wives. After spending long hours in the fields all week, the farmers were exhausted. So, when the farmers went to church services on the weekends with their wives, they'd constantly be nodding off. The wives would bring along this long feather, called the "Tickler" and tickle their husbands under the chin with it if they began falling asleep, as a "reminder" for staying awake. Thus the term "Tickler File" was coined. It's a reminder for staying on top of our daily projects, tasks and activities.

- **Make a morning checklist.** Ever get all the way to work and realize you forgot to put on your wristwatch? This can be annoying. To avoid this from happening, make yourself a quick, morning checklist. Include anything you have to do before work—or school—and everything you must bring along with you.

- **What's his name?** In your address book, always include all names that relate to a particular address. For instance, if your friend's name is in your book as Alice Smith, if you know the rest of her family's names, include those too— her husband, her kids, her pets. If you need those names, they'll be easily available.

- **Make reference lists.** Make lists for accessing information that you'd find useful and put those lists in an easy-to-access place. Jot down good ideas on your reference lists as they come to you. This can save you hours. You won't have to waste time constantly looking things up or trying to remember.

- **Keep an "Events Folder."** To remember an upcoming concert, presentation or lecture that you're interested in attending, keep an "Events Folder" of the announcements you come across. Then, mark an RSVP date and the event date on your calendar. When the RSVP date comes around, decide if you really want to attend and if so look at the literature in your Event Folder and make any necessary reservations. Purge papers in this file regularly to keep it up-to-date.

Great idea!

I keep a tablet on my refrigerator with a magnet on the back. As I run out of something that I will need at the grocery store, I write it on the list. This keeps me from having to remember everything before I go to the store.

Trish Meixell
Newark, DE

- **Record yourself.** Use a tape recorder to instantly capture your thoughts and ideas. They work great in the car or if you have an idea in the middle of the night when the lights are off. A little hand held tape recorder is a wonderful gadget to carry around with you and record your thoughts, your parking space number or a phone number you see on a billboard.

- **Keep a pad and pencil by your bedside.** If you have a flash of inspiration in the middle of the night, you'll be able to jot it down.

- **Same day, same time.** Do similar tasks every day at the same time. You'll get into the habit of knowing that when 4:00PM rolls around, you have to start dinner or when it is 3:45PM you automatically remember to tidy up your home office desk.

Great idea!

Do you ever miss a medical appointment because those little appointment cards get tucked away in a wallet or buried in a pile in your desk drawer? I use a business card holder—the type that has three sleeves to a page—to file appointment cards in chronological order. I just flip it open to see what appointments are coming next.

Philip C. Richards
Logistics Management Specialist
U.S. Army Petroleum Center
New Cumberland, PA

- **Buy ahead and mail ahead.** Make a list of all recurring events you buy greeting cards for, such as birthdays and anniversaries. Put all January events together, all February events together and so on. Go out and purchase all of the greeting cards you'll need, for the entire year.

Write on your monthly calendar, on the 25th of each month, to send out all of the greeting cards for events being celebrated the next month. For example, on July 25th, mail out all your August cards. On August 25th, mail out all your September cards.

Since all of your cards will be pre-purchased and you only have to mail once each month, chances are all of your greeting cards will be sent out and received on time.

- **Use triggering devices.** These alert you when you're not sticking to your priorities. A watch with an alarm or kitchen timer set at half-hour intervals can work wonders.

Great idea!

Whenever I make an appointment and put it in my appointment book (i.e., hairdresser, doctor, plumber), I always put the phone number right besides it. Then if I need to cancel or change the appointment, I don't have to go searching for the number. This saves a lot of time and aggravation.

Fran Hackerman
Hamden, CT

- **Practice memory techniques.** There are a number of memory techniques available such as pneumonics or memory by association. Local libraries and bookstores have many books available on the subject.

- **The computer can help.** Use a computer program, such as Outlook™ to remind you when a deadline is coming up; or carry around a Palm Pilot™ to keep you on track.

- **Always store in one place.** One way to be certain you never forget where something is, is to have a designated home for it and to return that item to its designated home when you're done with it. For instance, use a key holder for your keys or an eyeglass case by your reading lamp for your reading glasses.

- **Write it down.** With the amount of things you have to remember in any given day, why should you try to stuff it all into your memory bank? When you want to remember something, the very best thing to do is write it down. When you need to recall it, it will be there for you in an instant.

- **Keep it together.** When you write down things you want to remember, keep them in one consistent place. Otherwise, you're going to spend a lot of time looking for your notes.

- **Maintain good health.** Eat healthy foods, get enough sleep and exercise. These are all important for your memory, staying focused and being alert.

- **Believe in yourself.** If you keep saying you have a bad memory, you'll probably continue to have a bad memory. It's important to have a motivated, "I can remember" attitude.

- **Send yourself email reminders.** There are many free email reminder services available. You type in what you want to remember, such as a birthday, anniversary or event and you then receive an email reminder when the date is approaching. There's a good reminder service available using the free calendar feature on Yahoo!

Great idea!

If I need to remember to leave the house or work with a particular item, I put my car keys with it even if it's in the refrigerator.

Carolyn Morrison
Rockville, VA

- **Set timers and alarms.** Take advantage of alarm clocks and timers throughout the day. Have to take the clothes out of the wash at 3:00? Set your alarm clock to remind you. Want to leave for the basketball game by 6:15? Set your timer to beep a few minutes before.

- **Use visual reminders.** Visual reminders can help you remember and focus. I especially like visual reminders for remembering goals. If your goal is to take a trip to a beautiful island in a few years, keep a magazine photograph of the island right on your desk. If your goal is to own your own business one day, find a picture or ornament that will help remind you of this goal each day.

- **Leave yourself a message.** Whenever you have to remember something, call yourself to leave a message on your answering machine. When you listen to your voice messages later, you'll be reminded. If you check your email daily, you can email yourself instead.

Great idea!

For appointments, I put a note on the bathroom mirror and everyone in the family makes sure that appointment is kept. We tried putting notes on the refrigerator, the front door, the TV frame and calendars and nothing worked as well as the bathroom mirror. Even guests have read and given us reminders and offers of a ride to the appointment if necessary.

Virginia Kessinger
Vancouver, WA

- **Use the Tickler System.** It will help you remember upcoming projects, special events and more. Use it religiously and I guarantee you'll never forget!

  You'll need:

  - ❖ 12 hanging file folders
  - ❖ 31 manila file folders
  - ❖ File folder labels
  - ❖ A pen or marker
  - ❖ A portable file box (only if you don't plan to use your filing cabinet or desk file drawer)

  To assemble:

  - ❖ Label 12 hanging file folders by month—Jan, Feb, Mar, etc. all the way to December.
  - ❖ Place these folders in a container that holds hanging file folders, such as a filing cabinet, a portable file box or portable file holder.
  - ❖ Label 31 manila file folders—in a different color than the hanging file folders—1,2,3,4, etc. all the way up to 31. The 31 file folders represent each day of each month.
  - ❖ Place all 31 manila file folders in the hanging folder for the current month. In other words, if the current month is May, put the 31 manila file folders in that month. If the current month is November, put the 31 manila file folders in that month.

  To use:

  - ❖ When you have a task or project you're not ready to start right now but would like to start in a few days or a few months from now, no problem! Slip the appropriate documents into the appropriate day—or month—and it will be there later when you need it. For example, if you have to do something on the 14th of the month, put the required documents in folder number 14 and add extra notes as needed.

❖ If you need to start the task before a certain day of the month, put a note in the folder a number of days ahead of the date that it's due. For instance, if a relative's birthday is coming up on August 20th and you want to send him a greeting card ahead of time, put a note or the actual greeting card in your Tickler System in folder number 10, for instance, and your card will make it to your relative on time.

❖ For items that are to be started in another month, put a note in the hanging file folder for that particular month. If the current month is December, but the task needs to be done in February, a note pertaining to that task should go in the folder labeled February. Be sure to give each paper a due date.

❖ You can even insert event tickets, permission slips and other papers that have to be checked on a particular date, into the appropriate folder.

❖ When the current month ends, all 31 manila file folders should be moved to the following month. Any papers that were in the hanging file folder for the month should be moved into specific days, based on the due dates you previously assigned.

❖ The first task on your To Do list each day should be to check your Tickler System. The system will not work if you don't get into the habit of checking it daily. If you're having difficulties getting into this habit, set an alarm to go off at a set time each day until you can do it without being reminded. Eventually, it will be very natural.

❖ Finally, if you have to reschedule a task or event, move the note from the date it's in, to another month or day in your system.

❖ You can also "roll" your tickler file every day. As you check each day, place the empty tickler file at the end of the files. Thus, if today is the 16th, process the papers for the 16th and place the 16 folder at the end of the files. Tomorrow, the 17 folder will be the first folder in the tickler system.

Chapter 60

Being Productive

- **Subtract steps.** Unload groceries from your shopping bag, directly into the refrigerator or pantry, instead of first putting them on the countertop.

  Put all of your cleaning supplies into one bucket and carry the bucket from room to room as you clean, rather having to walk back and forth to your cleaning supplies area.

  Fold clothes as you're taking them out of the dryer so they're ready to be put away.

  In other words, don't take many steps to complete a task that can be done in just a few simple steps.

Great idea!

I helped a friend develop a plan of action when she was feeling overwhelmed. The basic concept was to attack things one step at a time.

Break each task down into 15-30 minute increments:

Wash the dishes	15 minutes
Do laundry	30 minutes
Pay bills	20 minutes
Complete form	20 minutes
Total time	85 minutes

Pull together anything necessary to complete each job so there's no delay in beginning or a reason to stop. Do each task one at a time. Stop when the 15-30 minutes are up, even if not completely finished. Put that task aside and continue on to the next task. Carry over anything not completed to the next day. To her amazement, she was completing more tasks than ever before without feeling overwhelmed.

As for myself, a single mom with two active boys, I find this method allows me to get everything completed in a stress free manner with flexibility, which leaves me time for myself or activities with the boys. Friday night is Monopoly night!

Sharon Anson
Springfield Gardens, NY

- **Identify your tasks.** Each task you do each day, falls into one of four categories:

  A: I have to and I want to

  B: I have to, but I don't want to

  C: I don't have to, but I want to

  D: I don't have to and I don't want to

  A: I have to and I want to. Tasks that fall into category A are those tasks that are most likely to get completed. For instance, perhaps you have to go furniture shopping for the new unfurnished home you're buying.

  If you don't go shopping, you won't have a bed to sleep in or a sofa to relax on. It's a task that has to be done, but you also consider it a fun task. You already want to do tasks in this category, because your desire is incentive enough.

  B: I have to, but I don't want to. Tasks that fall into category B are tasks that you will complete, but are also those you may procrastinate a bit on. An example might be paying your phone bill.

  You have to pay the bill, but you don't want to. Likewise, you know if you don't, your phone will be turned off. Category B tasks require a bit more of an incentive, so be sure to attach pending rewards to these tasks. If you attach rewards you will have something to look forward to and enjoy when those tasks are completed.

  C: I don't have to, but I want to. Tasks that fall into category C either get done at the expense of other things getting done or they get put on the back burner. For instance, you may enjoy surfing the Internet, so you surf instead of doing laundry.

  On the flip side, you may enjoy scrap booking, but since it's not a major priority, it never seems to make it to your To Do list. If you always use Category C items as reward items for completing something else you have to do, you will always enjoy the benefits of doing these items. Also, these tasks will never be done at the expense of a priority item not getting done.

  D: I don't have to and I don't want to. Tasks that fall into category D should be eliminated from your To Do list. For example, perhaps you volunteer to act as a board member for your community town hall. You used to enjoy it, but you don't anymore. Nor do you have the time to dedicate to it anymore. This type of "don't have to, don't want to" task is something you should stop doing. Why take up your precious time doing something that you don't have to do and that is no longer in line with your goals?

Organizing Clinic

Question

I am always starting a project but never finishing it. I'll start to rearrange the kitchen cabinets and think that cleaning out the hall closet is of greater importance. My house is a wreck because of this. How do I stick to one project at a time?

Crystal Yob
Palm Bay, Florida

Answer

Crystal,

This problem that you're experiencing is a classic one. The personality style is called "Drop and Hop." You start one project, get distracted—whether by your own thoughts or outside interruptions—and you then hop to another project. As you already mentioned, this leads to unfinished projects and no sense of accomplishment. Here are three simple ideas to help you start and complete, your projects.

- **Don't set enormous goals.** Many people drop and hop because they get frustrated or bored with the enormity of the project at hand and decide it would be easier to do something else. To avoid this, don't give yourself enormous goals, like reorganizing the kitchen cabinets. Instead, break your goals down into small, manageable mini goals that you can complete in a small amount of time. Set a goal to organize one shelf in one kitchen cabinet at a time and you're certain to finish that task and feel a sense of accomplishment.

- **Get a reminder every 15 minutes.** It sounds like you have a number of organizing projects you'd like to do, so each project is calling out to you, trying to steal your attention away from the project you've chosen to work on. To keep your attention on one thing at a time, set a timer or alarm, to go off every fifteen minutes. When the timer sounds, if you've strayed from the project you were originally working on, come right back to it. Keep setting the timer until you've reached the mini goal you've set for the day.

- **Eliminate interruptions at all costs.** It's so easy to stray from a project, when the phone rings or a visitor stops by to shoot the breeze. When you're ready to work on a project, have your answering machine field your calls. Shut off the television. Put up a "Do Not Disturb" sign. Tell visitors to come back later. The less you're interrupted, the quicker you'll complete your mini goal.

- **Avoid attempting too much.** Anyone who thinks they have to accomplish everything yesterday, almost always end up with half finished projects and feelings of anxiety. While it's fine to include everything you have to do on your Master List, only pull a maximum of four to six items per day from that list and transfer them to your Daily To Do List and work on those. Be sure most of the items are high priority and just a few of them are lower priority.

Each day, focus only on those items on your daily To Do list and don't put anything else on that list until those items are complete. If you find that you always get all of your items done with time to spare, you may be able to put one or two more items on your list per day.

If you find that you're having difficulties finishing four to six items, then just put two to four items on your list instead. By the end of each day, you should be able to enjoy your evening, feeling good about everything you've accomplished.

Great idea!

Many people rush to various places, meetings, clients, kids' activities, personal appointments and social engagements. Information is always coming to us almost 24 hours a day, even during sleep. An idea slips in while waiting for your dentist, getting gas or during some down time. What to do?

Keep a little notebook with you at all times. This is your Master List. Put that idea down, write that phone number or add that new email address someone just gave you or even a wish. Later, you can transfer it to where it belongs and then cross it off your Master List. Some things will just stay in the notebook at your fingertips, but do make a clean page for the leftover information and dispose of your crossed-off list.

Gerrie Beck, Professional Organizer
Kensington, MD

- **Break it down.** Rather than being overwhelmed by a huge task, break it down into manageable chunks. For instance, don't focus on organizing your bedroom. First, focus on organizing the top of your dresser. Next, focus on organizing a shelf. Finally, focus on organizing under your bed and so on.

- **No excuses.** Be careful you're not using more enjoyable tasks as excuses for not getting things done.

- **Alternate.** Sandwich difficult tasks in between fun tasks. In doing this, you'll always have a task to look forward to after the more difficult task is completed.

- **Divide and conquer.** No matter what project you have ahead of you, the best way to avoid getting overwhelmed is to divide it into small, manageable tasks. For instance, if you have ten boxes of paper to plow through, go through just one box at a time and tell yourself you'll work for a mere ten minutes.

If you get through the ten minutes and you wish to work for another ten minutes, great! If you'd prefer to take a break after that first ten minutes and come back to the project later or tomorrow, that's fine too.

As long as you work on your project a little bit at a time, you'll be that much closer to its completion. This "divide and conquer" approach helps to alleviate stress and ensures your project is constantly moving ahead.

Great idea!

I organize projects into rolling luggage cases of various sizes. Not only does it keep everything together, organized and clutter free with all the necessary tools at hand, but I can move the project around to whatever part of the house I feel like working in, even outside on the back patio. I can change them out as the projects change, while others are permanent, like the one I use for my music classes.

G Fior
Cincinnati, OH

- **Do what you dread most.** Don't procrastinate on tasks you hate to do. If you hate returning phone calls, balancing your checkbook or doing laundry, make these the very first tasks of your day to get them out of the way. You'll feel good that they're done and the rest of your day will be smooth sailing.

Great idea!

I clip and sort grocery coupons while watching my favorite TV shows. I save money and don't waste time on commercials, all at the same time! I keep my coupons in an index box with dividers that are sorted by the grocery store aisle. So, when I take my coupons to the market with me, I can go aisle-by-aisle and not waste time looking for the coupons I need.

Tina Escobar
La Quinta, CA

- **Use index cards for goal setting.** Perhaps you've always wanted to take a cruise or learn a new language or plant a garden. Goal setting will help you get there.

Grab a bunch of index cards and write a specific goal on each—anything you can think of that you really want to do.

Then, arrange the cards so that the goals you most want to achieve are on top and the less important goals follow. Next, write deadlines on each of your top three cards, break each goal down into mini-goals and schedule time to achieve each of them.

- **Pack a project.** Every minute of the day is so precious and yet, endless hours are wasted standing in line, being on telephone hold, sitting in the doctor's or dentist's office, awaiting a client or friend who is meeting you for lunch or sitting in the car to pick up a child or spouse.

    This wasted time is the perfect reason to always make sure you pack a project. In other words, always have something with you to do, wherever you are bound to be waiting.

    If you're leaving your house, put the project you're working on in your purse, briefcase or a tote bag. If you're on telephone hold fairly often, put your project in a basket and leave that basket right near your phone.

    Whenever you catch a few free minutes, work on your project. While you're waiting, you can balance your checkbook, work on a cross-stitch craft, write letters, catch up on your reading, update your planner or work on any number of other projects.

- **Make standard lists.** Make standard lists for things like groceries, instructions for the babysitter, instructions for the house or pet sitter or a note for the UPS delivery person when you're away, so you don't have to write them up each time you need them.

- **In your cell phone.** Program frequently called numbers into your cell phone, such as your spouse's cell number, your child's pediatrician or your local pizza shop. They're good numbers to have available when you're out.

- **Set up 10-minute "When I have time" goals.** One of the oldest phrases in the book is, "I'll do that, when I have the time." Problem is, that time never seems to come. If you *really* want to do something, the time can generally be found pretty easily. For example, if you just won an all-expenses paid trip to the land of your dreams, you'd probably find time to fit it into your busy schedule without much of a problem.

    So, it's time to begin fitting in those things you want to do and 10-Minute Goals can help. Schedule ten minutes each day to catch up on your reading or to begin learning that foreign language or to spend having fun with your children. Then, work on those goals when the scheduled date and time rolls around.

Chapter 61

Procrastination

- **Laziness?** Do people procrastinate because they're lazy? Sometimes yes, and sometimes no. For instance, if you have to organize your bedroom and you know exactly what to do, but you'd rather sleep, in most cases that would be considered laziness.

  But if you're not organizing the bedroom because you are so overwhelmed you don't know where to start, then that actually has nothing to do with laziness. This book doesn't cover laziness, but it does cover legitimate reasons why people procrastinate.

- **The perfectionist trap.** Perfectionists often put off starting something because they feel if they can't finish it all at once, there's no sense even starting it. Unfortunately, this is a good way to have a To Do list that's a mile long. Try saving your perfectionist tendencies for something extremely important and try to ease up on some of those tendencies for things that aren't quite as important. In addition, if you have to vacuum the entire house, but don't have time to finish it, concentrate on vacuuming one room perfectly. You don't have to eliminate your perfectionist tendencies, but you're still getting things done.

- **Make segments.** If you're procrastinating on something because you find the project as a whole to be very overwhelming, break that project up into manageable segments. For instance, instead of trying to do everything you have to do for your child's upcoming birthday party, take care of just the invitations. The next day, take care of making a shopping list. The next day, shop for decorations. You get the idea. When you give yourself smaller tasks that are easily handled, the project moves ahead and you can avoid getting overwhelmed along the way.

- **Get a helping hand.** When you find yourself procrastinating on something, get someone else involved who can either help you out or cheer you on. Every once in awhile, we all need some support.

- **Does it really have to get done?** What's the worst thing that will happen if you don't do the task you're procrastinating on? If the result will be something major like you'll have creditors chasing after you or your car will likely run out of gas the next time you're driving, then obviously the task needs to be done. But, if the result will be nothing important, then you may be able to just take that item off your To Do list completely.

- **Set a reward.** Sometimes things get done faster when rewards are attached to them. Next time you find yourself procrastinating on something, tell yourself you'll do something you really enjoy as soon as you finish that project, or a part of that project. Mini rewards along the way, along with a more major reward for completing that task or project, may be all the motivation you need to get going on it.

- **Just do one a day.** If you have a long list of items you've been procrastinating on, maybe it would help you if you just choose one of those items to focus on at a time. Choose one, and work on that one thing. Don't even think about the other things until this one is done.

- **Make up your mind.** Very often, procrastination occurs when you can't make up your mind about something. For instance, perhaps you want to buy a digital camera, but you can't decide what model to buy. A good solution is to make a chart of all the models you're considering (across the top of the page) and all the features you're looking for (along the left side of the page). Use checkmarks in between to mark the features available on the particular models. Sometimes, just having a visual can open your eyes to the most appropriate solution.

- **Pro/Con List.** A Pro/Con list is another tool to help you stop procrastinating on decisions. Using one sheet of paper per possible decision, make 2 columns, one for Pros and another for Cons. List all the Pros and Cons for each possible decision. The decision that has the most Pros, is likely to be the decision you should choose to make.

- **Write it down.** Make it official by recording on paper, what needs to be done. When it's written down, it's more concrete, and there's a greater chance you'll start and complete it.

- **Tell someone.** Tell a friend, associate or loved one what your plans are. Discuss decisions that need to be made with others. Ask a friend or spouse for some ongoing motivation. Sometimes an outside perspective may be all you need to get started.

- **Schedule.** Establish a regular time each day to work on your goal, project or task. Be sure it's an area where you're not likely to be interrupted. Burn a wonderful smelling candle in that room, open a window, or do something to give your environment a pleasant, inviting reason to be there.

- **Post reminders.** Keep your goals in front of you. Post reminders of your goals and deadlines where you can constantly see them.

- **I'll only do this if . . .** Make something you normally do and enjoy contingent upon doing the avoided task. For example: "I will not watch my favorite television program until I complete Part A of my project." By the way, no fair cheating!

Chapter 62

Prioritizing

- **Quantity is not as important as quality.** When you prioritize, you're determining what needs to get done and in what order you should perform those actions. Very often, one may concentrate on getting lots of easy tasks done. But just because you're crossing off tons of items on your To Do list, doesn't necessarily mean you're completing the important stuff——the tasks that will help you achieve your goals.

- **Look into the future.** What do you want out of life? Do you want to play guitar well enough to be able to perform for your children? Do you want to travel the country? Do you want to have a beautiful vegetable garden in your backyard? While it is certainly important to get your day-to-day things done, it's also important to schedule in time for activities that will help you achieve the higher level goals you've set for yourself.

- **Make a Master List.** This is simply a long running list of everything you want to accomplish. It's in no particular order, but is essentially a holding place and a reference so you don't forget any activity and so that you're not trying to remember everything that needs to get done.

- **Assign A, B or C.** Assign each activity one of the following letter codes:

  - ❖ A - Those activities that are important AND urgent and will impact you greatly if you don't accomplish them right way.

  - ❖ B - Those activities that are important to be done, but not urgent. You have time to accomplish them before they have a great impact on your life.

  - ❖ C - Those activities that may be nice to do sometime, but if you don't do them, you wouldn't be terribly disappointed.

- **It's not set in stone.** Your letter assignments may change over time. Just because you assign a B priority to one of your activities today, doesn't mean it has to stay a B priority. It may turn into an A priority or a C priority in the future. Use your priority assignments as a guide, but don't be reluctant to change them if the need arises.

- **Focus.** Now it's time to focus on just a few activities listed on your Master List. You'll want to include a mixture of activities on your Daily To Do list. I recommend you choose three A priorities, two B priorities and one C priority. So each day, you'll have a total of 6 activities to focus on.

- **Make a schedule.** Schedule in time for each of your priorities, leaving some free time throughout your day for getting daily things done (dusting, cooking, etc.) and for rest and relaxation.

- **Morning, noon and night.** In general, you'll want to schedule so that you actually get those A priority tasks done, no matter what. I find that if I do my top priority tasks first thing in the morning and get them out of the way, then it's pretty smooth sailing the rest of the day.

  However, some people are able to better focus in the afternoon or the evening, so A priority tasks are sometimes better left for this time of day for them. No matter what time of day you choose to focus on your A priorities, be sure you don't allow anything except dire emergencies to take over the time you originally scheduled to complete those priorities.

- **If something comes up . . .** There are going to be times when you decide to do something in place of the activities you have initially assigned. For instance, the other day I had some activities planned for the afternoon, but a friend called and asked if I wanted to go to a local event with her in town. I weighed my options. I still had one B and one C priority on my list and I knew if I went to the event that these would not get done today. I decided to meet her at the event, and complete the B priority I had assigned when I returned home afterwards, and I also decided to move the C priority to tomorrow.

  Of course, while I do allow for flexibility in my schedule from time to time, I don't make a habit out of doing this. Most of the time, I stick to getting my priorities accomplished unless something very palatable arises that is important enough to me to push my originally assigned activities to another day.

- **The next day.** You will always want a total of six activities on your Daily To List. These should be three A priorities, two B priorities and one C priority. If you can never get 6 completed, then try for three—one A priority, one B priority and one C priority. If you do not accomplish one or more of today's priorities, you should then put them on tomorrow's To Do List.

- **Reward yourself.** If you follow this system, you will get an enormous amount of important things done and you'll more easily be able to reach your goals. As you get things done, particularly your A priorities, reward yourself along the way. For instance, you can sprinkle mini rewards throughout your day, such as a walk in the park or an outing with a friend. A more major reward should be enjoyed when you accomplish something big, such as passing a major exam or remodeling a room in your home.

Chapter 63

Reducing Interruptions

- **Log your interruptions.** Ever start working on something, get distracted and start working on something else—just to discover later that you never completed that first task you intended to do? If so, you're not alone. This drop one project, hop to another tendency is a common one that many people share.

  Next time you begin working on something, set a timer to sound off in ten minutes and then begin working on your first project. When the timer goes off, determine if you're still working on your first project.

  If you are, that's great. If not and you haven't yet completed that first project, stop what you're doing, jot down what interrupted you, re-set the timer and get back to working on your first project. Repeat this process throughout the day.

  At the end of the day, read through your list to determine what interruptions caused you to get distracted—television, unexpected visitors, phone calls and so on. Once you know what these interruptions are, you can then work on eliminating them so the same things don't distract you tomorrow.

  For example, perhaps you'll turn off the TV, screen your phone calls or ask those visitors to return at a later time.

- **Use your voicemail or answering machine.** Answering the telephone every single time it rings is one of the most common daily interruptions. Allow your voicemail or answering machine to field your calls when you're working on something that requires focused attention. Then, get back to your callers if you wish later on.

- **Make rules.** Sometimes you need peace and quiet to complete a task, such as when you're writing out your bills, making a call to a physician or simply taking a few minutes to catch your breath and clear your mind. If you have a spouse, kids or someone else living in your home, interruptions are probably a part of life.

  However, some times are meant to be free of interruptions. During those times, tell your family members you can't be interrupted, occupy kids with something else or get someone to help out and watch the kids for you until you have had a few minutes to complete whatever it is you need to do.

- **Give written guidelines.** A big reason so many people are constantly interrupted is because he or she is the only person that knows how to do certain things. My friend Andrew, for instance, always does the laundry in his house, but he recently assigned his son, James, to do this task each day.

Every time James has a question such as what temperature the wash water should be set to or if a particular fabric can be washed with towels, James has to interrupt his dad to ask. All Andrew would have to do to prevent these interruptions, is to write up some simple guidelines for James and post them near the washing machine.

- **Tell it like it is.** If you're working on something that cannot be interrupted, simply tell any family members, visitors or callers that you're working on a very important project and you'll get back to them as soon as you're done with it. Hopefully, most people will get the message.

- **Be firm.** If every time you say you can't be interrupted, you allow interruptions anyway, people will know that you're not very serious. If you say you can't be interrupted and someone tries to interrupt you, do not allow it. Don't take the call. Don't let the visitor in. Put up a do not disturb sign and lock the door. Give your kids a specific time when you'll be able to assist them so they'll know what to expect.

- **Tune out.** It's easy to get interrupted or distracted if the television or radio are constantly on. When you're working on something that needs your attention, turn them off and get to work in a quiet setting.

- **Establish a schedule.** If family members and friends know when you're available, they'll be less likely to interrupt you during times that you may need to be focused.

- **Give a list.** If you want to be interrupted for some things, but not others, make a list. Your list may say to only interrupt you if Sally calls or if a particular neighbor comes calling. This way, your kids or partner will know your intentions.

- **Work elsewhere.** If you have to get some home paperwork done, but you can't seem to get it done at home with all the constant noise and interruptions, why not take what you have to do to a local park, a quiet coffee shop or the library?

- **Respect others.** If someone else doesn't want to be interrupted, such as your daughter working on an important school project, respect her wishes too. This way, when the tables are turned, she will respect your wishes back.

Chapter 64

Respecting Your Time

- **It doesn't have to be all or nothing.** While you may consider helping someone out, that certainly doesn't mean you have to do it all. For example, rather than serving on a committee, you may volunteer to make reminder phone calls or to type up the newsletter.

- **Barter.** If someone asks you to volunteer your time, ask this person to volunteer her time right back. For instance, if your friend asks you to babysit tonight, ask her if she can drive your son to school tomorrow.

- **No guts, no glory.** If you have no intention of saying "yes," don't avoid the issue by saying, "maybe" or "if I have time." While this may temporarily alleviate your guilt, it's unfair to the other person and you'll be wasting time fretting over what excuse you're going to give to this person. Just say "no." And don't feel guilty because you'd rather spend some quality time with your family or you need some personal time alone.

- **Postpone your "Yes" answers.** Before agreeing to every request for your time, postpone your decision. When someone asks you if you could do something, tell that person you will get back to him or her later after you've had time to check your schedule.

  Go home. Think about it. Give yourself a chance to determine if you have the time, interest or energy first. If you truly want to do it, call the person and say "yes." If you don't want to do it, contact the person and say it won't fit into your schedule right now.

- **Shorten phone conversations.** Here are three ideas that will help you get off the phone and start getting things done:

  ❖ **Warn them about your time limits.** Know someone who can talk for hours? Sometimes you just don't have the time. Next time she calls, right at the start of the conversation, tell her you've only got five minutes to spare right now. When those five minutes have passed, tell her it was wonderful talking, but you've got to hang up for now.

  ❖ **Set an egg timer.** Many phone calls get lengthy because you get so involved with the conversation that you lose track of the time. This can be both time-consuming and expensive. Set an egg timer for a specified amount of time (5-15 minutes serve most conversations well) and politely end the call when the timer goes off.

- ❖ **Prepare ahead of time.** Before you make your calls, make a list of the items you want to cover. You're not wasting your time or the time of the person on the other end of the line, trying to remember things during the conversation.

- **Do it because you want to.** While there are some situations that are to be considered emergencies—such as helping an ill relative or friend—there are many other requests for your time that you don't have to do.

  The best rule of thumb is to choose those activities that you truly want to do—those things that will make you happy. If someone asks you for your time and you find yourself thinking, "Oh, no," then don't do it.

- **Slow down.** Who wants to go through life feeling rushed all the time? Every individual should have enough time to read a book, take a hot bath or slowly sip a glass of cool lemonade. If you're always rushing through life, there will be no time to truly savor it.

- **Schedule in fun.** In order to achieve a balanced life, one must schedule both work and fun activities. Just like you plan definite time to go to work, visit a doctor or get a haircut, so too should you make an appointment to enjoy a hobby, go swimming or have a nice dinner out with your spouse or loved one.

- **Have a heart to heart.** If you're always on time, but another person is always late to meet you, after two back-to-back occurrences, it's probably time to speak with that person and clear up this matter. Otherwise, it's bound to cause ill feelings later on. Perhaps it's difficult for this person to meet you at 3:00 due to his work schedule, but would definitely be on time if you scheduled your time together to begin at 4:00. Maybe a different day of the week could make all the difference in the world. Have a heart-to-heart with this person and come to some compromise that you both can live with.

- **Who's in control?** Yes, occasionally you will have to wait for someone else. Perhaps you always find yourself waiting at your doctor's office or your hair dresser—even though you have a scheduled appointment. However, even in these situations, you can still be in control of your time.

  One possibility is calling the doctor's office, for example, and asking if the doctor is running behind schedule. Some medical offices will allow you to come in a half hour later if the person you need to meet with is running late.

  Another alternative is to bring something with you to work on while you're in the waiting room. I often bring my laptop, some magazines or notepaper while I'm waiting for my appointments. This way, I always have something to keep me busy if needed.

Chapter 65

Bill Paying

- **Set up a bill paying area.** Decide on a dedicated place to collect, review and pay your incoming bills. Designate that area to be your permanent bill paying space. Every time you write out your bills, do so here.

- **Tear, tuck and store.** When you get a bill in the mail, tear open the envelope over a recycling container, discarding any flyers or other promotions. Tuck the bill into the return envelope and then store the bill in your bill paying system.

- **Use a bill paying system.** As soon as you get bills in the mail, they should immediately be placed into a bill paying system. All of your pending bills are then ready to be paid once a week or once every two weeks. Use that same bill paying system to store paid bill summaries, making sure that each category is in its own folder or envelope.

  Doing this makes it very simple to look something up when necessary. We have a product available called the Easy Bill Paying System. For more details, please visit: www.getorganizednow.com/ezbill.html

- **Create a workable bill payment and money management system.** You can do this with a calculator, pen and paper; or you can go the more sophisticated route by using one of the money management, computer software programs available, such as Quicken™.

- **Get it to remind you.** If you do decide to use money management software, you can set it up to automatically remind you of upcoming payments and invoices due. It can also help you print out your checks, keep track of your expenses and provide you with detailed reports of your transaction history.

Great idea!

A lot of companies like banks and utility companies are offering electronic statements. I sign up for as many of these e-statements as I can and save them all to a specified folder on my computer. Come the end of the year, all I have to do is burn these statements onto a disk and I will have all of my records in one convenient place. I'll also be saving tons of storage space.

Stacy Creed
Phoenix, AZ

- **Do your research.** Research before purchasing money management software. Find out how each of the programs can help you and how they compare with each other. While some of the more expensive programs offer a multitude of features, you may not really need all of the extra bells and whistles.

- **Don't lose track**. Keep on top of checks you write or you'll never know how much is in your account. Enter the check information into the check register, before tearing out the check. If you use money management software, get the details for the checks you wrote out each day into the program that night.

- **Back up.** Be sure to always back-up your money management computer files—keep an extra copy—on floppy, CD-Rom or zip drives. Better to be safe than sorry.

- **Balance your checkbook monthly.** In order for you to have a good idea of how much money is sitting in your checking account, what checks have cleared and any errors that you or your bank may have made, you must balance your checking account. It really doesn't take that long if you balance your checkbook the same day your statement and/or cancelled checks arrive back from the bank each month. In fact, if you use a computer program, you can do this task very quickly.

- **Mark it paid.** After paying a bill, mark it "paid" with the date and confirmation number if you're given one. Purchase a stamp/inkpad set that allows you to change the date and mark your paid bills effortlessly.

- **Keep everything nearby.** Keep essential bill paying supplies and tools in close reach. This may include your computer, a calculator, your checkbook, pens, envelopes, a letter opener, self-stick return address labels and postage stamps.

Great idea!

When recording my checkbook activity I like to use colored pens. For instance, I use green for deposits, purple for withdrawals, black for written checks, red for any bank related activity and pink to check off things. This is a great help when reconciling and also helps lighten the task of working on your checkbook. It's not so boring.

Robin Bennett
Pilot Mountain, NC

- **Set up a monthly budget and schedule.** Set consistent time aside at least twice a month to pay your bills (e.g. the 8th and 22nd of each month.)

- **Get automatic.** You can pay some companies without ever writing them a check. Some companies can automatically deduct your payments from your checking account each month if you like.

- **Avoid math errors.** The American Bankers Association confirms that the single largest reason people overdraw checking accounts is math errors. It's very easy to make a mistake in math calculation when doing it manually or even with a calculator. Money management software can be an effective, time saving tool that can eliminate many, if not all, math calculation errors. If you prefer to calculate with a calculator, always double-check your work.

- **Reverse the process.** Most people first write out a check and then add the information to their check register afterwards. Instead, before you write out a check, first write all of the necessary information in your check register. Only when you're done, should you then begin writing out your check. Do this and you'll never miss an entry in your check register again.

> **Great idea!**
>
> Always have two stamp booklets inside the front of your checkbook. This makes it handy and easy to get your bills ready for mailing.
>
> Diane Iannaccone
> North Babylon, NY

- **Pay online.** If you have a modem, you may be able to pay many of your bills online, without leaving your office or home. In addition, companies such as American Express, allow you to view your balances, review recent charges and download transactions—all in minutes.

- **Buddy up.** One person can be in charge of writing out all the bills and another person can double check that everything is written out correctly and that calculations are accurate. This is a great way to reduce the chance of an error occurring.

- **Don't overpay.** Just because your bill states you owe a certain amount, doesn't necessarily mean it's correct. My husband and I have caught several errors over the years that would have cost us significantly more than what we owed, had we not questioned the amount stated before we paid.

- **Add a few bucks.** Consider adding a little more when you're paying your mortgage, car payment or credit card statements. You may be able to greatly reduce your finance charges and/or the length of time you owe.

Great idea!

Years ago, I had to look for a check number to give to a company to prove that I had paid the bill. It took me a while going through check registers and such. No more. I log each bill paid each month in a one-subject 3-ring binder that you can find for about $.25 each. I fill it with approximately 100 sheets of loose-leaf paper.

Then, I use one page per month. I list each bill, date paid, check number, and amount paid. The heading is simply Month and Year. I set this up ahead of time for regular bills such as mortgage, electric and telephone. It's a real time saver and space saver as well.

I use the front and back of each page and it will hold ten years of bills. No more looking for the check numbers.

In addition, after balancing your checking accounts each month, put the range of checks used on the outside of the envelope, filing most recent to the front. Looking for that cancelled check is a snap!

Debra Cote
Gonzales, LA

- **Open a checking account.** If you usually pay your bills with money orders, consider opening up a checking account. Many banks now offer free checking and you'll save time having to get money orders every time you need to pay a bill.

- **Add the details.** When writing out a check to pay a bill, always include the account number or any other pertinent numbers or details in the note field on your check.

- **Mail on time.** Always mail your bills a minimum of one week before the due dates. You'll help ensure your bills arrive at their destinations on time and you won't incur late fees.

- **Share the system.** While it's best to have one person in charge of paying the bills, make sure your spouse or other authorized adult knows your system for doing so. In case you cannot do the bills for a particular time period, another person will be able to do so for you.

Chapter 66

Credit Cards and Purchases

- **Consolidate whenever you can.** Rather than having a bunch of different credit cards, consolidate all of your expenses on one single credit card, preferably one that has a low finance rate and perhaps one that offers cash back or airline mileage on every dollar you spend.

  This can result in less confusion over which card to use, it can give you a better idea of how much debt you're accumulating, it may give you more back for your dollar and you'll only have to write out one payment check per month.

  Most businesses take Visa, MasterCard and/or American Express. Fewer cards allow better control, thus saving you time and money.

- **Trade them.** Rather than using credit cards, use debit cards instead. You can only spend what's currently in your account.

- **Register them.** If you absolutely must have a number of credit cards, register them with a company that will cancel them with one phone call if they're stolen or lost.

- **Make a list.** Make a list of your credit card numbers—name of the card, card number, expiration date and any listed phone numbers. Keep this list in a safe, inconspicuous area, so it can be retrieved in an instant in the unfortunate event of a loss.

- **Don't carry all of them.** Don't carry all of your credit cards everywhere you go. Keep a few major ones in your wallet—Visa, MasterCard, American Express and/or Discover—and leave the rest at home. If you need to go to a particular store, bring only that store's credit card.

- **Buy yourself gift cards.** Purchase gift cards to use in your favorite stores and restaurants each month, for the amount of your monthly budget. If you have a monthly budget of $100 for eating dinner out at restaurants, you might buy four gift cards in the amount of $25.00 each at your favorite restaurants. If you have a monthly grocery shopping budget of $300, buy yourself a supermarket gift card in that amount.

  Use your gift cards when you go out to eat or when you shop. Once your gift cards are used up, that means you've reached your budget for that month. At the very end of the month, get new gift cards for the following month.

- **Pay more than the minimum.** The only way you're going to reduce your credit card debt is to pay more than the minimum required. Of course, you have to stop charging too. If your credit card debt is very high, stop putting purchases on your credit card until the debt is paid off.

- **Make payments on time.** If you don't send in credit card payments on time, you're going to pay hefty fees. Put your credit card bills into your bill paying system and pay them prior to the due date. If you have a hard time remembering to check your bill paying system, write out the payment the second you get the bill in your hand and immediately mail it out.

- **Cut them up.** If you're knee deep in credit card debt, do yourself a favor and cut up all your credit cards today. Once all your debts are paid off, limit yourself to one major credit card.

- **Close the accounts.** You can also call your credit card companies and request that the accounts be closed to further charges. You can continue to make payments but you will not be adding to the balances, which will reduce your debt.

- **Organize your expenses, as you spend.** Want to know how much you spend each month, so you can determine your monthly spending budget? As you spend, just record that expense. This can be called your Expense Summary. A computer program like Quicken or a simple spreadsheet is great for this purpose or you can certainly do this with paper and pen.

- **See the big picture.** Consider not only the cost of the item itself, but also all related costs. Take the time to think out your purchase, on paper. For example, if you're buying an expensive car, determine if you can afford future repairs, fuel costs, insurance and so on.

Great idea!

When I purchase something, but decide not to keep it for whatever reason, I put the receipt back into the store bag and hang the package on the knob of the door that leads to my garage. This allows me to return the item soon because I see it each time I leave the house.

Years ago, when I had an item to return, I would store it in a closet, which often resulted in finding the item months later. Some stores will only give you store credit after a certain length of time. Now that I use the door hanger method, I don't get stuck with credit vouchers. Instead I receive a cash refund.

Esther Chavez
Highland, CA

- **Think before buying.** Before you make your next purchase—furniture, appliance, electronics—be certain that you'll really use it. Will it save you time? Will it help you reach your goals? Will it make you happy? Do you have a home for that particular item in mind? Beware of impulse buys.

- **What's your pleasure?** Write down what you're looking for in the product/service—size, benefits, features and price. Then, give your list to sales clerks and let them show you what products/services meet your needs.

- **Bargain or waste of money?** Before you purchase something just because it's on sale, think again. If it's on sale, but you don't need it, it's not a bargain.

- **Use a comparison chart.** When you're planning on buying an expensive item, a simple grid comparing features and benefits will help you make the right decision.

- **Read reviews.** The Internet is a wonderful resource for getting details on a variety of products and options. Read reviews on specific company Web sites and independent opinion message boards.

- **Ask for a gift receipt.** When you purchase something to be given as a gift, always ask the store clerk for a gift receipt. Gift receipts don't include the price of the item, but can be used to make a return if necessary. I usually tape the gift receipt right inside the recipient's greeting card, so they can make a return or exchange if they wish without asking me for the receipt.

- **Corral your receipts.** Anytime I buy something, I immediately put the receipt in a shoebox—unless it's for a high-ticket item. If something needs to be returned, from a grocery store, department store or small retail store, I will know exactly where to find the receipt. I weed this box out as soon as it's full.

- **Keep store discount cards handy.** Many stores, especially grocery stores and book/music stores, provide discount cards when you shop at that store. Try to keep all of these cards in one place in your purse or wallet. Wallet-sized photo cases are perfect for storing these cards. Key-chain sized versions should be kept on one key chain, or stored flat inside a wallet-sized photo case.

- **Reference your list.** On one sheet of paper, type up the names of the people you buy for often, along with helpful information such as shirt size, favorite colors, favorite hobbies and so on. Keep this one sheet tucked into your wallet for handy reference whenever you're shopping for gifts.

- **Don't toss it in the bag.** Rather than allowing sales clerks to toss your purchase receipts in your shopping bags, instead ask them to hand the receipt to you. Tuck them all into one area in your purse or wallet, so you can remove all of them at once when you arrive home. This will ensure they don't get lost.

Chapter 67

Taxes

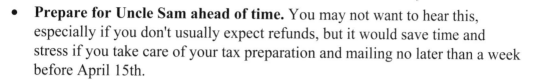

- **Prepare for Uncle Sam ahead of time.** You may not want to hear this, especially if you don't usually expect refunds, but it would save time and stress if you take care of your tax preparation and mailing no later than a week before April 15th.

  In addition, there are a few simple things you can do to help yourself prepare and to avoid your accountant's despair as ten boxes stuffed with receipts are literally dumped onto his or her desk. By the way, if you do bring boxes of disorganized receipts to your accountant's office and you expect him to sort through them, you usually will be expected to pay extra for this service.

- **Keep your tax-related stuff together.** Before tax season, you'll start to receive tax related information from your job and your bank. Keep all of these tax-related papers in a labeled file folder. When you're ready to do your taxes, you won't have to search for the papers you need.

- **Organize your receipts.** Keep all of your day-to-day receipts in categorized envelopes. You will be able to quickly and easily match up charges with your credit card statements, find receipts for returns you may need to make and have everything in one area to take to your accountant for tax preparation.

Great idea!

When I write a check for a tax-deductible item, I draw a circle around the amount in my checkbook. When doing my income taxes, it is easy to pick out proper items in connection with filing my taxes.

Jo Anne Boykin
Austin, TX

- **Income and expenses.** Have a system for recording your income and expenses. Whether it's a sophisticated computer-generated system or a simple notebook, having these numbers readily on hand will simplify things at tax time. Each month, just keep track of all money coming in and all money going out. You can itemize, but have these two totals at the end of each month.

- **Set up a purchase reference.** Each year, set up categorized envelopes for receipts from items and services you purchased. Some of these categories are:

Health Care, Clothing, Home Improvement, Automotive, Business Meals, Entertainment, Travel and Education.

Then, whenever you make a purchase, slip the receipt into its appropriate categorized envelope. All the information will be at your fingertips for the entire year.

At the end of the year, file all of the categorized envelopes away and start new envelopes with the same categories again for the upcoming year.

- **Don't mix business with pleasure.** If you have a home-based business, be sure to keep your business tax records separate from your personal tax records. The same goes for your checking account. Have one for business and another for personal.

- **Write it off your taxes.** You may be entitled to a sizable tax write-off for items you donate to charity. Always ask for a receipt to prove your donation and speak with your accountant about writing that donation off.

Great idea!

In Canada, the law requires one to keep income tax records for six years. In a plastic file box, I keep seven hanging folders: one for the current tax year and six for each of the previous six years. The seven folders are labeled: current year, current year minus 1, current year minus 2, current year minus 3, current year minus 4, current year minus 5 and, finally, current year minus 6.

Throughout the year, as I receive tax receipts for dividends, interest earned and more, I put them in the "Current Year" folder. When tax time rolls around, all the records I need to prepare the current year tax declaration are in my "Current Year" folder.

After I submit my taxes and receive back from the tax department my "Notice of Assessment," I destroy the records in the "Current year minus 6" folder and move "Current Year" records to the "Current year minus 1" folder, "Current year minus 1" to "Current year minus 2" folder and so on.

I also made up a checklist of my tax receipts and the date when I received them. Each year whenever I receive a tax receipt for dividends earned, I tick it off the list. When all the items on the list are ticked off, I know it is time to prepare my taxes again. These two simple techniques have made preparing my taxes almost painless.

Bob Benjamin
Ottawa, Ontario

Chapter 68

Organizing to Save Money

- **Organize your savings efforts.** Deduct a fixed amount from each paycheck and immediately deposit it in the bank.

- **Buy gift cards.** Budget the amount you can afford to spend at your local restaurant, movie house or clothing store. Then, buy yourself gift cards in pre-determined amounts. When the card runs out, you've reached your budget for the month. Start over again next month. This organized system ensures you can enjoy your favorite treats, but never go over budget.

- **Form a babysitting co-op with other parents.** Rather than paying for babysitting, find other parents in your area who are willing to babysit at least one day each week. If you find five (one for each weekday), you'll have a few free hours to yourself at least four out of five days!

- **Buy the same socks for your kids.** When a mate is lost, it won't matter. If one sock is lost, there will be plenty of others to match it.

- **Beware of duplicates.** When cabinets, pantries and refrigerators are disorganized, it's difficult to see what you have and what you need. For instance, you may have hair spray stashed in a bathroom cabinet, but since that cabinet is so full, you can't see it immediately.

  After rummaging for a few minutes, you determine you need more hair spray. So, you go out and buy more, just to later discover you already had this product buried in your cabinet. You just spent money you didn't need to this week.

  Save money by getting those cabinets organized. Don't overstuff them. Put small items into baskets so they don't fall to the back of the cabinets. Use stackable shelves to increase your storage space and to make what you have more visible. Use Lazy Susans in cabinets too. They can be an enormous help.

- **Don't be late.** If you don't send in your bill payments on time, you're most likely wasting money. Most companies charge late fees and interest for bills that are not paid by the due date.

  When you receive bills in the mail, just tossing them on a table or desk isn't a good idea. They're going to get lost.

  Use a bill paying system, such as the *Get Organized Now! Bill Paying System*, to hold all pending bills in one consistent place. Schedule a bill paying date once a week or once every two weeks to pay invoices due.

Do this religiously and you will be saving money you would have paid in late fees and interest—money you could put into your savings account.

- **Know your supermarket schedule.** Some supermarkets double your coupon values when you shop on certain days of the week. Others give you discounts depending on what day certain groceries arrived. Still others have discounts if you shop late in the evening, especially for perishable items like those in the bakery and deli departments. Learn more about the grocery store where you shop. Organize your shopping schedule around these cost-saving days!

- **Surf and save.** Quit wasting time and money driving all over town looking for the best bargains. Search for bargains on the Internet instead. You'll be able to search for exactly what you're looking for without leaving the comfort of your home or office. Less wasted gas. Less wasted time. Less wasted money.

- **Keep them in the car.** Do you find you're always cutting out coupons for restaurants and stores, but also always forgetting to bring them with you? Ever go out to a restaurant and then remember that you actually had a coupon but left it at home? Stop forgetting to bring those coupons by just leaving them in the car.

  Keep an accordion file folder, that's divided into several sections, organized by store or restaurant. You're probably more likely to run out to the car to get the coupon, than go all the way home. In other words, you'll get your discounts.

- **Rent instead.** Rather than spending money on things you use once, such as DVDs or a spray painter, consider renting them instead. When you're done, you bring them back. You'll spend less and you won't build up clutter in your home.

- **Barter.** Rather than spending money on a product or service, barter with a friend, relative or associate. For instance, borrow your friend's snow blower to clear the way for your holiday company and babysit for your friend in return.

- **Share.** If you have a really good neighbor, you may consider sharing things like the lawn mower, snow blower or leaf blower. Perhaps you buy the lawn mower and your neighbor buys the snow blower. Of course, this requires a true friendship and patience if the other person is using the item when you want to use it.

- **Take the doggie bag.** When you go out to dinner, if you have leftovers, take them home with you rather than sending them back with the waiter. You'll save yourself cooking time tomorrow or you'll have a ready-made lunch to bring to work.

- **Get it on the way.** Try to run several errands at once starting at the errand that's furthest away and working your way back. You'll save fuel costs by not making individual runs back and forth from home.

- **Keep track of subscriptions.** Most magazines want you to renew years early, but just because you like a magazine today, that doesn't necessarily mean you'll still like it two years from now. Learn how to read your subscription label so you know when the subscription really runs out. Wait until the last minute to renew—this is one of the few situations that I actually do recommend that you wait. Magazines will often give very special "Last Chance" offers that you can take advantage of. You can also use these "last days" to determine if the magazine is truly worth re-subscribing to.

- **Spend to save.** Very often, buying the least expensive product or service will end up costing you more in the long run. For instance, it's much less expensive to buy a high quality lawn mower that will last for 15 years, then to buy a very inexpensive model that you'll have to keep replacing every few years.

- **Go by the list.** Make a list before you go shopping and only get those items on your list. Avoid browsing and being tempted to buy anything that didn't make it to your list, and you'll only spend what you originally intended.

- **Use what you have.** Designate a few "use what you have" weeks on your calendar. During those weeks, don't go shopping for groceries, craft materials, clothing and so on. Instead, be creative and try to use things that you already have in your house. Most people can do just fine skipping a few weeks of buying and you'll save an entire week's worth of spending cash.

- **Reserve early.** When it comes to air travel, you will usually get lower-priced seats if you order your tickets up to eight weeks in advance. Of course, you can also get good rates at the last minute. But when it comes to travel, I never wait until the last minute. I want to be absolutely sure I can get the dates and times I want.

- **Inventory your clothes closet.** Never go clothes shopping without organizing your closet. If you don't, how will you know if what you already have in your closet will do?

For instance, maybe you think you need a new outfit for an upcoming business engagement. It may cost you significantly for a new pair of pants and a new blouse. However, you may already have a nice looking blouse stashed in your closet that you never wear because you've forgotten it's in there.

Organize your closet. Donate clothes you don't like or that don't fit. Gather those clothes that you could wear, but currently don't because you don't have shoes or other pieces that match.

Chapter 69

Organizing on a Budget

Save that Raisin Bran box. Forego more expensive magazine boxes and make your own out of cereal boxes. Just cut out one of the narrow sides. You might even cover it with contact or wrapping paper—or have your kids decorate it.

- **Store those tiny things.** Need to organize smaller items, such as earrings, extra buttons or push pins? Ice cube trays, muffin tins or egg cartons are perfect for keeping everything sorted. Place some in your drawers and these smaller items will always be handy. Margarine tubs can hold office supplies, small kitchen items like corn-on-the-cob holders and loose change you might need for the bus or for tolls.

- **Organize with inexpensive boxes.** While I generally suggest sturdy, plastic, see-through containers for storage, for the budget conscious, that may not be an option. If this is your situation, you can certainly use good old cardboard boxes. Just make sure you clearly label the contents in each.

- **Use small, shallow boxes as dividers.** If you have a long, shallow desk drawer, chances are it's filled with an assortment of paper clips, pens, tacks, and loose change. My first suggestion is to pick up an organizing tray, but if you'd rather save some money, there is a very frugal solution.

  Gather small shallow boxes—the type that jewelry or bank checks often come in. Most people have these floating around the house. Empty out the desk drawer and line up these boxes inside, arranging them so that there are no open spaces.

  You now have the perfect sorting system for all of those loose desk items. By the way, before you put anything back into that drawer, toss out anything you no longer need or can no longer identify!

- **Hook it.** Often, wall space is forgotten about. But you can free up so much space in your cabinets, on your dresser, in your garage and so on, if you always think about how you can use your walls. The solution is to use hooks—very inexpensive and available at all hardware stores. Hang your pots, pans and teacups. Hang photo frames. Hang bikes. You get the picture.

- **Baby food jar magic.** Clean out those jars, remove the labels and you have the perfect storage containers for nails, screws, nuts, bolts, buttons, loose change, paper clips, elastic bands and so much more. The best thing is, they're transparent, which means you can easily identify everything inside at a glance.

- **Make an instant bag holder.** Use an empty cube-style tissue box to neatly store plastic grocery bags.

- **Go undercover.** Use space under a table for storage. Then, cover the table with a pretty tablecloth or quilt.

- **Wipe out!** Empty baby wipe containers can hold anything from first aid, to craft items to crayons.

- **Nice mug.** Rather than investing in pen and pencil holders, why not use some of those extra mugs you know you have stored in your cupboard? Same goes for empty jelly or canning jars.

- **Know when to fold 'em.** Fold a left-tabbed file folder inside out to make an instant right-tabbed folder.

- **Make it newsworthy.** Don't want to spend money on wrapping paper? Wrap gifts in newspaper instead. Finish them off with a pretty ribbon. Your gift packages will be both interesting and festive.

- **Print your calendars.** Some computer software programs, such as Publisher, and many sources on the web, allow you to print your own calendars out each year for free. Just insert them into a binder and you'll be all set for the new year.

- **Shop around.** When seeking baskets, containers or other storage items, don't buy the first ones you see. Instead, do a bit of price shopping first. Don't forget to look in the newspaper inserts either. Very often, stores like Walmart and Target run sales on organizing items.

- **Make one-pot recipes.** Search online or in cookbooks whenever you can for recipes you can make in one single pot. This will save you money on washing extra dishes.

- **Use the library.** Stop piling tons of books in your house and make use of the public library. If you really like a book that you read, you can always then just purchase that one for your home library.

- **Ask a store clerk.** Very often, liquor stores, shoe stores and other merchants will be willing to give you extra boxes—for free. So definitely ask around before buying them.

- **Try empty film canisters.** Empty film canisters are perfect for storing pins, buttons, tacks and other small items. Sort your things into these small organizing wonders, press on the top and stick a blank label around the outside. Then, label each canister to identify the contents. Finally, store these canisters in a box to keep them all together.

Chapter 70

Computer Smarts

- **Pre-print labels or envelopes.** Don't type out or write names/addresses on envelopes to the same people day after day. Use your computer to preprint batches of labels ahead of time. Keep them stored alphabetically in a file near the area where you do your mailing. I have pre-printed labels addressed to my parents and my sister since I mail to them quite often. My husband has pre-printed envelopes to pay the mortgage each month.

- **Put the tower on the floor.** If your computer has a tower type CPU, you will save desk space by putting the tower on the floor. Just be careful that the unit is securely positioned and that it's properly grounded. Your computer manufacturer may even be able to sell you appropriate stands.

- **Clip on some light.** Use a clip-on light in your computer center. It takes up little space, can be easily moved and provides just the right amount of lighting to get your work done.

- **Add a shelf.** Instead of leaving your keyboard on your computer desk, install an under-the-desk sliding drawer/shelf. It will neatly hold your keyboard, while allowing you the extra space.

- **Take a short cut.** Use computer shortcut keys for functions you use frequently. The less keystrokes you have to use, the less time you'll waste.

- **Here are some quick Word Shortcuts:**
  - ❖ Select text: Shift + Right Arrow, Left Arrow, Up Arrow, or Down Arrow to highlight text
  - ❖ Copy selected text: Ctrl + C
  - ❖ Cut selected text: Ctrl + X
  - ❖ Paste selected text: Ctrl + V
  - ❖ Undo your last action: Ctrl + Z
  - ❖ Select all the text within your document: Ctrl + A
  - ❖ Bold text: Ctrl + B
  - ❖ Italicize text: Ctrl + I
  - ❖ Underline: Ctrl + U
  - ❖ Decrease font size: Ctrl + Shift + <
  - ❖ Increase font size: Ctrl + Shift + >
  - ❖ Change font: Ctrl + Shift + F, then use the arrow keys to reach the new font
  - ❖ Change font size: Ctrl + Shift + P, then use the arrow keys to reach the new font size
  - ❖ Create page break: Ctrl + Enter

- ❖ Create new document: Ctrl + N
- ❖ Open My Documents window: Ctrl + O
- ❖ Close a document: Ctrl + W
- ❖ Save a document: Ctrl + S
- ❖ Print a document: Ctrl + P
- ❖ Preview what you're about to print: Alt + Ctrl + I

- **Here are some quick Excel Shortcuts:**

- ❖ Move right to left, cell by cell: Tab
- ❖ Move up and down, cell by cell: Enter
- ❖ Erase data in current cell: Backspace
- ❖ Return to the beginning of the row: Home
- ❖ Enter the date: Ctrl + ; (semicolon)
- ❖ Enter the time: Ctrl + Shift + : (colon)
- ❖ Start a formula: = (equal sign)
- ❖ Check the spelling of titles or words within the cells: F7
- ❖ Find out about the style within the cell: ALT + ' (apostrophe)
- ❖ Display the Format Cells dialog box: Ctrl + 1
- ❖ Apply the general number format: Ctrl + Shift + ~
- ❖ Turn numbers into dollars: Ctrl + Shift + $
- ❖ Make numbers a percentage: Ctrl + Shift + %
- ❖ Apply a border: Ctrl + Shift + &

Great idea!

I used my computer to organize the grocery list on my refrigerator according to the grocery store I usually frequent, so I can go straight through the store without backtracking.

My family knows to mark an item on the list as soon as it is used up.

At the bottom of the list, I have space for items I can't find when I go to that store, so I remember to buy them at another store that week. Likewise, if it is something I don't need in a hurry, I just put it on next week's grocery list.

Merry Pruitt
Columbus, OH

- **Buy with storage needs in mind.** When purchasing a computer desk or unit, consider the accessories you're going to need to store, such as CD-Roms, manuals and disks. Then, purchase a unit that meets those needs.

- **Lifelong learning.** Don't let your computer sit around just gathering dust. If you are not familiar with its uses, take a class, read some books or get a friend to help. It's amazing how much time it can save you.

- **Take a stand.** An effective organized printer stand is one that holds your printer, but also holds printer paper and perhaps a drawer for your printer manual and disks.

- **Make an index.** Create a word processing file index for each directory or folder on your computer. Indicate the name of the file and a couple of words to describe it. Next time you're searching for a file, you won't have to open up each one individually. You can just go to your index and search for words that match what you're looking for, using your "Find" feature.

- **Keep disks safe.** Use disk holders to hold your diskettes and zip drive disks. If you don't, they're likely to get lost or damaged.

- **You don't have to stretch.** Keep those disks and CD-Roms you use most often near the computer and within easy reach.

- **Same info on each disk.** Keep the same type of information on each disk. For instance, all of your family letters could be on one disk and all letters to businesses you've used on another. Don't mix information.

- **Find them quick.** Organize CD-Roms and computer disks. Use color-coded labels to label your data. Keep them in dust free holders. The disks you use most often should be in the front and easily accessible. Label disks and CD-roms clearly.

Great idea!

For cleaning your computer keyboard, telephones and light switches, use baby wipes. They are easy to use and heaps cheaper than the expensive computer cleaning wipes. They're also kinder on your hands.

Veronica Reid
Hamilton, Waikato, New Zealand

- **Back up your stuff.** Don't run the risk of losing everything on your hard-drive, in case of a computer crash or malfunction. Back up your vital files on disk once a day.

- **Save, save, and then save again.** When working on a long document, save it every ten to fifteen minutes. This way you won't waste time having to redo everything in case of a power loss or malfunction.

- **Create a computer binder.** As you receive instructions or solutions to problems you've run into that are computer-related, insert them into your binder. You'll end up with your own personal computer reference.

- **Keep similar files together.** I like keeping all of the files that are of a similar category all together. For instance, all of my photo files begin with photo???.jpg and all of my letters begin with ltr???.doc.

- **Keep your filenames consistent.** Develop a naming scheme for all of your files and stick with it. For instance, you might always name your files with a short letter category code, a short description, and the proper extension, such as auto-maint.doc, auto-repairs.doc, family-health.doc and family-education.doc.

- **Give it a tune up.** Just like your house needs regular cleaning, so does your computer. Run your computer maintenance program on a regular basis to keep your computer running efficiently. ScanDisk, Disk Cleanup and Disk Defragmenter are usually available on Windows-based systems by clicking Start, Programs, Accessories and System Tools. You can run these manually as you wish, or use the Task Scheduler to run them automatically.

- **Keep a list.** Maintain a list of computer software names, serial numbers and technical support information. You'll be able to access it quickly without having to rummage through tons of paperwork.

- **Arrange your desktop.** Line up the icons on your desktop according to name, size, type or the programs you use most often. You can do this manually, or right click your mouse from the desktop and choose Arrange Icons to do so automatically.

- **Sub-Divide.** Use folders and sub-folders on your computer. For instance, I have a main folder called Photos and within that folder, I have distinguishable categories such as Family, Friends, Vacations and Seasonal. That's broken down easily enough for me to find what I'm looking for. Occasionally, I might break those sub-categories down even further, such as Cruise and Boston for my Vacations Folder. However, I generally avoid too many sub-categories as this could tend to get both too intricate and too confusing.

Chapter 71

Web Surfing

- **Maximum memory.** Make sure your computer has plenty of memory and a fast modem. Ensure your online service has high-speed Internet connection capabilities. Your time is valuable and will slip away with slow, ineffective tools. I can't begin to tell you how much more efficient my life became when I went from a land line to a cable line.

- **Bookmark it.** When you visit a web page that you want to return to, bookmark it. If you're an America Online user, store this Web site in your "Favorite Places."

  If you're on another online service, save the Web site as your service provider allows. If this option isn't available to you, make a list of the web addresses and the titles of the web pages. Keep this list near your computer for quick reference.

- **Note the time of day.** Sometimes, the time of day that you choose to surf the web has a lot to do with how productive your web surfing time will be. If the Net is really busy, it will take you much longer to get from one web page to another. If you run into this problem, try surfing earlier or later in the day.

Great idea!

Because you should use different passwords for everything, I use index cards filed alphabetically to record account numbers, user id's passwords and Web sites. I have sent this idea to many places and they all think it's great!

Nancy Greene
North Haledon, NJ

- **Learn search specifications.** Learn both basic and advanced search specifications when using search engines such as Yahoo or Google. You'll be able to find what you need quickly and without having to sift through hundreds of results. For instance, if I'd like to find dog training tips on Google, I would probably type in: "dog training tips" with quotes around it. This will limit my search to dog training tips and not all categories related to "dogs," "training" and "tips" which would result in much more than what I actually need.

- **Make your favorite your home page.** If there's a web page you always visit, make that your Internet browser's default page. For instance, if you visit www.getorganizednow.com often, set Internet Explorer or another browser so that you always go to that page every time you go online.

Great idea!

Usually, when I find an interesting Web site in a magazine or newspaper, I note it down. I have a small notebook assigned especially for this task. This way, I won't have to keep the magazine or tear out the page, which will only create more clutter.

Carol Gonzalez
New York, NY

- **Be careful.** Don't download anything from an unknown source or you run the risk of downloading a dangerous computer virus.

- **Do something else.** Open up another window when you're downloading something. Rather than twiddling your thumbs waiting for it to finish, you can open up another window and work on something else at the same time.

- **Where in the world is it?** When you do download something, make a note of the filename and the folder you're downloading it to so that you can find it quickly later on.

- **Eliminate the http:// and www.** You'll be able to get to most web pages without using these codes. For instance, if you type getorganizednow.com into your web browser, it will take you quickly to my site.

- **View in text mode.** If you frequently visit a Web site that is very picture-heavy and takes forever to load, but has great information, you may want to view the Web site in text-mode only. Check your browser's help menu to determine how to do this with your system.

- **Work offline.** Ensure the page you're viewing on your browser is the newest version by holding down your CTRL key and hitting F5. This action will load the newest version of the page, while bypassing your cache.

- **An easier way to scroll.** Rather than scrolling up and down to peruse a web page, simply use your Page Up and Page Down keys instead.

- **Give them a passport.** I found this excellent Cyberspace Passport idea from the Federal Trade Commission and the National Association of Attorneys General:

❖ Children act more responsibly when they know the rules. That's why you may find the idea of a parent-child contract helpful when it comes to using the Web. Here are some rules of the "virtual" road, along with a sample Cyberspace Passport for children who accept the rules. You and your children may want to develop others.

These rules are for my safety. I will honor them when I go online. I can go online:

  ➤ _____ (Time of day) for _____ (How long)

  ➤ It's ___ OK ___ not OK for me to go online without a parent.

  ➤ I understand which sites I can visit and which ones are off limits.

  ➤ I won't give out information about myself or my family without permission from my parents.

  ➤ My password is my secret. I won't give it to anyone.

  ➤ I will never agree to meet an online pal, or send my picture, without permission from my parents.

  ➤ I know an advertisement when I see one. I also know that animated or cartoon characters aren't real and may be trying to sell me something or to get information from me.

  ➤ I will follow these same rules when I am at home, in school, or at the library or a friend's.

- **Empty your cache.** Every time you visit a Web site, your computer stores that site on your hard drive. The more full your cache gets, the slower you'll be able to browse. Empty your cache every day after you finish your web surfing. Check with your browser provider or look in your browser's Help Menu to determine how to do this on your system.

- **It's what you think.** Generally, especially for big companies, the Web site addresses are the company name. For instance, JC Penney's Web site is jcpenney.com, Sears Web site is sears.com and Amazon's Web site is amazon.com. If you want to visit a company Web site, first try typing in what the address is likely to be, before you spend time looking it up on a search engine.

- **Google to the fullest.** I mainly use Google when I search on the web. Did you know you could add a Google toolbar to your browser, block annoying pop-ups and have Google automatically fill out forms for faster online shopping so you don't have to keep typing in your name, address and credit card number? It's true and I love this feature. Just visit http://toolbar.google.com/ and download the Google toolbar to your computer—for free!

Chapter 72

Email

- **Schedule two email checks per day.** Rather than checking for email every time your email reminder sounds or on the hour, schedule two 15-30 minute email checks per day. Use this time exclusively to delete, respond to and organize your email.

- **Skim and delete.** When I retrieve mail, I immediately skim the subject lines and delete anything I know I don't need. This eliminates 50% or more of the email messages I receive. Once I do this, I then respond to the email messages that can be answered in a sentence or two. At that point, all you should be left with are those messages that require a bit more time to handle. This is a less overwhelming method of getting through your inbox each day.

- **Use your address book.** Use your online service's virtual address book if you have one to store frequently used email addresses and whom they belong to. They'll be on hand when you need to email someone.

- **Create your own.** If your online service doesn't come equipped with a virtual address book, create a computer or paper list of common email addresses and whom they belong to.

- **Beware of virtual clutter.** Just like paper, email can soon turn into clutter. Delete messages as soon as you handle the action necessary or as soon as it is no longer useful.

- **Sort them.** For those email messages you wish to keep, sort email within the program by topic or person.

- **Store them in your program.** If your online service is equipped with a Personal Filing Cabinet, you can store important email right within the online software program.

- **The joke's on you.** Don't forward tons of jokes and other such things to friends and associates. An occasional joke is fine, but a volume of them is a waste of time; time that could be much better spent.

- **Cc or Bcc.** If you have an email message that you'd like to send to a number of different people, don't send them individually. Send them all together as a group. You define what email recipients belong to a specific group.

- **Make the subject specific.** Always put specific subject headings in your email messages. With the volume of email the average person receives these days, your subject must really stand out and be specific to get noticed ahead of all the other email.

- **Be wary of attachments.** Be careful of opening files that have been attached to email, unless you're absolutely sure there isn't a virus attached. Take every precaution you can, otherwise, you're going to spend a lot of time trying to recover lost files on your computer. Use virus protection software.

- **Think simple.** Don't spend too much time changing email font styles, sizes, colors and background colors. It's highly likely that your recipient won't have the same capabilities as you and won't see any of your fancy changes.

- **Wait a minute.** I set up my email program so that mail I write first gets put into my Outbox, rather than sent immediately. This gives me one or more chances to go back and change something I've written before it gets sent out. Once I'm definitely ready, I just choose the "Send All Mail" option.

- **Mark message urgency.** If you're sending an email that requires quick attention by the recipient, most email programs will allow you to mark your email as URGENT. However, don't do this all the time, otherwise you'll be seen as "crying wolf." In other words, if you say that everything is urgent, after a while, people will stop believing you.

- **Set some limits.** Email has really opened up the lines of personal communication. You might now email people every day, that before email you wouldn't have spoken to in a week or more. It's wonderful that we're so connected, but occasionally it is necessary to set some ground rules. For instance, for friends and family members I email often, I usually set a 5-10 minute limit on my email messages to them. Whatever I don't tell them today, I can always tell them tomorrow. With my sister, I usually email her once or twice a week to keep in touch, and if there's something urgent, I just call her on the phone.

- **Don't set yourself up.** Beware of getting on spam lists in the first place. Avoid posting your email address on public Web sites. Only sign up for newsletters and email from trusted sites that promise not to sell or share your contact information.

- **Set up rules and alerts.** Spam comes in fast and furious these days, if you allow it to. Some email programs provide automatic spam filters, although you have to be careful because sometimes mail that isn't spam gets filtered into your spam mail folder. You can also set up your own personal email filters in most email programs. Check your email provider's help menu or contact them for more information if necessary. The less time you have to spend dealing with spam, the more time you'll have for your more important email messages.

- **Set up a Temporary Folder.** In some cases, I need to keep an email for reference for a short amount of time, such as if I requested something from someone and am waiting to receive it. I don't like to keep these messages in my Inbox, because they're in "waiting mode." So I drag and drop them into a Temporary Folder, which I weed out once a month. This way, it doesn't end up with thousands of messages. This is also a good reminder method if you come across an email message that has not yet been handled.

- **Set up a Shopping Folder.** If you shop online quite a bit, you might want to set up a Shopping Folder. When you order something and you get a confirmation email, or any message that relates to your order, you can simply save it in your Shopping Folder. You'll then have something to reference while you're waiting for your order. In fact, I usually keep email in that folder for approximately 2 months after my purchase, just in case I want to return something. After 2 months, however, I weed this folder out.

- **Have a good outlook.** I use Outlook as my email manager. Besides all of the wonderful email capabilities, it is also equipped with a personal calendar, a contact database, a task list, a journal and other great features. I used to use Outlook Express, but I've come to enjoy all the additional benefits of Outlook.

- **How many accounts?** I have two email accounts—one that I use as my primary account, and one that I use as a backup account. If you have more than one account, it could become very confusing. Consider having all of your email forwarded to your main account so you don't miss anything. In addition, try to always send mail from your main account so as not to confuse your message recipients.

- **Don't SHOUT?** When you type all letters as capital letters, in essence, you are shouting at your reader. Use all caps sparingly, if at all, in your email.

- **Use emoticons.** 97.8% of human communication is non-verbal, such as smiles, frowns, body gestures and hand movement. When it comes to email, sometimes the written word can be taken incorrectly, sometimes even offensively. Emoticons, such as smiley faces and winks can indicate some emotion in your email and often eliminate your message being taken in the wrong way.

Chapter 74

Reading

- **Make a commitment.** If you want to keep up with your reading, you have to commit to some reading goals. First, determine how much time you're willing to dedicate to reading. Many people can commit anywhere from 15 minutes to an hour each day.

- **Be consistent.** Set a consistent time each day to read. Perhaps you'd like to read first thing in the morning, while you're having breakfast. Maybe later in the day works better for you. Schedule this time on your calendar and don't allow that time to be used for anything else.

- **Don't go overboard.** If you are good about keeping your reading commitment each day, but you still have too much in your To Read pile, then you most likely are being over ambitious with how much you can realistically read with the time you've committed. If this is the case, either increase your reading time or decrease your reading material.

- **Make it stand out.** If you enjoy reading newspapers and magazines, but find you have trouble getting through them before the next issue arrives, read with a highlighter. Quickly skim through the publication, scanning each page and highlight all headlines that are of interest to you. Then, go back and read only those articles.

- **Tear it out.** If you don't have time right now to read those articles that you highlight, you may want to tear out the pages, put them in a To Read folder and schedule a time to read them later on. However, you need to set time each day or each week to read everything in your folder. Otherwise, you're just going to be tearing out countless articles that never get read.

Great idea!

Magazines piling up? Can't find that certain article? When browsing through a magazine, always have a bright highlighter handy. Then when you read something that you will want to save or check on later, highlight it right away. Later it will jump right out at you as you just flip the pages. You won't have to read the entire magazine just to find want you want.

Madolyn Hayne
Clarksville, VA

- **Bring it along.** If you're planning on spending your day out, put your day's reading materials into a file folder. Then, whenever you have the opportunity during the day, your reading material will be easily accessible. Some opportune times to read are while waiting in someone's office for an appointment, while riding on the train or bus, or when waiting in line at a check out counter.

- **Don't feel you have to finish it.** If you start reading a book just to discover you're not enjoying it, and it's not imperative for you to read it for business or school, don't feel like you have to continue with it. Don't allow it to take up time you could be using to read something you truly enjoy.

- **Start a book chat.** A great way to read a book is to do so, with the intention of sharing what you've read with someone else. Book chats are great for this purpose. A group of people agree to read a particular book, and then you all meet three or four weeks later to discuss the book in detail. It's a fun way to get different perspectives. Plus, since you have to complete the book by a certain date, it encourages you to read a little bit each day.

- **Set a limit.** If your dilemma is reading too much and not having time to do anything else in your day, set a time limit for reading, such as an hour in the morning, or an hour before you go to bed.

- **Books on tape.** There are many books-on-tape available to listen to these days. Check out the titles at your local library or bookstore. They come in all genres and may be a welcome change when your eyes are feeling strained, or you're relaxing at the beach.

- **Don't say the words.** When you read out loud, or even whisper the words to yourself, you will read much slower. Read with your eyes and mind, rather than your lips, and you'll read much more efficiently.

Great idea!

I try to keep a set of sticky notes nearby when I look at a new magazine. If I see a recipe or idea I think I would like to keep, I jot it down on the sticky note and put it on the front of the magazine. When I dispose of old magazines, I know which ones I read and then tear out the articles that I indicated on the sticky note.

Peggy Duke
Columbia, MD

- **Read reviews.** I rarely buy a book before I've had a chance to read reviews from both media and customers, and sometimes you can even read a chapter of the book online. If you purchase on Web sites like Amazon or Barnes and Noble, very often there are reviews and or testimonials to help you in making your decision about whether to buy a book or not. This allows me to buy online without the need to physically go to a bookstore to flip through a book.

Great idea!

When reading a newspaper or book, keep a dictionary nearby. You'll be able to look up an unfamiliar word in a jiffy.

Jude Abrigo
North Bergen, NJ

- **Get on the net.** If you have to research a particular subject, the Internet could offer you a lot, in addition to books in bookstores or libraries. Learn how to use the various search tools to narrow your searches, so you don't end up with tons of information that's of no use to you.

- **Don't believe everything you read.** Just because something is in print, doesn't necessary mean it's true or false. Verify any information you read before you believe it or discount it.

- **Read with the kids.** One way to ensure your younger children are reading is to schedule reading time with them. Make it a fun, family-affair with lots of books and snacks. Also, discuss each book after completion. Sharing with others almost always makes the content more interesting and offers good conversation subjects.

- **Make a visit to the doctor.** If your eyes feel strained, you get headaches when you read, or the words on the page seem blurry, you may need to get your vision checked. Make an appointment today.

- **Get it done.** If you have to read a book by a certain date, check to see how many pages are in your book. Then take that number and divide it by the number of days before your deadline. You'll then know how many pages you must read each day to complete your book prior to the deadline.

Chapter 74

It's a Family Affair

- **Involve everyone.** Enlist family members to help serve and prepare dinner. Give everyone a specific task such as chopping the veggies, preparing the salad or setting the table.

- **Make them responsible.** Make it a rule in your home that whoever makes a mess is responsible for cleaning it up.

- **Pass out the assignments.** Pre-assign after-dinner cleanup duties to each family member such as clearing the table, loading the dishwasher or taking out the trash.

- **Make a chore chart.** Develop a Family Chore Chart of routine daily chores and hang it on the fridge. It should include a list of common household chores—taking out the trash, walking the dog, dusting—along with the date due and the family member responsible for getting it done.

  An erasable board is a good choice, since you can then easily rotate assignments for variety. Assign tasks to each member of your family. Have them check off jobs as they are completed.

- **Pick a task.** Get a pack of index cards. On each one, write down one daily thing that has to be done around the house (i.e. wash dishes, fold clothes, load the dishwasher.)

  Each day, have each family member draw a few cards. Those are the chores that person is responsible for that day. Divide evenly. If you have 12 daily chores and four family members, each person draws 3 cards. This also works well for weekly or monthly chores.

  If someone wants to swap chores with another family member, that's OK—as long as both parties are agreeable.

- **Pick a chore.** Get yourself a dry-erase board and jot down a list of chores that must be done for the week. Each day, have each member of your family choose a chore to do. When they're done with the chore, they should erase it from the board. When one can choose a chore, rather than get stuck with the same chore each week, it's a bit less boring.

- **Reap the rewards.** While it's important to get the entire family involved in getting and staying organized, it's also important for everyone to reap the rewards of their efforts. Once a week, institute a "No Chore" day and hold a family outing, or barbeque or "Just Relax Day" instead.

Organizing Clinic

Question

My husband has two areas in our home that are his—his office in the basement and the whole garage. These two areas are so messy that it stresses me out to even go there. What's even worse is that he can never find anything, but he still won't clean it up. He keeps everything for future use. I am embarrassed when people come over and try to keep them out of those areas, but invariably he has to show them something and takes them there. I would clean and organize it myself, but I don't know what he wants or needs. Can you help?

Joan Sieving
St. Louis, MO

Answer

Dear Joan,

Have you spoken to your husband about your frustration with these two areas? I don't mean nagging, but rather a heart-to-heart? Perhaps if your hubby knew how much stress this was causing you, then he would be more willing to "clean shop" a bit. Maybe he's not sure how to get these areas organized or feels too overwhelmed to do it himself. In this case, you might offer to organize with him. In doing so, nothing important will be tossed.

Concentrate on storage so your husband doesn't think you just want to toss out all of his stuff. Wall space is often forgotten. Shelves and hooks can do wonders for conquering chaos. In the end, since you've said these two rooms are his responsibility and the rest of the home is yours, it's really up to your husband whether or not the disorganization is bothering him enough to do anything about it—unless it's posing a safety or fire hazard.

Post signs on your basement and garage that say "Bob (or whatever your husband's name is) Is Responsible For Keeping This Area Neat and Organized." That will either embarrass him into cleaning up or will at least give your guests a chuckle when they visit. Finally, to ease your stress, steer clear of these areas.

- **Play the "disappearing act" game.** This game is perfect for families with young kids. If the parents always pick up the toys and dirty laundry, the kids will never learn how to do these tasks on their own. Instead, set a timer for 10 minutes.

Have the kids run around picking up their things and putting them away. If they get everything done by the time the timer sounds, they win small prizes, such as being able to choose that afternoon's video to watch or baking cookies with mom or something else fun and enticing.

- **Create a filing system for your child.** It can hold artwork, rock star photos, blank paper and notes from family and friends. Use a portable filing container that is capable of holding hanging files and that can be transported someplace else if necessary. The ones with handles are nice, since they can be transported to different homes or on vacation. Some of these containers have snap-shut compartments for pens, pencils, clips and other supplies.

- **Post a family calendar.** Stop wondering when your husband is going on that fishing trip, when your son's soccer games are scheduled or when the family vacation is taking place. Post a large, erasable annual calendar on a wall in the mudroom or the laundry room.

  Fill in all events you're aware of for the year. Then, ask your family to fill in any additional events such as soccer games, birthdays or field trips. Everyone will know the schedule and you'll prevent conflicts from arising.

- **Create a Family Message Center.** Use a corkboard, message paper and push pins. Place it in a prominent place, such as the kitchen. Instruct everyone that all messages, phone and other, should be placed and retrieved on this board. If you have a large family, divide the message board into sections for each name. Once a family member has retrieved his message, he is responsible for removing it.

- **Log calls.** An alternative to the corkboard mentioned above is to put a five subject notebook right near the phone. Each person gets his or her own tab and that's where phone messages, or any other messages for that matter, can be written. Everyone is responsible for checking his or her section each day and for entering messages in the appropriate section(s).

- **Schedule a 10-minute pick up.** Control the chaos. Schedule a consistent, 10-minute pick-up session each night. Set a timer to sound an alarm in 10 minutes. While the clock is ticking, all family members are responsible for clearing out and putting away their belongings from the main family area. When the timer sounds, you're all done. Give yourselves a warm round of applause for all you've accomplished.

Organizing Clinic

Question

I subscribe to your email newsletter and love it. I'm a fanatic about organization. Unfortunately, my husband of 10 years is not. I have tried everything to help him get organized. Nothing works. He does well for about a week and then says he has no time or it is too hard to change and he goes back to his old ways. Do you have any suggestions for helping him to change?

Ann Green
Cleveland, OH

Answer

Thanks for the nice compliment. Here are a few ideas that may help:

- **Be specific.** What organizing means to you, may mean something completely different to your husband. Just telling him to be more organized is not going to result in much. If you want him to put his laundry in the hamper in the laundry room, that's specific. If you want him to hang his coat in the closet when he gets home from work, that is also specific. The more specific you are, the more he'll know what you're asking of him.

- **It takes at least 21 days to break a habit.** Work on your husband slowly. Don't expect him to change everything he has been doing for a lifetime, overnight. Choose one battle at a time. For instance, work on just one improvement until he's doing it consistently, like putting his keys on the key rack or putting books back on the bookshelf when he's done with them.

- **Don't nag.** Nagging is one of the worst ways to get someone to do something. Instead, let him know how important it is to you when he washes a dish or glass he just used. He may tend to do it more, if he knows it really makes you happy. Be appreciative and do something for him every so often that shows your appreciation.

- **Make a deal.** Tell your husband that if he does something for you, you'll do something for him. For instance, if he remembers to keep the dresser clear of papers without being asked, you'll help him out by waking up to walk the dog once or twice a week. Sometimes it takes a little incentive.

- **Pick your battles.** Some things are just not worth getting upset over. If your hubby's sock drawer isn't exactly what you would call organized, let it go. It obviously doesn't bother him and as long as you don't open his drawer, it shouldn't bother you.

- **Clean and organize with your child.** Rather than nagging your child to clean his or her room, do it together as a team. Come up with six specific things that need to be organized, such as the clutter under the bed or a dresser drawer or the toys strewn about. Then, have your child choose two of those areas—one for him or her to do and one for you to do.

  After your areas are completed, choose the next two and so on until all six chores are complete. Afterwards, do something enjoyable with your child, like playing outside for a while or having a milk and cookie break together. It will give you quality time with your child, the room will be a lot cleaner and more organized and it will also be teaching responsibility that will be of enormous help later in your child's life.

Great idea!

When our children were still at home, we allocated the inside of one kitchen cupboard door to each member of the family. On the door we taped each child's school schedule or adult's work contact info and a "wish card" for what they might like for birthdays or Christmas. We attached a large clip to each door to hold pertinent papers such as announcements from school, boy scout call lists and book club member lists. Our children now have families of their own, but my husband and I still use "our" doors to house papers we need to refer to and, of course to maintain our wish lists.

Mara Ambrose
Frederick, MD

- **Make it visible.** Hang an erasable Month-at-a-Glance calendar and erasable marker on the refrigerator or on a wall where they won't be missed. Have each family member jot down upcoming meetings, appointments, trips or other events. In doing so, the entire family will be well informed and will be able to plan their schedules accordingly.

- **Beep, beep.** Get a beeper attachment for family keys. Clap to activate the beeper when keys have been misplaced.

- **Set an example.** Set a good example for your children by being organized yourself. When parents are not organized, kids are being sent the wrong message. Everyone must play the organizing game for it to work.

- **Hang a bulletin board.** Hang a bulletin board on one of your kitchen walls and divide evenly with colored tape so that each family member of your household has his or her own section. Each section should be stocked with pushpins. This is the perfect area for family members to leave notes or phone messages for each other. Instruct each person to post messages here and to check for messages at least once each day.

- **Make family dates.** Schedule frequent dates with your spouse, children and significant others. Write these appointments on your calendar and do everything you can so that they don't have to be rescheduled or put on the backburner. Effective organization ensures you don't ever forget to make time for those you love.

- **Multi-task.** Do multiple activities simultaneously. Go for a walk in the park with your spouse and/or children. You'll be communicating, exercising and possibly planning for that long needed vacation—all at the same time!

- **Create a Family Only Hour.** Designate a minimum of one hour per week as "Family Only Hour." This is the perfect time to catch up with each other, conduct family meetings, play a game or plan an event. Everybody must show up and participate for this to be productive and successful.

- **Record and zap.** You and your family are not locked into watching television programs only when they're scheduled. Take advantage of the VCR. Record what you're interested in and watch these programs when convenient for you and your family. Zap through all the commercials later and save time.

- **Make the most of dinnertime.** Shut off the television during dinnertime and use that time more constructively. Consider having each family member share something they've learned today.

Great idea!

My kids are slowly starting to get into sports, clubs and other extracurricular activities. I am a single mom who works full-time, is going back to school and also belongs to various organizations.

To keep track of our very hectic schedule, I have purchased four different colors of small sticky notes to use on our calendar.

Pink is for my daughter's appointments, purple is for my son's, blue is for mine and yellow is for miscellaneous. When an appointment comes up, depending on who it's for, I write it on the appropriate color and stick it on our calendar.

This way I can see at a quick glance who has what coming up for the week. Also, if something gets cancelled or rescheduled I can easily take the sticky note off and not have to scribble up my calendar!

Heather Ziegler
Flanagan, IL

- **Set specific times.** If you want your kids to do specific chores at specific times, give them an exact time or a time range. For instance, if you want the trash put outside immediately after the table is cleared, make that point known. If you want the mowing done on Saturday morning, be sure your teenager knows that the mowing must be done between 10:00AM and 12:00 noon on Saturdays.

- **Pets are family too.** Be sure your pets are tagged and licensed. If necessary, put a fence around your home and be sure all family members know to close the gate so the pet does not escape.

- **Photo behind photo.** If you have kids in school, you'll probably get an 8" x 10" portrait each year for each child. Store each child's portrait in his or her own frame, with the latest portrait on top. They'll all be in one place and you can look through each photo every year when you add a new one.

- **Catch up with the kids.** If your children come home hungry after school, give them a quick, nutritious snack that doesn't require lots of cleanup. A bowl of fruit or some raw veggies and cheese are healthy choices. This is also a great time to catch up on your child's day at school, sign permission slips and review homework assignments.

Great idea!

To keep school, scouts and sports information together, I use a looseleaf binder with tabs—one for each child. When I receive a paper I need to keep, I use a three-hole punch and place it in the binder in the appropriate section.

After I started this method, I didn't lose things on the fridge or accidentally throw something away or forget something special. In addition, I belong to several organizations and use this binder system concept for keeping my information together.

Renee Shelfer
Pelham, AL

Great idea!

My husband works very long shifts (leaves at 4:00AM and gets home at 8:00PM) and I think of all sorts of things I want to tell him or ask him about taking care of while he's away. However, when he gets home, he only has about 30-40 minutes to eat, relax, and head to bed to get up again at 3:15. During that time, I can never think of all the things I wanted to say and I'm tempted to keep chatting while he's trying to fall asleep. Or I remember again when he's gone and get frustrated that I have to keep postponing actions.

So I have a bright yellow folder marked "For Jim (look/discuss)" in a spot he knows to look. Any mail he needs to see goes in there after I open it in addition to any papers he needs to take care of. After he looks at them or does what he needs, he pops them into the next folder, my Action file, so I can take the appropriate action.

Bills go in there for him to see as they arrive. Then he marks what to pay when and puts them in the Bills file (same location) for me to handle.

I also attached some paper to the inside left of the file folder and marked it, "Tell Jim." During the day, when those little flashes of insight hit, I flip the file open and jot them down where he will look. As we discuss them, one of us crosses them off.

At the other end of the same flap (turn folder upside down), I have paper marked, "For Jim to do," where I jot down things I need from the storage shed at his convenience.

This puts all the communication info in one spot, where he knows to look, and keeps all the paperwork at my desk (since I do most of our family's administrative work, at his request).

Vicki Bentley
McKenney, VA

Chapter 75
Children

- **Rewards and consequences.** Children are swayed by: 1. Desire for gain (rewards) and 2. Fear of loss (consequences).

  - ❖ **Rewards.** Tell your children that if they do what you want them to do, within the time frame you set, you'll reward them. Maybe make their favorite meal tonight, offer to play a game with them or let them stay up a half hour later.

  - ❖ **Consequences.** Tell your children that if they don't do what you want them to do, within the time frame you set, then there will be consequences. Send them to bed earlier than usual, put their toys in an out-of-reach "Holding Box" where they can't touch them for a few days or tell them they can't go out to play until the chore has been completed.

- **Play the Round-up Game.** Set a timer for five minutes. Then have each child grab a basket and run around picking up everything out of place. Have small prizes—ice cream, trading cards, stickers—depending on how much they can pick up within five minutes.

- **The spirit of giving.** Have your children sort through their toys and give to other less fortunate children. They'll be making room for new toys, plus contributing to another child's happiness simultaneously. For every toy they give up, eliminate one of their chores for the week or make their favorite meal for dinner. To make it more real for your kids, give them a choice of charities that they can donate to.

- **Color their world.** If you have more than one child, consider the color-coding system. Choose one consistent color for each child—or have your children choose their own color if they can do so without arguing with each other. Then, whenever you buy a toothbrush, hairbrush or comb, buy the designated color for each child. You'll experience fewer fights over what belongs to whom.

- **Lower the lists.** Post chore lists at eye level for kids. Have them check off each chore as they complete it. Use a washable board for the chore schedule and erasable markers.

- **Stick on picture labels.** Young kids who can't read can still learn to put their toys away. Label their toy boxes and toy storage containers with pictures of the contents, such as a picture of a teddy bear where stuffed animals go and a picture of blocks where blocks go.

- **Assign a home.** Ensure that your children have a place for their things—toys, clothing, books—and they know where that place is. Otherwise you're going to have to put everything back yourself.

- **Make it easy for them to learn.** Teach children how to do things for themselves, but make sure you help them to succeed. For example, if you want them to set the table every night, sketch out a diagram on paper for them to follow. It will save you time, plus it will help your children learn and grow.

- **Give them responsibility.** Instruct your children to clean their rooms at least once a week and to help with dinner every night. Put this on a written schedule. It will help enforce the importance of responsibility.

- **Prepare for leaving.** Ensure each child's book bag and backpack is packed with everything needed for school, day trips and other outings. Leave the bags near the door so they're not forgotten.

- **Hang low.** Lower clothes closet rods to your children's eye levels to encourage them to hang up clothing on their own.

- **Stow the stuff.** Removing dozens of stuffed animals off the bed each day is time consuming for you and your children. Toy hammocks hung in children's rooms, toy chests or shelves are great for keeping the cute critters organized and out of the way.

- **Shelve it.** Instead of stacking toys in boxes, install shelves in children's rooms. Your children will more easily find what they're looking for, plus you'll prolong the life of the toys.

- **Filing systems aren't just for adults.** Assist your children in setting up their own files. Get them brightly colored hanging file folders, along with manila files and labels. Some categories might be:
  - ❖ Poetry
  - ❖ Artwork
  - ❖ Assorted paper
  - ❖ Greeting cards from close family and friends
  - ❖ Rock star photos/facts
  - ❖ Blank greeting cards
  - ❖ Birthdays and other events
  - ❖ Stickers

- **Teach the rule of 25.** Teach them that once a file has "25" papers inside, they should first toss something out before inserting anything new—or start an additional file folder.

- **X-ray vision.** See-through containers, which come in various sizes, are better than opaque ones. Children can locate their things without having to empty each box to find something.

- **Method of transport.** Give each of your children a handled tote bag to transport toys from room to room or to bring with them during travel.

- **Tape it on.** Securely tape your child's signed permission slips to his schoolbooks so there's little chance they will get lost.

- **Prep the book bag.** Teach your child to put completed homework in her book bag, but watch her do it until she regularly does it on her own without supervision. Make her a checklist if necessary.

- **Kittens and mittens.** Are your children always losing their gloves and mittens? Sew a long piece of yarn between each pair. Run it through their coats, inside and out both sleeves. They'll never lose them again.

- **Corral toys.** To help keep toys under control use a toy box with a lid. A closed lid means children must ask to get toys out. An open lid means they are free to take one or two toys out at a time.

- **Make it off limits.** If your children refuse to organize the toy area when asked to, declare it off limits for a few hours. Enforce these measures every time you ask them to clean up and they don't.

- **Use the rule of 2.** Only two toys are allowed out at any one time. This will help to keep toys under control.

- **Institute a Holding Box.** When a toy or another item is left out of place, take it and place it in the Holding Box. The rule: no matter what day the item went in, it must not be retrieved again for seven days—or five or three depending on your aggravation level. If you treat this system seriously, it should work like a charm.

- **Storage for small stuff.** Clear, shoe bags hung in a closet will store children's action figures, hair accessories, playing cards, jacks, crayons and other small items. Kids can then find what they want at a glance.

- **Label it.** Label each child's hat, gloves, eyeglass case and book bag with their name and address. When something is misplaced at school, teachers will have the necessary information they need to return lost belongings to the appropriate student.

- **Bag in a box.** Store small, easy-to-lose game pieces, toys and puzzle pieces in Zip-lock bags. Keep these bags in the game boxes.

- **Give them a display area.** Hang a corkboard in each child's room so that he can display his drawings, favorite photographs and other papers.

- **Putting things in perspective.** Many people are sentimental about keeping their children's artwork and toys, but it really helps to determine what you should and should not be sentimental about. After all, if you keep 10 things a year for two children for 16 years, you'll end up with 320 items!

- **Alternate bath nights.** Unless young children have been playing in the mud, it may not be necessary to bathe them every night. Consider switching to every other night.

- **Use a tablecloth.** Whenever your child is going to do anything messy, such as color, paint or play with clay, lay a plastic tablecloth underneath him. You won't find artwork on your rug later. Better yet, if it's nice outside, move these messy activities out of the house.

- **Make clean-up time fun.** If your kids feel that putting their toys away is a chore, they're not going to want to do it. Make it fun by singing songs as they clean up or holding clean-up contests for small rewards like stickers.

Great idea!

I like to keep our kids toys in clear containers, but these containers can be costly. As I was cleaning out my son's closet, I came across the vinyl bag that the mattress pad came in. It was perfect for his Imaginext Battle Castle and it fits under his dresser perfectly. Everything fits in the bag and it had a pouch to put the assembly instructions in as well. Please note that due to the plastic, I would only recommend this for older children

Maureen Kaiser
Galena, OH

- **Make a list of sitters.** Make a list of potential baby sitters with their names, addresses and phone numbers. Keep it near the phone.

- **Hire help and get things done.** Babysitters are not just for when you're going out. If you need time with your spouse, hire a babysitter to care for young children in another room for two hours a night.

- **Make a checklist for the babysitter.** Include important instructions and phone numbers. Hang it on the refrigerator. When not in use, keep this checklist in a file for the next time you need it.

- **Organize a co-op.** Get together with other families and organize a Babysitting Co-op. Each family is responsible for so many hours of watching the kids.

- **Get organized when you babysit.** Pick up a few kid-oriented movies at the video store. Have popcorn and juice boxes on hand. Once children are pre-occupied, they are more likely to be quiet and calm, resulting in a fun night for the kids and a less stressful job for you.

- **Set a barrier.** If you just organized a room, don't thwart your efforts by allowing your children to devour it. Close doors and gate off areas you've just organized and cleaned. At least it will stay clean and organized for a day or two.

- **Keep treasures at home.** Never allow your child to bring his or her favorite toy out of your home, unless that toy is very easy to replace. There's too good of a chance of it getting lost.

- **Keep big books at bay.** Children's books can be large and unwieldy. To keep them under control, hang a shelf and put the books between bookends. An alternative is to use large baskets.

- **Freeze.** Set an egg timer for three minutes and have the children race around the room picking up toys or getting chores finished before the timer sounds. When the timer rings, everyone must "freeze." If they don't beat the clock, set the timer again and have another freeze session. When they beat the timer, reward everyone for a job well done, perhaps with a treat of cookies and milk.

- **Set a good example.** If your bedroom or the rest of the house is a wreck, your child won't understand why her room has to be organized. If you want your kids to be organized, you have to first be organized yourself. That goes for your spouse too if you're married.

- **Be enthusiastic.** If you're always complaining about your chores, your child will probably follow suit.

- **Give your kids a chore checklist.** Write down chores that would be appropriate for their ages and laminate the checklist. Have your children do each chore, while checking off items on their checklists. Tell them when they show you the completed checklist, after you've inspected and all is OK, they can then do something fun, like have a friend over or go to the park. By the way, have fun making the checklist. Cut out cartoon characters or fun pictures representing the chores. Don't make it look like a boring business checklist.

- **Age appropriate chores.** Make up a list of chores that are appropriate for each of your kids, depending on their age category. Next to each chore, designate a point value (10 points, 20 points, etc.) for chores that are completed.

  On the bottom of the list, indicate possible rewards for when the kids reach 100 points, 200 points, etc. Every time a chore is completed, your child gets the points for that particular chore.

  He or she can build up his or her points and turn them in for rewards like movie tickets, a trip to the book store or staying up a half hour later.

- **10-minute tasks.** Think up a bunch of 10-minute cleaning tasks and write each on small sheets of multi-colored cardstock or cut-up index cards. Put the small cutouts in an opaque paper bag and shake it up. Each day, have each child draw a task from the bag. That task becomes the one thing that child must do before he or she goes out to play.

- **Clean up together.** Clean up with the kids so you're all spending time together. Make it more fun with energetic music. Encourage dancing and cleaning at the same time, so your kids see this time as fun and entertaining.

- **Be specific.** Saying "clean your room" is general and vague. Chances are, you won't get what you want. Saying "put your dirty clothes in the hamper" or "remove the dishes from the dishwasher" is more specific, helps ensure your child understands what you mean and doesn't give them "wiggle room."

Great idea!

I'm a mother of six children and four grandchildren. When I ask the kids to pick up their toys, we make it a counting game. In doing so, they are learning their numbers and picking up toys the fun way.

Peggy Pierce
Cheshire, MA

- **Praise.** Always praise your child for a job well done. Really show your appreciation. That will encourage future chores to be done well. And if your child does something on his or her own, without being asked, do something extra special for your child since he/she made the extra effort. This will encourage him/her to do things without being asked later.

- **Don't yell; remind.** Don't yell at kids if they don't remember to do a chore you asked them to. Kids have short attention spans. Instead, firmly remind them of what they need to do and give them a specific deadline.

Be sure you have consequences for chores that are not completed when you told them to have them done, like not allowing them to play a video game or use the computer until the chore(s) is done.

Great idea!

When my son was a Cub Scout and Boy Scout we needed to keep up with ID card size documents for each rank and for each badge for future documentation for his Eagle Scout Rank. Using a three-hole binder filled with vinyl sheets used for baseball cards helped to keep these cards safe. If anything got slightly out of chronological order it could be easily reorganized.

Eileen Carman
San Diego, CA

- **Pay for performance.** Base your kids' allowances on the number of chores they complete. If they complete between five to seven chores they get one set amount, eight to ten chores they get another set amount and so on. Less than five chores, they get no allowance this week. Sad, but fair.

> ### Great idea!
>
> I have two tips I'd like to share.
>
> 1) If your child has a favorite story, record yourself reading it to him. When there is a sitter, when it's too late to read a story, or when your child has trouble falling asleep, play the tape for him. He will be soothed and comforted by your voice, as well as enjoy hearing himself on tape where he laughed, made a comment, or read a word or two of the story. It's also a great time saver if one parent is out of town, and multiple young children need to be put to bed.
>
> 2) Make your own "Crustables" peanut butter and jelly sandwiches. My sons love to eat peanut butter and jelly in their lunch each day. On Sunday nights, I make eight to ten peanut butter and jelly sandwiches, put them each in their own plastic sandwich bag and stack them in the freezer. Each night when I prepare their lunch, (or in the morning if I forgot to do so the night before), I just pluck a sandwich out of the freezer and half the work is done. The sandwich slowly defrosts prior to lunch and is just as fresh as if you made it that same morning. Try it yourself and see!
>
> Janet Pace
> Loveland, OH

- **Block out time.** Your kids need schedules too. Block out consistent times each day for the morning routine, chore time, homework time, fun time and bedtime.

- **Early to bed, early to rise.** Set consistent nap times, bed times and wake up times for your kids. Teach kids as early as you can how they can tell time so they know they shouldn't be hopping into your bed way before their wake times and so they're aware that bedtime is approaching at night.

- **Schedule a Hop-To-It Hour.** Make a designated hour of the day "Hop to It Hour." During this hour, everyone, including yourself and your spouse, uses this time to clean or organize something. Actually have little kids "hop" to the toy chest as they put things away to make it more fun. It teaches kids that everyone in the family has a responsibility to keep a clean environment.

Kids Artwork

- **Find the diamonds.** Rather than keeping every single piece of artwork your child creates, sit down with your child on a regular basis and ask him to choose the one or two he likes best. By the end of the year, you should have no more than five pieces of artwork that your child believes to be his "best" pieces. This will help keep the artwork under control and will still give you an opportunity to save his creations for future memories.

- **Take photos.** A picture is worth a thousand words. Take photos of the artwork that your child creates and keep these photos in a scrapbook. Even if the artwork is later discarded for space purposes, you'll still have the memory!

Great idea!

For those not sure what to do with the mountains of artwork their children bring home from school each day, here is what I do. I hang each project on my kitchen cabinets during a particular school month. At the end of the month, I have my daughter stand in front of the artwork and take a picture. The photos get saved and the artwork gets dumped.

In doing this, not only do you get to keep all the projects preserved for years to come, but you also get to see what your child looked like when she made them. The best part is you only have nine photos (one photo for each month of school) to file, box or add to a scrapbook instead of an overabundance of artwork.

Monica Bosse
Roselle, IL

- **Use a file storage box.** Office supply stores carry portable file boxes that hold hanging file folders. These generally have a cover and a handle for easy portability. Help your child create her very own filing system. Perhaps one file folder for second grade artwork, one for third grade artwork and so on. Now, all the drawings and any type of artwork that is flat, will be kept safe and organized. You'll even be teaching your child filing skills. It's never too early.

- **Keep it contained.** For other artwork that does not lie flat, the perfect container may be a large, plastic container with a lid. Your child will have a space for shadowboxes and other artwork that won't fit into a file folder. Again, be choosy. If you keep every single piece of artwork your child brings home for the next 15 years, your house is going to be overflowing with it.

Great idea!

Use your kids' artwork as gift-wrap. It's festive for the recipients and your kids will be so proud of the homemade wrapping paper. In addition, ask them to help make a card for the extra-special, homemade touch.

Caroline Sarian Meisel
St. Louis, MO

- **Hang it.** Get your child his very own artwork bulletin board so he can display his favorite artwork in his bedroom. When organized on a nice corkboard, this really adds a nice touch to a child's room. Plus, your child can very easily switch one piece of art, with another.

- **Tame supplies.** If your child produces a lot of artwork at home, she probably has tons of crayons, markers and other art supplies. Keep it all in a portable box, light enough for your child to be able to transport it from one room into the next. In addition, separate and organize the supplies into separate quart-size plastic bags before putting them in the box. This will keep everything organized and easily accessible.

Great idea!

Now that my kids are starting preschool and kindergarten, I'm beginning to collect quite a pile of worksheets and artwork. I wish I could keep every precious "work of art," but they take up too much space. So I decided to scan all of the papers and burn them onto CD.

When I'm feeling nostalgic, I just pop in a disk and have a slide show. My oldest likes it too because his younger sibling can't tear up his work. I'm also thinking of cutting and pasting them into scrapbooks as backgrounds and borders.

Meena Verma
Richmond, British Columbia
Canada

- **Give the perfect gift.** Kids artwork makes the perfect gift for grandma, grandpa, sister Jane, Aunt Sue, Uncle Jim and so on. Rather than buying gifts for your child to give to family members, encourage them to give their creations away as special gifts to special people.

Great idea!

Use a portable file box and hanging files for kids keepsakes. Label them:

1. Schoolwork
2. Artwork
3. Awards/Certificates
4. Medical/Health
5. Photos
6. Friends and Family
7. Keepsakes
8. Hobbies/Sports
9. Large Artwork and Non-Paper Keepsakes - store in a bin or under the bed box.
10. Vital Records - Keep copies here and originals in a fire safe box.

Allison Carter, The Professional Organizer & Speaker
www.theprofessionalorganizer.com/

- **Pizza delivery.** Make friends with your local pizza restaurant and ask them for a few clean pizza boxes. These are wonderful for storing kids artwork that doesn't fit in a file folder. Give one pizza box to each child and make him or her responsible for keeping it weeded out when it gets too full.

- **Wall of Fame.** Designate a wall in your child's bedroom, family room or other area that is to be used as the display wall for kid's artwork. If you don't want to hang directly on the wall, hang string and clothespin the artwork to the string. Once the wall is full, decide which artwork can be filed or discarded.

- **Frame it.** Choose one or two of your child's treasures each week or each month, and frame them. Your kids will be delighted to see their artwork on the walls in a main room, and you'll be amazed how much better scribbled pages look when they're in a nice frame.

Great idea!

I use my child's painting as the mat behind photos of him, I frame them and we can enjoy his art work along with his photo.

Joanne Wiggins
Langley, BC, Canada

Chapter 76

Teenagers

- **Give a little, get a little.** If your daughter asks you to drive her to soccer practice, ask her to water the plants.

- **Take the loot back.** If you pay your teenager an allowance, pay yourself a set amount out of his allowance for any items belonging to your teenager that you have to pick up for him, like a coat tossed over the sofa or dirty clothes tossed on the floor in his closet. This should give him the message that you mean business. An alternative is for every item you have to pick up for him, he then gets another chore tacked on.

- **Be sure they like it.** To encourage your teenager to keep her room clean, be sure it's a room that she really enjoys being in. Have her choose her own paint color. Have her help shop for a dresser she loves.

- **Put a TV in his room.** Tell him he can watch TV, as long as he cleans up his room at the same time. If he doesn't comply, remove his TV privileges.

- **Give them a prize.** For every day you don't have to nag your daughter to clean her room, give her a point. Once she has reached a set amount of points, she gets something for all of her efforts, like a sleepover with a girlfriend or pocket money to use at the mall.

- **Make it specific.** Just telling your teenager to "clean his room" is not very specific. You have to specify exactly what you want. If you want him to vacuum his room on Monday, tell him. If you want him to dust his room on Tuesday, say so.

Great idea!

I use a multiple rack pants hanger with movable arms to hang my teenage daughter's jewelry. The bottom arm holds necklaces, then bracelets, then hoop earrings and finally rings on top.

Only bracelets that do not have a clasp pose any problem and we just pull them through the middle of the other bracelets to take them off the arm. This hangs on the inside door to her closet on an over-the-door hook.

It is easy to see everything as she decides on her outfit for the day. Plus, we aren't continually trying to untangle necklaces. Works great!

Karen Blevins
Garden Ridge, TX

Chapter 77

Baby and Toddler

- **On the clock.** With a baby in the house, consistent feeding times are essential. Newborns have to be fed on demand, but once your baby is around four months old or so, a schedule can definitely be set. To remember to feed your baby at the same times each day, wear a watch with a timer to jog your memory.

Great idea!

Being a new mom certainly has its rewards, but you are bombarded with coupons and gifts for the new baby. One organizing tip I have is I keep all baby-related coupons and vouchers in one envelope or plastic bag in the diaper bag. I also keep a second plastic bag for receipts and gift receipts with baby items on them. I know where to always find it if I have to exchange or return a baby item. Pint and quart-size plastic bags are great because they are see-thru and waterproof.

Also, I like to keep a stash of diapers, wipes and change of clothing in a small caddy in the car. If there is ever a time we need diapers at the day care or if we forget to restock the diaper bag, we have a mobile nursery in the car. I have a minivan and I use the very back row of the van as a changing and nursing station. This makes life a whole lot easier.

Erika Steele
Lawrenceville, GA

- **Pre-pack a baby bag.** It should include a blanket, diapers, moist towelettes, a small toy, a change of clothes, plus a list of any last minute items. When you have to leave with the baby, you'll be all packed and ready to go.

- **Quiet please.** When going out to a restaurant with your infant or toddler, be sure to bring a fluffy toy along for her to play with—instead of noisy keys that will disturb others. You might also want to attach it to the highchair with a piece of yarn or ribbon so that, when she tosses it, it won't go very far and you can retrieve it easily.

- **Double duty.** Why carry both a purse and a diaper bag? If virtually every trip you make out of your house is with the baby, combine your purse contents into your baby's diaper bag. You'll only have one bag to grab when you leave the house.

- **Keep them informed.** If you're expecting a baby soon, make sure that the vital people—spouse, partner and other family members—can be notified quickly. If you don't have cell phones, you may want to rent a few beepers when the time is near.

- **Always have a diaper bag ready-to-go.** I always had my baby's diaper bag filled with five diapers, a travel pack of baby wipes, diaper rash cream, a travel-size baby powder, plastic bags (to toss dirty diapers in), an extra outfit, a sweater, two receiving blankets, a few small toys, a bib, an extra adult shirt (for those times when baby decides to spit up on you) and a changing pad. When I had to leave the house, I just added some food and milk and was all set. If I used any of the things in the diaper bag, I would re-stock the bag that same day and store the bag in the closet for next time.

- **Bring a portable DVD player.** When going on a long drive, bring along a portable DVD player with your toddler's favorite shows. Your son or daughter will be entertained, and you won't have to put up with whining. Another great place for a portable DVD player is a restaurant. Once your toddler is done eating, just put on his or her favorite show. You'll be able to finish your meal and possibly even order dessert before the little one begins to get restless.

- **Hire a babysitter.** If you're having difficulties getting anything done at home because you're always tending to your baby and/or toddler, consider hiring a babysitter to come into your home for an hour or two a day. You'll be giving yourself some time, and your kids will get used to being around someone else occasionally.

- **Teach them early.** Toddlers as young as 18 months are capable of helping you clean and organize. Little ones usually love putting away blocks, picking up magazines and other small chores. My daughter, at two years old, helped me put clothes in the clothes dryer.

- **Picky eaters.** Avoid too many non-nutritious snacks during the day to encourage your child to eat what is served for dinner. Make it known that at dinnertime, everyone sits at the table and eats what's served. Don't cook separate meals for your toddler, unless you're eating something very spicy or something that doesn't agree with your toddler's digestion. You'll just be encouraging picky eating habits.

- **It's potty time.** Potty training will be accomplished a lot quicker if you focus your attention on it. My advice is go right to underwear, not pull-ups, so your child is more aware of what's happening and is more likely to want to go on the potty, rather than sitting in wet clothes. You can always add a vinyl underwear cover if you're concerned about your carpets.

Chapter 78
Finding Time for You

- **Take a class online.** If you want to learn something new, but don't have time to sit in a classroom, take a class online. There is no commuting and you can set your own schedule.

- **Do one or two things and do them well.** Rather than volunteering at every school, church organization or work activity, pick one or two things and focus your efforts on those. If someone else requests your time, let this person know you're already committed to one or two activities and cannot take on another.

- **Schedule Play Time in Your Life.** Life is not about working every single minute. What a shame if you never have a single moment to enjoy a new fallen snow or the twinkling stars in the sky. Yet, so many people stay at work for endless hours to get more projects and tasks completed—long after everyone has gone home. Others spend every moment of the day cleaning, running errands and doing other household projects.

  Life is not about working harder. It's about working smarter. It's about doing what you have to do in a way that leaves you with enough time to enjoy your life, your loved ones and the activities that interest you. Think about your day and your current schedule. If you don't have a moment to spare, then something is wrong.

  Start by scheduling your "work time" and your "play time" just like teachers have young kids do in school. Stick to that schedule each day. Most people just have their work time scheduled, but play time often gets put on the backburner.

  Actually write your play time down on your daily schedule. If you schedule it to be between 7:00 and 9:00 at night, then use that time to play—whether that means spending time with your kids, visiting a friend, enjoying a hobby or relaxing and reading a book.

  Be careful. If you don't schedule a definite date, that time will most likely be used up with some form of work, whether that means working late at the office or catching up on household tasks. Keeping a healthy balance between work and play will ensure well-rounded, fulfilling, enjoyable days.

- **Creating time pockets.** A time pocket is a specific length of time within your day or week, that is set aside to do something. Here are two examples of how you can use time pockets in your life:

A) You're waiting for some extra time to magically come into your life to begin learning how to speak French. That time never seems to arrive. By the way, it never will—unless you make that time. So, you set up a "French Time Pocket" from 8:00 to 9:00pm on Mondays and Fridays and you use this time to begin learning French. Nothing except a major emergency should interfere with your French Time Pocket and within a few weeks, you should begin to have a beginner's French vocabulary.

B) You love to surf the Net, but you're spending three hours each night doing so and you can't get anything else done. The dishes are piling in the sink, the laundry is overflowing and the dust bunnies have taken over your furniture. Get everything back in control by scheduling an "Internet Time Pocket" of 10:00 to 10:30 each night. That will give you 210 minutes per week to surf the Net, but you'll also have plenty of time to catch up on your cleaning.

Whether you are not spending enough time doing something or you're spending too much time doing something, creating time pockets in your life can help.

- **Make a scheduled appointment with yourself.** Sometimes, it's just necessary to take some time for yourself, whether that involves you working on a favorite hobby, reading something you enjoy, taking a walk while dreaming about your future or relaxing on the sofa and watching a movie. Other commitments can easily take over your time. But if you want time for you, you have to make time for you.

Grab your planner and schedule in a minimum one-hour of "you" time each week just as you would schedule specific dates and times for your medical appointments or any other important appointment. If it's scheduled in, you'll know not to make any other appointments or commitments for that specific hour each week. Time taken for you is time well-deserved and is vital for healthy body, mind and spirit.

- **Tame your To Do list.** Your To Do List should not be ten pages long. Good time management is picking and choosing those items that are truly important and saying no to those that are not important at all. Force yourself to limit the amount of items on your To Do List.

Scheduling your day is an art definitely worth perfecting. A balanced schedule—one that equally distributes both work and play—is worth striving for. If you're spending all your time working and little or no time playing, then it's time to tame your To Do List and take back your time.

- **Set a time budget.** When it comes to making purchases, most people have an idea in their minds of what they're willing to spend. You probably wouldn't walk into a shoe store and say, "I will buy that pair of shoes no matter how much they cost." If the salesperson says the shoes cost $400, most people would not buy them. That's because when it comes to making purchases, people set a budget in their minds of how much those shoes are really worth to them.

But what about when it comes to how you spend your time? Do you sometimes spend more time on certain tasks than they're really worth? For instance, when it comes to cleaning your home do you spend an hour each day doing so? Two hours? Three hours? More than three hours? Is dusting really worth that much of your time? What about your other projects and appointments? How much is that time worth to you?

We all get the same amount of time each day—24 hours. At least eight of those hours are allocated to sleeping. So, we all have approximately 16 hours when we're awake. By setting a time budget for certain activities, you will always ensure your time is being spent on what is most important to you, your family and your future.

How much time are you willing to invest with a spouse or loved one? How many hours will you allocate to working, cleaning, exercising, eating or watching television? Before doing anything, ask yourself how much time you're willing to invest. Write those time investments down so you're able to reference them regularly. Then, stick to your time budget. Time isn't an unlimited currency, so be sure to spend it wisely.

- **Join a book club or a quilt club.** Planned activities that you enjoy doing are less likely to be cancelled then personal time you set up for yourself at home.

- **Team up with your spouse.** You and your spouse both need personal time. Why not ask him to watch the kids for a few hours one day a week, and then you do the same for him another day during the week. You'll both have time for hobbies, outings with friends or just to relax and enjoy a book.

- **Find some things you enjoy.** So many people don't take time for themselves because they simply don't know what to do with extra time. One way to combat this is to do a little soul-searching and make a list of things you might enjoy doing. When your scheduled free time arrives, just choose something on that list. You'll never know if you enjoy something unless you do it once or twice.

- **Learn to say no.** If you're always doing something for someone else, you'll never find time for yourself. This is not to say you should say no to every request that comes your way, but it's occasionally OK to say no if by doing so that means you'll be able to do something for yourself.

Chapter 79

Travel and Vacations

- **Directions TO your place.** Over time, there will be a number of people who are going to ask you for directions to your home or office. Rather than writing them out every single time you're asked, you will save a lot of time by having these already written or typed out.

  Write or type out driving directions from all points—east, west, north and south. Then, make copies of these directions and file them in a file folder marked "Driving Directions." Whenever someone asks, you can quickly pull a copy out of your file folder and fax or mail it to him.

  In addition, keep a word processing or text file on your computer. If the person asking for directions has an email account, you can copy and paste the directions into an email and send to that person.

> ### Great idea!
>
> I travel a great deal and don't have time to re-invent the wheel so to speak when packing a bag. So I have a series of lists that enable me to delegate packing to staff, friends and family if need be, such as a two-day bag, a four-day bag, a week-long bag, a fortnight bag and a month-long bag. Some useful traveling tips:
>
> - Always carry plastic shopping bags. They are excellent for holding damp laundry, wrapping anything wet and keeping anything dry.
>
> - Drink plenty of water and get enough sleep.
>
> - Always carry foam earplugs so you can sleep properly when traveling.
>
> - I keep a record of the serial, reference and registration numbers of all my insurance policies, bank accounts and personal and professional information in a single word document on my computer. At any time I can access it and it would be on hand should emergencies or other needs arise.
>
> Charles Boyle
> Townsville, Queensland, Australia

- **Directions FROM your place.** Whenever you visit a relative, client, friend, business or event that you plan to visit in the future, jot down how to get to that destination from your home or office. After your trip, file the directions away in your "Driving Directions" folder. When you need those directions in the future, they'll be waiting for you in your filing cabinet.

> ## Great idea!
>
> My husband and I use our car and truck with trailer often for travel and our interests (nature and archaeology) and travel needs require good organization in our vehicles. We use old canvas briefcases to store various necessities such as picnic supplies, first aid kits, travel games, books, toys for the grandkid, business supplies, extra clothes and emergency food.
>
> The briefcases are durable, roomy, cheap ($1-$2 at garage sales), and enable easy organization. We have a first aid bag, an emergency bag, a picnic bag, and a book and game bag. These bags also stash easily in corners, under seats and in the trunk. We use old luggage tags to identify the contents.
>
> Dinah Ackerson
> Concord, CA

- **Know where you're going.** Prior to leaving for any trip, be sure you have maps with you. Either get free trip planners from an automobile association such as AAA or get free maps and driving directions from the Internet. Even if someone gives you directions, it's always good to have additional maps as a backup, especially if you happen to hit a detour that the person who gave you directions was not aware of. If you use a road map, highlight your intended route.

- **Pack and then reduce by half.** Most people bring way more than what they need when going on a trip. If this sounds like you, it's time to lighten your load. Determine the number of days you'll be away and bring clothing for only half of those days.

  For example, if you're going away for eight days, bring enough clothes for four days). Wear each outfit twice or mix and match different tops with different bottoms so you look different each day. Be sure the pants or skirts you bring along easily match with lots of different tops.

- **Bring a goodie bag.** When traveling with small children, always bring a goodie bag that includes a few toys and non-perishable foods. When the kids start to fidget, you'll have a quick solution.

Great idea!

When going on a trip, I type up a one sheet travel itinerary by date that has airline information, car rental information and confirmation and hotel address, phone and confirmation. E-tickets and hard copies of reservations are attached to this one page sheet and I keep all these in a clear plastic folder. The folder either has a snap or string close, to keep contents secure. It is reachable at all times during my trip. I can grab the envelope and with a quick glance through the plastic, see where I am supposed to be and have phone numbers in case I need to call. When I need to pull a document, it is in the folder.

This works for one individual going on a trip or a whole family, keeping everything together in one secure place, handy at all times.

Using this plastic folder helps during the trip. We throw all our receipts in the folder so that they are in one place. If it is a business trip, all your receipts can be matched up against your credit card statement. If it is a personal trip, all your receipts can be matched up against your credit card, so you get a view of what your trip cost in total. The plastic folders can be reused over and over again.

Chris Mara
Woodridge, IL

- **Tame with games.** Create some games that the children can play. They could count all the white cars that they see or count state license plates. If you prefer, pick up some store-bought travel-sized games for them.

- **Have a sing-along.** Plan ahead. Find some audiocassettes that your children will enjoy. Have them help you pick them out. Then, everyone can sing along.

- **Listen to a book.** Pick up a few at the bookstore or have your children pick out their own. You can either play each cassette out loud on the vehicle cassette player or each child can use their own Walkman and listen to his or her personal choices.

- **Watch TV.** Install a TV in your vehicle that runs on a dashboard cigarette lighter. These can be a little pricey, but if you are on the road often and television is the only way to get some peace, it may be worth it. You may also want to consider a portable DVD player so you can pop in your kids' favorite movies. My husband and I paid $200 for one of these, and it's one of the best investments we've ever made for our sanity when going on family trips and outings.

- **Do a hobby.** Crayons and a coloring book, crossword puzzles, embroidery and electronic games can be fun activities for your kids and an excellent way to make it to your destination in a state of peace, rather than stress.

- **Start early.** Once you determine where you plan to go, begin gathering everything you need to make your trip a pleasant one. Need a passport? Apply at least three months ahead of time or you'll pay extra for express delivery. Secure your airline reservations at least eight weeks prior if traveling abroad. The closer it gets to the date you want to leave, the more the tickets may cost.

  Reserve hotel and car rentals well ahead of time to ensure your reservation is accepted. Get maps, surf the Net and speak with others to get specific travel tips for the areas you're visiting.

- **Call ahead.** Contact your hotel ahead of time to find out what their amenities are. If they have a hair dryer in each room for instance, you won't have to bring yours along. If they have laundry facilities, you can pack even less since you'll be able to do wash while you're there. If they have exercise facilities, you may want to bring some sneakers along. It's better to know ahead, so you're prepared.

- **Use a packing list.** Come up with a list of everything you need to take with you when traveling. Organize each item by genre such as clothing, toiletries and financial. Make copies of this list, so you can reference it for each trip you take.

  As you're packing, check off each item on your list as you put it in your suitcase. Finally, pack your list and use it on your last day of vacation or business trip, so you remember to take everything back home with you.

- **Keep a toiletries bag packed.** If you travel often, rather than having to gather toiletries every time you travel, keep a toiletry bag packed with shampoos, deodorant, and other travel-sized items. Stock this bag or refill travel-sized containers as soon as you return from your trip.

- **It leaked.** Store anything that may leak in a plastic Ziploc baggie. If you're not sure whether or not it will leak, err on the side of caution.

- **Take an empty suitcase.** If you're the type of person who shops when you travel, bring along an extra suitcase. You'll have the perfect place to put your souvenirs and gifts purchased during your trip.

- **Make a schedule.** Find out what you wish to do at your destination before you get there. Make yourself a schedule for each day based on specific criteria such as the days and times a particular store or museum is open. If you wish to switch some events around when you get there, that's okay. At least you'll have something to reference, so you're not wasting time wondering what you should do or what's open on what days.

- **Call me while you're away.** Most hotels charge an arm and a leg for making long distance calls. Some cell phone plans require you to pay roaming charges if you're outside your regular calling area. Buy a prepaid phone card before your trip and bring it with you. You can either use it from your hotel phone or a pay phone.

- **Carry one on.** If you're taking an airline or other mass transit to your destination, always carry on a small carry-on bag that contains your prescription medications, some of your cosmetics, a toothbrush/toothpaste duo, your cell phone, a change of underwear and a good book. Just in case your luggage doesn't make it when you do, you'll have your important items with you.

- **Bring some food onboard.** If allowed, bring some food onboard with you when you travel. You won't have to pay the high fees for getting an airline meal. Plus, you can better stay within your personal nutrition guidelines.

- **Travel buddies.** If you are traveling with a spouse or friend, each of you should pack an outfit in each other's luggage. That way, if one of you loses your luggage, the other person has a back-up set of clothing in his or her luggage.

- **Fly non-stop.** It may cost a bit more, but you'll save tons of time. If you have kids, you'll also save tons of aggravation.

- **Bring proof.** If you have young children flying free, don't forget to bring along their birth certificates. Airlines generally ask for proof and if you can't prove it, you may have to buy a seat.

- **Bag it.** If you don't plan on washing your clothes while you're away, be sure to pack an empty plastic bag so your dirty items can be kept separate from your clean clothes.

Great idea!

I keep packing lists, but mine are by type of trip. I have a cruise list, an overseas list, domestic travel list, and one for adventure travel. I also have a pre-trip To Do list, in chronological order by when it needs to be done.

Jessie Lang
Spokane, WA

- **Pay the toll.** Keep empty film canisters in your car for holding change for tolls. Tape a specific coin to the top of each film canister so you can easily identify the coins inside. If you have a digital camera, you probably don't have film canisters. Just use any small canister with a lid or keep a small

Tupperware container in your car. Inside, keep change separated into plastic Ziploc baggies.

- **Keep receipts together.** Whenever we go on a trip, we bring a plain, white #10 envelope with us. Whenever we spend anything, we write the date, purchase price, store and item(s) on the front of the envelope. We keep all receipts inside the envelope. When we get home, we have everything we need to determine how much was spent and on what. Once you're done figuring this out, you don't need to keep the individual receipts unless you need them for tax or expense purposes.

- **Do laundry.** If you're staying somewhere that has laundry facilities, do yourself a favor and do a load of wash every few days. I never have to do catch-up laundry when I return from a trip. I always do whatever I can right in the hotel and only clean clothes get packed into our return suitcase.

- **Don't over schedule.** Otherwise, you'll spend a lot of time running and a little time enjoying. Pad time in between activities and be flexible. It is easier to relax if you aren't constantly on the go.

- **Safety first.** Make two copies of your itinerary—one for yourself and one for family members who are not traveling with you. Those at home will be able to contact you in case of an emergency.

- **Familiarize yourself.** When traveling, especially when traveling abroad, familiarize yourself before you leave with geography, some very basic language and currency conversion.

- **Play catch-up.** As long as you're not driving, travel time could easily be used for catching up on some business work, reading or letter writing. Laptops have made it easy to bring your work along with you if you choose. Magazines or a good book can be tucked into your carry-on for reading while you're on the road, on a plane or later while you're in bed at a hotel or a relative's home.

- **Journal it.** If you scrapbook or like to remember your vacations vividly, bring a journal so you can take notes during your trip. You may want to give your kids a journal too.

- **Get someone to keep watch.** Whenever we go away, we always have a neighbor stop by to pick up the mail and to check to be sure everything is OK at our house. In addition, we always set our house alarm before we leave.

- **There's no place like home.** Before you leave for vacation, clean your house, wash all of your laundry and make your bed. When you arrive back home after your vacation, your home will be a welcome haven.

Chapter 80

When to Hire Help

- **You can't get started.** In the event you're too overwhelmed to start getting organized, are not physically able to get organized or don't have the time to figure out productive, efficient systems, you may consider hiring a professional to assist you. There are actually people who will come to your home or office and work with you to get it organized. These people are called professional organizers.

  To find a professional organizer in your area, you can first look on my Web site, as I have a pretty comprehensive listing available by area of the United States, Canada, Mexico and abroad. The direct link is www.getorganizednow.com/po-dir-index.html

  Or, you can check out the National Association of Professional Organizers on the following link: www.napo.net

- **You have to be there.** A good professional organizer will always request you work with her (or him) side by side. She will not usually do the job alone, especially because you will have to assist in the decisions regarding what gets kept and what gets tossed.

  Plus, the professional organizer will determine those systems that best meet your personality and needs and will train you how to use these systems well into the future.

- **Invest in tomorrow.** Since professional organizers are independent contractors, they set the price and it can range anywhere from $15 per hour to $250 per hour, depending on the organizer's education, skill, experience and expertise. Typically, you will spend anywhere from $35-$65 per hour if you need your home organized.

  If that amount seems high, just imagine how wonderful you're going to feel when the clutter is gone, your schedule is worked out or your stress is has vanished. It's an investment in your future.

- **What about the future?** Many people acknowledge that a professional organizer can probably help them today. But what about tomorrow? What if they can't keep it up, after spending all that money?

  Your investment should be a bit of an incentive to stay organized. In addition, some organizers offer follow-up assistance or follow-up services at reduced rates.

- **Weekend warriors.** Some professional organizers are willing to work with you on the weekend. This is especially helpful if you work a 9 to 5 schedule. Others may come in early in the morning and still others may work late at night. You'll have to work it out with the person you hire. Interview several professional organizers to determine who can best work with your schedule.

- **Use your answering machine.** Whatever time you schedule the professional organizer to work with you, it will be a lot more productive if you eliminate any possible interruptions. Allow your answering machine to take calls for you. Close the door to the room you're working in. Get a babysitter to watch the kids. If the organizer keeps getting interrupted, the job is going to take much longer and it's going to end up costing you more money.

- **Get quotes.** Get quotes from several professional organizers in your area. Meet with them to determine who can best meet your needs and budget. Don't only use money as a factor. Use years of experience, references, the person's portfolio and personality as criteria too.

- **Is everything included?** When a professional organizer quotes you, it's generally just the organizer's time and expertise in that figure. If you need file folders, containers, computer disks, or other supplies, that's usually extra. Sometimes the organizer will assist you in getting these extras, while other organizers require you to pick up these items yourself prior to your first session.

- **Ask them to consult.** If it's just a little bit of advice you need and not necessarily organizing sessions, ask a professional organizer what he charges to consult with you. Many charge an hourly consulting fee and maybe that's all you need to get going.

- **They're well rounded.** While professional organizers are known for typical organizing projects, such as uncluttering a room or creating a filing system, there are many who specialize in more unconventional projects. Some professional organizers are personal shoppers, others organize photos, and yet others might help with packing or unpacking services during a move.

- **Just call me bashful.** Please, don't be embarrassed about having to contact a professional organizer. Believe me when I say, your home is most likely not the most disorganized home they've seen. And even if it is, professional organizers are known for being kind, understanding, gentle and more helpful that you can imagine. If you feel you need the help of a professional organizer to start getting organized, do yourself a favor and hire one today.

Chapter 81

Reducing Stress

- **Take time to stretch.** Take one-minute stretching breaks throughout your day. This little act can help you take a physical and mental break.

- **Play with your pet.** Studies show that people who have pets have less stress in their lives. Whenever you're feeling stressful, play some Frisbee with your dog or pet your cat.

- **Make a clean sweep.** Sweep the floors, sweep out the garage, sweep the sidewalk and sweep out negative thoughts. Hanging on to frustration and anger will surely drain your energy and bring you down. For every negative thought that enters your mind, force yourself to think of three positive things—you'll be training your mind to re-focus. In fact, as you're sweeping out your home, think of all the negative energy you're sweeping out too.

- **Stop what you're doing.** If you're super-busy and find yourself getting overwhelmed with all the tasks and projects you have to do, the best thing to do is stop what you're doing—at least for a few minutes. It's vital to take a deep breath and a step back to be sure a) you're working on the right things and b) you're working as efficiently as possible.

- **Be realistic.** The other day, someone asked me if I would volunteer my time for an event. I quickly glanced at my busy schedule and graciously declined the offer. I realized immediately that if I took on this additional project, that I would be in a major time-crunch. While others may expect you to be super-human, the truth is that everyone has limitations. Know yours and be realistic about how much can actually be completed accurately in any given day.

- **Keep a running record.** There are always going to be things that need to be done. Always have a Master List so you can jot these things down. This running list serves as a memory tool, so you can free your mind to concentrate on the task at hand.

- **Take your pick.** Once you have a Master List, use it to write up a Daily To Do List. Wisely choose four (or five or six—whatever you can handle each day without getting overwhelmed) things from your Master List and put those items on your Daily To Do List. Work on those four items and don't put another four on that list until those initial four are completed.

- **Make your environment more pleasant.** Surrounded by papers and mail? Clear your work area, even if you have to put everything to the side for now. Are your kids interrupting you? Give them a project to do to keep them occupied. Not enough light? Add a lamp or paint the room a lighter color. Put on some pleasant music. Light a scented candle. The bottom line is, the more pleasant your environment is the more relaxed you're going to feel.

- **Sandwich in rewards.** After we did a bunch of yard work the other day, my husband and I went out on the front patio and relaxed with some lemonade while we flipped through our favorite magazines. After I write my organizing columns for the media, I often take a refreshing walk around my neighborhood. Sandwiching enjoyable rewards in between work can make your day productive, stress-free and fun.

- **Take some thinking time.** Sometimes it's necessary to just sit back in a chair and take some time for quiet reflection—perhaps about goals, maybe about how you would tackle a particular project. No matter what, just taking some time for thinking will help you to slow down and relax, rather than jumping right into something you're not sure about.

- **Play with your kids.** Time goes by so quickly, and if you have children, you probably already know that they're growing up by leaps and bounds right before your eyes. Don't let the time slip by without enjoying some quality time with your children.

- **Be realistic.** Don't try to take on more than you can handle, otherwise you're bound to get overwhelmed. Learn to say no when your plate is full.

- **Exercise.** Building just 20 minutes or so of exercise into each day can reduce stress and make you feel more energetic.

- **Enjoy a hobby or two.** Hobbies allow you to get away from the daily grind and give you time to be creative. Why not try out knitting, scrapbooking, stamp collecting, photography or quilting?

- **Spend time with friends.** Good friendships allow you to talk about things in your life—both good and bad—so you're not holding everything in. Sometimes just having a cup of coffee with good friends may be just what the doctor ordered.

- **Slow down.** Life goes fast enough. Don't try to rush it even more. Take things slowly, one small step at a time.

- **Play some games.** Get together with family members and/or friends and play some board games once in awhile. These often end up in laughter, which can be an excellent stress-reducer.

- **Schedule 10-minute luxuries.** Don't forget to schedule a few 10-minute luxuries per day to do something nice for yourself. Sometimes the day is so rushed and chaotic, that it's easy to forget the really important things like family, health, spirituality, personal time and so on. Take that 10-minute vacation every day. You deserve it!

Chapter 82

Goals and Personal Achievement

- **Make them concrete.** Don't keep your goals in your head alone. Get them down on paper and you'll make them more concrete.

- **Don't keep them to yourself.** Tell all family members and close friends about the goals you plan to reach. When you tell others, you may actually be more committed to reaching that goal.

- **Make your goals SMART.**

  - ❖ **Specific:** Your goals must be specific. For instance, saying that you'd like to spend more time with your kids is too general. However, saying that you vow to spend one hour of quality time with your kids each Wednesday and Friday, immediately following dinner, is very concrete and specific.

  - ❖ **Measurable:** Goals that are worked on and achieved, are those that can be measured and tracked. When you think of making a resolution, think in terms of numbers. Perhaps you'd like to lose weight. Thinking in numbers, you might state that you'd like to lose five pounds—one pound per month for the next five months. Or possibly you'd like to go on a short vacation. Thinking in numbers, you may state that you'd like to save $100 per month, so you can go on a bed and breakfast weekend in June.

  - ❖ **Attainable.** You can certainly make challenging goals, but don't make them so difficult that they're going to be almost impossible to achieve. You can always break your goals down into smaller, mini-goals. For instance, if you'd like to put aside $50 per month, make a resolution to set aside $12.50 per week.

  - ❖ **Realistic.** You might want to be a pro golfer this year, but if you haven't even started training yet, then this goal is going to be unrealistic and unattainable. Instead, set more realistic goals, such as taking a few basic golf lessons or playing golf once per week on Tuesdays for practice.

  - ❖ **Timely.** The word "someday" is indefinite. Yet, often people say they have so many things they'd like to accomplish ... someday. Goals with no start or end date in mind never get accomplished. Be sure all of your goals have both a deadline and a starting date. For example, you might say you'd like to change your job. Your deadline might be March, 2008 and your start date might be next week—determining what you'd like to do, seeking available positions, etc.

Chapter 83
Staying Motivated and Organized

- **Create a visual.** Many organizations that wish to reach a financial goal for a charity cause will draw a vertical thermometer, with incremental goals written along the side of the thermometer starting at the bottom with zero and at the top with, let's say, $20,000.

  As each mini goal is met, they fill in the portion of the thermometer up to the number they have reached. This gives everyone an excellent visual of how close the organization is to reaching its goal.

  You can do the same for goals you're trying to set in your life. A simple sheet of poster board and a thick magic marker is all you need.

  Draw your own thermometer, indicating your own starting point, incremental goals and completion point. Describe the goal at the very top and then attach the poster to a place you'll see clearly every day.

  Fill in your thermometer as you complete each mini goal and you'll have a wonderful visual that will help keep you on the track to success.

- **Set the stage for your life.** So many times I've heard people say they want to learn how to play a musical instrument, learn a foreign language, draw, take a vacation or any number of things that would be enjoyable. But at the same time, very often it's all talk and no action.

  There are so many things in life to enjoy, but our time on this earth is limited. Be proactive in setting the stage for the rest of your life. Each week, set at least one goal and begin working towards reaching that goal, even if it's only for a few minutes each day. Don't let your life pass you by without doing the things you've always meant to do.

- **Triumph in your accomplishments.** Whether you've just completed a 10K run or you've just organized your medicine cabinet, be proud of yourself for the things you accomplish each day. What's the sense of doing something, if you can't truly enjoy the satisfaction of having done it?

  Every accomplishment is a stepping-stone for your next accomplishment. The more satisfied you are with yourself, the more you'll want to do.

- **Make a "Free Time Bag."** When you have some free time, don't spend it running throughout your house looking for something to do. Instead, pack yourself a "Free Time" bag and leave it in an easily accessible place.

  A tote bag can hold favorite magazines, crossword puzzles, a crocheting project you're working on, the book you're in the middle of reading, stationery and a pen to write letters to your friends and brochures for future vacation destinations. When you have free time just grab your bag and you're all ready to enjoy time at home, in the yard or in a local park!

- **Count your blessings.** Each day, think of at least ten things that make you really happy to be alive—your spouse, your children, your pet, your garden, your health, your home, the moon, the ocean, flowers, trees, puffy clouds—whatever you can think of that makes you smile.

List these ten things each morning, before you start off your day. Carry this list with you and refer to it throughout the day, especially at those times when you might be feeling a bit stressed. Your list can be a constant provider of positive energy.

Great idea!

This is something I have wanted to do for a long time, but you've made it so easy for me. I greatly enlarged and printed out the quotes from your inspirational page on your Web site, bought an 8" X 10" Lucite frame and put a quote a week up in our kitchen. This is great, because it is a good discussion point and it also helps me to explain and teach the values I want to instill in them.

Sara Newell
Grosse Pointe, MI

- **Eliminate the obstacles one day at a time.** What's holding you back from enjoying each day? The ever-growing pile of laundry? The kitchen table stacked with mail? A cluttered living room? A calendar jam-packed with stuff, much of which you don't even want to do? A demanding job?

No matter what the obstacle is, it can be overcome. But you can't expect to overcome all of your obstacles immediately. It takes time, but little by little, you can get rid of each one.

Focus on one of those obstacles each week. For instance, if the laundry pile is bothering you, why not work on that problem this week? Do a load of laundry each day until it's done. If the living room is cluttered, have a 15-minute clean-up session with your family, until it's less chaotic.

You get the picture. The obstacles will only go away, once you decide to focus on getting rid of them.

- **Have a party.** That is an "organizing party." Make it progressive. Invite five or six people over to your home and have them help you organize your _____ (you choose the area). Next month, the organizing party moves to one friend's home and so on. Make this a recurring party each month and the whole bunch of you will be super organized.

Great idea!

I find that the biggest favor I can give myself is not only to accomplish something everyday, but to make a list of what I accomplished yesterday!

Shirley Fichera
Chester, CA

- **Seize the day.** Choose one day each week and on that day jot down the words, "Seize the day!" on your calendar. When that day arrives, do something spontaneous that you wouldn't normally do, but is something you could do in one day.

  Perhaps you might go bowling, go on a picnic, take a dance lesson, or flip through a book about astronomy. Since the things you choose can be experienced in one day with very little preparation, you'll be more inclined to do them.

  Likewise, doing something you don't normally do can pull you outside of your comfort zone, add excitement to your day, give you the opportunity to experience something new and build your self-esteem.

- **Declare an "Organizing Day."** Designate one day each month, "Organizing Day." Put it on your calendar. When this day arrives, make a concerted effort to organize your office, unclutter your home, slay the raging, paper beast, thin out your file folders or donate unwanted items. Organize. Organize. Organize. Then organize some more.

- **Schedule a party.** Choose one weekend for you and your family to do nothing but organize your house. Schedule a party for the weekend following your organizing weekend. Invite others over in advance. You'll be forced to organize since guests will be coming. And why not? You'll want to show off your newly organized house, won't you?

- **Take it outside.** The weather is just beautiful and you want to be outside, but you have chores to do. A dilemma? It doesn't have to be. Take your chores outside.

There are tons of things you can do in your own backyard. Read your mail, balance your checkbook, polish the silverware, write a letter by hand or on your laptop, make some calls on your cell phone, peel potatoes—the list is endless.

- **Ask for little reminders.** Ask a friend or loved one to check on your organizing progress once every week. Choose someone who can boost your spirits and who won't give up asking you until he or she sees you're doing so well that you no longer need to be asked.

- **A little at a time.** If you wait to organize until you have the time "to do the job right and in its entirety," you'll never get started. Organize yourself by listing tasks you can complete in shorter periods of time. Then schedule those tasks and do them.

- **Gather a cheering section.** If you are having a hard time motivating yourself to organize, perhaps a friend, family member or associate would be willing to help. Since they won't be emotionally attached to your clutter, they may be able to encourage you to get rid of it easier. Maybe you could barter with them.

- **Pay someone to help you organize.** There are many professional organizers available if you choose. If you're on a tight budget, perhaps you could hire a student for a few hours to help.

- **The joy of organizing.** Would you rather be ironing or relaxing outside on a sunny day enjoying the fresh air? No matter what work-related tasks you're doing, whether it's ironing, paying the bills, filing papers or clearing out your inbox, chances are you'd rather be doing something else. That's just natural.

Just being organized in itself will allow you to enjoy more sunny days, your favorite hobbies, your family and friends and everything else you enjoy, just by helping you get the work-related tasks done more efficiently.

One of the ways I use to get those work-related tasks done a lot quicker is to make those tasks more enjoyable to do.

Now, I know you're probably thinking that there's no way to make ironing more exciting. It's boring. It's drudgery. The trick is to make the task you're doing not boring, but something you can actually tolerate—or even enjoy.

For instance, when I fold laundry, I generally do so while watching something interesting on television. Obviously, it's easy to fold and watch TV at the same time. I actually associate folding laundry with giving myself a TV break. I get to enjoy a program and get my task done at the same time.

Jenny, one of our newsletter readers told me that when she's dusting, she puts her favorite "dusting music" on. To her, dusting music meant loud, energetic, dance-type music. She said, "I barely feel like I'm dusting and I even get my husband to join my dusting party on occasion. It's so much fun!"

Kevin, another one of our readers, tells me he used to hate washing the car. But one day his seven-year old son asked him if he could help out and ever since then, Kevin washes the car with his son once every week. Kevin said, "It gives me the time to talk to my son and share his life on a regular basis. My son just loves it. In fact, to make it even better, we always go out for a soda or ice cream cone afterwards. It gives us something special to look forward to each week."

Ally, another reader, used to hate to file at work. Therefore, it would constantly pile up. She determined that one of the reasons she wasn't filing was because the file folders were worn, tattered and smelled very musty. She dreaded even the thought of filing. Then one day, Ally decided to toss those old file folders and she went out and got herself some new file folders—in pink, her favorite color! Ally said, "What an enormous difference it made. It's amazing how such a small thing can change your attitude. I never have piles of filing to do anymore. I do it on a daily basis!"

Whenever you're dreading something that needs to be done, just think of possible ways you could make it better. With just a little bit of thought and creativity, you can make virtually any task less daunting and even more joyful.

- **Take a mini-vacation.** Whether it's going for a walk through the park, sipping lemonade on your deck, going to the mall or taking a swim, a ten-minute mini-vacation each day will help keep you stress-free and energized.

- **10 minutes a day, keeps the clutter away.** Take ten minutes at the end of your day to tidy up. You'll be ready to start fresh the next day.

- **Go to our site.** Take advantage of the most effective organizing publications and tools. Hint: Visit my Get Organized Now! Web site. Updated weekly, it includes lots of great stuff to help you. www.getorganizednow.com

- **Go to our forum.** Post a question or share your favorite ideas on the Get Organized Now! Discussion Forum. Simply visit the Get Organized Now! Web site and click on the "Forum" link. Our reader community offers great questions and advice. Sharing helps all of us achieve greater organizational success!

- **Keep this book nearby.** It's not meant to be read once and then stored on a shelf, but rather to be read and referenced whenever you need a refresher on staying organized.

Chapter 84
Final words

I hope you have enjoyed this journey we've taken together. Please let me know how you're doing in your efforts to get and stay organized. Write to me with your success stories. I would love to hear from you.

Keep this book handy for future reference. Whenever you need a brush-up, just read a few chapters.

If you think of ideas or tips that are not in this book, please submit them to us. We'll consider printing them in a future update. You can submit your ideas on the following link:

www.getorganizednow.com/readertip.html

Visit the Get Organized Now! Web site each day for new ideas, tips, articles, checklists, e-courses and motivation. Hang out in our free discussion forum, frequented by thousands of people around the world, to ask questions, share ideas or to get a dose of motivation.

I wish you the best of luck and success on your path to a stress-free, pleasant, fun, exciting, productive organized life.

In the final chapter of this book, I leave you with the 10 Commandments of *Finally Organized, Finally Free.*

Maria Gracia
Get Organized Now!
www.getorganizednow.com

Chapter 85

The 10 Commandments of Finally Organized, Finally Free

I _____
(your name)

on this date _____
(date)

do hereby solemnly swear to accept and abide by the following 10 Commandments so that I can be *Finally Organized, Finally Free*.

I. Thou shalt not get overwhelmed, but shall go forth and be organized with baby steps.

II. Thou shalt not give yourself the disadvantage of generating clutter, physical, virtual or mental, for it will trap you into living a life of chaos.

III. Thou shalt always have a place for everything and thou shalt put everything back in its place immediately.

IV. Thou shalt always write it down and never commit details to memory alone.

V. Thou shalt banish obstacles barring you from reaching your dreams. Thou shalt achieve your dreams by always having a vision, a goal and a deadline.

VI. Thou shalt not attempt to do everything yourself, lest you will exhaust yourself. Seek help from family members, friends, associates and professionals.

VII. Thou shalt spend a minimum of ten minutes each day organizing, tidying, planning and scheduling.

VIII. Thou shalt not procrastinate. Do what you say you're going to do, when you say you're going to do it. Control your destiny.

IX. Thou shalt take care of yourself and your health. Thou shalt make time for you and your loved ones. Thou shalt strive to have a positive "Can Do" outlook on life. Thou shalt have fun by designating and enjoying rewards for all your effort.

X. Thou shalt respect your time, by not allowing unnecessary interruptions and not accepting every single request for your precious time.

Contributors

The following people have been instrumental in the writing and editing of this book.

- **Reader Contributions.** We have a special area on our Web site where Web site visitors can contribute their own organizing tips and ideas. We have thousands of excellent, truly unique, ones in our archives. We are thrilled to print many of these tips in our books and publications.

  A big "Thanks," to all contributors. Your personal insights have greatly enhanced *Finally Organized, Finally Free for the Home*.

- **Joe Gracia: Senior Executive Editor.** Joe Gracia began his marketing career over 30 years ago. He is an expert in both traditional offline marketing as well as marketing on the Web. Over the past 13 years, he has made his clients literally millions of dollars in increased sales and profits with his unique approach to small business marketing and management techniques.

  After receiving his degree in Marketing and Advertising Design in 1976, Joe entered broadcast media; first with Public Television (PBS), and then, through the years, with both ABC and CBS television affiliates. As an advertising designer and then Director of Advertising Design for 14 years, Joe learned some tremendous marketing lessons by working with thousands of small business owners on their marketing strategies and advertising.

  In 1990 Joe left broadcasting to start Effective Business Systems, a small business consulting firm, specializing in helping small business owners develop simple, but effective, low-cost and profitable marketing systems to replace the costly and wasteful systems commonly in use. Joe's consulting practice quickly grew as word spread about the dramatic sales increases his strategies were producing for his clients.

  When Joe asked one new client to set a sales goal for her $300,000 business, she said, "I would love to grow my business to one million dollars in annual sales within the next four years." Just 24 months later, Joe's client celebrated the achievement of her goal—two years ahead of schedule! By the fourth year, she was fast approaching two million in annual sales, and still growing.

  Another client wanted to double her sales, and then sell her business for a healthy profit. In 1999, her goal of doubling her business was achieved, and in January of 2000 she signed the papers for the sale of her business. All achieved with the help of the marketing techniques Joe shared with her.

  In 1997 Joe set a goal to make his marketing expertise available and affordable for all business owners, no matter how big or small their budget.

His plan was to put all of his marketing expertise, and effective marketing methods—the same simple marketing methods he was using to help grow his current clients' businesses—into written form.

In 1999 the project was completed. He called it *The Give to Get Marketing Solution*. Finally, Joe was able to share his "tested and proven," low-cost techniques for attracting customers not just with hundreds of business owners, but with literally thousands across the country, and around the world.

In 1997 Joe and his wife, Maria, brought their business and marketing experience to the Internet by co-creating the Get Organized Now! Web site.

Joe applied his marketing expertise to the design of the site, as well as the overall marketing strategy of the site. Maria actively hosts the site and with the help of Joe's marketing strategy has grown the site into one of the most popular and successful organizing Web sites on the Internet.

On October 1, 2000, Joe founded a new company division called Give to Get Marketing. His Give to Get Marketing Web site is designed to educate small business owners in a wide variety of marketing principles including effective strategies and proven marketing systems. Visit his Give to Get Marketing Web site at: www.givetogetmarketing.com

When he's not working, Joe enjoys spending quality time with his wife and daughter, playing guitar and reading—especially anything with historical significance.

- **Laura Sherman: Senior Executive Editor.** Laura, a freelance editor, has an excellent "eye for detail". She lives in Watertown, WI with her husband, Alan, and three wonderful children, Abby, Emma and Jack.

  Laura graduated from the University of Wisconsin-Madison in 1989 with a degree in English.

  Active in her community, Laura has served on the board of the Watertown Newcomers and Neighbors Club in positions including Treasurer and Social Coordinator.

  She enjoys being outdoors in the warm weather and you'll frequently see her gardening or reading, while enjoying the company of her kids. She plays violin, attends monthly book chats and plays a mean game of Bunco!

  Laura understands the great benefits of clutter control, and holds regular rummage sales throughout the year to "lighten up."

- **Maribel Ibrahim: Associate Editor.** Maribel C. Ibrahim is a freelance writer and stay-at-home mom residing in Severna Park, Maryland. After thirteen years as an Industrial Engineer for two Fortune 500 companies, she traded in her briefcase for a diaper bag.

Maribel and her husband Omar recently welcomed their first-born son Aidan. Sampson, their iguana, is very jealous, but is gradually making the adjustment to the new addition.

Maribel is a lifetime member of Weight Watchers, a La Leche League member and a vocalist for the Magothy United Methodist Church Praise Band. Maribel's monthly column, MomTalk, featured in the Severna Park Voice, provides moms with tips on organizing, finances, fitness, home management and family resources available in the Severna Park area. You can visit Maribel online at www.abundantlivingnow.net or via email at MomTalk@abundantlivingnow.net

- **Jodi Arrowsmith: Associate Editor.** Jodi Arrowsmith is a lifelong resident of Bay City, Michigan. She has been married to her husband, Rob, since 1993 and they have two boys, Evan and Adam. Jodi has worked for a Bankruptcy Attorney and Trustee as a "Trustee Administrator," since 1993. Her job consists of reviewing all Trustee cases in her bosses care to be sure that they are actively administering all assets of each file in a timely manner. Jodi processes all documents, does her own filing, maintains dates to follow up, as well as updates all case records with all banking transactions.

Much of Jodi's volunteer time is spent at her parochial school and church: She listens to children read, monitors various lessons in the computer lab on Fridays, is a PowerPoint Multimedia Projection System technician for her church service and serves on several committees at the church/school. She also served as a volunteer bookkeeper for her children's school daycare.

Jodi has been a Moderator on the Get Organized Now! forum, since 2002. She enjoys seeing new friends progress from chaos toward peace of mind. As Jodi says, it's a work in progress!

- **Diana Romagnano: Associate Editor.** Diana lives in Elgin, IL. She has four kids, Louis Jr., Sam, Lucy and Sabina and four grandsons, Louie, Rudy, Andrew and Nathan. She also has two grandkitties, Lynde and Sylvester. Diana is retired and enjoying things she put off when her children were home and she was a busy working mom and wife.

Her hobbies and interests include a love of organizing, cross stitching, card making, crocheting, reading and going out to lunch with friends. She was born in Chicago and loves the city, but has moved to the country and loves that also.

Diana retired shortly after her husband Lou died and her Mother moved in with her. She enjoys having her mom and her daughter living with her. They call themselves the "Golden Girls" minus one!

Diana enjoys working as a moderator on the Get Organized Now! forum and helping people. She loves when they start to see an improvement in their lives. She says the forum has helped her through a very devastating time in her life and changed her into the person she is today. Diana says she could not have done it without Get Organized Now! and the wonderful people involved with the site. The other thing she has learned over the years is to take time for herself each and every day. It changes one's entire outlook—reading, stitching or just sitting and thinking. She says that we all deserve it and definitely need it in our lives.

- **Lynne Poindexter: Associate Editor.** Lynne Poindexter was born and raised in Philadelphia, Pennsylvania. She is a corporate paralegal for a satellite television communications corporation. Lynne is a member of her church's choir. She is a big movie buff with a movie library of over 1,000 films.

  She moderates the Get Organized Now! forum and enjoys her ongoing quest of getting organized. Lynne enjoys line dancing and has been taking classes for over two years. She is a member of a line dance and social club. Her other interests include, sewing, cross-stitch and miniature dollhouse building.

- **Bonnie Stonebraker: Associate Editor.** Bonnie and her pastor husband currently live in Washington State with their granddaughter and are preparing for an early 2005 move to Montana. Their daughter lives in western Washington and her son and his family, wife Kris, sons Ben and PJ live in Kansas. Bonnie was born and raised in New England and is currently employed as a project manager in the aerospace industry.

  Bonnie is a member of the choir, a substitute ringer in the handbell choir, and Junior High Youth Advisor at church. She also enjoys sewing, knitting, and card-making. She is currently learning to use the embroidery machine, which was a gift for her college graduation. Her major milestone was to complete her college education prior to turning 50, which she accomplished in early 2004.

  She is also a moderator on the Get Organized Now! Discussion forum and has benefited greatly from the support there. She has forged friendships with the other forum members, some via email, some via telephone calls and others in person.

- **Katrina Cole Slaughter, Associate Editor.** Katrina was born and raised about 35 miles west of the Nation's Capital. She has not strayed very far from the place of her birth, except for an 18-month stint in Northeast Georgia. With parents who are in their 70's and a teenage son, Matt, Katrina happily moved back home to Virginia in April 2004.

Using her free time wisely, Katrina is an active member of GRACE Bible Church, where she serves as a Pre-School Praise teacher and participates in the women's programs. She was the inaugural Chapter Coordinator for the Loudoun County Chapter of CHADD (Child and Adults with Attention Deficit/Hyperactivity Disorder). Katrina finds great joy when helping those around her.

- **Margaret Witherington, Associate Editor.** Margaret was born and lives in Southern, Ontario, Canada. She has been happily married for 36 years. She is the proud mother of three wonderful children.

  Margaret enjoys volunteering as a moderator on the Get Organized Now! Forum and helping people. She loves to help them get started on their organizing journey. She also loves the camaraderie with the other moderators on the site.

  Margaret's hobbies and interests are knitting, crocheting, organizing, moderating and camping. She is very honored to be helping with this book.

About the Author

Maria Gracia, founder of Get Organized Now!, specializes in helping people get better organized to live the kind of stress-free life they've always dreamed of.

During Maria's ten years with Dun and Bradstreet's Nielsen Media Research in New York, Maria worked as a marketing, organizing and management specialist.

Throughout her tenure, she managed the data analysis department, worked with hundreds of television stations and advertising agencies and developed effective, productive systems for her clients and staff.

Today, Maria, her husband, Joe, and their beautiful daughter Amanda Grace, live in Watertown, Wisconsin. Joe and Maria own and operate their company, Effective Business Systems. Maria founded Get Organized Now! as a division of the company in 1996.

The Get Organized Now! Web site is currently visited by over a million people per year. Maria has hundreds of thousands of people on her Get Organized Now! newsletter list.

Specializing in peak time and space management, Maria has over 20 years of organizational experience. Her broad range of skills covers clutter control, planning, scheduling, peak productivity, records management, space planning, time and paper management, filing systems, computer oriented-organizational systems and more.

Maria Gracia has appeared at, wrote for, or has been interviewed by hundreds of international, national and local media and organizations such as Woman's Day Magazine, Country Living Magazine, Access Magazine, USA Today, Staples and hundreds of television and radio stations.

Maria is the author of the *Finally Organized, Finally Free* series. Her books have been read by thousands of people all over the world. In addition, she has created a variety of other helpful organizing products, sold worldwide, which can be found in her Get Organized Now! Store on her Web site: www.getorganizednow.com

On the homefront, Maria is a huge proponent of family time and enjoys as much time as possible with her husband Joe and daughter Amanda. She has served on the board of the Watertown Newcomers Club in a number of positions including President, is an avid scrapbooker, attends monthly book chats and enjoys cooking, traveling and entertaining.

Other Products Available from Get Organized Now!

Finally Organized, Finally Free – For the Office
If you loved Finally Organized, Finally Free – For the Home, you will definitely love Finally Organized, Finally Free – for the Office. You'll discover tons of tips and ideas to help you get your office and your life organized, including how to banish office clutter, better manage your time, be more productive and more!

The Easy Organizer
It's not just a planner. It's much, much more! Loaded with easy-to-use forms to help you eliminate those notorious scraps of paper and consolidate all of your home-related data into one place so you can find your info when you need it.

The Easy Bill Paying System
Pay your home-related bills on time, easily organize your statements and conveniently keep track of your expenses with this simple, but powerful, system.

The Ultimate Guide for Professional Organizers
This comprehensive guide contains everything you need to know about starting, running and growing your professional organizing business, while making a great profit! If you've ever dreamed of owning your own professional organizing business, this guide is the only one you'll need.

Give to Get Marketing Solution
Have a small to medium-sized business or thinking of starting one? Kick start your marketing program into overdrive with this all-encompassing guide that will help you develop a solid strategy for attracting customers to your business.

The Christmas Holiday Planner
A must-have planner to help you get and stay organized for a stress-free, enjoyable holiday season.

My Oh-So-Organized Filing System
It's not just a filing system. It's a filing system AND an organizing system rolled into one. Includes 510 color-coded category labels and 150 additional blank, color-coded labels ready to be applied to your file folders. Category labels are designed to cover any family's paper organizing needs. Comes with an extensive User Guide, and a Bonus Tickler Reminder File System that covers an incredible 17 years.

For more information about any of these products, please visit: www.getorganizednow.com and click on the STORE link.

Your Tips, Ideas and Comments

Write to us
Do you have an organizing tip, success story or comment you'd like to share? We'd love to hear from you. Feel free to write to us at:

Get Organized Now!
611 Arlington Way
Watertown WI 53094

Please include your name and full mailing address on all correspondence. If you send an organizing tip or a success story, we may publish it, along with your name, city and state as the contributor, on our Web site, in our newsletter, in a media press release or in one of our future products.

Spelling or link corrections
While careful care has gone into the writing and editing of this book, there's always the possibility that we may have missed something. In light of this, if you happen to notice a spelling error or a Web site link that no longer works, please feel free to write to us at the above address. We'll then have the opportunity to correct it in future printings. Please be sure to include the page number where you located the error.

Grammatical corrections
As far as grammatical errors, Maria Gracia has always said, "I write the way I speak. If I followed every grammatical rule there was, my writing would be awfully stiff and stuffy. My main concern is that I get my point across." But feel free to write to us about any grammatical error that truly bothers you and we'll bring it to Maria's attention for consideration.

Correspondence
Although we do respond personally to some of our mail, due to the thousands of email messages we receive each week, we regret that we can't respond personally to every single one we receive. However, please be assured that we do read and consider all correspondence.

Index

A

B